CN00945993

Effervescent Adventures with Britannia

EFFERVESCENT ADVENTURES WITH

*B*RITANNIA

Personalities, Politics and Culture in Britain

Edited by Wm. Roger Louis

I.B.Tauris
London · New York

Harry Ransom Center
Austin

Published in 2017 by I. B. Tauris & Co Ltd
6 Salem Road, London W2 4BU
In the United States of America and Canada, distributed by
Palgrave Macmillan, a division of St. Martin's Press
175 Fifth Avenue, New York NY 10010
www.ibtauris.com

Harry Ransom Center
University of Texas at Austin
P.O. Drawer 7219
Austin, Texas 78713-7219

Copyright © 2017 by British Studies
University of Texas at Austin

All rights reserved. Except for brief quotations in a review, this book,
or any part of it, may not be reproduced, stored in, or introduced into a
retrieval system, or transmitted, in any form or by any means, electronic,
mechanical, photocopying, recording, or otherwise, without the prior
written permission of the publisher.

The paper used in this publication meets the minimum requirements of
American National Standard for Information Sciences—
Permanence of Paper for Printed Library Materials

ISBN 978-1-78831-185-4 hardcover
ISBN 978-1-78831-186-1 paperback

Library of Congress Control Number: 2017913399

Print production by Studio Azul, Inc., Austin, Texas

Table of Contents

List of Authors

Sarah Beaver is a Fellow of All Souls College, where, as Bursar, she has been responsible for its administration since 2008. Formerly a civil servant, she spent most of her career working in the Ministry of Defence. After the Falklands crisis, she prepared evidence for a parliamentary inquiry into the handling of the press and public information during the conflict. Her later appointments were as Director General for operations and overseas garrisons, including the Falklands.

Barnaby Crowcroft was educated at the London School of Economics, Yale, and Harvard, where he is currently completing a PhD in the Department of History. His research has been supported by the Social Science Research Council, the American Council of Learned Societies, and the John Clive Memorial Fund. He is the author of articles in publications including the *Historical Journal* and the *Times Literary Supplement*.

Richard Davenport-Hines is a former Visiting Fellow at All Souls College, Oxford. His biographical subjects include W. H. Auden, Marcel Proust, Lady Desborough, and Maynard Keynes. He has edited Hugh Trevor-Roper's wartime journals and his correspondence with Bernard Berenson. Recent books include studies of the Profumo Affair and of the sinking of the *Titanic*. His latest book is *Traitors: Communist Espionage and the Making of Modern Britain* (2018).

Caroline Elkins is Professor of History and of African and African American Studies at Harvard University, and Visiting Professor of General Management at the Harvard Business School. Her book *Imperial Reckoning: The Untold Story of Britain's Gulag in Kenya* was awarded the Pulitzer Prize for General Nonfiction in 2006. She is currently completing a book on violence and the British Empire in the nineteenth and twentieth centuries.

Joseph Epstein is the author of more than twenty-five books. Two recent works are *Frozen in Time* (2016), a collection of short stories, and *Wind Sprints* (2016), a collection of his shorter essays. *Snobbery: The American Version* was published in 2002. He was the Editor of Phi

Beta Kappa's *The American Scholar* magazine, 1974–98. In 2003 he won the National Humanities Medal of the National Endowment for the Humanities.

John D. Fair, whose career has straddled the fields of British history, physical culture, and the American South, taught at Auburn University–Montgomery (1971–97). His publications include *British Interparty Conferences* (1980), *Harold Temperley* (1992), *Muscletown USA* (1999), *The Tifts of Georgia* (2010), and *Mr. America* (2015). He teaches and does research at the Stark Center for Physical Culture and Sports in the Department of Kinesiology at the University of Texas.

Patrick French is the inaugural Dean of the School of Arts and Sciences at Ahmedabad University, and Professor for the Public Understanding of the Humanities. He has a visiting position at Cambridge University. His biography of V. S. Naipaul, *The World Is What It Is,* won the Hawthornden Prize and the National Book Critics Circle Award in 2008. He is the author of *Younghusband* (1994) and is now writing the authorized biography of Doris Lessing.

S. J. D. Green is Professor of Modern History, University of Leeds, and Fellow of All Souls College, Oxford. He gave the Birkbeck Lectures in Ecclesiastical History at the University of Cambridge, 2013–14; a revised version of the lectures is being prepared for publication. His many books include *Religion in the Age of Decline* (1996) and *The Passing of Protestant England* (2011). He is currently completing a narrative history of All Souls, from 1850.

Rosemary Hill is an historian of art and ideas. Her biography of A. W. N. Pugin, *God's Architect* (2007), won the Wolfson History Prize. She is a contributing editor to the *London Review of Books,* Fellow of the Royal Society of Literature, Quondam Fellow of All Souls College, Oxford, and a member of Historic England's Blue Plaques Committee. Her current research is on antiquarianism in the Romantic period.

Michael Holroyd is the author of biographies of Lytton Strachey (2 vols., 1967–68), Augustus John (2 vols., 1974–75), George Bernard Shaw (4 vols., 1988–92), and the actors Ellen Terry and Henry Irving (2008). He has been President of the Royal Society of Literature and Chairman of the Society of Authors. In 2007 he was awarded a Knighthood for services to literature. He is married to the novelist Margaret Drabble.

Steven Isenberg was Visiting Professor of Humanities at the University of Texas at Austin for several years. He has taught and lectured at Berkeley, Yale, Davidson, and Oxford. Before that, he was chief of staff to New York mayor John V. Lindsay, publisher of *New York Newsday*, vice president of the *Los Angeles Times*, executive director of the PEN American Center, and interim president of Adelphi University. He is an Honorary Fellow of Worcester College, Oxford.

Boisfeuillet Jones, Jr., studied at Harvard, 1964–68, and was President of the *Harvard Crimson*. As a Rhodes Scholar at Exeter College, Oxford, he earned a D.Phil. in History. At Harvard Law School, he was an editor of the *Harvard Law Review*. He worked at the *Washington Post* for thirty-two years, rising to become Publisher and CEO. He left the *Post* to be President and CEO of MacNeil-Lehrer Productions, producer of *PBS NewsHour*, 2012–14.

Paul Kennedy is the Dilworth Professor of History at Yale. He has published or edited nineteen books on the history of British foreign policy and Great Power struggles. His best-known work, *The Rise and Fall of the Great Powers* (1987) has been translated into twenty languages. His most recent book, *Engineers of Victory* (2013), looks at problem solvers during World War II. He is at work on a book about sea power and global transformations, 1939–45.

Andrew Lownie was educated at Magdalene College, Cambridge, where he was Dunster History Prizeman and President of the Union, and at Edinburgh University. A literary agent, he is a Fellow of the Royal Historical Society, a former Visiting Fellow at Churchill College, Cambridge, and President of the Biographers Club. He serves on the Advisory Council of Biographers International Organization. His books include a literary guide to Edinburgh and a life of the writer John Buchan.

John M. MacKenzie was a professor of imperial history at Lancaster University (1968–2002). He holds honorary professorships at the Universities of Aberdeen, St. Andrews, and Edinburgh and is visiting professor at the University of the Highlands and Islands, Scotland. He was editor-in-chief of the Wiley Blackwell *Encyclopedia of Empire* (4 vols., 2016), and among his recent books are *Museums and Empire* (2009) and the co-edited volumes *Exhibiting the Empire* (2015) and *Global Migrations* (2016).

Kenneth O. Morgan has been Fellow and Tutor at The Queen's College, Oxford, and Vice-Chancellor in the University of Wales, and is now Visiting Professor at King's College, London. He is a Fellow of the British Academy and a Labour peer. His thirty-five books on British, Welsh, and American history include the *Oxford Illustrated History of Britain* (over one million copies sold) and biographies of Lloyd George, Keir Hardie, James Callaghan, and Michael Foot.

Annamaria Motrescu-Mayes is based at the University of Cambridge as a visiting lecturer in new media anthropology in the Division of Social Anthropology, an affiliated scholar and guest lecturer at the Centre of South Asian Studies, and Fellow and Tutor at Clare Hall. She is a visual and digital humanities scholar working on British imperial studies and issues of racial and gender identities. Her current research draws on visual culture, cognitive psychology, and postcolonial studies.

Susan Napier is the Goldthwaite Professor of Rhetoric at Tufts University, where she teaches courses on science fiction, film, and fantasy literature. Previously she held the Mitsubishi Heavy Industries Chair of Japanese Studies at the University of Texas at Austin. She is the author of four books and numerous articles. Her book on the Japanese animator Hayao Miyazaki will be published in 2018.

John Prados is a senior fellow of the National Security Archive in Washington, D.C., and director of its CIA documentation project. He is the author of more than thirty books, most recently *The Ghosts of Langley: Into the CIA's Heart of Darkness* (2017). His other books on the CIA include *Safe for Democracy* (2006) and *The Family Jewels* (2013). Four of his books, including *The Ghosts of Langley*, have been nominated for the Pulitzer Prize.

Jane Ridley studied at St. Hugh's College, Oxford, and Nuffield College, Oxford. She is Professor of History at Buckingham University. She won the Duff Cooper Prize in 2002 for *The Architect and His Wife,* a biography of her great-grandfather Edwin Lutyens. Her other books include *Bertie: A Life of Edward VII* (2012) and *Queen Victoria* (2014). She is working on a biography of King George V.

Reba Soffer was a Professor of History at California State University, Northridge. Her works include *Discipline and Power: The Universities, History, and the Making of an English Elite, 1850–1930* (1995), and *History, Historians, and Conservatism in Britain and America* (2010). She has received fellowships from St. Catherine's College, Oxford, the Guggenheim Foundation, and the National Endowment for the Humanities. She is a past President of the North American Conference on British Studies.

Martin Stannard is Professor of Modern English Literature at the University of Leicester. His works on Evelyn Waugh include *The Critical Heritage* (1984) and a two-volume biography (1986, 1992). His biography of Muriel Spark (2009) was shortlisted for the James Tait Black Memorial Prize. He has also published on Kingsley Amis, Ford Madox Ford, Graham Greene, and Philip Larkin. Currently he is Executive Editor of Oxford University Press's forty-three-volume *The Complete Works of Evelyn Waugh*.

Steven Weinberg holds the Josey Regental Chair of Science at the University of Texas, where he teaches in the Physics and Astronomy Departments. His research has been honored with the Nobel Prize in Physics and the National Medal of Science. He is a member of the National Academy of Sciences and Britain's Royal Society. The author of both scientific treatises and books for general readers, he wrote on the pre-modern emergence of physics and astronomy in *To Explain the World* (2015).

Geoffrey Wheatcroft is a journalist and historian. He studied Modern History at New College, Oxford, and joined the *Spectator* in 1975. He writes regularly for the *Spectator,* the *New York Times,* the *Wall Street Journal,* and the *New York Review of Books.* His books include *The Randlords* (1995), *The Controversy of Zion* (1996), *The Strange Death of Tory England* (2005), *Le Tour* (2007), and *Yo, Blair!* (2007).

The editor, Wm. Roger Louis, is Kerr Professor of English History and Culture and Distinguished Teaching Professor at the University of Texas at Austin, an Honorary Fellow of St. Antony's College, Oxford, and a past President of the American Historical Association. His books include *Ends of British Imperialism* (2006). He is the Editor-in-Chief of the *Oxford History of the British Empire.* In 2013, he was awarded the Benson Medal of the Royal Society of Literature, and in 2016 he delivered the Weizmann Memorial Lecture.

Introduction

WM. ROGER LOUIS

In introducing another volume of adventures—*Effervescent Adventures*—I am once again reminded of the wisdom of the Cambridge mathematician G. H. Hardy, who wrote that the pain of having to repeat himself was so excruciating that he decided to end the agony by offering no apology. In the spirit of the adventurous refrain—more, still more, yet more, penultimate, ultimate, resurgent, irrepressible, resplendent, and now effervescent—I once again follow his example. This book consists of a representative selection of lectures given to the British Studies seminar at the University of Texas at Austin. Most of the present lectures were delivered in the years 2015–17.

Lectures are different from essays or scholarly articles. A lecture presumes an audience rather than a reader and usually has a more conversational tone. It allows greater freedom in the expression of personal or subjective views. It permits and invites greater candor. It is sometimes informally entertaining as well as anecdotally instructive. In this volume, the lecture sometimes takes the form of intellectual autobiography—an account of how the speaker has come to grips with a significant topic in the field of British Studies, which broadly defined means things British throughout the world as well as things that happen to be English, Irish, Scottish, or Welsh. The scope of British Studies includes all disciplines in the social sciences and humanities as well as music, architecture, and the visual arts.

Most of the lectures in this collection fall within the fields of history, politics, and literature, though the dominant themes, here as previously, are literary and historical. Occasionally though rarely, the lectures have to be given in absentia. In such cases, the lectures or at least substantial parts of them are read and then critically discussed. The full sweep of the lectures will be apparent from the list at the end of the book, which is reproduced in its entirety to give a comprehensive idea of the seminar's evolution and substance.

In 2017, the British Studies seminar celebrated its forty-second year. The circumstances for its creation were favorable because of the existence of the Humanities Research Center, now the Harry Ransom Center, at the University of Texas. Harry Ransom was the founder of the HRC, a Professor of English and later Chancellor of the University, a collector of rare books, and a man of humane vision. Through the administrative and financial creativity of Ransom and subsequent directors, the HRC has developed into a virtually unique literary archive with substantial collections, especially in English literature. Ransom thought a weekly seminar might provide the opportunity to learn of the original research being conducted at the HRC as well as to create common bonds of intellectual interest in a congenial setting of overstuffed armchairs, Persian carpets, and generous libations of sherry. The seminar was launched in the fall semester of 1975. It has remained consistent in its dual purpose of providing a forum for visiting scholars engaged in research at the HRC and of enabling the members of the seminar to discuss their own work.

The sherry at the Friday seminar sessions symbolizes the attitude. The seminar meets to discuss whatever happens to be on the agenda, Scottish or Indian, Canadian or Jamaican, English or Australian. George Bernard Shaw once said that England and America were two great countries divided by a common language, but he understated the case by several countries. The interaction of British and other societies is an endlessly fascinating subject on which points of view do not often converge. Diverse preconceptions, which are tempered by different disciplines, help initiate and then sustain controversy, not end it. The ongoing discussions in British Studies are engaging because of the clash of different perspectives as well as the nuance of cultural interpretation. Though the printed page cannot capture the atmosphere of engaged discussion, the lectures do offer the opportunity to savor the result of wide-ranging research and reflection.

I am grateful to Philippa Levine, the Co-Director of British Studies, for help in sustaining the program. The seminar has two University sponsors, the College of Liberal Arts and the Harry Ransom Center. We are indebted to the Dean of Liberal Arts, Randy Diehl, for his support and especially for allocating resources for the program of Junior Fellows—a few assistant professors appointed each year to bring fresh blood, brash ideas, and new commitment to the program. We are equally grateful to the Directors of the HRC, Tom Staley and his successor, Stephen Enniss, for providing a home for the seminar. I wish also to thank Frances Terry, who has handled the week-by-week administrative detail from early on in the seminar's history. I am indebted to Kip Keller and Holly McCarthy for their steadfast assistance in many ways.

The seminar benefits especially from the support of the Creekmore and Adele Fath Foundation. When Creekmore Fath was an undergraduate at the University of Texas in the 1930s, he valued especially the chance to exchange ideas and become friends with faculty members. The Fath Foundation now enables the seminar to offer undergraduate and graduate scholarships and generally to advance the cause of the liberal arts. The students appointed to scholarships are known as Churchill Scholars. The Churchill Scholars, like the Junior Fellows, not only contribute to the vitality of the seminar but also extend its age range from those in their late teens to their nineties.

For vital support we continue to thank Mildred Kerr and the late Baine Kerr of Houston, John and Susan Kerr of San Antonio, Becky Gale and the late Edwin Gale of Beaumont, Custis Wright and the late Charles Alan Wright of Austin, Althea Osborn, David Osborn, and the late Robert Osborn, and the two dozen stouthearted members of the seminar who have contributed to its endowment. We are indebted to Dean Robert D. King for his help over many years. I again extend special thanks to Sam Jamot Brown and Sherry Brown of Durango, Colorado, and Tex and Charles Moncrief of Fort Worth.

THE CHAPTERS—MORE PRECISELY, THE LECTURES—are clustered together more or less chronologically and thematically. In the first, **Richard Davenport-Hines** exhumes the circumstances and reputation of Jack the Ripper as a serial killer. In the autumn of 1888, at least three middle-aged prostitutes in the East End of London near Whitechapel were viciously murdered, usually with skirts raised to their stomachs and sometimes their intestines ripped out by cuts possibly made with a surgical instrument. Who was the killer in fact? Davenport-Hines discusses the evidence and the widespread terror as well as the demoralization of the police and the public reaction to the murders. He draws the reader's attention to contributing circumstances, including the squalor of the East End. Above all he separates the actual murderer from the mythology created by "Ripperologists." In examining the murders as they appeared in the contemporary newspaper press and later in various literary works, he explains how the Ripper inspired an excellent novel admired by Gertrude Stein and Ernest Hemingway as well as a film by Alfred Hitchcock. The principal question turns out to be not so much the killer's true identity as how to explain the Ripper's fame as an historical and literary phenomenon.

Throughout his life, George Bernard Shaw demonstrated a consistent preoccupation with physical fitness, bordering on obsession. **John D. Fair** points out that he was a teetotaler and vegetarian, emphasizing in plays, essays, and other writings the ruination caused by drink. He sang while walking four miles a day, he enjoyed both cycling and motorcycling, and at one point he developed a physical fitness routine with the former heavyweight boxing champion Gene Tunney, who believed that Shaw's vegetarian diet and healthy lifestyle kept him "radiantly healthy, buoyant and exceptionally fit." For his part, Shaw wrote, "Gene Tunney is among the very few for whom I have established a warm affection. I enjoy his company as I have that of few men." By developing the theme of wit and wisdom converging with health and well-being, Fair proves to be a guide to the paradox of Shaw's life and work, which was lodged as much in the body as in the mind.

Evelyn Waugh's visits to America in the late 1940s were significant beyond the reason that he succeeded in leaving Americans entirely confused about what to make of such a patronizing and snobbish visitor. **Martin Stannard** explains that he began "the oddest quest of his life." In 1947 he discovered, in his own phrase, "literary gold" in a Southern California cemetery for pets. In the next year, he began, by correspondence, a shared spiritual struggle and friendship with the American monk Thomas Merton. During Waugh's visit to America in 1948, he visited small Catholic colleges, conferred with Merton in person, and witnessed in New Orleans "a dense crowd of all colours and conditions" moving to the altar. He later wrote of "the heroic fidelity of the Negro Catholics." Beneath the impression that he liked to give of an arrogant Englishman with a stiff white collar and bowler hat carrying a rolled umbrella, Waugh contemplated contrition, compassion, and humility. In Stannard's interpretation, it kept him sane.

Patrick French places his subject, V.S. Naipaul, in the context of British biographical writing, which at its best is historically informed, accurate, and fair-minded. It is not always easy for his readers to take a fair-minded or balanced view of Naipaul, though most would probably acknowledge as unforgettable, perhaps even as works of art, his novels *A House for Mr. Biswas* (1961) and *A Bend in the River* (1979). Mr. Biswas is largely drawn from Naipaul's father; and *A Bend in the River* reveals his conservative views on European colonialism, along with his radical, pessimistic vision about the future of Africa and other parts of the world formerly under European colonial rule. With a Churchillian ring, Naipaul writes of a post-British Raj where Indians defecate on the hills, on the riverbanks, and on the streets. The *New Yorker* referred to French's biography of Naipaul as "masterly and mournful." His assessment here will certainly make readers wish to return to Naipaul not only for the pleasure of his novels but also to understand why many readers in postcolonial societies find him so perplexing.

Scotland and Japan have two authors in common separated by at least a century. **Susan Napier** argues that the work of Robert Louis Stevenson and the movies of Hayao Miyazaki are characterized by dual personality: *Dr. Jekyll and Mr. Hyde,* and Miyazaki's *Starting Point,* a memoir that reveals him as caught in tension between the pre-1945 Japanese Empire and the American occupation of Japan. Another point of comparison is Scotland as culturally distinct from England as Japan is from the West. In another sense, Stevenson's *Treasure Island* finds a distinct echo in Miyazaki's *Animal Treasure Island* (leading to over a dozen movies). Miyazaki is explicit: *Treasure Island* is a "foundational text." In the Miyazaki version, the granddaughter of the Captain is "feisty, cute, and smart"—a twentieth-century feminine twist compatible with Stevenson's Jim, who fends for himself with "youthful resilience." Miyazaki's work is inspired by Stevenson yet is strikingly original, especially in the questioning of the nature of the "treasure." Robert Louis Stevenson is faring well in Japan.

Reba Soffer asks whether the popular fiction of Dorothy Sayers and Michael Arlen sustains the idea of a new and radical era of the 1920s, in bitter reaction to the conduct and consequences of the Great War. Sayers became celebrated for her detective series about Lord Peter Wimsey. Arlen became instantly famous after the publication of *The Green Hat,* in which the central figure, Iris Storm, personifies a new spirit of rebellion. In *Gaudy Night,* one of Sayers's most famous detective novels, she portrays the aristocracy as anachronistic, idle, and self-indulgent. Sayers and Arlen were quite different writers, but their novels convey a common theme of individuals breaking away from irrational traditions. Perhaps the most unusual revelation in the piece is Joseph Stalin's connection with Arlen's novel.

Joseph Epstein points out that the success of the *Encyclopaedia Britannica* can be explained by the quest for self-improvement. We are all autodidacts. The encyclopedia had humble beginnings, three volumes published in Edinburgh in 1768–71. It rose to great heights with the ninth edition (1875–89), "one of the splendid achievements of the Victorian age," and reached its pinnacle in the eleventh edition of 1910–11, which Epstein describes as the last great encyclopedia. As a result of its success, anyone writing entries was regarded as the leading authority on the subject well into the twentieth century. The *Britannica* subsequently had a curious and checkered history, but one remarkable feature was the salesmanship. It was marketed door-to-door, a complete set on the installment plan, with a bookcase thrown in at no extra charge. Responsibility for the project eventually wound up at the University of Chicago, which from 1943 to 1973 earned royalties of $47.8 million (roughly $260 million in current dollars). Its future is rather bleak. With the advent of the Internet, anything can be looked up. Readers may be surprised at Joseph Epstein's connection with the *Encyclopedia*.

Boisfeuillet Jones, Jr., asks why some newspapers are faring better than others in the transition from traditional newspapers to digital editions. On the American side, he draws examples mainly from the *New York Times,* the *Washington Post,* and to some extent the *Los Angeles Times* and the *Wall Street Journal*. On British newspapers, he focuses principally on *The Times,* the *Guardian,* and the *Telegraph,* and to a lesser extent on the *Financial Times* and *The Economist*. The common denominator is the effort to build revenue through a variety of digital paid subscriptions. One way in which print newspapers have coped with a decline in revenue is to increase the single-copy price. For the *Washington Post,* the increase has been from 25 cents to $2.00. The *Financial Times,* the *Guardian,* and *The Economist* have vigorously expanded internationally with digital as well as print editions. As in the past, good management and aggressive reporting as well as accuracy and fairness will determine the future of both print newspapers papers and digital copies, but will it matter whether newspapers survive as they have been printed traditionally?

Since the British Foreign Office traditionally referred to its colleagues in the Secret Intelligence Service (MI6) as "friends," it seems fair to rescue from clichéd use the term "cousins" as a description of the relationship between the CIA and MI6, though it was usually meant with considerable irony. **John Prados** points out that the principal point of conflict between the two agencies was the future of the British colonies, on which the Americans pressed for independence at a pace that the British believed to be injudicious and dangerous. In the post-war years, the CIA and MI6 bumped along easily enough in intelligence collection because the British had MI6 stations round the world. In joint operations they fared less well, often because of conflicting aims. In the overthrow of the Iranian government in 1953, the British let the CIA claim credit, which after the revolution of 1979 seemed a wise decision. In the Congo in 1960, the CIA attempted to poison the prime minister, Patrice Lumumba, while MI6 tried to bolster him. Both were saved from further embarrassment by Belgian mercenaries, who murdered him. In the many other joint endeavors, none was as fraught as the Falklands conflict: the CIA withheld intelligence from Britain because of regional ties to Argentina. Prados concludes that both intelligence agencies would have learned more about the dangers of interrogation during the Northern Irish trouble and in Iraq if they had listened more to each other. But on the whole, the relationship between the cousins continues to be mutually advantageous.

In some ways, Guy Burgess is the most elusive of the Cambridge Five spy ring. The significance of his espionage is hard to measure. Russian intelligence officers regarded him, from their vantage point, as the best of the lot. **Andrew Lownie** has put in years of research to assess his personality and the motives for treason. He has studied records ranging from those of the Old Etonian Association to the FBI to the Russian archives, when they were opened for a short time in the 1990s. Burgess seems all the more paradoxical because he was a British patriot who betrayed his country yet thought of himself as a Soviet agent who served his adopted country. He belonged to the Reform Club; he loved English literature; but he was slovenly in dress and did irreparable damage when drunk. There is a connection here with another chapter: Burgess was the lover of Harold Nicolson. Lownie leads the reader to the ultimate question, what to make of him in view of the accumulated evidence and the conflicting motives?

Guy Burgess defected to the Soviet Union in 1951. Over a quarter of a century later, the art critic Anthony Blunt confessed to having been a Soviet spy. **Steven Isenberg** discusses a recent novel by John Banville, *The Untouchable,* which presents a stand-in for Blunt as an art critic, double agent, and homosexual aesthete of the 1930s generation at Cambridge. In Banville's novel, Blunt is refracted through the novelist's imagination and becomes Victor Maskell, the pariah of the book's title. He is "outed" by Mrs. Thatcher into public humiliation. Isenberg assesses the novel's verve and originality, and its theme of the compulsive appeal that communism had for Blunt and others of the Cambridge spy ring. He quotes the questions posed to Maskell (Blunt): "Why did you spy for the Russians? How did you get away with it?"

S. J. D. Green explains the transformation of All Souls College, or at least of its reputation. Well into the twentieth century it was part of the establishment. At various times its members included Lord Halifax, Foreign Secretary and then Ambassador to the United States; Geoffrey Dawson of *The Times;* and Lawrence of Arabia. It did not admit undergraduates. It stood for the best in all branches of knowledge except the sciences. It was particularly strong in history and law. By the 1930s, it reached its height of influence, "an intellectual aristocracy" shaping world affairs, so it was believed, and charged with the destinies of the British Empire. It served as the model for Princeton's Institute for Advanced Study and Harvard's Society of Fellows. Yet by the 1960s the college had fallen into the doldrums. What are the reasons for the decline of the myth that All Souls was composed of the fifty brightest men in England? Perhaps the beginning and end of the alphabet: "A is for All Souls, and alike the Athenaeum . . . Z is for the Zeitgeist, that threatens the lot."

Guglielmo Marconi was the electrical engineer who invented long-distance radio transmission as well as the shortwave radio. He is an example of the Victorian, or rather Italian-Irish, self-made man. He spent long periods of time in England, where he was regarded by some as the "perpetual outsider" but to others as the "favorite outsider." **Paul Kennedy** explains that his success came from a combination of technological insight, skilled and sophisticated organization, and business acumen. In 1912, the wireless operator on the *Titanic* enabled the Cunard liner *Carpathia* to rescue some 700 passengers. In an era in which electricity and science, nationalism and colonialism, all appeared as major themes, Marconi's law of signaling distances in the radio-telegraph system claimed a prominent place.

In 1948, Harold Nicolson looked back on some of the turning points in his life, including his resignation two decades earlier from the Foreign Office to become a writer, with only minor success; and his recent defeat in a parliamentary election, which ended his political career. He enjoyed close friendships and a successful but sometimes turbulent marriage to Vita Sackville-West. But he was at loose ends. **Jane Ridley** describes the critical lifeline thrown to him when Sir Thomas Lascelles invited him to write the official biography of George V. He was granted unrestricted access to the Royal Archives. But there was a condition. He could not "descend to personalities." He was expected "to omit things and incidents that were discreditable." It would be a spoiler to mention how he transcended those barriers to write, in the words of David Cannadine, "a model for royal biography."

The whig interpretation of history is usually taken to mean viewing the past through the eyes of the present with similar moral judgment—a practice deplored by historians. As a scientist, **Steven Weinberg** finds that there is a different way of looking at it. Copernicus and Newton after all have been proved to be right. It is difficult but necessary to trace the slow and difficult progress that has set scientists on the right path, or in other words "progress toward truth." Scientists as well as historians need to be skeptical of grand designs and simplistic elucidation of the present from "lessons of the past." But they also need to confirm from past conclusions that there are laws of nature equally binding on all places and times. Whig historians of science need to keep their eyes on the past as well as the present.

In discussing paintings and other images of the British Empire, **Annamaria Motrescu-Mayes** presents illustrations as "visual manuscripts" that provide their own historical insight. Contemplating what an artist chose to ignore, include, exclude, or censor provides the viewer with a critical perspective on both the image and what it reveals through its historical significance. In one of her more striking examples, Sir Joseph Paton's original painting of the Bibighar Massacre depicts "maddened Sepoys, hot after blood" and threatening English ladies. A later version adjusts the image to replace the Sepoys with a group of Scottish soldiers appearing to rescue the terrified British women and children. This is but one example of the ways in which the chapter argues that a full understanding of the empire requires taking into account visual images created by both the colonizers and the colonized.

One remarkable feature of British propaganda during World War II is the extent to which it was both true and sensible—in line with the government's decision to be "as full and truthful as possible in order to be believed." **Rosemary Hill** is quick to point out that nevertheless there were some dubious points, for example, that eating carrots would help one see in the dark. There were also paradoxes: the British stood alone, yet it was a source of pride that the empire symbolized the collective British people throughout the world. A major problem arose when the Soviet Union suddenly became Britain's ally in 1941. Posters and broadcasts emphasized a "People's War"—coincidentally, one in which women would have the chance to play "the role which they deserve." The chapter concludes with an assessment of the artists who created the wartime posters, including one with a quotation from Charles Lamb translated into Farsi. What impression might it have made in the Persian Gulf?

In a slightly revised version of the Weizmann Memorial Lecture given in October 2016 (subsequently re-inflicted on the British Studies seminar), **Wm. Roger Louis** discusses the ideas and decisions of Ernest Bevin, the Foreign Secretary of the Labour Government of 1945. Bevin described himself without bragging as one in a million; he was the most powerful member of the Attlee cabinet. In Zionist ideology, he ranks only a rung or so below Hitler. He attempted to block or severely curtail the creation of the Jewish state. His principal adversary in England was Richard Crossman, Member of Parliament and editor of the *New Statesman,* who expressed revulsion at the attempt to deny a home to a people who had suffered unspeakable atrocities under the Nazis. At a critical stage of the controversy, Bevin asked Crossman whether he had been circumcised. Bevin had a constructive, positive plan for the future of the Jews, which today seems sensible, but at the time fell on deaf ears.

In an original comment on the Suez crisis of 1956, **Barnaby Crowcroft** asks how it might have looked from the vantage point of anti-Nasser Egyptians. A successful British military operation in the Canal Zone would probably have brought about a revolt of Egyptian army officers. The result would not necessarily have been another military government. A small but effective group of right-wing British politicians and former members of the secret service made contact with a range of prominent Egyptians who had been dismissed or otherwise ill treated by the Nasser government. They included former civil servants, military officers, and judges as well as journalists and businessmen who had previously benefited from a stable relationship with the countries of western Europe. Crowcroft has discovered British plans for "a broad-based successor administration" that would be nationalist but not anti-British. How realistic was this assessment? Crowcroft's answer takes into account American as well as British contemporary evidence and concludes with a sharply revisionist comment by Henry Kissinger.

To what extent were violence and such methods as torture endemic in colonial regimes? Using an example from the Arab Revolt of 1937–39, **Caroline Elkins** argues that the British in Palestine systematically deployed "limitless violence" in such a way that martial law evolved into emergency regulations giving sweeping powers beyond statutory colonial law—a process that can be traced from the Boer War at the turn of the century to the Easter Rising of 1916 and the Amritsar massacre of 1919. She uses the story of Jamal al-Husayni, who was President of the Palestine Arab Delegation to the

League of Nations, to tell the overall story of repression, including "interrogations, tortures, aerial shootings." She sustains the indictment by tracing emergency powers that became the model for post-1945 counterinsurgency campaigns. When complaints and accounts of atrocities reached officials in the colonies and then the Colonial Office or War Office, "nothing, legally, was required to be done." In 1939, as a last example, British officials were less concerned about the deaths of Arab villagers, some of whom had been locked in cages as a form of punishment, drinking their own urine to survive, than they were about this news reaching Indian nationalists.

Rudyard Kipling fiercely guarded his privacy. In his autobiography, *Something of Myself,* he in fact revealed little about himself. He wrote only briefly of his early years in England, little more than describing the misery he experienced in a school that resembled, in his own phrase, a prison house. He was bullied and beaten but found an escape in reading books. Here **Michael Holroyd** has picked up a clue. Reminiscing a half century later, Kipling mentions a book by a Mrs. Ewing entitled *Six to Sixteen.* But he failed to give the subtitle: *A Story for Girls.* Kipling discovered not only that schools for girls were just as vicious and humiliating as those for boys, but also that he had found a kindred spirit. He read the book not once but twice, in school and fifty years later, taking in every word. His thoughts reveal a different personality from that of the champion of empire.

In a sweeping survey of the history of the British Empire, **John M. MacKenzie** makes the distinction between "ramshackle" and "rampaging," different ways of viewing the process of expansion from minimal influence to extensive control and authority. He uses as one illuminating example the case of David Livingstone, the Protestant missionary whose exploration in Central Africa led eventually to "a shoestring, ramshackle administration" that in turn became a colony and still later the independent country of Malawi. Different types of empire existed at different times and in different places and could evolve in different ways.

In commenting on the war in the Falklands, **Sarah Beaver** writes as a former civil servant. At the outbreak, she had no idea that she would be witnessing from the heart of the government the most critical conflict for the British in the second half of the last century. Part of the fascination of her account is the way in which she found herself organizing meetings, drafting replies to hundreds of inquiries, coping with a computer system that by today's standards would be regarded as primitive, and running up and down the stairs because the elevators (or lifts) were too slow. She witnessed, sometimes directly and sometimes indirectly, such major developments as the First Sea Lord, Sir Henry Leach, stating emphatically that a task force of some 28,000 men and 100 ships could retake the islands, and Mrs. Thatcher's immediate response. Her assessment of the Prime Minister is one of striking features of the chapter.

The worst thing since Suez? **Geoffrey Wheatcroft** argues that the long-awaited Chilcot report on Iraq is a damning indictment of Tony Blair and the entire British government. In what he describes as comic subplot to an unfunny story, Blair ignored advice about the probability of a calamitous invasion and exclaimed, "That's all history . . . This is about the future." This part of the story ends with his comment to George Bush, "I will be with you, whatever." Wheatcroft raises large questions about nuclear weapons, Islamic terrorism, and the statement by the United Nations inspector Hans Blix that he had found no weapons of mass destruction in Iraq. The reader will learn of the parallel Victorian episode of Lady Gwendolen Cecil's ruthless comment on Disraeli and how it applies to Blair as well. Finally, Wheatcroft comments on Blair's public attempt to answer the Chilcot report. It is an excruciating story.

Painting an ultimately bleak picture of Britain after Brexit, **Kenneth O. Morgan** sets out the argument as follows. After the referendum of 1975 linking Britain with Europe, a new element entered the debate, one that had been dormant for many centuries: English nationalism. Especially within the Conservative Party, it expressed itself as Euroskepticism. In the referendum of June 2016, passion rose on the Leave side, especially over the issue of immigration. The strongest Leave vote came from older, middle-class people in Southern England. The outcome signified profound historical change. At this point, the reader will discover key constitutional issues opened up by Brexit, as well as its significance for Scotland and Ireland. The chapter concludes with the question, how will post-Brexit Britain be regarded worldwide? Lonely and rudderless? The idea of Britannia taking the lead in a new "Anglosphere" seems an appropriate way to bring the volume to a close, though Morgan brings us a sad ending.

"The Discovery of 'Jack the Ripper's' First Murder," *Famous Crimes Past and Present*, vol. 2, no. 15, c. 1903.

1

Jack the Ripper

RICHARD DAVENPORT-HINES

London's most infamous serial killer was known as the "Whitechapel murderer" or "Leather Apron" until on 27 September 1888 the Central News Agency received a red-inked, defiant, semiliterate letter signed "Jack the Ripper." This letter was probably a hoax concocted by news agency staff. It is suitable that he is known by a name devised in a journalistic stunt, for he was the first criminal to become a figure of international mythology through the medium of global communications. The indivisibility of his crimes from the reporting of them is shown in a few words of a Cabinet minister, Lord Cranbrook, who on 2 October noted: "More murders at Whitechapel, strange and horrible. The newspapers reek with blood."[1]

The Ripper was almost certainly male, probably right-handed, unmarried, employed, and possessed of either some anatomical training or enough education to study surgical textbooks. He was perhaps a foreigner. Although all his victims (possibly barring one) were destitute and drunken prostitutes, he did not rape or penetrate them; nevertheless, there was a sexual element to his homicidal excitement. He was daring, energetic, hate ridden, cruel, and perhaps obsessed with wombs. Evidence for his age and appearance from those who claimed to have seen him is inconclusive and contradictory. Nothing is certain of his life except for a few violent hours during the summer and autumn of 1888.

There was much routine violence against women in Whitechapel, an area of the East End. Early on the morning of Tuesday, 3 April 1888, following the Easter bank holiday on Monday, Emma Elizabeth Smith, age forty-five, was attacked in Osborn Street. A blunt instrument, possibly a stick, was thrust into her. She died in the London Hospital the next day. Her death is sometimes reckoned as the first in the series of crimes perpetrated by the Whitechapel murderer, but was probably an unrelated street robbery and rape by several ruffians.

Between 1:50 and 3:30 a.m. on Tuesday, 7 August 1888 (again after a Monday bank holiday) Martha Tabram (b. 1849), alias Turner, who was also known as Emma, was stabbed thirty-nine times on the first-floor landing of the communal stairs of the George Yard Buildings, a block of model dwellings off Whitechapel High Street. Her clothes were disarrayed, and her lower body was exposed. Police investigations focused on an unidentified private in a guards regiment with whom Tabram had reportedly gone to George Yard shortly before midnight on 6 August. Some criminologists insist that Tabram's killer was an unidentified soldier; others identify this crime as the first of the series attributed to Jack the Ripper.

There is no controversy that at about three in the morning on Friday, 31 August 1888, the Whitechapel murderer killed Mary Ann (Polly) Nichols (b. 1845) in the entrance to a stable yard in a narrow cobbled alley called Buck's Row, off Whitechapel Road. As with Tabram, her skirts were raised almost to her stomach. Her abdomen was savagely ripped open, and her throat cut; her private parts were twice stabbed. She had, however, probably been throttled before the stabbing and mutilation. After her murder, suspicions focused on Jack Pizer (c.1850–1897), a Jewish slipper maker who for some time had been bullying prostitutes and was known as "Leather Apron"; he was eventually detained and eliminated from the inquiry.

The next victim was Annie Chapman, alias Annie Siffey (b. 1841). She was murdered (probably at 5:30 a.m.) on Saturday, 8 September 1888, in the backyard of 29 Hanbury Street, Spitalfields, an area near Whitechapel. This was the only one of the serial killings committed in daylight. An eyewitness who saw the killer picking up his victim described him vaguely as shabby-genteel, foreign looking, and about forty years old; a neighbor apparently heard him stifling her cries and throttling her to insensibility or death. Chapman's throat was severed, and her body mutilated. Some of her organs were removed from the scene, and her rings were wrenched off. The perpetrator seemingly had some knowledge of anatomical or pathological examinations; a small amputating knife or a thin, sharpened butcher's knife was probably used.

Police street patrols of Whitechapel and Spitalfields had been increased after the Tabram murder and were soon intensified until the district was almost saturated with police at nighttime. After Nichols's murder, when journalists raised the specter of a homicidal lunatic stalking his victims through Whitechapel, Inspector Frederick Abberline of Scotland Yard, who had an extensive knowledge of the area, was sent there to coordinate the divisional detectives investigating the prostitute murders. Generally, the police were reasonably efficient, though bewildered. The press sensation following Chapman's murder, however, raised bitter recriminations against the Metropolitan Police. Some of these attacks were intended to injure politically the Home Secretary, Henry Matthews, or to retaliate against the stern police treatment of Irish nationalists, socialists, and the East End unemployed. The situation was exacerbated by Sir Howard Vincent's guidelines for the Criminal Investigation Department, which required secretiveness on the part of police officials in unsolved cases. Resentful of this policy, journalists resorted to ploys and dodges that impeded police investigations. There was a popular outcry for a large government reward to be offered for information on the killer, but the Home Office was set against this practice, which it knew could draw false information or induce the framing of innocent parties. The police nevertheless were showered with information from the public about lunatics, misfits, and unpopular neighbors. Chapman's death raised suspicions of Jewish ritual murder, and crowds assembled in Whitechapel streets and threatened Jews. This resulted in Samuel Montagu, MP for Whitechapel and a pious Orthodox Jew who was fearful that wild rumors could be a pretext for anti-Semitic outbreaks, offering a reward of £100 for the murderer's capture, and in the formation (largely by Jewish tradesmen) of the Mile End Vigilance Committee. Larger rewards were later offered.

Probably between 12:40 and 1 a.m. on Sunday, 30 September, in Dutfield's Yard, flanking the socialist (and mainly Jewish) International Working Men's Educational Club, at 40 Berner Street, Elizabeth Stride (b. 1843), a Swede, prone to drink but not a habitual prostitute, was murdered. A meeting of 100 members had recently ended in the club, where those who had not dispersed were singing. Stride's throat was cut, but her clothing was undisturbed. Her expression was peaceful, and she still clutched in her left hand a packet of aromatic breath sweeteners wrapped in tissue paper. Some

Ripperologists discount Stride as one of the serial killings because the corpse was not extensively slashed or mutilated, but it is more likely that the killer was disturbed before completing his work. A passerby gave evidence suggesting that there were two men involved in this killing. Another witness, who saw a member of the socialist club carrying a small black bag while leaving the yard, started the legend of Jack the Ripper carrying a doctor's bag.

After murdering Stride, the killer went three-quarters of a mile eastward (twelve minutes' walk) to Mitre Square, off Aldgate, within the eastern boundary of the City of London. In the southeast corner of this square, near a warehouse yard and some derelict or empty houses (the darkest corner of the square, favored by prostitutes and their clients), between 1:30 and 1:44 a.m. on that same morning, he murdered Catherine Eddowes (b. 1842), alias Kate Conway or Kelly. She had been discharged from the Bishopsgate Street police station (where she had been held for drunkenness) only forty-five minutes before her corpse was discovered. She was found lying on her back with her clothes disarranged. Her throat was cut and her stomach opened. Further terrible mutilations were made, and again the murderer took organs away. He showed ruthless efficiency on this occasion, for he had only a quarter of an hour between two police patrols to inveigle his victim into the square, kill and mutilate her, and escape. The police reacted swiftly to the discovery in Mitre Square, but the killer fled eastward, apparently stopping to leave a piece of Eddowes's bloody and fecal-stained apron at a stairwell entry at 108–19 Wentworth Model Dwellings, Goulston Street, where he chalked a message:

> The Juwes are
> The men That
> Will not
> be Blamed
> for nothing.

The chairman of the Mile End Vigilance Committee received a parcel (16 October) putatively containing a portion of Eddowes's kidney, together with an unsigned letter headed "From Hell," purportedly from the murderer.

From the night of the double murder, the police investigation became even more conditioned by public unrest and reactive to the press. The police were demoralized by false leads and failure. Relations became strained between Matthews and the commissioner of the Metropolitan Police, Sir Charles Warren, who reported to the

FINDING ᴛʜᴇ MUTILATED BODY IN MITRE SQARE

Fig. 1.1. "Finding the Mutilated Body in Mitre Square," *Illustrated Police News*, 6 October 1888.

Home Office on 17 October, "I look upon this series of murders as unique in the history of our country";[2] Warren resigned a few weeks later. The press agitation reached its shrillest pitch during October 1888, when there were no Whitechapel prostitute murders: the pseudonym Jack the Ripper of the probably inauthentic letter publicized by the Central News Agency achieved worldwide notoriety in the early days of that month. This name represented a state of mind rather than an individual: that mentality being a paroxysm of horror, fear, and fascinated disgust.

In the aftermath of the Chapman murder, a German hairdresser named Charles Ludwig was apprehended (18 September), and the evidence against him seemed powerful until the double murder was committed, while Ludwig was in police custody. Other suspects at this time included Jacob Isenschmid, an insane Swiss pork butcher; Oswald Puckridge (1838–1900), a trained apothecary who had recently been released from the Hoxton House Lunatic Asylum and had threatened to rip people up with a long knife; and three medical students, including John Sanders (1862–1901), who had attended

London Hospital but had become insane. It was speculated whether the killer was a member of a barbaric sect, a mad Freemason, a black magician, a dipsomaniac, a notoriety craver, a jewel thief, a midwife or abortionist, a person or persons intent on inciting anti-Semitism (many details of the Stride and Eddowes murders could be construed as intended to incriminate Jews), or a religious monomaniac. Sir George Savage (who suspected "*post-mortem* room and anatomy room porters") hypothesized that "imitative action may have come into play," and that the murders were maniacal acts of emulation by more than one killer, including someone bent on "world regeneration."[3] A looser speculation is that the killer was a social reformer such as Thomas Barnardo (who met Stride on 26 September) hoping to shock the national conscience about slum conditions. Certainly, Whitechapel became the cynosure of 1888. The Church of England clergyman Lord Sydney Godolphin Osborne, in a description typical of the time, characterized its inhabitants as living in "godless brutality, a species of human sewage, the very drainage of the vilest productions of human vice" and called for a concentrated philanthropic effort.[4]

On Friday, 9 November 1888, (perhaps between one and four in the morning) the Whitechapel murderer killed Mary Jane Kelly (b. 1862) in her room at a common lodging house, Miller's Court, off Dorset Street, Spitalfields. Her body was found almost naked on her bed, her throat cut. Since the murderer was secure in her room, without fear of interruption, he had time to cut her to pieces by the light from her fireplace. The mutilations were horrific, apparently undertaken in an atrocious frenzy.

Kelly is usually treated as the last victim of the Whitechapel murderer. His death, incarceration in an asylum, or emigration may have terminated the crimes. (The deaths of Alice McKenzie, whose throat was cut between 12:25 and 12:50 a.m. in Castle Alley, off Whitechapel High Street, on 16 July 1889, and of Frances Cole, whose throat was cut under a railway arch in Swallow Gardens at 2:15 a.m. on 13 February 1891, have been tentatively attributed to the Whitechapel murderer.)

Over 130 suspects are listed in *The Jack the Ripper A to Z* (1991). Sir Melville Macnaghten of the Criminal Investigation Department believed in the guilt of Montague Druitt (1857–1888), a barrister and schoolmaster who drowned himself in the Thames after the Kelly killing. Another police official, Sir Robert Anderson, suspected Aaron Kosminski (c. 1864–1919), a Polish Jew working in Whitechapel as a hairdresser, who was confined in Colney Hatch Asylum in 1891. Inspector Frederick Abberline of Scotland Yard, the most impressive detective involved in the investigation, suspected Severin Klosowski (1865–1903), a Pole who had studied surgery and immigrated to England in 1887. Klosowski (who originally worked as a hairdresser in Whitechapel) was a Roman Catholic who masqueraded as a Jew; under the name of George Chapman, he was executed for poisoning his three common-law wives between 1897 and 1902. Chief Inspector John Littlechild specified an unbalanced woman-hating American quack, Francis Tumblety (c. 1833–1903), who absconded abroad while on police bail after Kelly's death. Tumblety and perhaps Klosowski are the most plausible suspects. The guilt of an unidentified Jewish ritual butcher is also tenable. Sillier accusations include the eldest son of the prince of Wales, Albert Victor, Duke of Clarence and Avondale; his tutor, James Kenneth Stephen (1859–1892); the physician Sir William Gull; the painter Walter Sickert; and Dr. Thomas Neill Cream (1850–1892), an abortionist hanged for poisoning Lambeth prostitutes. Several Ripperologists accuse a fish porter named Joseph Barnett (1860–1927), who was in love with Kelly and was supposedly trying to frighten her off the streets.

The Ripper was the first sexual serial killer to command international notoriety: he inaugurated the modern consciousness of such crimes. Since 1888, the phenomenon has proliferated: in England the atrocities of an unidentified serial killer of prostitutes in Notting Hill and Shepherd's Bush (1964–65), and of Peter Sutcliffe, the Yorkshire Ripper (1976–80), are comparable to the Whitechapel murders. Though the Victorian public had always reveled in the sanguinary details of murder, and popular journalism had always striven to shock, Jack's nightmarish mutilations were recognized in 1888 as new and strange. In an epoch when a glimpse of a woman's ankle could seem indecent, the violence of his mutilations was blasphemous. His attacks were reported in explicit, pitiless detail of a kind that would be rendered impossible a generation later by voluntary journalistic self-censorship. The detectives' policy of not confiding their progress to journalists resulted in reporting that was often wild, irresponsible, and mendacious; accurate reports were contradicted with seeming authority by jealous or mischievous journalistic rivals. At their breakfast tables, the British were confronted with the mechanisms of the vilest sexual homicide. After the Eddowes murder, a "sweet-natured and kindly-souled" middle-class girl who had been forbidden "to read *Adam Bede*" was invited to east London, and asked enthusiastically, "'Shall we pass Mitre Court?'"[5] Knowledge of the crimes affected everyone, and there was no return to innocence.

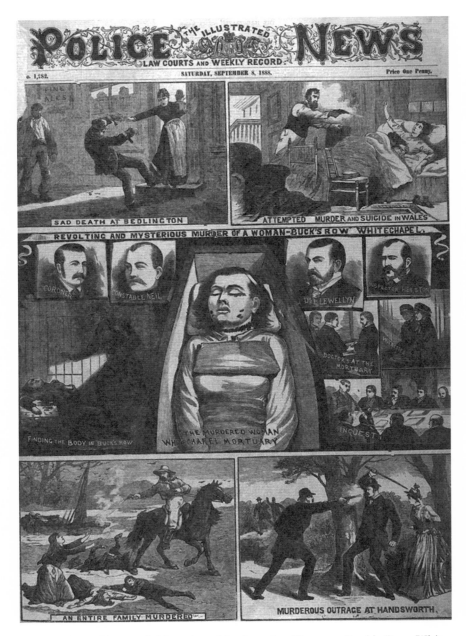

Fig. 1.2. "Revolting and Mysterious Murder of a Woman—Buck's Row, White-chapel," *Illustrated Police News*, 8 September 1888.

Jack the Ripper is partly a literary phenomenon. There was already a vigorous political and quasi-scientific debate among the intelligentsia in 1888 about the body, the city, and degeneration theory. The Whitechapel murders occurred two years after the publication of Robert Louis Stevenson's *The Strange Case of Dr. Jekyll and Mr. Hyde* and of Richard von Krafft-Ebing's *Psychopathia Sexualis,* and two years before the publication of Oscar Wilde's *The Picture of Dorian Gray.* The graffiti clue left after the Eddowes murder seems adapted from an incident in Arthur Conan Doyle's *A Study in Scarlet,* published a few months earlier in *Beeton's Christmas Annual.* Much contemporary doggerel developed about the Ripper. Later, Leonard Matters's unreliable *The Mystery of Jack the Ripper* (1930) launched a massive literature of Ripperologists: some of it exploitative, asinine, or tawdry, but other books more fascinating. The crimes inspired one excellent novel, Marie Belloc Lowndes's *The Lodger* (1913), admired by Gertrude Stein and Ernest Hemingway, and first adapted for the screen by Alfred Hitchcock in 1926 (starring Ivor Novello); the film has been remade three times. Phyllis Tate turned *The Lodger* into an opera (1960). A cognate novel is Colin Wilson's *Ritual in the Dark* (1960). By 1977 there were twenty films reflecting the Ripper story. The Ripper crimes influenced Frank Wedekind's plays *Erdgeist* and *Die Büchse der Pandora* (and hence Berg's 1937 opera *Lulu*), as well as Bertolt Brecht's *Dreigroschenoper.*

The identity of Jack the Ripper will likely never be known. He is nonetheless firmly established as one of those indelible British characters that continue to fire the imaginations of artists and audiences, amateur enthusiasts and dedicated professionals, worldwide. Unlike Sherlock Holmes, Tarzan, or James Bond, however, the Ripper was all too real, as were his crimes, and as were his victims.

Fall Semester 2016

A version of this lecture appeared in the *Oxford Dictionary of National Biography.*

1. *The Diary of Gathorne Hardy, Later Lord Cranbrook, 1866–1892: Political Selections,* ed. N. E. Johnson (Oxford, 1981), p. 716.

2. Stewart Evans and Paul Gainey, *The Lodger: The Arrest and Escape of Jack the Ripper* (London, 1995), p. 112.

3. George Savage, "Homicidal Mania," *Fortnightly Review,* 50 (Oct. 1888), p. 463.

4. *The Times,* 18 Sept 1888.

5. S. A. Barnett, "East London and Crime," *National Review,* 12 (1888–89), p. 437.

George Bernard Shaw, 1888. © National Portrait Gallery, London.

George Bernard Shaw and Physical Culture

JOHN D. FAIR

> *Mens sana in corpore sano* is a foolish saying. The sound body is a product of the sound mind.
>
> *Man and Superman*

On his way to becoming the most prolific modern playwright and man of letters, George Bernard Shaw contended that he had earned fifteen reputations, but neither he nor his many biographers consider him a physical culturist, despite his life-long obsession with bodily functions. The most obvious example is his fourth novel, *Cashel Byron's Profession* (1886), in which the hero acquires the fighting prowess of the heavyweight boxing champion Gene Tunney. It provided, according to Benny Green's 1978 study, an opportunity to demonstrate the "viability of the life force" and mind over matter. Thus, readers were attracted to the "spectacle of Life imitating Art."[1] Playing on this incongruity in "Pugilist and Playwright," Stanley Weintraub observed that this "process of life imitating art had become complete, for Tunney was the boxer become gentleman, Cashel Byron come to life."[2] In Jay Tunney's retrospective account of his father, *The Prizefighter and the Playwright*, he explains that "you had this paradox of a fighter who loved books, and Shaw loved the paradox because he himself was a paradox."[3]

The biographer Michael Holroyd identifies a deeper source of this trait in Shaw's attempt to escape from a frightful and loveless childhood. Shaw typically "put on the spectacles of paradox," by which he could turn "lack of love inside out" and conjure "optimism out of deprivation."[4] But Holroyd devotes little attention to Shaw's lifelong struggle with his physical self. Sally Peters successfully weaves pertinent details of Shaw's physical life into her 1996 study, but its destination, through the mythical vehicle of the life force, is spiritual. Indeed, most Shaw scholars portray Shaw's life as concentrated in the mind rather than the body, but his obsession with the latter is inescapable.

The earliest indication of this propensity appears in the memoirs of Edward McNulty, Shaw's classmate at a Dublin day school in the 1860s. Shaw's passion was drawing, fostered by visits to the National Gallery, where he admired depictions of humans with exaggerated muscularity and a resemblance to the figures of Michelangelo. Seeking to improve his and McNulty's drawing skills, Shaw devised a scheme to study the human form in his apartment, where they would alternate as nude models. Although such encounters might appear to reveal homosexual tendencies, they might not, given Shaw's enduring fascination with the unsexed nude and his lack of inhibition in revealing his unclothed body before cameras. Not unrelated to this physical awareness was a deepening concern for his well-being, drawn from lack of parental nurture. Most disillusioning was the hypocrisy of his father, George Carr Shaw, who while professing to be a teetotaler, was a dipsomaniac. Nor did Shaw find an adult model in his maternal uncle, William Gurly, a common drunkard and inveterate smoker, or solace from his mother, Bessie, who seemed devoid of maternal instincts.

The curse of alcohol is most apparent in Shaw's early novels. After 1878, forsaking his hapless father, he joined his mother, who was pursuing a music career in London. In his first novel, *Immaturity,* written in 1879 but unpublished until 1930, Shaw compensates for his family's moral failings and his lack of strong physical qualities by leading his main character (Smith, a clerk) to ballet, the most athletic of the arts. At a performance at the Alhambra theatre, the prima ballerina seems to become a veritable fairy. Afterward, her gymnastic skills obsess Smith. His ability to resist converting the dancer's physical artistry to sexual attraction, the ultimate form of bodily expression, Shaw considered a mark of genius.

His insights on genius stemmed from years of intellectual incubation in the British Museum Reading Room and exposure to Arthur Schopenhauer's *World as Will and Representation* (1819), in which Shaw learned about the unconscious forces governing human behavior. What he discerned from Schopenhauer was a possible escape from physical existence. Although an imperious will exercised tyrannous control over mankind, it could be neutralized through the strength of imagination and a level of knowledge that would inspire acts of genius. Artistic creation best exemplified this kind of insight. A Platonic idea based on eternal verities, it included for Shaw the medium of literature. Reinforcing Shaw's new ideas was his exposure to Percy Bysshe Shelley, who revealed the evolution of death into creative life and inspired his conversion to vegetarianism.

The theme of rejuvenation is evident in the transition between Shaw's second and fourth novels. In *The Irrational Knot* (1880) the plot centers on the unreasonableness of marriage, the relationship between alcohol and death, and the physical failings of a stage singer, dancer, and actress named Susanna Conolly, who had all the makings of genius. There was seemingly nothing she could not accomplish, but she took to drink—champagne by the gallon, from morning till night. No longer fit for society or marriage, Susanna flirted with death. The end came with a fall, bottle in hand, at a New York boardinghouse.

Ruination by drink appears only sparingly in *Cashel Byron's Profession,* which emphasizes vigor, good health, and the triumph of genius. Shaw creates the image of a strapping youth whose "broad pectoral muscles, in their white covering, were like slabs of marble." To Cashel's female admirer, Lydia, he was "the statue man," a paragon of manly strength and beauty. Cashel had "executive power," a Schopenhauerian concept that meant more than "merely living," but having the instinct to "act up to your ideas." Thus, in boxing, "you want to know how to hit him, when to hit him, and where to hit him; and then you want the nerve to go in and do it." For comparison, Shaw cites "a man in the musical line named Wagner, who is what you might call a game sort . . . wins his fights, yet they try to make out that he wins them in an outlandish way, and that he has no real science." Having defeated a slugger in the ring, Cashel displayed the nature of genius to his female admirer as champion of the world and a gentleman: "Where will you find his equal in health, strength, good looks or good manners?" The final didacticisms in *Cashel Byron* draw its author toward his emerging intellectual commitments—socialism and creative evolution. From Lydia, with eyes fully opened to the dignity of the common man, emerges a belief in "the doctrine of heredity": "I think my impulse towards a man strong in body and untroubled in mind a trustworthy one." It was "a plain proposition in eugenics."[5] As a template for the progress of humanity, a sound body seemed a fitting prerequisite for a sound mind.

A glimpse at the impact physical culture had on Shaw's personal life is possible through diaries he began keeping in 1885. Besides attending boxing matches, he trained with a boon companion, Pakenham Beatty, and even entered a championship. He bought a pair of five-pound dumbbells. He ate his vegetarian meals at a restaurant called the Wheatsheaf and used a spirometer to test his breathing. With income from his father's life insurance policy, he purchased an outfit of sanitary wool clothing, popularized by the clothing reformer Gustav Jaeger, that allowed the skin to breathe. Shaw celebrated his twenty-ninth birthday with Jenny Patterson, a widow who provided his first sexual experience. Starting in 1886, he kept a separate entry on his health. A persistent concern was colds and an inability to rise early, but he also complained about boils, eye floaters, nausea, loose bowels, headaches, and laryngitis, which hampered his public speaking. Most frustrating was his vulnerability to carnal desires. It disgusted him that trifling about women consumed a great deal of energy. However much he styled himself a philosopher, he was susceptible to the biological life force.

At this juncture, he read Samuel Butler's *Luck, or Cunning, as the Main Means of Organic Modification?* (1887), ironically, on the same day he recorded having sex with Jenny twice and staying till one in the morning, thereby jeopardizing his commitment to early rising. What he ascertained from Butler was a twofold affirmation of purposeful existence—the relationship between heredity and memory, and the infusion of design into organic development by which even physical characteristics could be purposely transmitted. In trying to refute Charles Darwin's attempt to eliminate mind from the evolution of the universe, Butler subscribed to a version of intelligent design whereby bodily form became the solidified state of an idea or memory. In accordance with his belief in God's omnipotence, he contended that organic modification resulted from cunning, not luck. Although Shaw had abandoned organized religion, it still permeated his convictions and personal conduct. It was exemplified in his purity of lifestyle and his notion that men should leave the world a better place than they found it. Shaw's concept of the life force can be viewed as a tenet of a secularized religion.

By 1888, Shaw's preoccupation with health had fostered a better understanding of the body-mind connection. Though heartened by an absence of colds, he became depressed over an aching jaw and remained low in health and spirits until the spring of 1889. From this slough of despond, Shaw was drawn into the spiritual realm by the writings of Schopenhauer on genius, Nietzsche on the superman, and the otherworldly strains of Richard Wagner. That their ideas were pullulating in Shaw's mind is evident in a letter to Hubert Bland in which he formulates "the spirit of the will," which, unlike Darwinism, was more akin to humanism than science. The ordinary man "supposes his life to be a mere matter of logical consequences from a few bodily appetites and externally appointed 'duties' with their attendant pains and penalties."[6] Yet Shaw was constantly vigilant of his own bodily functions. So closely did he monitor his health habits that one suspects hypochondria, but Weintraub insists that "he was in excellent health for his place and time."[7] Indeed, after leaving the worldly Jenny one evening, he was exhilarated by a walking race with two soldiers in the park, which he won. Life for the ordinary man might be the consequence of a few bodily appetites, but Shaw, with his abstemious lifestyle, could envision a higher level of being made possible by his own physical resources.

To attain bodily perfection, Shaw paid attention to his diet, which excluded such appetizing staples as meat, alcohol, coffee, and tea. But there remained a nagging sense that diet, even a vegetarian one, had to be complemented by exercise. Thus, he invested in a pair of skates in December 1891. By January, Shaw was mentally "incapable of work and craving for exercise." He took long walks around Hyde Park, and in August he engaged in more vigorous exercise. In addition to walking and swimming, he had a long game of cricket, followed by a round of tennis. "This violent exercise . . . wrenched and strained every muscle in my body external and internal; and I was unable to move without pain afterwards." By year's end, he needed rest and rejuvenation but wanted "bodily exercise badly."[8]

Concurrently, he was drawn to a higher source of inspiration through the writings of Schopenhauer. He consumed a couple of books in July 1891 and reread them on the train on 24 January 1892. He wrote to the actress Florence Farr three days later on the nature of genius in terms that closely corresponded to Schopenhauer's distinction between genius and talent. Whereas talent was a form of excellence manifested in versatility and acute reasoning, "the genius beholds another world," one perceived more intuitively, in "greater purity and distinctness."[9] These ideas, rooted in physical reference points, provided Shaw a better sense of his own life and a template for constructing his superman.

In 1893, his commitment to exercise increased as he took to walking frequently. Bicycling presented a new challenge that Shaw eagerly embraced. Over the next several years, he cycled about city and country, sometimes with reckless abandon. The Argoed, a Victorian country house in Monmouthshire, Wales, where he stayed in the summer of 1895, provided ample opportunities for vigorous exercise. Unaccustomed to shoving his machine up steep hills and descending at blistering speeds, he suffered several mishaps. By the summer of 1896, Shaw was pedaling for four hours daily, still driving himself at a superhuman pace, overexerting his fragile physique, and enduring the consequences. In March 1897, he took an evening ride of "eight or nine miles at wild speed on the bike; and the next morning I was again a wreck." After another speeding casualty, he described himself as "a ludicrous spectacle, like a badly defeated prizefighter." But he presumed himself to be "as fit as ever" and "better for the adventure in nerve."[10]

In the spring of 1898, Shaw declared to Beatrice Webb that he was in "almost superhuman condition—fleshless, bloodless, vaporous, ethereal, and stupendous in literary efficiency." But after a ride to Ealing, his left foot swelled to the size of a leg of mutton, and he broke his arm. Confined to crutches and a wheelchair, he continued to exercise by hobbling up and down stairs. After multiple recoveries and relapses, Shaw emerged weary but in a physical-culture frame of mind, declaring to Beatty his intention to delve further into the noble art of boxing and to investigate how evolutionary theory was propagating the "decay of the human intellect" by turning from the "truth of Lamarckism to the mechanical rationalism of Natural Selection." Shaw's faith in creative evolution coincided with the struggles of "the Grand School," he told the drama critic William Archer, those "who are building up the intellectual consciousness of the race": "My men are Wagner, Ibsen, Tolstoy, Schopenhauer, Nietzsche, who have . . . nobody to fight for them." Archer corrected him, "You are *their* man."[11]

Shaw's subsequent conception of a superman was a composite of numerous intellects of his day and an attempt to project man into a higher, nonphysical reality. In *Man and Superman,* Shaw uses a debate between Don Juan (the earthly hero) and the devil to illustrate how man creatively evolves through the life force ultimately to form a race of supermen: "We agree that we want superior mind; but we need not fall into the football club folly of counting on this as a product of superior body." Given the choice between "a race of athletes and a race of 'good' men, let us have the athletes: better Samson and Milo than Calvin and Robespierre." But the superman would be a product of the biologically superior or "intelligently fertile," who could propagate "the partisans of the Superman." Although it would necessitate elimination of the unintelligent and the voluptuary elements from the evolutionary process, genius was not the exclusive preserve of the upper classes. Fulfillment of his utopian dream of allowing the working classes access to the corridors of wisdom would require an overhaul of society along lines promoted by the fashionable eugenics movement. Only through selective breeding could socialism and human evolution be achieved. His formula for advancing the species echoed Schopenhauer's views on heredity (à la Plato) that an improvement of humanity might be attained "not so much by instruction and culture as rather upon the path of generation." He advocated a State Department of Evolution, with a Cabinet seat and revenue to fund state experiments. It could even entail a chartered company to improve human livestock. Such radical solutions hinted at flirtations that Shaw would later have with totalitarian regimes.

Flirtations for Shaw at this time, however, were limited to young women, who often sought his company as a sage. His physically unfulfilling marriage to Charlotte Payne-Townshend made him vulnerable to the life force embodied in Erica Cotterill, with whom he assumed an avuncular role not unlike that portrayed in his most famous play, *Pygmalion*. Responding to a compliment from her about his youthfulness in 1907, Shaw explained that his body "persists incongruously in the usual course": "Every two years or so, my spectacles become too weak; and I have to get new ones. My hair gets whiter: I have gold plates and artificial teeth in my mouth: my feet seem a longer way off; and when I race down a hill or cross a stream on stepping stones I am not quite so sure that they will go exactly where I mean to place them." Further attention to his body was necessitated by serious bouts of lumbago in April 1912. From Shropshire, where he was visiting friends, he told Charlotte that he had worked hard for five hours: "We chopped and hacked and piled up heaps of furze bushes for burning like three field laborers. Every muscle in my body is racked: the lumbago is no longer perceptible because I am all lumbago from top to toe."

In June, Shaw became afflicted with the severest worldly affliction when he fell "head over heels in love" with the widowed Mrs. Patrick Campbell, who would play Eliza Doolittle in *Pygmalion*. In the ensuing torrent of love letters, he professed to be her "utter captive." He seemed deliriously happy. In his newfound exhilaration, Shaw bought a motor bicycle and rode seventy-seven miles on his initial journey, despite having never ridden one. All went well until he approached a "bad corner" near his home at Ayot St. Lawrence: "I went into the bank, and fell one way whilst the machine happily fell the other. I only broke its lamp, and I broke nothing." When Campbell broke off their relationship, Shaw was devastated.[12] Physical exertion in the form of long-distance bicycle trips to Essex, Coventry, and Scotland likely served as means of alleviating his emotional pain.

While Britain was absorbed with war, Shaw's views relating to healthful living were publicized in America by *Physical Culture* magazine. Its editor, Bernarr Macfadden, introduced him as an ascetic and "almost everything apart from the common-place in thought, manners and life." For three successive issues in 1915, readers were exposed to Shaw's wit and wisdom in his play *Getting Married.*[13] In 1916, the magazine offered Shavian advice on health and humanity in the essays "You and Your Doctor" and "The Folly of Vivisection," and in 1917 by a five-month series entitled "What's Wrong with Marriage?" Later Macfadden visited England and treated Shaw to a short film of himself working out. In 1936, when Shaw and his wife traveled to America, they met Macfadden in Miami and the health reformer John Kellogg at his sanatorium, in Michigan. Yet in retrospect, Shaw was dismissive of *Physical Culture,* which gave "far too much prominence to advertisements of overmuscled strong men."[14]

The boxing champion Gene Tunney held an attraction of a different kind. Shaw was a leading intellectual who was obsessive about his body, and Tunney was a practitioner of physical fortitude who craved intellectual fulfillment. They had a close intellectual compatibility: Tunney was attuned to Schopenhauer and had read Butler's *Way of All Flesh* before winning the heavyweight championship from Jack Dempsey in 1926. Mesmerized by the fight, Shaw obtained every newspaper and watched every film that covered it. Tunney seemed to embody the life force to Shaw, who deemed his victory a measure of intelligence. After retiring from the ring, Tunney visited England and, according to his son, was "electrified" by Shaw. Tunney believed Shaw's vegetarian diet kept him "radiantly healthy, buoyant and exceptionally fit." Their friendship was sealed by visits to an Italian resort, where they shared vigorous exercise. "Gene encouraged him to walk briskly for 20 minutes a day" and to "inhale deeply through his nose for 12 paces, hold his breath and exhale slowly through his mouth, repeating the process 15 times to sweep impurities from his body." Their favorite morning exercise was swimming, even in cool weather. After a cold shower, "the former world's heavyweight champion and the Irish playwright glided easily through the water for long distances." Another exercise was singing together while walking, especially vigorous pieces by Wagner and Handel, while they "reflected on the nature of life."[15] Unlike the emergent political supermen on the international scene, Shaw could personalize his admiration of Tunney. As the biographer Frank Harris noted, Tunney was "another of Shaw's gods, a man of action. . . . You can write Shaw's inner convictions and hidden aspirations in terms of Lenin, Mussolini, and Tunney."[16] In *Heartbreak House* (1919), Shaw suggests the need for a strongman to steer the ship of state.

In the post-war years, as Shaw approached seventy, he befriended other young men of daring. "As his vigour declined," observes Holroyd, "so his need for vicarious exploits through younger men-of-action-and-letters intensified." Shaw was captivated during the 1920s by the rising political star Oswald Mosley, whose "radicalism and unorthodoxy" led him to abandon the Conservative Party for Labour and to form his own New Party. Mosley seemed capable of heroic deeds. Holroyd asks: "He was athletic and quick-minded, part child and part strong man—could this be the superman whose advent Shaw had been prophesying?" Eventually, Mosley self-destructed by attaching his British Union of Fascists to the cause of Benito Mussolini. Another fallen star for whom Shaw had an affinity was T. E. Lawrence, whose heroic deeds in the Middle East

Fig. 2.1. Gene Tunney and George Bernard Shaw, 1929. Getty Images.

encapsulated the life force as Shaw would depict it in *Saint Joan* (1923). Lawrence often stayed with Shaw, who edited and proofread his *Seven Pillars of Wisdom* and gave him a motorcycle.[17] Like Tunney, Lawrence regarded Shaw as his idol and even changed his name to T. E. Shaw.

Back to Methuselah (1921), a five-play metabiological swan song, was intended to be a sequel to *Man and Superman*, or a "second legend of Creative Evolution." In it, Shaw argues that the effective governance of civilized societies is not possible within the normal human lifespan. The life force enabling creative evolution requires time: "Mankind is by no means played out yet. If the weightlifter, under the trivial stimulus of an athletic competition, can 'put up a muscle,' it seems reasonable to believe that an equally earnest and convinced philosopher could 'put up a brain.' . . . If on opportunist grounds Man now fixes the term of his life at three score and ten years, he can equally fix it at three hundred, or three thousand." Shaw accepted the Lamarckian view that "living organisms changed because they wanted to." Creative evolution was possible through "deliberate human selection," not Darwin's circumstantial selection. While phenomena of "use and disuse, of wanting and trying, of the manufacture of weightlifters and wrestlers from men of ordinary strength," were familiar facts, they were puzzling as subjects of thought. In the march of progress, "mankind gains in stature from generation to generation, from epoch to epoch, from barbarism to civilization, from civilization to perfection." But it was the cumulative growth of the intellect, not the body, adds the She-Ancient in *As Far as Thought Can Reach,* the final part of *Back to Methuselah:* "It is this stuff [*indicating her body*], this flesh and blood and bone and all the rest of it, that is intolerable. . . . The day will come when there will be no people, only thought," she believed. "And that will be life eternal," responded the He-Ancient. The sculptor Martellus agreed: "The body always ends by being a bore."

Yet Shaw showed no less awareness of his physical being during his seventies, despite his yearning for intellectual fulfillment. How paradoxical that the most flagrant of corporeal pleasures should be so deeply etched in Shaw's association with the intellect. "I liked sexual intercourse," he told Frank Harris, "because of its amazing power of producing a celestial flood of emotion and exaltation of existence which, however momentary, gave me a sample of what may one day be the normal state of being for mankind in intellectual ecstasy."[18] In a 1929 interview for *Physical Culture,* Henry Neil deemed him in perfect condition. "Body and brain are matched to a remarkable degree in a rapier-like keenness. He is a live wire, a human dynamo." These sentiments were echoed in Hollywood during the Shaws' round-the-world tour in 1933. Film celebrities were attracted as much by his unique diet as by his acerbic wit. A *Screenland* photo showed "literature's 'bad boy'" refusing to act his age, being escorted around MGM Studios by the actress Marion Davies, who "has all she can do to keep pace with him."[19] Shaw was also photographed in later years while bathing in the buff. Though aware of the health risks of sunlight, he believed in dispensing with unnecessary clothing, thinking it promoted, like excessive eating and drinking, too much comfort and encouraged prudery.

As Shaw entered his ninth decade, he became more aware of his mortality. Though suffering from pernicious anemia, angina pectoris, locomotor ataxy, and anorexia, he maintained a daily exercise routine of sawing firewood. Even death took a physical-culture turn for Shaw. In September 1950, while trimming branches in the garden at Ayot, his favorite form of exercise, he fell on the pathway and was rushed to the hospital with a broken femur. Although the subsequent operation succeeded, doctors discovered a kidney and bladder malfunction, requiring Shaw to wear a catheter and cast. He responded to well-wishers that he just wanted to die and be gone as quickly as possible. "His mental worry about his kidney trouble killed him as much as the illness itself," Holroyd concluded. "I believe in life everlasting; but not for the individual," Shaw uttered as he neared death.[20]

Bernard Shaw could hardly be considered a physical culturist in any traditional sense. As a general rule, he eschewed bodily pleasures and would rarely admit that the body controlled his impulses or intellect. Sally Peters repeatedly stresses his disdain for the body: "Paradoxically, to emphasize vegetarianism was to emphasize what Shaw wanted to forget—the body, the essence of the material world."[21] Thus, his aversion to the world's foremost symbol of physical perfection of the time is understandable. "Eugen Sandow wanted to overmuscle me," he told George Viereck in 1926, "but I told him I never wanted to stand my piano on my chest, nor did I consider it the proper place for three elephants. I remained a weakling; but I am alive and Eugen is dead. Let not my example be lost on you, nor his fate. The pen is mightier than the dumbbell."[22] Physical strength for its own sake held no special place in Shaw's hierarchy of desirable traits. Nor did competitive sports hold much allure. In the 1930 *Who's Who,* Shaw contended that cricket symbolized what was wrong with England. Holroyd admits that Shaw's achievement, like that of Beatrice Webb, was "built on repression of the body."[23] As Shaw reminded Viereck in 1934, "The mind makes the body: watch your mind."[24]

Yet Shaw was obsessed with the body, especially his own body, and engaged in lifelong dietary and exercise regimens to sustain it. Regardless of what he sometimes maintained, his practices were classic examples of physical culture. As a vegetarian and teetotaler who eschewed tobacco and stimulants, he condemned physicians and wore sanitary wool clothing. Always a "sturdy walker," as his secretary Blanche Patch observes, he also regularly engaged in swimming, cycling, motoring, log sawing, hedge trimming, and, occasionally, tennis. None "was undertaken lightly for pleasure; the aim of each was to increase the efficiency of his existence."[25] Furthermore, physical fitness and a healthy lifestyle were values he promoted for others. Prizefighters, who held a special fascination for him, often appear in his writings. No sports more dramatically defined character to him than boxing, wrestling, and fencing. While Shaw visualized an ideal world as a state of mind over matter, his real world consisted of matter over mind.

The body also served as the basis for his conception of the superman. In this respect, he followed the lead of Schopenhauer, who emphasized the body's importance for human regeneration. "Sexual passion is the kernel of the will to live, and consequently the concentration of all desire," Schopenhauer contended; it was manifested mainly in "an effort to sustain the individual; yet this is only a step to the effort to sustain the species."[26] As a conduit for the will, the body provided the essence of being from which Shaw drew the anti-Darwinism of Samuel Butler, and the grounding for his attraction to the like-minded voices of Nietzsche, Ibsen, Wagner, and Henri Bergson. But for one fixated on the importance of heredity to the progress of the species, Shaw's platonic marriage and repeated statements of aversion to sex contradicted the very premise that would make creative evolution of the intellect possible. For a man of many paradoxes, it was the ultimate paradox.

Fall Semester 2015

1. Benny Green, *Shaw's Champions* (London, 1978), pp. xii–xiii, 194.
2. Stanley Weintraub, *The Unexpected Shaw* (New York, 1982), p. 45.
3. *Republican American,* 3 Dec. 2010.
4. Michael Holroyd, *Bernard Shaw* (New York, 1998), p. 9.
5. Bernard Shaw, *Cashel Byron's Profession* (London, 1930), pp. 37, 89, 91, 207, 233.
6. Dan H. Laurence, ed., *Bernard Shaw, Collected Letters* (London, 1965), I, p. 228.
7. Stanley Weintraub, ed., *Bernard Shaw: The Diaries* (London, 1986), I, p. 454.
8. Ibid., II, pp. 784, 847–48, 782.
9. Laurence, *Collected Letters,* I, p. 332.
10. Ibid., I, p. 823.
11. Ibid., II, pp. 50, 225, 352, 356.
12. Ibid., II, p. 731; III, pp. 87, 95.
13. *Physical Culture,* Oct. 1915, pp. 20–33.
14. Laurence, *Collected Letters,* IV, p. 14.
15. Jay Tunney, *The Prizefighter and the Playwright* (Richmond Hill, 2010), pp. 58, 139, 163, 171.
16. Frank Harris, *Bernard Shaw* (New York, 1931), p. 141.
17. Holroyd, *Bernard Shaw,* pp. 539–41.
18. Laurence, *Collected Letters,* IV, p. 192.
19. *Screenland,* June 1933, p. 13.
20. Holroyd, *Bernard Shaw,* pp. 788–91.
21. Sally Peters, *Bernard Shaw* (New Haven, 1996), p. 73.
22. Laurence, *Collected Letters,* IV, p. 14.
23. Holroyd, *Bernard Shaw,* p. 154.
24. Shaw Papers, Harry Ransom Center, University of Texas, 46.3.
25. Blanche Patch, *Thirty Years with G. B. S.* (New York, 1951), p. 281.
26. Schopenhauer, *World as Will and Idea* (London, 1891), pp. 3, 314.

Evelyn Waugh, 1955. Photo by Kurt Hutton. Getty Images.

3

Evelyn Waugh in North America

MARTIN STANNARD

E velyn Waugh once remarked, on hearing that a friend had un-
dergone a successful operation for lung cancer, "It is a typical triumph of modern science to find the only part of Randolph that is not malignant & to remove it."[1] The friend, of course,
was Randolph Churchill, Sir Winston's son, with whom Waugh had
an erratic comradeship. The remark was typically Waugh: savaging
with paradox someone for whom he had felt affection, hating the
modern world. By 1947, the year of his first visit to America, he had
wounded most of his friends. He had tried to bully John Betjeman
and Lady Diana Cooper into Catholicism; he had condemned Olivia
Plunket-Greene, the woman who had brought him to the Church,
as a traitor to the faith; he had lampooned Cyril Connolly in mor-
dant literary reviews. When, two years later, Nancy Mitford enter-
tained him in Paris and he conscientiously insulted all her friends,
she asked him why he needed to be so cruel. "You have no idea,"
he replied, "how much nastier I would be if I was not a Catholic.
Without supernatural aid I would hardly be a human being."[2] This
much-quoted remark from Christopher Sykes's biography is often
set alongside another. Hilaire Belloc, after a visit from Waugh, described him as "possessed." Waugh's American experience, however,
reveals a much more sympathetic character.

In 1944, after Waugh broke a leg while learning to parachute,
the army gratefully allowed him extended leave, during which he
wrote *Brideshead Revisited* (1945). Appearing with the Armistice, it

transformed his career. In America, it was a Book-of-the-Month
Club selection. At a time when most of his countrymen were suffering the austerities of the aftermath, Waugh became rich, and he
had the Americans to thank. In 1947, he traveled to Hollywood to
negotiate the film rights for an additional $100,000.

After a few days in New York, Waugh and his wife, Laura, entrained
on the luxurious Twentieth Century and headed for Chicago. His
American agent had stockpiled $3,500 in pocket money for them,
$2,000 of which Laura had already spent on clothes. Waugh had
purchased Champagne, brandy, and sherry to take west, assuming
that nothing of reputable quality would be available in the desert.
Most New Yorkers, he thought, were barbarians; but some, he had to
admit, possessed a certain chic: the train was undeniably luxurious,
its cuisine excellent. True, it was "all thin alluminium and one hears
coarse native laughter through the walls."[3] But there was something
appealing about the childlike seriousness of Americans, something
healthy in their sense of temporary habitation. "*Non habemus hic ma-
nentem civitatem*" ("Here we have no abiding city"); death at the el-
bow; life as brief exile from felicity—these religious preconceptions
had channeled Waugh's skepticism since 1930. In the dining car,
pulling out of Chicago, he had explained to the maître d'hôtel that
he was a foreigner, and had received a curt and pleasing response:
"We're all foreigners in this country."[4] Waugh liked that man.

Alec Waugh, also a writer, had made New York his professional
base after the war, and reported Evelyn's exploits to their mother,
a lonely widow living in a Highgate maisonette. "Evelyn's appearance at [Pasadena] station," he wrote, "was fantastic. The sun was
shining, tropical flowers were in bloom, all the young people were
dressed in shorts and slacks and open shirts and there was Evelyn
in a stiff white collar and a bowler hat, carrying a rolled umbrella."[5]
California was like nothing Evelyn had ever seen. As he stared impatiently from the window of MGM's limousine, the only compari-
sons that sprang to mind were Egypt and Abyssinia—Cairo with a
dash of Addis Ababa. He was equally surprised by the comfort of
the Bel Air Hotel. But fortunately there was something to complain
about. The suite that had been booked for him was not available.
An old man, a regular customer, had suffered a paralytic stroke
and could not be moved. Each morning, Waugh would appear in
his bowler to demand access. Each morning, the flabby young manager apologetically refused. "Your guests' health," Waugh replied
one day, "is no concern of mine,"[6] and he stepped up the attrition.
Even the hard-boiled film magnate who had arranged the visit was

shocked by this. Mr. Waugh, he told Peter Quennell, "had gravely disappointed him."[7]

This, of course, was precisely Waugh's intention. On the train, he had been advised to hold out for considerably more than they were offering. Thus it was that in the Petronian luxury of Louis B. Mayer's house, he declaimed: "How wise you American are to eschew all ostentation and lead such simple, wholesome lives. This really is delightful. Who'd even *want* to live in the main house when he could have this charming gatehouse instead!"[8] And all this from a smiling, cherubic face. "I can tell you," someone reported, "it was all rather unnerving. Now we don't quite know how to deal with him, even on a business level."[9]

Business with Mr. Waugh was clearly going to be difficult. He had taken one look at Hollywood studio life and decided that none of these savages was going to monkey with his magnum opus, $100,000 or no $100,000. All saw *Brideshead* as a love story. None recognized the theological implications. But how to escape from the deal without repayment of expenses? Fortunately, the Hayes-Johnson dicta (that is, the Hollywood Production Code) came to the rescue. As a form of moral sieve, their function was to eliminate impurity from moving pictures. When the *Brideshead* script was condemned as likely to undermine the conception of Christian marriage, Waugh, with the excuse he needed, refused changes.

From this point, he instructed his MGM driver to take him not to the studio but to the pets' cemetery and to its elaborate counterpart for the defunct plutocracy. He was gripped. "I am entirely obsessed by Forest Lawns [*sic*]," he wrote to his agent, "& plan a long short story about it. I go there two or three times a week, am on easy terms with the chief embalmer & next week am to lunch with Dr. HUBERT EATON himself. It is an entirely original place—the *only* thing in California that is not a copy of something else." MGM had supplied introductions; Hubert Eaton, the "visionary" founder, provided guided tours of the grounds and embalming rooms. Here Waugh saw the loved ones propped up and painted. The place symbolized for him the paganism at the heart of the American Dream: if Forest Lawn was California, and California was America, America was the cemetery of the humanist fallacy. Primed with artistic enthusiasm, he returned to England and wrote *The Loved One* (1948) quickly. Its American reception surprised him. His agent had advised against American publication. Both had expected ructions. In fact, nearly everyone admired it, and Waugh had to think again about the "barbarism" of that powerful audience across the pond.

Fig. 3.1. *The Loved One* (1948), by Evelyn Waugh.

THE HOLLYWOOD VISIT SHOWS WAUGH at his worst: snobbish, patronizing, vindictive. But an unaccustomed humility began to appear in his correspondence afterward. He was growing ashamed of
his neurotic outbursts, struggling to cultivate the virtue he chiefly
lacked: compassion. And behind this spiritual struggle lay a then-
obscure figure: a young American monk, Thomas Merton. The
rights to his autobiography, *The Seven Storey Mountain,* had been offered to a friend of Waugh's, Tom Burns. Burns, a publisher, had
passed the book on to Waugh for an opinion. But Waugh, it seems,
had read the book and was already in contact with Merton. Waugh
had suggested cuts. Merton was delighted. Waugh was the writer he
most admired. "I need criticism," the young monk replied, "the way
a man dying of thirst needs water,"[10] and from these formal beginnings a close friendship took root. Waugh edited the British edition,
Elected Silence (1949). He cut about a third and, with typical artistic
modesty, remarked in his foreword only that this "very remarkable
Autobiography" had been "very slightly abridged," refusing even to
say by whom.

It was an odd friendship with Merton. They met only once. As
often in Waugh's later life, the relationship was conducted by post.
Waugh sent him books on prose style and discussed writing like a
benevolent schoolmaster. Merton, bewildered with gratitude, was in
literary matters a penitent to Waugh's confessor. But their discussions quickly broadened to include the spiritual life—and here roles
were reversed. Merton never knew the burlesque masks with which
Waugh defended his privacy so fiercely, only a humble, self-lacerating
soul tortured by his own sense of sinfulness. "Like all people with
intellectual gifts," Merton wrote, "you would like to argue yourself
into a quandary that doesn't exist. Don't you see that in your anxiety
to explain how your contrition is imperfect you are expressing an intense sorrow that it is not so—and that is true contrition."[11] Waugh
remained unconvinced and saw his spiritual condition as parlous.
But there was, at least, something he could do to assist the faith,
something penitential. "It seems to me likely," he wrote to *Life* magazine, "that American Catholicism may help save the world,"[12] and
he proposed a lengthy article on the subject. Waugh had already
planned a lecture tour in January 1949. *Life* agreed to fund a pre-
liminary tour for Waugh to discuss American Catholicism with the
bishops and professors. And so it was that in November 1948 he set
off on his second trip to the States, and his only one without Laura.
The contract was arranged so as to be almost entirely discountable
as expenses. Pietas and tax avoidance thus magnificently combined,
Waugh began the oddest quest of his life. Less than a year after

Fig. 3.2. Thomas Merton, in his study. Photo by John Howard Griffin. Merton Center, Bellarmine University.

completing *The Loved One,* he was returning to the country his book had savaged in search of spiritual enlightenment.

He didn't spare himself: New York, Boston, Baltimore, Kentucky (to visit Merton), New Orleans (all by train), and home, exhausted, at the end of December. In a benign mood, stepping ashore at Southampton, he broke a golden rule and allowed an interview. The next day, an article appeared entitled "Waugh Doesn't Like the U.S. but Tolerates Its Dollars": "Evelyn Waugh told the British Press today that 'it is almost impossible for a man to lead a good life in the United States' but admitted that he was going back next month for a series of lectures at $550 apiece . . . 'They heat their rooms to seventy-five degrees, then nail down the windows so that you suffocate. . . . Their radios are on all day. And they talk too much.' . . . Mr Waugh said that he was relieved to be back in England because he was afraid that should he die in the United States, the Morticians Union of America would refuse to bury him because of . . . *The Loved One.*"[13]

He should, he knew, have known better than to have attempted comic irony with journalists, but somewhere between the beatific vision and the fleshpots, he was caught with his dry soul hungering for contrition to ease the burden of his faith. All that remained to him was a form of the cenobitic life: the retreat to his country house; the stocking of library and garden; Laura and the farm; the embellishment of the place; the education of his children; the construction of a huge, grim, and solitary jest from what was left of his life and the hope that death would not be unduly delayed. Waugh was only forty-five in December 1948, but he was a very old man. He wanted to die.

Waugh's version of the "monastic" life could appear amusing to the popular press in the Age of Austerity. His incoming correspondence, however, immediately demolishes any charges of hypocrisy. He quietly distributed tens of thousands of pounds to charity, including large checks to a family of very distant relations who had become displaced persons in the European camps. Before leaving for the States, Waugh had sent Father Caraman's *Month* a free short story that directly concerned such refugees and the author's military experience in Yugoslavia. It dealt with a British officer's frustration and guilt as he tried to release a party of Jews from a DP camp run by the Partisans. The text was eventually spliced, almost intact, into *Unconditional Surrender* (1961). As with *A Handful of Dust* (1934), Waugh began his trilogy at the end, and the title of the story, "Compassion," suggests both a major thematic concern of *The Sword of Honour* and the focus of Waugh's spiritual struggle.

CONTRITION, COMPASSION, HUMILITY—these things he prayed for. But resisting vanity was difficult during the lecture tour that followed. Waugh and Laura docked in New York at the end of January 1949, and were greeted by a firestorm of publicity. *Scott-King's Modern Europe* (1947) and *Work Suspended & Other Stories* (1948) were about to be published. Catholic America was still humming with controversial debate about Graham Greene's *The Heart of the Matter* (1948), a novel that Waugh addressed directly in his talk. The title was "Three Vital Writers," G. K. Chesterton, Ronald Knox, and Greene. "The U.S.A.," Waugh said in his advertising material, "is assuming the leadership of the 'West,' which historically was formed by Christianity, predominantly Catholic Christianity. The 'West' is incomprehensible unless one understands the CHURCH—which is identical everywhere: a single supernatural body. Great diversity, however, exists in this essential uniformity . . . English Catholicism is the natural bridge of understanding between American and European Catholicism. The particular character of the CHURCH in England can best be illustrated by examining the lives and work of three eminent Catholic writers." Coming from almost anyone else, this might have seemed a dreary diet. Coming from the celebrated author of *Brideshead* and *The Loved One,* a close friend of Greene, it was a showstopper. Packed houses greeted him everywhere—and he did not disappoint them.

Waugh's first two engagements were not modest affairs: at the Waldorf Astoria and New York Town Hall. Robert Craft, the conductor and writer, was at the latter. "It was," he recorded, "the coolest performance of the sort I have ever seen, even though he disparages it." Several days later, Craft tried to discuss the lecture over dinner, having engineered a meeting between the Great English Novelist and the Great Russian Composer. Stravinsky was in town.

Craft invited the Waughs to his hotel. They arrived, spectacular in evening dress: "Mrs Waugh . . . fair and lovely, Mr Waugh pudgy, ruddy, smooth-skinned, rather ramrod and poker-faced." Waugh was awkward and defensive, eyeing the composer of *The Rite of Spring* with undisguised suspicion. Craft made the introductions and maneuvered uneasily between the two couples. When he tried to draw out Waugh on the lecture, conversation was quickly deflected. Despite Waugh's rage at that newspaper report from Southampton, he proceeded to reinforce the statements he had denied: his rooms were too hot; the fervent hope of the Morticians' Union, he insisted, was that he should die on American soil. Mr. and Mrs. Stravinsky, disconcerted, sank into hushed conversation in Russian. No one was fooled by her elaborate display of rummaging in her bag, pretending to talk about cigarettes. Clearly, they were discussing the Waughs.

It was a block and a half to the restaurant on a freezing night. Waugh stumped along, glum and coatless. His spirits seemed marginally to rise with the discovery of a funeral parlor but quickly dropped again on entering Maria's—dark and crowded, no one else in evening dress. Craft feared the worst but soon discovered how quickly wine and good Italian food could warm Waugh's heart. He began to act gallantly with Mrs. Stravinsky and, turning the conversation to the Church, was delighted by the composer's response. "Here," Craft noted, Stravinsky shone, "showing himself to be at least as ultramontanist as Mr W., at least as well read in Chesterton and Péguy, and at least as prone to believe in the miraculous emulsification of Saint Januarius's blood." Thus encouraged, the Stravinskys admitted to having read and admired Waugh's complete works. Another palpable hit, and another Waugh began to emerge, "as magnanimous and amusing as the old one was unbending and precise." Ultimately, the evening was triumphantly convivial. There was only one further hiccup. Mrs. Stravinsky invited the Waughs to the forthcoming premiere of her husband's *Mass*. No, no, Waugh said abruptly, it couldn't be done; tickets for return passage already booked. And lest they press the point: "All music is positively painful to me."[14]

It was the same everywhere Waugh went in America. A chain of conflicting anecdotes followed him from Baltimore to New Orleans: he was frank and convivial; he was dismissive and discourteous; he was the prophet of doom and the celebrant of faith. Certainly, the Americans did not know what to make of him. And when, on the one occasion that he crossed the border to speak, in Windsor, Ontario, the Canadians were equally baffled. Moving on to Chicago and Milwaukee, Waugh found it increasingly difficult to disguise his boredom with the Midwest, and in an effort to discover something amusing, had written ahead to John Pick of Marquette University. Could he arrange for Waugh to meet some Indians, preferably on a reservation? Unfortunately, the reservations were hundreds of miles away. The best Pick could offer was waxwork figures in the Public Museum. Wholly unsatisfactory: Waugh wanted them alive. "After I met him and Mrs Waugh at the train I tried to take them to see the sights of Milwaukee—but instead he paid attention to the conversation of two of my students in the front seat of the car; one . . . was telling the other that his family were vacationing in Florida and had sent him a small . . . alligator. Waugh asked: 'Do you feed it shells to harden its skin? . . . Rather fond of it, aren't you? . . . Do you miss it when you're at classes? . . . Where do you keep it?' The student said, 'Well, in my room, of course.' 'Why, at Oxford,' Waugh replied, 'we would have had to keep it in a kennel.'"[15]

Waugh was a master of embarrassment. Forewarned, Professor Pick had made scrupulous arrangements for the dinner party: the silver was polished, the wine chilled, the candles lit. "All went well," Pick reported, "till toward the close of the meal he whispered—audibly—to . . . Laura across the table making queer gestures with wiggling his fingers. She tried to ignore him and conversed more and more audibly with her dinner partner. Waugh repeated. Repeated again. Finally, Laura saw what his predicament was and said, 'Evelyn, to the kitchen tap, my dear, to the kitchen tap.' . . . I had thought of every detail except the finger bowls."[16] Apparently, the only source of fascination for Waugh was Catholic gadgetry—the commercialization of pietism, such as devices for counting rosary beads. "Another anecdote from the Springfield town-diocese shop," he wrote later to Merton. "A traveller came in with a new type of plastic crucifix and said: 'Its great advantage is that it is so strong that you can throw it on the ground and stamp on it.'"[17] That found its way into the *Life* article and might have seemed perfectly in keeping with a generally flippant approach. What the public could not see, however, what he would never allow them to see, was the sincere missionary purpose of his tour. He was not trekking round glamorous institutions, but often small, independent Catholic universities—and for the second time. Everywhere, he made himself available to the press. The whole business was purgatorial to him, particularly so because the more he saw, the more presumptuous his project appeared. No coherent history of Catholicism in America existed, and he had undertaken to cover this massive subject in a magazine article. Waugh returned to England profoundly depressed by the prospect of *Life*. The six thousand words of "The American Epoch in the Catholic Church" took him the best part of three months to complete—astonishingly slow by his standards—and in the end, he thought it a failure: drearily pedagogic. In fact, when it appeared in September, it met with huge success and revealed a depth of humble piety in Waugh that few Americans suspected. He had been widely reported as hating their country. Here he was springing to its defense.

Shortly after finishing his article, Waugh read Merton's *The Seeds of Contemplation* (1949) and wrote to him about it: "I am greatly impressed by your assurance. You write as if you had been a director of souls for a lifetime. Except perhaps that an experienced director would not press the need for contemplation on all so eagerly. . . . But don't you think that most souls are of slow growth? Is it not the most precocious child whom the parent loves most? Is there not a slight hint of bustle and salesmanship with which you want to scoop us all into a higher grade than we are fit for?"[18] There can be little doubt that Waugh was referring here to himself: a soul of painfully slow growth, a prodigal son. His precocity was deeply ingrained, incurable, the necessary attack on boredom. He may not have been "possessed," but he was a tormented man. He hurt people and somehow could not stop himself from doing it. It was the power to hurt that made him a writer and exerted a demonic fascination on his friends. In this way he had chosen his friends, testing their resilience, and a form of their love for him became the craving to be one of those he would not injure. Of late, however, his judgment of the gap between tease and injury had become erratic, and this distressed him. He believed in the power of evil. Like St Augustine, he wished to be made good—but not yet.

If he could not be good and was constitutionally incapable of being careful, he could at least use his literary power in the service of the Church. "The American Epoch" is penitential in its austerity. Jokes are sparse. Waugh conscientiously foregrounds the whole range of his prejudices against America, only to demolish them as ignorance. The Church was universally in a minority, constantly threatened by "enemies inside and outside her body." What mattered was that "Catholics are the largest religious body in the United States, the richest and in certain ways the most lively branch of the Catholic Church in the world . . . firmly grounded in a neutral, secular state."[19] One of the more moving sights of his tour, he says, was in New Orleans: Ash Wednesday, the Roosevelt Hotel packed with tourists oblivious of the significance of Lent. "But across the way the Jesuit Church was teeming with life all day long; a continuous, dense crowd of all colours and conditions moving up to the altar rails and returning with their foreheads signed with ash. And the old grim message was being repeated over each penitent: 'Dust thou art and unto dust thou shalt return.' One grows parched for that straight style of speech in the desert of modern euphemisms."[20]

The phrase "all colours and conditions" is significant. To make his American argument coherent, Waugh had to qualify the hierarchical principle on which so much of his thinking had been based. He was examining here the root of his prejudice against the common man. He does not overcome it, but he does at least confront it. In America, most Catholics were the descendants of slaves or of impoverished immigrants from the Old World. Many were still poor. Their faith was associated in the popular mind with a redundant heritage, "with the smell of garlic and olive oil and grandfather muttering over the foreign-language newspaper." Europeans, Waugh warns, should be cautious of sneering. He praises "the heroic fidelity of the Negro Catholics" and defends humble piety. "Without help from the State . . . the poor have covered their land with schools, colleges and universities, boldly asserting the principle that nothing less than an entire Christian education is necessary to produce Christians. For the Faith is not a mere matter of learning a few prayers and pious stories in the home. It is a complete culture infusing all human knowledge." In the context of the Church, and there was for Waugh no other context, he had learned a form of humility. No humanist argument could convince him of the merits of egalitarianism, but he had to accept that in the eyes of God all men were equal: "A youth who is inarticulate in conversation may well be eloquent in prayer. It would be an intolerable impertinence to attempt to judge . . . God alone knows his own." In the present phase of humanist, competitive materialism, he suggests, contemplatives are the powerhouse of faith: "The Church and the world need monks and nuns more than they need writers. These merely decorate. The Church can get along very well without them." Nothing could be further from the implicit connection between aesthetic taste and faith that permeates *Brideshead,* and in this chastened mood he returned eagerly to work on what he thought his "masterpiece," a novel that had already been five years in the making: *The Quest of the Empress Dowager,* or *Helena* (1950), as it became.

EIGHTEEN MONTHS LATER THE NOVEL was complete, and the birth of his seventh and last child, Septimus (8 July 1950), marked a milestone in Waugh's life. Beyond that, the final, fragile connections with the world of his youth broke. Even his faith had changed in character, hardening, contracting to the dry kernel of dogma that alone, he believed, kept him sane. Looking back over his forty-seventh year, he felt the latent enthusiasm that had fueled a lifetime's jokes was all but exhausted. The opening of a new decade represented to him only the end of an era, the point at which he seems to have moved from the boyish to the senescent, omitting middle age altogether. His last trip to America, for the publication of *Helena,* was his last jeu d'esprit.

Waugh and Laura arrived at the Plaza in September 1950 to the jubilant greetings of mink-coated Catholics and a fanfare from the press. Eighteen days of lecture-less luxury restored him from torpor to sustained high spirits for the last time in his life. Wherever he went, the conversation bubbled with fantasy, expense seemed limitless, and he bathed in adulation. *Helena,* just released, was going well. The climax of the trip was a party at the Plaza to celebrate the master's birthday. Anne Fremantle was dazzled: "I felt as though I was swallowing three canaries . . . It was all most gala and glorious . . . You touch these shores, & presto, life is a party & we all dance as though at the Waterloo Eve Ball."[21]

He left New York triumphant, his novel a best seller, his apostolic mission complete. He never returned, but he never reneged on his belief that America would act as the focus of Catholic Christendom during the dark years that lay ahead. The glitter and pace of New York, however, were no longer for him. Unlike his brother or Nancy Mitford or Graham Greene, he could not live as an expatriate, and he sailed back, an old man of forty-seven, to defend the faith on the European front. "I have felt so feeble in recent weeks," he wrote to Nancy two months later, "that at last I called in a doctor who took my blood-pressure & pronounced it the lowest ever recorded—in fact the pressure of a 6 months foetus. In an access of sudden hope I said, 'Does this mean that I shall die quite soon?' 'No,' said the doctor. 'It means that you will live absolutely for ever in deeper & deeper melancholy.'"[22]

Spring Semester 2016

This lecture is based on material in Martin Stannard, *Evelyn Waugh: The Later Year, 1939–1966* (1992).

1. *The Diaries of Evelyn Waugh,* ed. Michael Davie (London, 1976), Mar. 1964, p. 792; hereafter *Diaries.*
2. Christopher Sykes, *Evelyn Waugh: A Biography* (London, 1975), p. 334.
3. *Diaries,* 3 Feb. 1947, p. 672.
4. *Diaries,* 4 Feb. 1947, p. 672.
5. Alec Waugh to Catherine Waugh, 22 Feb. 1948; Boston University Library.
6. Peter Quennell, "Speaking of Books: Evelyn Waugh," *New York Times Book Review,* 8 May 1966, pp. 2, 23.
7. Ibid.
8. Marguerite Cullman, "A Waugh-Time Memory," *Harper's Bazaar,* Feb. 1963, pp. 109–110, 162.
9. Ibid.
10. M. Louis Merton, OCR, to Evelyn Waugh, 2 Aug. 1948; British Library.
11. Merton to Waugh, 22 Sept. 1948; British Library.
12. Evelyn Waugh to John Shaw Billings, 3 Sept. 1948, in *The Letters of Evelyn Waugh,* ed. Mark Amory (London, 1980), p. 283; hereafter *Letters.* Waugh's contact at *Life* was Clare Booth Luce (wife of its owner), to whom he had been introduced by Randolph Churchill.
13. *New York Herald Tribune,* 31 Dec. 1948, p. 11.
14. Robert Craft, "Stravinsky and Some Writers," *Harper's Bazaar,* Dec. 1968, pp. 101–2, 105–6, 108.
15. John Pick to Frederick J. Stopp, 13 Dec. 1954; Cambridge University Library.
16. Ibid.
17. Waugh to Merton, 27 May [1949]; reprinted in the *Evelyn Waugh Newsletter,* 3, no. 1 (Spring 1969): p. 1.
18. Waugh to Merton, 28 August [1949]; in ibid., p. 2.
19. "The American Epoch in the Catholic Church," *Life,* 19 Sept. 1949, pp. 135–38, 140, 143, 144, 146, 149–50, 152, 155.
20. Ibid., p. 382.
21. Anne Fremantle to Evelyn Waugh, Feast of Christ the King [29 October 1950]; British Library.
22. Waugh to Nancy Mitford, 6 January [1951]; *Letters,* pp. 343–44.

V. S. Naipaul, c. 2000.

4

V. S. Naipaul and the British Tradition of Biography

PATRICK FRENCH

Vidyadhar Naipaul was born in 1932 in Chaguanas in the Crown Colony of Trinidad, the grandchild of indentured laborers from India, and from this inauspicious beginning ended up as a knight of the realm, a winner of the Nobel Prize in Literature, and one of the great writers of the last century. His papers (and those of his first wife, Patricia) were sold to the McFarlin Library at the University of Tulsa in Oklahoma in 1993. I was asked by him to write his biography in 2001, and agreed on the condition I could have full and exclusive access to his archives, quote from them freely, interview him, and write without restriction. These conditions were accepted by him and honored at every stage. The substantive part of the Tulsa archive, which formed the basis of *The World Is What It Is* (2008), consisted of V. S. Naipaul's personal documentation. It made for an extraordinarily rich set of primary sources for a literary and historical biographer.

In the case of Patricia, the most important find was a diary she kept from 1972 to 1995, running to hundreds of thousands of words, written by hand in twenty-four large notebooks, some of which were not legible. It appeared her husband had not read this diary, but was aware it had been written. Although not a clear or well-structured narrative, it felt reliable, and contained no discernible inventions. V. S. Naipaul's archives contained stories, memorabilia, and letters written by his father, Seepersad Naipaul, and other family members, including his siblings; his own literary notebooks from the mid-1950s; illuminating day-by-day correspondence with Patricia during the years leading up to their marriage and afterward; a large collection of press cuttings; professional and personal correspondence; his working notebooks from almost all his journeys from the late 1960s onward, including those to Argentina and parts of South America, the West Indies, the United States, Congo and parts of West Africa, and repeat trips to India, Pakistan, Iran, Malaysia, and Indonesia; a good collection of photographs and other images; audio and video material dating back to the 1960s, mainly of radio interviews and television programs about him; and full sets of bank statements, accounts, tax records, and other financial information dating to the 1970s. Naipaul had archived his working life scrupulously since his late teens. He told me in an interview on 26 January 2004 that he had sought to preserve everything: "I kept it for the record. I am a great believer in the record, that the truth is wonderful and that any doctored truth is awful . . . I destroyed nothing . . . I have great trouble reading other people's autobiographies because I feel it is doctored."

During the research and writing of *The World Is What It Is,* I used radio scripts from the BBC show *Caribbean Voices,* preserved on microfilm at the British Broadcasting Corporation Written Archives Centre in Caversham, and official records from Trinidad, which revealed information about the status of his family and in particular his maternal grandmother, whose landholdings made her one of the richest East Indian woman in Trinidad. I did oral interviews with around eighty people in Britain, the United States, Argentina, India, France, and the West Indies. Only two people refused to participate: Harold Pinter and Derek Walcott, who told me over the phone that he did not want to add to the legend of Naipaul. I also did twenty or so interviews with V. S. Naipaul himself.

Some of the thinking I used in planning the biography can be expressed in five critical questions I asked myself as I went along: What were the external forces—familial, social, personal, financial, racial, professional, political—acting on Naipaul? What were the internal impulses that made him behave in a particular way, and how did they link with larger external forces and expectations? How were such events connected with the process of literary creativity, and how was that reflected in his work? Were the versions of his own actions that he created in his fiction and nonfiction accurate? And was it possible to find linked lives within his peer group that placed the principal's biographical story into a larger social and historical context?

When it came to writing the biography, I decided that the running commentary provided by the interviews I had done with Naipaul, some of which covered the same ground from different angles, could be placed alongside versions of events drawn from contemporaneous writing in the archives. Actuality could be compared with memory to demonstrate the human imperfection in any subjective account of emotion. To give one example: Naipaul's refusal to buy his wife a wedding ring appears to have come from a fear of marriage and the consequences of marrying someone of a different ethnicity, as well as from a psychological denial that he was actually getting married. He retrospectively rationalized his decision: "I had no interest in jewellery. I didn't think it was important. I simply had no money." I took this to be an instance of memory, in the form of self-justification, seeking to flatten the actuality.

Wherever possible, I placed new information in the nexus of historical, cultural, social, and literary studies. It was essential that the reader be able to picture the physical context in which Naipaul lived at formative periods and to see how other people responded to similar situations. To take an example from his childhood: "Vegetarian food from their own land—pigeon peas, okra, rice, pumpkin, potato, spinach, green fig, chick peas, breadfruit, all spiced with masala in an approximation of north Indian cuisine—was cooked communally by the Mausis [maternal aunts] in a dingy, blackened kitchen. Men and boys dressed in shorts and shirts, the shirts usually made from flour bags, and wore long trousers when working in the fields. Barefoot around the house and yard, outside they wore 'washekongs'—(Salim collects a pair in *A Bend in the River:* 'from *caoutchouc,* the French word for rubber, being patois for canvas shoes.'")[1] Returning Naipaul to his roots through the physicality of his past, and hence his own historicality, was central to my intention as a biographer.

Naipaul's literary career has lasted for more than sixty years, an abnormally long time for a writer. His work was first broadcast on the BBC Colonial Service in 1951, and he is still writing. Because of this longevity, his critical reputation has been through phases that can be loosely periodized: he was ignored, patronized, embraced, rejected, and re-embraced. Naipaul liked to present himself as displaced by history, and suggested this had made him uniquely insightful—implying that he was driven by objective, external forces rather by internal psychological or practical compulsions. The idea that he was a rootless, stateless, hyper-perceptive global observer linked—collusively, I felt—with a British (and later with an American) critical reaction placing him *inside* the canon, in what could be perceived as the empire making good in an act of self-conscious postcolonial generosity. While noting his unique triangulation between Trinidad, Britain, and India, I tried to show that Naipaul was created not only by historical circumstance but also by personality.

I wished the reader of the biography to be able to discover the material conditions and challenges faced by Naipaul as mediated through individual experience in an extraordinary and at times impossible cultural journey. It was apparent from the childhood material archived in Tulsa that self-masking was an aspect of his personality, but it was only after interviews with his contemporaries in Trinidad that I was able to place this into a larger social context. Naipaul's primary mask from the early 1960s until the late 1990s (when he consciously sought to recover his "Indianness," or his Indian heritage) was that of the unassailable, detached global author whose talent overcame every obstacle. Creating this image meant cloaking aspects of his creolized past in the West Indies and denying that he had faced the same hazards, pressures, and prejudices as any other person of color seeking to become established in the chauvinistic Britain of the 1950s and 1960s. It is indeed arguable whether, at that time or later, a writer and thinker in his position could have succeeded in his grand ambition except by taking a tangential or tricksterish route. His triumph, won at times by manipulating the well-being of others, was an act of conquest.

Naipaul emerges more plausibly out of an established Caribbean lineage rather than a British tradition. For example, in the year of his birth, 1932, C. L. R. James arrived in the United Kingdom for the first time. A black Trinidadian man who had been to the same school that Naipaul would attend, Queen's Royal College, James was, in the words of Kenneth Ramchand, "confident about his intellectual superiority, and apparently able to live comfortably with a quota of discrepant attitudes and interests." James wrote articles that were published back home in the *Port of Spain Gazette* about the Bloomsbury set, and commented that that since "the English native is so glum and dull and generally boorish in his manners . . . any man of colour who is not repulsive in appearance, has good manners, and is fairly intelligent, is a great favourite with the girls."[2] In his style and cultural approach to the imperial metropolis, James was one of several intellectual and social models for Naipaul the nascent writer.

Other Caribbean figures alongside James provided a guide: Alfred

Mendes, Albert Gomes, Herbert de Lisser, Jean Rhys, and Claude McKay. In Naipaul's accounts in fiction and nonfiction, his father, Seepersad, is presented as the sole local exemplar. Though I share Naipaul's high estimation of Seepersad's literary work, he was not the only key figure in his son's life, education, and literary career. I sought to foreground what was omitted in the paternal creation myth found in *A House for Mr. Biswas* (1961), "Prologue to an Autobiography" (in *Finding the Center*, 1984), and other works. Given his father's fragile mental health, the determining influences of Naipaul's early life were, crucially, women: his widowed maternal grandmother (who controlled the extended family and its finances), his mother (who was "a strong woman with a strong personality," according to her eldest daughter, Kamla), and Kamla herself, who was his closest ally and emotional sounding board during his childhood and afterward.

Once Naipaul reached adulthood, women remained a driving influence. His girlfriend and later wife, Patricia, was central to the process of his writing development, his physical well-being, and his psychic survival. During the course of a long marriage, he displayed his weaknesses and wounds to her to an intense degree, and yet chastened her for being aware of this hidden aspect of himself. Their punishing embrace was central to the creative process that gave rise to books such as *The Mimic Men* (1967), *The Enigma of Arrival* (1987), *A House for Mr. Biswas,* and *A Way in the World* (1994). After 1972, a different but connected relationship with Margaret Murray developed, which was to be closely tied to his writing of later works such as *Guerrillas* (1975) and *A Bend in the River* (1979), and to a new and often aggressive development of female characters in his fiction.

I WANT TO WIDEN OUT NOW from Naipaul to a substantive idea of what biographies can do, and their position in relation to the study and writing of history. They can overlap vividly with multiple societies in a way that local or national histories usually cannot. The traveling human is the perfect vehicle through which to see world history and, in the case of the soldier and explorer Francis Younghusband, the writer Doris Lessing, and V. S. Naipaul, imperial history. Rather than being only about its subject, a biography opens a range of linked accounts of personal experience, both through others' perceptions of the subject and through the flaws of a human life, which never conform to a strict pattern. In biography, you always find the unexpected: people who hold inconsistent opinions or who do not comport with our idea of what such a person "should" have been thinking at a particular time. A biographer must use the same standard as an historian in collecting and analyzing information and showing connections between people, places, and ideas. Biography brings in contingency—the idea that life is unpredictable. With Younghusband, Lessing, and Naipaul, who traveled between regions and cultures, it is possible to tell a global historical story through what is nominally the experience of a single person.

English biography in the seventeenth and eighteenth centuries was considered a casual and maverick form. Even Boswell's *Life of Samuel Johnson* (1791) was considered improper for its use of anecdote and novelistic description. In the nineteenth century, such biographies gave way to works in multiple volumes that entombed their subjects and projected imperial, moral, and economic authority. They were filled with extracts from letters and texts, often compiled by the children or the admirers of the deceased. As Thomas Carlyle wrote in revolt: "How delicate, decent is English biography, bless its mealy mouth!"[3] A response to the nineteenth-century style came in 1918 with Lytton Strachey's *Eminent Victorians,* which started a persuasive vogue for the debunking life. His contagious books were as much about style as content, a gossipy counterpart to the stolid books that preceded them. Although Strachey's books are entertaining, they were the work of an un-radical, ironic insider, and his approach has been too influential. His self-consciousness was accompanied by what was then called the "New Biography," which saw the biographical form as mutable because the modern age was mutable. This trend extended across Europe, its central figures being Strachey, André Maurois, and Emil Ludwig.

This shift was followed and to an extent overtaken in the mid-twentieth century by psychobiography, a reductive method that melded a theory of human improvement with the art of the historical chronicle. Leon Edel on Henry James, or George Painter on Marcel Proust, believed in "keys"—the oddly enduring idea that a clever biographer could "unlock" a subject by discovering crucial moments or influences. As Ray Monk, the biographer of Bertrand Russell, has argued, if a biographer seeks to make an argument that the subject of a book must be seen in a certain way, it puts too much focus on the author's ideology and not enough on the subject's. Or to express it another way, Freud's writing on Leonardo da Vinci's childhood tells you more about Freud than it does about Leonardo. Biography grew to be seen as suspect by historians in part because tools such as psychoanalysis did not guarantee a reliable outcome. Now, scientific research suggests the coherent "self" that twentieth-century biographers sought to discover and depict may not exist. What is a life? What is a self? In Buddhism, self is an illusion that must be dissolved. Modern cognitive science to an extent backs this view, namely, that from the perspective of neuroscience, the brain and body are constantly in flux.

Strachey's version of biography, exacerbated by Edel and later swamped by first-person memoirs, diminished the seriousness of its status. The final takedown came in the 1990s with Janet Malcolm's picking apart of Sylvia Plath's biographers, a move that coincided with the takeover of English literature departments by theory, which contained a logical, Barthesian hostility to the biographical. Malcolm inserted herself into the battle between Plath, Ted Hughes, Hughes's sister Olwen, and assorted chroniclers. The methodology of the form was criticized, too, by scholars like the structuralist philosopher Pierre Bourdieu, who denied the *possibility* of writing the history of one life as a coherent whole. For Bourdieu, biography was an illusion, and the subject could not be distinguished from the surrounding society.

Continental European biographical mores were more mainstream and linked with the professional writing of history, although the German tradition was later adjusted for being representative of a project with an unfashionable need for national role models. In much of Europe today, biography has a higher status in the academic world than it does in Britain and United States. But as Susan Ware has noted, "Hardly anyone talks about the actual craft of writing biography. Biographies just seem to emerge *ex nihilo* in print, with no discussion of the choices and challenges of research, organization, interpretation, and voice. The apparent assumption is that historians and writers should just know how to create a biography."[4] From the 1970s, it became accepted that it was necessary to cover every area of a biographical subject's life, including the sexual, which led in some cases to significant insights into human behavior. It was a period that has been called a golden age of biography. Roughly parallel to this came an effort to recover or reconstitute "missing" parts of history, and there emerged subgenres such as group biography, family biography, and, most significantly, feminist biography. Books such as Claire Tomalin's *The Invisible Woman* (1990) or Brenda Maddox's *Nora* (1988) needed to be published because Nelly Ternan and Nora Joyce had been written out of history. Mothers, wives, sisters, daughters, and lovers exist at every point in time, so biography, inevitably, contains vital discoveries for social history, the history of emotions, and the stories of the once peripheral.

Yet questions about the status of biography are still raised, and probably no historical form has been more vigorously attacked. For the view from academia in the 1960s and 1970s, let us cite Geoffrey

Elton. In *The Practice of History* (1967), he wrote that biography was "a poor way of writing history," since the biographer was obliged to "give much weight to those private relationships and petty concerns which have little to tell the historian." The historian "should not write biography—or at least should not suppose that in writing biography he is writing history."[5] Although Elton was being cantankerous, he was reflecting a mainstream view at the time, which was that life writing was a suspect way of looking at the past. Stanley Wolpert wrote: "Fawn Brodie, a great biographer-historian, was almost denied a full professorship in UCLA's history department by several now-departed professors who considered her biographies nothing more than 'action' or 'fatuous gossip.'"[6] Today, we accept that emotions and gossip matter. History is no longer studied as a series of events or as detached diplomacy. It is a mark of how far methods have changed that historians now want to know why ordinary people did what they did, to understand their feelings, motivations, aesthetics, impulses, personalities, and self-perceptions, along with the influence of material culture. I would suggest the development of intellectual history is often intimately linked with biography.

The case for the prosecution has also been made, volubly, by writers and artists. George Eliot called biography "a disease of English literature." Rudyard Kipling said it was "Higher Cannibalism." Henry James was wary of the "post-mortem exploiter." Vladimir Nabokov spoke of "psycho-plagiarism." Germaine Greer has labeled biographers "the intellectual equivalent of flesh-eating bacterium," and biographies as "pre-digested carrion." The list of writers who have, in fictional form, disparaged the biographer is long: Philip Larkin, A. S. Byatt, Penelope Lively, Kingsley Amis, Alison Lurie, Philip Roth, Hanif Kureishi, and Saul Bellow. William Golding's character Professor Rick. L. Tucker is to be found rootling through dustbins. Bernard Malamud's cipher of a biographer, William B. Dubin, leads the author to conclude: "All biography is ultimately fiction." These characters in hot pursuit bear no resemblance to a contemporary biographer, who, rather than pursuing sensation, is often swamped by material and plied with too much information by "friends" of the subject. As Michael Holroyd wrote: "No serious biographer working this century will have failed to lay down some ethical foundations for his craft."[7] The fear that writers feel of biography may stem from an idea of moral perfection, which itself comes from societies entangled in ambiguous social standards. Many of the people listed above had an aspect of their life about which they felt embarrassed or ashamed, and were nervous of being misrepresented, misunderstood, misbiographized.

Kafka's executor, Max Brod, famously published *The Trial* after the author's death despite having been asked to destroy it, along with all his work. In the case of Younghusband, I literally snatched a stash of his letters from the jaws of a dog in Dorset. Gustave Flaubert was insistent that a writer's life should not be considered in any reading of his work. Charles Augustin Sainte-Beuve, a founding figure in modern literary criticism, had included biographical aspects in his work, seeing the overlap between the literary and the process that created books. Proust, in what Ann Jefferson has called his "famously ferocious" essay "La Méthode de Sainte-Beuve," was adamant that the habits and vices of "the social self" should not be confused with "the writer's self."[8] He wanted to preserve a distinction. In his Nobel lecture, Naipaul responded to Proust's judgment on Sainte-Beuve with comments that became creatively useful to me when I was conceiving the biography: "All the details of the life and the quirks and the friendships can be laid out for us, but the mystery of the writing will remain. No amount of documentation, however fascinating, can take us there. The biography of a writer—or even the autobiography—will always have this incompleteness."[9]

To do our job, we become magpies and rely on observation and a grab bag of information, culled from wherever we see it. In his *Life of Samuel Johnson,* Boswell noted how Doctor Johnson "rolls in his gait, going zigzag to and fro, like a ship rolling and tacking in a heavy sea, and swinging his arms backwards and forwards as he shambles along." I did something analogous in *The World Is What It Is,* trying to capture the way the literary critic Francis Wyndham walked: "Popular, gentle, solitary and eccentric, Wyndham lived with his mother, wore heavy glasses and high-waisted trousers, gave off random murmurs and squeaks and moved with an amphibian gait." The physicality of the subject must run alongside his or her creative development.

If biography is to be theorized and accepted as central to the writing of history, it requires total context: social, cultural, material, political, personal, and economic information. Giovanni Levi recognized the importance of the surrounding social history: since we do not know, for example, much of Diderot's youth, we must recover the world in which he moved: "This biographical practice rests on an implicit hypothesis which can be formulated as follows: whatever its apparent originality, a life cannot be understood only by means of its distinctive or unique qualities, but on the contrary, by returning each apparent abnormality back to the norms by demonstrating it has a place in an historical context which accommodates it."[10] A persuasive biography rests on an intuitive emphasis on the inner life

that produces individual agency. It requires a measure of intellectual nerve and agility: a biography cannot be a compendium, but
neither can it be an act of self-projection. A fictive biography may be
great imaginative literature, but it is not a biography. A life cannot
be told in isolation. It must be situated in world history, and in the
case of Naipaul, Younghusband, and Lessing, in imperial and postcolonial history. The subject of a biography can serve as a symbol
for broader issues affecting a culture. Younghusband is representative of a common eccentric strand in late British imperialism; Naipaul's extraordinary but contested success in literary and cultural
life reveals the struggles of a community of midcentury migrants;
Lessing has been represented as speaking for a generation.

IN *HISTORY AT THE LIMIT OF WORLD-HISTORY*, Ranajit Guha argued: "If the writing of history were to ground itself in such historicality [the stories people tell about themselves], it would have a
subject matter as comprehensive as the human condition itself. The
world would open up with all of its pasts ready to serve for its narratives. No continent, no culture, no rank or condition of social being would be considered too small or too simple for its prose."[11] In
its contemporary state, biography can act as a subgenre of history,
providing a wormhole view into the past: in Naipaul's case, it can be
a route for understanding the human effect of British imperialism
and the way relationships between people play out in a disturbed
creative process.

   In the instance of Doris Lessing, her transfer from colonial Southern Rhodesia (where she spent her childhood as the daughter of
poor farmers who had been persuaded by the British Empire Exhibition of 1924 to try their luck in Africa) to the metropolis of 1950s
London (where she cut a swathe through multiple social restrictions) acts as a reflection on the functioning of empire. Like the
subject of Linda Colley's *The Ordeal of Elizabeth Marsh* (2007), Lessing was a woman in transit. Biographically, she links with the long
twentieth century: the First World War (in which her father had his
leg blown off, altering the lives of his future children), the making
of the modern Middle East (she was born in colonial Persia), late-
imperial expansion in Africa (Rhodesia was the ultimate late settler colony), the consequences of nationalism and communism, the
genesis of modern feminism, and changes in the accepted structure
of the nuclear family, as well as rival interpretations within Islam
(she became a follower of a branch of Sufism) and the postcolonial
eclipse of white political power in Africa.

   Francis Younghusband was a soldier, spy, imperial administrator, and mystic whose peculiarity and failure to fit into an expected pattern made it possible to use his story to give an account of late British imperialism, when it was at its most intense and delusional. Many colonial administrators in his era appear to have been impersonating one another, operating in a virtual society where they were expected to conform to a stereotype. What Naipaul refers to as "mimicry" by the first generation of indigenous postcolonial leaders was also used by the later generation of British imperialists—acting a role to protect their status and to enable them to function in distant societies that they often misunderstood but nominally controlled.

Coming back to the life of V. S. Naipaul: by the late 1990s, his reputation was low in academia, but in the twenty-first century it rebounded. A crucial reason was that history itself returned with a vengeance in 2001, after the attacks of 9/11. Far from being at an end, history became a driving force in modern global politics. Movements built on ancestral identity took the place of an earlier postcolonial, and predominantly nationalist, impetus. The techniques of postcolonial theory began to appear dated. Naipaul's books on Muslim responses (and specifically on non-Arab Muslim responses) to modernity, which had been seen as disproportionately gloomy, appeared prescient. Even his opponents acknowledged that his opinions were based on repeated travels and prolonged interviews in the societies about which he was writing—Iran, Pakistan, Malaysia, and Indonesia—over a long period. A renewed interest in Islam, in the effects of globalization, in displaced ethnic diasporas, and in the impact of past events and inherited identity on the present returned Naipaul's work to the critical forefront. His case provides a clear demonstration of the West being approached from an unusual and even opposite direction—from the periphery—rendering the familiar ideological moves of postcolonial theorists outmoded.

The British or Anglo-American biographical tradition is a remarkable one, with much to recommend it, notwithstanding my suspicion of the tendency for such biography to be incorporated as a supplement to the mainstream, in the tradition of Lytton Strachey. We should be aware of the singularity of this tradition, which rests on a degree of continuity that does not exist in many cultures. In biography, the individual provides a pivot around which interdisciplinary approaches to history might cluster. It should be seen as a historical discipline in its own right, and one with a unique ability to cut across standard forms and to reveal the world.

Spring Semester 2017

1. Patrick French, *The World Is What It Is: The Authorized Biography of V. S. Naipaul* (London, 2008), p. 26.

2. C. L. R. James, *Letters from London,* ed. Nicholas Laughlin (Port of Spain, 2003), p. ix.

3. Quoted in the *London Review of Books,* 19 July 1984.

4. Susan Ware, "Writing Women's Lives: One Historian's Perspective," *Journal of Interdisciplinary History,* 40, 3 (Winter 2010), pp. 413–35.

5. G. R. Elton, *The Practice of History* (London, 1967), pp. 134–35.

6. Stanley Wolpert, "Biography as History: A Personal Reflection," *Journal of Interdisciplinary History,* 40, 3 (Winter 2010), pp. 399–412.

7. Michael Holroyd, *Works on Paper: The Craft of Biography and Autobiography* (London, 2002), p. 19.

8. Ann Jefferson, "Sainte-Beuve: Biography, Criticism, and the Literary," in *Mapping Lives: The Uses of Biography,* ed. Peter France and William St. Clair (Oxford, 2002), p. 136.

9. V. S. Naipaul, "Two Worlds," Nobel Lecture, 2001. Available at www.nobelprize.org/nobel_prizes/literature/laureates/2001/naipaul-lecture-e.html.

10. Giovanni Levi, "The Uses of Biography," in *Theoretical Discussions of Biography: Approaches from History, Microhistory, and Life Writing,* ed. Hans Renders and Binne de Haan (Leiden, 2014), p. 69.

11. Ranajit Guha, *History at the Limit of World-History* (New York, 2002), p. 22.

Hayao Miyazaki at the Venice Film Festival, 2008. Photo by Thomas Schulz. Robert Louis Stevenson, c. 1900.

Where Shall We Adventure? Hayao Miyazaki Meets Robert Louis Stevenson

SUSAN NAPIER

> *Where shall we adventure, today that we're afloat?*
> *Wary of the weather and steering by a star?*
> *Shall it be to Africa a-steering of the boat,*
> *To Providence, or Babylon, or off to Malabar?*
> Robert Louis Stevenson

> *Basically there is such a thing as Treasure Island. We don't know what the treasure is but it exists.*
> Hayao Miyazaki

From *Robinson Crusoe* to *Lord Jim,* adventure stories have been at the heart of literature, and English literature in particular, at least until the early twentieth century. Even today they remain a core part of much children's literature and of mass entertainment in general. Steeped in action and in larger-than-life deeds of derring-do, they take place in the borderland spaces of the sea, the wilderness, or, more recently, in a galaxy far, far away, and involve exotic Others for the protagonists to engage with, confront, and measure themselves against.

In the late twentieth century, however, adventure stories developed a bad reputation. Critics and scholars came to see the popular "boys' adventures" stories of nineteenth-century Great Britain, such as *King Solomon's Mines* or *The Coral Island,* as upholders and even enablers of an imperialistic, hegemonic master narrative of white domination over the rest of the world. All the accoutrements of adventure—the ships, the maps, the weaponry—were seen as sinister aids in the quest to dominate the marginalized Others who inhabit the worlds the adventurers voyage to. Martin Green, for example, describes adventure stories are "the energizing myth of English imperialism."[1]

This lecture refines the interpretation of the adventure story structure as an upholder of imperialism, through a discussion of two creators of adventures whose work to some extent subverts this vision. These creators are the Scottish writer Robert Louis Stevenson and the Japanese animator Hayao Miyazaki. Both artists build on a genuine enthusiasm for and skill in devising enthralling adventure tales to subtly undermine the triumphalist quest narrative that their work initially seems to uphold. In both cases, the text in question is *Treasure Island,* Stevenson's 1889 novel and Tōei Cinema's 1971 animated adaptation, *Animal Treasure Island* (*Dobutsu Takarajima*). Both artists celebrate the excitement and endless possibility inherent in the adventure story format even as they question the structure that *Treasure Island* is based upon—that is, the quest for treasure.

At first glance, however, Robert Louis Stevenson (1850–1894) and Hayao Miyazaki (1941–) would seem to have little in common. The former is a Scottish writer, born in Edinburgh, who lived at the height of the British Empire and spent the final days of his short life as a frequently ill, perhaps tubercular, expatriate in the South Seas. The latter is a Japanese animation director and manga artist, born in Tokyo in the last years of the Japanese Empire and still energetically riding the waves and whirlpools of the early twenty-first century.

This summary description leaves a great deal out, not least the truly surprising number of elements that the two creators have in common. Most obvious is the fact that both men are exceptional world builders who range across a wide array of sources to create immersive works of art, frequently in two major genres, the adventure story and the fantastic. Furthermore, both artists' most famous works were, at least initially, viewed as child oriented, since the audience for the fantastic and for adventure was long assumed to be children or young adults. Stevenson and Miyazaki both benefit and suffer from this perception, benefiting financially and professionally from their art's popularity, but suffering from the arrows of critics unable to believe that children's entertainment or popular culture in general needed or even deserved to be taken seriously.

In fact, as critics are increasingly discovering, children's entertainment, perhaps especially fantasy and adventure, can reveal depths and layers that are indeed deserving of critical attention. What Stephen Donovan says of Stevenson, that he "ranged across the fields of imagination, commercialization, childhood, and maturity, as well as the class and national politics of mass culture," applies equally well to Miyazaki.[2] Like Stevenson's writings (which have been translated into an enormous number of languages), Miyazaki's works have achieved a global reputation, beloved by children and adults for their rich and propulsive narratives, which stir the imagination without sacrificing psychological depth or moral values.

An important similarity is that both creators are, at some level, outsiders in relation to the dominant culture. While it would be a preposterous stretch to say that nineteenth-century Scotland was as culturally different from England as twentieth-century Japan was from the West, it is worth noting that Stevenson was highly aware of his Scottish identity and its distinction from Englishness. This comes across most clearly in an essay from Stevenson's posthumous work *In the South Seas* (1896), in which the writer perhaps semi-ironically notes his similarity to the Polynesians because of his country's superstitions and savagery. It is also possible to speculate that Stevenson experienced the uneasiness of being a Scot in the dominant British Empire from early on. His famous horror story *The Strange Case of Dr. Jekyll and Mr. Hyde,* although usually read as a portrait of psychological barbarity or a veiled treatment of perverse sexuality, can be seen as an image of split or distorted cultural identity as well.

This is not to say that Stevenson was consciously anti-English. Although his later works can legitimately be read as anticolonialist, in many ways England was a cultural treasure trove to him. In a nostalgic essay that Stevenson published in a late memoir, he talks about the profound appeal of the toy theaters manufactured by Skelt in London. These beautifully constructed miniature theaters functioned not simply as stages where the young boy could hone his considerable storytelling powers, but also as miniature models of a fantasy "England" that inspired Stevenson all his life, a magic costume box of England's trademark architecture, scenery, clothes, furniture, and so forth. As an adult, Stevenson remembered Skelt's depiction of "the castles sit[ting] upon the hill," the "cottage," the "nautical" inn with "the gun and powder horn," ultimately summing up this vision with the memorable statement "England, when at last I came to visit it, was only Skelt made evident. To cross the border was, for the Scotsman, to come home to Skelt."[3]

IF ENGLAND WAS A TOY THEATER to a young Scots boy from across the border, how much more of a fantasyland must it have been to a young Japanese boy growing up in Tokyo. The years when Miyazaki grew to maturity were ones of personal and social turmoil. Miyazaki (born 1941) and his family experienced the devastation wrought by the Allied bombings of Japan, including the nuclear devastation of Hiroshima and Nagasaki, as well as the profound cultural dissonance of growing to adolescence under the U.S. occupation. Miyazaki has said little about the occupation except to mention that the American soldiers offered chocolate and chewing gum, but he "didn't take them."[4] What Miyazaki did take was the solace offered by English literature. Like Stevenson, Miyazaki grew up with serious illness, although in this case the affected person was his mother, Yasuko, who was bedridden with tuberculosis for nine years from the time her son was in elementary school until the end of high school. Not surprisingly, Miyazaki found escape and compensation in books, particularly English children's books.

The importance of English children's literature on the director's imagination comes across clearly in a compendium that Miyazaki published in 2010 of fifty of his favorite children's books, including each book's cover illustration and the director's brief commentary on them. Twenty of the titles are English, by far the most books from a single nation (only two are from Japan). Most are adventures stories, such as Arthur Ransome's *Swallows and Amazons* series—tales of sailing and camping in the Lake District—or fantasies such as *Alice in Wonderland*. Beyond the adventure narrative, Miyazaki seemed particularly entranced by the landscapes of English literature. About *Swallows and Amazons,* he writes longingly of a "dazzling summer" and a "glittering lake" on which "one's very own boat caught the wind and one sailed off wherever one wished."[5]

Miyazaki's Occidentalism was not unusual. As his longtime producer Toshio Suzuki said of the director and his contemporaries, "They all loved Europe."[6] But what is impressive is his unusually detailed and wide-ranging incorporation of the landscape and culture of England and western Europe in many of his films. Just as Stevenson imaginatively plundered the castles, cottages, inns, and landscapes of England, many of Miyazaki's works offer up castles, cottages, and English and European scenery. In the director's *Castle in the Sky: Laputa,* (1995; based partly on Jonathan Swift's *Gullivers' Travels),* the Welsh landscape is featured, and the Welsh miners' strike under Thatcher becomes part of the story's backdrop.

But Miyazaki's "Euroworld" had a dark side too. Stevenson, a Scot, could humorously refer to the "superstitions" and "savagery" of the Scots, but he was still a white man from just across the border. The identity of a modern Japanese in relation to the West is a far more complicated one. Alone among non-Western nations, Japan had never been colonized, and its extraordinarily successful modernization and Westernization program ultimately excited the West's grudging admiration, even fear, especially after the Japanese military had grown powerful enough to allow the nation to begin its own program of imperialist domination and colonization. But the success of Japan's drive to emulate the West wrought enormous psychic costs. The great early twentieth-century Japanese writer Natsume Sōseki described his country as undergoing a national nervous breakdown, and in Miyazaki's time the devastation of the war followed by the total demise of the Japanese Empire added to this sense of complex cultural unease.

By the time Miyazaki and some animator colleagues first visited Europe in the 1960s, Japan had once again awed the world by achieving a decade of unprecedented double-digit growth and was driving toward becoming the world's third-largest economy. But cultural insecurity still weighed on the Japanese. At one point, Miyazaki and a group of colleagues went to Visby, Sweden, hoping to obtain permission from the Swedish children's author Astrid Lindgren to animate her popular *Pippi Longstocking* series. They were refused, and at least one of Miyazaki's colleagues speculated that perhaps the Swedish writer did not want "Japanese" artists taking over her property.[7] A more personally traumatic moment occurred in Switzerland when Miyazaki saw a "dirty-faced" short-legged person coming toward him on a city street, only to discover that it was his own reflection in a shop window.[8] In an eerie coincidence, this story echoes almost exactly an anecdote told by Sōseki, who had gone to live in London in 1901, determined to show the English that he could appreciate and analyze English literature better than native speakers, only to end his sojourn lonely and despairing. In his later writings, Sōseki remembers a "yellow dwarf" coming toward him down a London street, only to discover, like Miyazaki, that it was his own reflection.[9]

Sōseki did not abandon literature, and indeed went on to write an Arthurian romance based on the tragedy of Lancelot and the Lily Maid of Astolat. Miyazaki was even more ambitious, appropriating European and, especially, English literature and transforming it into idiosyncratic cinematic visions, highly entertaining works of art that can be seen to both compensate for and criticize their Western sources.

Miyazaki's and Sōseki's uncannily similar experience, however, illustrates the complex identity of a modern Japanese facing the West, what Margherita Long has described as the despairing sensation summed up by, "You must be like me. You cannot be like me."[10] This frustrating imperative informs both the substance and the style of *Animal Treasure Island,* a movie that follows in the tradition of the many cinematic versions of the novel even as it transcends them, using the medium of animation to take the work in some surprising directions. While Miyazaki was not the director of the movie—at the time it was made, he was still quite a junior animator—his influence on the film's visual style and narrative form has been clearly credited, and he is the sole author of the manga comic edition that accompanied the movie's release.

Stevenson's *Treasure Island* is one of the fifty books that Miyazaki put on his list of favorite children's literature. Miyazaki writes: "How many many stories, films, comics and games about looking for treasure have been inspired by this book," and exhorts his readers, "This is a really entertaining story. You won't be sorry to have read it. It is a foundational text."[11]

Miyazaki is quite correct. The novel has been made into sixteen movie and television versions, including two from the Walt Disney Company. Its 1950 version, the company's first full-length live-action film, features Robert Newton in an indelible portrayal of the pirate leader Long John Silver. Newton's over-the-top performance became a benchmark for future pirate portrayals, but although memorable, it does not capture the darkness and moral ambiguity of the original character. Nor does the movie as a whole convey the shadowy subtext of Stevenson's novel. This is probably because for much of the twentieth century, *Treasure Island* was viewed as a conventional though entertaining boys' adventure story, a coming-of-age novel of young Jim's encounter with pirates and treasure. With the advent of postcolonial studies, critics came to see it as yet another imperialist narrative whose iconic treasure map is simply a trademark of Western exploitation.

It has only been in the last couple of decades that scholars have begun to discover subtler shadings in this narrative, partly because of the increasing appreciation of Stevenson as a Scottish writer and therefore someone more likely than an Englishman to take a skeptical view of British colonialism and empire. A careful reading of the text suggests that even in this early work, Stevenson was doing far more than simply celebrating adventure. Most obvious is the extreme and genuinely shocking violence in the story, in particular a scene when Jim, hiding in the bushes, hears the shriek of a man being murdered and then watches in horror as Long John Silver casually dispatches another man, first with his stick and then with a knife to the back. Silver's uncanny occupation of a position between gentleman and pirate gives rise to the possibility of Stevenson's subtly satirizing the figure of the English gentleman. Even more revealing is Stevenson's vision of the other authority figures in the story, most notably Squire Trelawney, who comes across as a fool that ends up putting his friends' lives in danger.

Perhaps the most compelling argument that *Treasure Island* is not an imperialist celebration is the low-key presentation of the treasure. Although technically the object around which the quest revolves, its discovery is rendered anticlimactically. Rather than a sumptuous heap of baubles unearthed through digging, it was carted away and hidden, stolen, perhaps ironically, by a man who is probably insane. Even more surprising is the ending, which is far from a call to further adventure. Back at home, Jim expresses a desire never to see the "cursed island" again, and the reader is not privy to what he does with his share of the loot. *Treasure Island* may have spawned many similar narratives in popular culture, but few of them have captured its ambiguous chiaroscuro of light and shadow.

It is possible to argue that Miyazaki is one of the artists most responsible for continuing Stevenson's aesthetic, narrative, and even political sensibility into the twentieth and twenty-first centuries. Besides working on *Animal Treasure Island,* the director used *Treasure Island* as an important source for one of his major films, *Castle in the Sky: Laputa* and as a more hidden inspiration for such films as *The Castle of Cagliostro* (1979), *Porco Rosso* (1992), and *Ponyo* (2008). Miyazaki resembles Stevenson most obviously in his consistent ability to craft compelling tales of plucky young characters engaging in stirring exploits amid exotic settings. More interesting, however, is his ability to call Western cultural tropes into question by skillfully appropriating them, leaving the audience intrigued rather than comforted.

Miyazaki's clearest engagement with *Treasure Island* is *Animal Treasure Island,* the 1971 animated film that he worked on at Tōei, one of Japan's premier animation studios. Tōei's stated ambition was to become the "Disney of the East," and the studio incorporated many Disney trademarks such as cute sidekicks, wholesome upbeat narratives, and bouncy musical numbers, all of which show up in *Animal Treasure Island.* It is also very likely that Tōei was honoring an earlier Japanese appropriation of the novel, the manga artist Tezuka Osamu's 1946 comic book *New Treasure Island,* an immensely popular work that has been described as a "goulash of *Treasure Island, Robinson Crusoe* and *Tarzan.*"[12]

Perhaps surprisingly, given its multilayered media legacy, *Animal*

Treasure Island is quite entertaining. Although I would not recommend it as anyone's first experience of a Miyazaki movie, it contains a number of elements that have become trademarks in the director's subsequent oeuvre. The film retains Jim as the central protagonist and stays true to Stevenson's characterization of him as a brave and inquisitive youth able to stand up for himself against adult provocation. This vision of youthful resilience unencumbered by adult authority is a motif that Miyazaki has consistently showcased throughout his work. The elimination of adult authority figures allows for what Adam Gopnik, in speaking of children's literature, calls the "fantasy of autonomy."[13] Miyazaki is sharply aware of the value of this "fantasy," pointing out in an interview, "One of the essential elements of most classical children's literature is that the children in the stories actually fend for themselves."[14]

Some of the most dramatic moments in Stevenson's story occur when Jim does in fact "fend for himself," slipping off to board the pirates' ship or sneaking back at night to an armed stockade, but adult authority always hovers in the background. In *Animal Treasure Island,* Jim is left even more on his own, since the film gets rid of the entire host of authority figures who populate the novel. Instead, we find him, apparently an orphan, sailing off in search of treasure on a little ship accompanied only by his sidekick, Glan, and, in a rather bizarre touch, his baby brother.

In lieu of adults, *Animal Treasure Island* offers the viewer one significant new character, Kathy, the young granddaughter of Captain Flint, whose treasure and treasure map kick off the story's action. Feisty, smart, and cute, Kathy stands at the beginning of a long line of what is now recognized as one of Miyazaki's central contributions to the adventure story, his featuring of strong independent female characters. Miyazaki is also known for not depicting romantic relationships between his characters, and *Animal Treasure Island* adheres to that as well. Kathy and Jim eschew romance to become comrades in arms against the pirates who capture them on their hunt for treasure. The film does contain an ode to the romance of adventure itself, an appealing musical paean to the joys of exploration, complete with lyrics celebrating a vision of sailing off "to unknown countries" and "meeting unknown people."

The joys of meeting "unknown people" do not include pirates, apparently. The film follows tradition in making the pirates a thoroughly unpleasant group rendered all the more so by animation's ability to anthropomorphize animals. The pirates include a hapless walrus crew member, a scruffy wolf henchman, and a sarcastic monkey taskmaster. Most memorable of all is "Silver," an immense pig with a diabolical gleam in his eye and a hook for his arm but, unlike Stevenson's villain, two functioning legs. The pig Silver retains the cantankerousness, craftiness, and violence of the novel's Long John Silver but ultimately comes across as more a buffoon than Stevenson's compelling but sinister character.

On the one hand, the movie's use of animal characters is hardly surprising. Anthropomorphized animals have long been a tradition in animation, since as early as Disney's Mickey Mouse. Animal characters help defamiliarize and make fresh classic texts, whether *Treasure Island* or Disney's *Robin Hood*. Using animals also helps defuse violent acts that if portrayed by humans might be too disturbing.

But is possible to see other motives at work, especially when we consider who the animal characters portray. In *Animal Treasure Island*, it is only the pirates and not the heroes of the film who are made into animals, and a rather tawdry set of animals at that—brutal, pugnacious, and single-minded (and simpleminded) in their pursuit of treasure. Of course, pirates are not known for their civilized behavior, but it is interesting in this regard to return briefly to Miyazaki's compendium of the fifty best children's books, this time to his introduction to Daniel Defoe's eighteenth-century adventure classic *Robinson Crusoe*. While acknowledging the entertaining quality of *Robinson Crusoe*, Miyazaki is far less enthusiastic about it than *Treasure Island* or virtually any of the other entries. He writes, "This is a thrilling book but . . . when I read it as an adult something bothered me. If the hero had not had a gun he would have been in serious trouble. The white people who read this book rampaged through the world always with their guns, plundering treasure from other islands and countries and shooting people. I don't have a gun nor do I have any desire for one. So it's a fun book but a little disturbing nonetheless."[15]

In one of the more memorable episodes in *Animal Treasure Island*, the pirates board a civilian ship. Colorful scenes of "plundering" ensue as the pirates attack those on board (although with swords, not guns) and grab everything they can get their hands on—food, jewels, ladies dresses. In the song that accompanies this episode, the pirates chant, "Everything yours is now mine. / Oh yes! Oh yes!" with the "oh yeses" sung in English.

It may be too much to suggest that an "anti-colonial" perspective suffuses *Animal Treasure Island*. And in fact, Japan's relation to the West has been more ambiguous than that of most non-Western nations. But in light of Miyazaki's later discussion of *Robinson Crusoe*, it is at least intriguing that the animalized pirates engage in behavior that he attributes to "white people" and that the song's chorus is in English. Through animation, Miyazaki and his fellow animators may be briefly subverting the problematic duality of "You must be like me. You cannot be like me."

Jim and Kathy's freshness and innocence contrast strongly with the predatory and violent pirates and they remain unsoiled by the materialism around them.

The movie's end contains another contrast with the original novel. As previously noted, Stevenson's story ends on a somewhat down note with Jim returning from what he calls the "cursed island" with no indication that he has any desire to go adventuring again or that he has taken particular joy in the treasure.

Later Miyazaki movies, such as *Castle in the Sky: Laputa* and *The Castle of Cagliostro* explore this theme of the complexities of treasure and the problematics of the quest. Even in *Animal Treasure Island,* the treasure seems very much beside the point. Rather, the real "treasure" seems to be the glimpse of a world where children, joy, and adventure go seamlessly together once adult authority is vanquished. We see Jim and his sidekick, Glan, boarding their boat about to take off in search of a world where unknown people and unknown places are still objects of pleasure, excitement, and anticipation. In a final appropriation, this one incongruously American, the ship goes forth accompanied by a song whose lyrics include the English words "Go, Pioneer, Go."

Spring Semester 2017

The epigraph is drawn from Hayao Miyazaki, *Starting Point, 1979–1996* (San Francisco, 1996), p. 422.

1. Martin Green, *Dreams of Empire, Deeds of Adventure* (New York, 1979), p. xi.
2. Stephen Donovan, "Stevenson and Popular Entertainment," in *Robert Louis Stevenson: Writer of Boundaries,* ed. Richard Ambrosini and Richard Dury (Madison, 2006), p. 77.
3. Robert Louis Stevenson, "A Penny Plain and Twopence Coloured," in *Memories and Portraits* (London, 1887), p. 224.
4. Hayao Miyazaki, "Kenpo o kaeru nado mote no hoka," *Neppu,* July 2013, p .4.
5. Hayao Miyazaki, *Iwanami shonenbunkozo no 50 satsu* (Tokyo, 2010), p. 85.
6. Toshio Suzuki, interview, "'Ugoku shiro' no ichigen de anime wa hajimaru," *Eureka Tokushū,* 12 (2004), p. 51.
7. Yōichi Kotabe and Reiko Okuyama, interview, "Kare wa kaze o kitte, hashite inai to ki ga sumanaindesu," *Kinema muku Filmakers: no. 6, Miyazaki Hayao,* ed. Takeshi Yoro, p. 44.
8. Mitsunari Ōizumi, *Miyazaki Hayo no genten* (Tokyo, 2002), p. 125.
9. Natsume Sōseki, quoted in Masao Miyoshi, *Accomplices of Silence* (Berkeley, 1974), p. 57.
10. Margherita Long, *This Perversion Called Love: Reading Tanizaki, Feminist Theory, and Freud* (Stanford, Calif., 2009), p. 5.
11. Miyazaki, *Iwanami,* p. 91.
12. Frederik Schodt, *Manga! Manga! The World of Japanese Comics* (New York, 1983), p. 63.
13. Adam Gopnik, "Re-reading Children's Books" (podcast), 17 Aug. 2015, www.Newyorker.com/podcast/out-loud/re-reading-childrens-books.
14. Miyazaki. *Starting Point,* p. 341.
15. Miyazaki, *Iwanami,* p. 89.

Michael Arlen, 1930. Dorothy L. Sayers, early 1920s. Unknown photographer. Both photos © National Portrait Gallery, London.

6

Newer Images of Women and Men in the Interwar Decades

REBA SOFFER

D id the interwar decades perpetuate the traditions and habits of thought prevalent during the Great War, or were they the beginning of a new and radically different era? Among the kinds of evidence to which we turn, are novels especially revelatory, because they have more readers than any other kind of writing? Throughout the nineteenth century, novelists told stories in which the standards of appropriate behavior were well known and generally endorsed, even if not always practiced. In popular literature, conventional virtue, especially for women, was rewarded, and unconventional vice was punished. Whether or not that code conformed to private behavior, it echoed and reinforced prevailing public morality. Then, in the 1880s, as cultural, political, social, and economic contexts changed, authors of fiction began to reconsider private and public images of men and women. For some female writers, the suffrage movement was the catalyst for questioning their circumscribed domestic and professional opportunities. These women repudiated their limited access to higher education and argued vigorously for independence, satisfying employment, mobility, and rational dress. The concept of the New Woman became a cultural icon of the fin de siècle after it was coined, applauded, and made into a mission by the writer Sarah Grand in 1894. It was not only middle-class radicals who became New Women; so too did factory and office workers, who were depicted by Grand in her books and speeches as intelligent, educated, emancipated, and self-supporting.

Nearly a decade later, Emmeline and Christobel Pankhurst accelerated the drive for expanded feminine roles. Their creation of the Women's Social and Political Union in 1903 coincided with the movement of increasing numbers of women into white-collar jobs. Available employment, largely as nurses and shop assistants, still lacked prestige and was poorly paid. In the late nineteenth century, a minority had positions as librarians and teachers, and fewer still found low-level government jobs. All together, there were fewer than 200,000 of these aspiring women. By 1911, that number had increased to approximately 800,000, and it grew exponentially during the Great War as women replaced men in nearly every kind of work.

After the war, a great variety of novels competed for a newly voracious, enormously expanded, and almost universally literate reading public. Publishers recognized and exploited these markets, especially among women, by offering them "best sellers." These books, originally developed for soldiers at the front, were published, promoted, and distributed in commercial and public lending libraries at minimal expense to readers and maximum profit for publishers. Among them was the lost generation that had died during the war or never recovered from their ordeals. Wilfred Owen, who died while fighting in 1918, and Sigfried Sassoon, who was wounded, wrote poetry revealing the horrors of the war. Vera Brittain described nursing and caring for the dying and the survivors. Those able to come home, such as A. S. M. Hutchinson, Philip Gibbs, and Warwick Deeping, revealed the troubled transition of soldiers returning to a depleted society. Besides these war memorials, the radical and revolutionary literature of James Joyce, T. S. Eliot, Robert Graves, T. H. Huxley, and J. R .R. Tolkien appealed to an avant-garde with experimental forms and warnings of chronic misfortune. None of these writers' genres offered the entertainment and escape typical of the popular best sellers. Instead, their writing tended to be coupled with disillusionment. Evelyn Waugh, although a best-selling author, amused his audience by skewering individual incapacity and finding its remedy exclusively in the capaciousness of the Roman Catholic Church. The weak figures who squirmed through his novels were dim, unpleasant, unsuccessful, and doomed.

Dorothy Leigh Sayers (1893–1957) and Michael Arlen (1895–1956) differed from these other writers by providing narratives in which individuals overcame all kinds of restrictions to achieve and profit from expanded opportunities. They were contemporaries who never met, and their characters and stories were very different. In common, though, they featured individuals who became more responsible, successful, better, and self-sufficient women and men. Their heroes and heroines overcame social, cultural, and economic barriers, including class and gender. While both men and women read Sayers, Arlen's audience was heavily tilted toward women. Male reviewers lauded Sayers but tended to dismiss and ridicule Arlen. Women, especially those who had been independent during the war but returned to domesticity and dependence in the interwar years, could appreciate the liberated women central to both Sayers and Arlen. Each assumed that their readers had despaired of participating endlessly in the social, political, economic, psychological, and demographic consequences of the Great War. Instead, they offered them introspective inquiries into an improved future that could fulfill their expectations. Their focus was domestic. Britain's increasingly uncertain role in the new world was not interesting to them as novelists, because it was less immediate than daily life. With unprecedented book sales, Sayers and Arlen became international celebrities. They exploited their popularity further by writing plays, promoting movies, appearing in radio broadcasts, and lecturing.

Their backgrounds were very different. The only child of a clerical father, Sayers received the education and encouragement he would have given to a son. *Whose Body?*, the first of Sayers's thirteen Lord Peter Wimsey mysteries, appeared in 1923, and the following year Michael Arlen published his infamous *The Green Hat*. Originally named Dikran Kouyoumdjian, Arlen was the youngest and fifth child of an Armenian commercial family that lived in Bulgaria when Arlen was born. Five years later, they moved to Lancashire to escape the continued persecution of Christian Armenians.

Both authors thought of their work as serious "literature," and they felt unfairly excluded from the work and communities to which they felt entitled by virtue of their intellect, talent, and demonstrated capabilities. Arlen wanted desperately to be English. Beginning as an alien and lonely young writer in London, he always remained an outsider. Before *The Green Hat*, a character in one of his stories for the *New Age* magazine predicted presciently that "in spite of your English airs, you will always be a pathetic little stranger in a very strange land, fumbling for the key." Before Sayers became the first and most successful member of the Golden Age of mystery writers in the 1920s and 1930s, she discovered that her gender prevented her from finding a rewarding personal and professional life. Their resentment about their perceived and unfair rejection, personified in their novels, may have resonated deeply among returning soldiers and the unemployed or underemployed of both sexes.

While Arlen had no competitors, Sayers has often been compared with Agatha Christie, who wrote sixty detective novels and eventually became the best-selling author writing in English. Christie certainly encouraged her readers to think, and she gave them eccentric and attractive characters. But those characters never challenged values and behavior that were recognizably traditional and British. Unlike Wimsey and, later, Harriet Vane, Sayers's surrogate, Christie's detectives are hardly "newer" men and women. Their stories do not reflect Christie's own painful personal life, which was marred by depression, her mother's death, her husband's infidelities, and their divorce in 1928. Instead, her heroes and heroines enjoy achievement and status, and their personal lives are economically and socially secure, and rewarding. Christie's first novel, *The Mysterious Affair at Styles* (1920), introduces Hercule Poirot, a former Belgian police officer who is in London as a refugee. Clever, eccentric, and sexually neutered, he hardly represents British values. *The Second Adversary* (1922) launches Tommy and Tuppence, two bright young things falling into adventures. Her final detective, Miss Jane Marple, is a very traditional, clever, genteel little old spinster of comfortable means, who lived and detected in a picturesque village.

In contrast to Christie, Sayers situated all her central characters within a troubled post-war Britain recognizable to both urban and rural readers. Lord Peter Wimsey is a victim of shell shock as a result of his battlefield experiences, as was Sayers's husband, Mac Fleming. Wimsey and later Harriet Vane were derived from Sayers's own desires, disappointments, and experiences. Christie adhered scrupulously to the anti-sex code generally accepted by all the prominent Golden Age crime writers. But Sayers decided that Lord Peter Wimsey would be more interesting, as would everyone in the real world, with an active and rewarding sexual life. In *Unnatural Death* (1927), Sayers even skirted a lesbian relationship between her murderess and an innocent and foolish young woman, recognizably foolish not for her lesbian impulses but rather for her admiration of Arlen. When she introduced the highly intelligent, accomplished, and perceptive Vane, in *Strong Poison* (1930), she too was given a sexual life, a scandalous one.

After 1937, when Sayers was financially able to abandon detective novels, she devoted her self to theology, Christian humanism, literary criticism, essays, lectures, and her first and last love—medieval scholarship. Before turning to mysteries, she had written poetry and translated the long twelfth-century poem *Tristan* from the medieval

French. In all her writing, she investigated intellectual and moral dilemmas and their consequences. Although she was most proud of her translation of Dante's *Divine Comedy,* her reputation rests on the creation of Peter Wimsey and Harriet Vane and the unsettled and introspective lives that she gave them.

An only child with a loving but neurasthenic mother, Sayers was blessed with a father who taught her Latin when she was six and encouraged her to be an original and independent person. Until she was four, Sayers's father was headmaster of Christ Church Cathedral Choir School in Oxford, where she learned and retained a love of music. The family then moved to her father's new living in East Anglia. Taught by governesses until she was fifteen, she went to the Godolphin School in Salisbury. When she was nineteen, she won a scholarship to Somerville College, Oxford. In 1915 she was awarded first-class honors in modern languages and medieval literature, and in 1920 she was among the first women to receive an Oxford degree, choosing to become an M.A. But she did not find economic security until 1922, when she was hired by the advertising firm S. H. Benson. She worked for it until 1931 and mined her experiences there for the witty, satirical *Murder Must Advertise* (1933).

Sayers's life was far more adventurous and intrepid than the experiences she allowed her female characters. Only a few friends and her supportive family knew about her disastrous romantic interests. They included a passionate but unconsummated love affair with John Cournos, a Russian Jewish writer, who broke her heart. That was followed by a brief affair with a motorcycle and car repairman, Anthony White, who taught her to ride and repair motorcycles. He also provided sexual satisfaction and an illegitimate child, John Anthony, before riding off into the rain. Her pregnancy was never suspected by her colleagues or friends, because her figure was concealed effectively by voluminous clothing. When it was time to give birth, in 1924, she took a vacation for a few weeks. Only her Aunt Amy and her cousin Ivy Shrimpton knew about John Anthony, and they raised him with Sayers's financial support. In 1926, marriage to Mac Fleming, a journalist, gave her a happy and companionable few years until the effects of his physical and psychological war damage prevented him from working. Sayers supported Fleming until his death in 1950. John Anthony believed Sayers to be his cousin until Fleming and Sayers finally adopted the boy, when he was a teen. But he was not acknowledged as Sayers's biological son until after her death, when her will bequeathed him her estate.

When Sayers decided to write crime stories, she could have launched a series starring a newer kind of woman, much like herself.

Instead, she introduced a newer kind of man, who rejected anti-
quated traditions and understood and often attempted to remedy
the injustices still confronting women. Lord Peter Death Bredon
Wimsey, the second son of the 15th Duke of Denver, had as his motto
"Wherever my Whimsey takes me." Like Sayers, he was intellectual,
multitalented, multilingual, musical, and an Oxford first-class honors graduate. When Wimsey demonstrated his arcane knowledge of
forensic medicine, bibliophilia, languages, the laws of inheritance,
criminology, and forensic medicine, Sayers was displaying her own
erudition. Sayers also made him a recognized expert in areas she
never mastered, including cricket, martial arts, wine, food, cryptog-
raphy, burglary, Foreign Office diplomacy, and espionage. Sayers,
who had to work unceasingly to earn an income, made Wimsey an
aristocrat with the leisure, wealth, and position to do whatever he
chose. Although occasionally arrogant, Wimsey followed a chivalric
code of personal and social responsibility. He managed to be genuinely considerate, dispassionately thoughtful, reflective, and, above
all, honest—qualities opposed to Sayers portrayal of most of the aristocracy as self-indulgent, anachronistic, idle, unimaginative, and
dishonest. Although Wimsey can appear to be an annoying and silly
amateur, there is nothing amateurish about his highly skilled and
expert investigations. His mannerisms are adopted, he confesses, as
a disguise to make others trust him by assuming that he is frivolous
and not very bright.

Sayers gave Wimsey a butler-valet, Mervyn Bunter, originally his
sergeant in the Great War. Bunter, an intelligent, well-informed
super nanny, is every workingwoman's fantasy. Instead of scolding
or intruding, he anticipates and dispatches not only the mundane
but also the consequential aspects of daily life. An accomplished
photographer and a keen reader of human psychology, Bunter understands, appreciates, and assists his employer in their common
detective work. Charles Parker, a policeman, close friend, and ally,
becomes a chief inspector and Wimsey's brother-in-law. Although
Wimsey's aristocratic family tries to reject Parker because he has
only a normal secondary education and comes from a lower class,
Wimsey encourages the couple and blesses their marriage.

Sayers did not want to be considered a social critic. In her introduction to *Gaudy Night* (1935), she contends that "the novelist's only
native country is Cloud-Cuckooland," a place that has nothing to
do with the real world. Sayers's attempted separation from the real
world often conflicted with other commitments, such as her feminism. Her address *Are Women Human?* (1938) was incorporated into
a later book with the same title. Even so, she took no part in the con-

temporary suffragette movement. There is no mention of the 1928 extension of full voting rights for women in any of the mysteries, or of any other major political event, such as the General Strike of 1926. But her husband's war experiences made her sympathetic to shell-shocked men unable to adjust to civilian life. In *Whose Body?*, Wimsey experiences recurrent nightmares as a result of his service in the Great War as a commended major with a Distinguished Service Order. In *The Unpleasantness at the Bellona Club* (1928), an innocent man is suspected of murder because his war experiences continue to cause him to behave aberrantly. Wimsey's shell shock returns in *Busman's Honeymoon* (1936) because he condemns a murderer to death. That episode compels him to doubt that he will ever again solve another crime. This book was the last Wimsey mystery.

Try as she might, though, Sayers could not entirely ignore contemporary life, especially when women such as herself were involved. She recognized very clearly that their quality of life depended upon eliminating the uses and abuses of power. In the Wimsey series, Sayers concentrated on women who lack every kind of power and are prevented from developing and using their abilities and knowledge. She thought of herself and many of her female friends as a neglected intellectual elite condemned by obsolete traditions to unsatisfactory choices about who they were and how they ought to live. One option was marriage. But even when based on love, she feared both an exclusive focus on a husband's career and the intellectually impoverishing role of caring for their children. Married women sometimes appear in her books as victims of circumstances or of their own delusions. The other option for women was to remain single and suffer discrimination in their attempt to be financially secure. In *Unnatural Death* (1927), Wimsey establishes what appears to be a typing agency, the Cattery, led by the formidable Miss Climpton and staffed by discarded, intelligent, resourceful, brave women. Instead of pursuing "women's work," the Cattery's employees work for Wimsey as detectives by going where men are unable to go. In that novel, the brilliantly innovative killer is a woman.

Sayers returned to the conflict between domesticity and independence repeatedly. That theme is central to *Gaudy Night* (1936), which takes place in a fictional woman's college based on Sayers's Somerville. When Harriet Vane, the successful detective mystery writer and Newer Woman, is introduced in *Strong Poison* (1930), Wimsey ceases to be a male Sayers and becomes instead the model Newer Man. Some of the remaining mysteries are advertised on their covers as "A Lord Peter Wimsey mystery with Harriet Vane." An illicit sexual affair costs Vane dearly with her peers, but not with

Wimsey. He cheerfully admits to her that he had lovers, too, and had been told that "he makes love very nicely." In five more books, Wimsey continues to ask Vane to marry him because he wants an intellectual equal. Finally, Vane learns in *Gaudy Night* that she can love a man who values her mental and moral qualities as she values his, and in *Busman's Honeymoon* she finally marries him. Sayers, as Vane, envies the advantages of an academic sanctuary in an Oxford women's college, but rejects an exclusively intellectual life as only partially fulfilling.

SAYERS AND ARLEN MIGHT HAVE MET at Oxford, where Dikran Kouyoumdjian had been meant to go. He had begun his education at Malvern College, where C. S. Lewis had spent an unhappy year. Dismissed as an "Armenian Jew," Kouyoumdjian was isolated there. Vehemently denying that identity as oxymoronic, because virtually all Armenians were Christian, he shared the anti-Semitism prevalent in Britain then. Instead of going to Oxford, he impulsively went instead to the University of Edinburgh for thirteen months. There, he devoted himself to "general fecklessness." After moving to London, he wrote for Armenian journals and for the *New Age,* the literary journal funded in part by G. B. Shaw and edited from 1907 to 1920 by A. R. Orage. Besides Arlen, the journal published writers such as Katherine Mansfield and Ezra Pound. In 1920, Arlen achieved wider recognition with the collection of his autobiographical essays from the *New Age* titled *The London Venture.* He then began using the name Michael Arlen. In 1922, he became a British citizen, the same year that he published two short stories in the *English Review.* More than any other literary magazine of the 1920s, the experimental *Review* had a wider, more celebrated international audience, with contributors such as Joseph Conrad, D. H. Lawrence, Sherwood Anderson, and Anton Chekhov.

Why did *The Green Hat* bring Arlen such wealth and notoriety? It is a hyper-romantic novel of social and moral criticism whose central figure is a Newer Woman with the chivalric sensibilities and independence traditionally associated with the other sex. She was unique because she "met men on their own ground." There are no admirable Newer Men in the novel, and the young narrator, a surrogate for Arlen, laments their absence. Instead, the narrator witnesses and records the obsolete pre-war standards of the upper classes, which were perpetuated not only by the older generation, but also by the younger men of "Careless Days Before the War" fame. The heroine, the wearer of the green hat, is Iris Storm, whose surname summarizes the effect she had on both men and women. When the book appeared, there was speculation that she might have been modeled in part on Nancy Cunard, who had had a brief affair with Arlen. Cunard was very much an independent woman—a poet and political activist—an independence enabled by her good fortune in being the heiress to the Cunard Line shipping empire.

The unimaginably beautiful, immensely wealthy, twice-widowed Iris drives a yellow Hispano-Suiza, then a symbol of ultimate luxury. But she cannot enjoy her life because she was held responsible for the suicide ten years earlier of Boy Fenwick, her first husband. When she explains only that Boy died "for Purity," everyone assumes that on their wedding night Boy learned of her previous sexual adventures. Towards the end of the book, we learn that Boy killed himself because he had syphilis and that Iris chose to maintain Boy's reputation at the cost of her own. Iris meets the narrator for the first time when she comes to visit her doomed alcoholic twin brother, Gerald Marsh, who lives in a flat above. Gerald, blaming his sister for Boy's death, had refused to know her for the past decade, and never sees her again. There is a suggestion that Geralds's love for Boy was homoerotic. Later, after Gerald is arrested wrongly for annoying a woman in a park, he kills himself.

On the night that Iris is rejected by her brother, she sleeps with the narrator. She is described the morning after as "beautiful, grave, proud . . . neither shameful like a maiden nor shameless like a mondaine, nor showing any fussy after-trill of womanhood, any dingy ember of desire." The narrator learns throughout the book that Iris is being punished for her autonomy by the fossilized upper classes, "the warriors of caste and conduct." From her childhood, Iris has loved Napier Harpenden, but when they were both eighteen, Napier's father, General Sir Maurice, separated them. Napier was too weak and too dim to resist, especially after Boy's suicide, for which he blamed Iris. Years later, in a chance meeting, they resume their affair for one night. Three days later Napier marries Venice, the daughter of a powerful and very wealthy man who, according to Sir Maurice's plan, can further his son's career.

Unknown to Napier, Iris becomes pregnant, loses the baby, and almost dies in a prison-like hospital in Paris. Napier comes to see her, but Iris instructs the narrator, who has become a friend, to tell Napier that she has ptomaine poisoning. Believing what he is told, Napier returns to his wife. Since they all move in the same social milieu, Iris and Venice find themselves together at a picnic and swimming party. When Venice begins to drown, Iris risks her own life to save her rival. Afterward, Venice learns of Iris and Napier's love and selflessly encourages Napier to go off with Iris. In a vindication of the judgment of some critics in the 1920s that little in the book is credible, the two delayed lovers decide to live by their love and resettle in Brazil. On the day before their departure, Iris is summoned by Sir Maurice, who wants to persuade her to leave Napier. Arlen's promise that love changes people beyond imagining comes true when Napier displays his first signs of intelligence and perception. Without warning, he becomes newly articulate and self-aware: "Here I am at thirty, a nothing without even the excuse of being a happy nothing, a nothing liked by other nothings and successful among other nothings, a nothing wrapped round by the putrefying little rules of gentlemanly tradition. And, my god, they are putrefying." Iris, insisting that her protection of Boy's reputation was "the only gracious thing" she ever did in her life, then drives her car into the oak tree where she and Napier had conspired futilely as young lovers. Iris's suicide shows her to be a Newer Woman capable of the kind of heroic self-sacrifice traditionally possessed exclusively by men.

The Green Hat received an overwhelming and very satisfying reception. The rush to buy green hats in order to identify with Arlen's heroine was so great that none of the manufacturers could keep up with the demand. But Arlen's popularity with the larger reading public moved him even further away from the approval of the literary intelligentsia, which he desperately craved. This was especially true and very painful for Arlen in his relations with D. H. Lawrence, who had greatly influenced him and whom he saw, reverently, as that " strange and great man." Arlen was strongly struck by Lawrence's signature embrace of emotions, instinct, spontaneity, and passion, and he adopted Lawrence's anti-intellectualism as a leitmotif in *The Green Hat.* Never intended to be a modernist manifesto, *The Green Hat* did explore many of the sexual and social dilemmas that troubled modernists like Lawrence. In 1927, Arlen joined Lawrence in Florence, where he received a disappointing welcome. While they were together, Lawrence was writing the third and final version of the unprecedented, sexually explicit *Lady Chatterley's Lover.* Lawrence inserted Arlen into the revised narrative as Micaelis, Lady Chatterley's occasional lover, derided as "a little mongrel arriviste and uneducated bounder of the worst sort" whose only real passion was social success. Worse yet, Lawrence portrays him as sexually incompetent because he left his partners unsatisfied. In real life, Arlen was uniquely appealing to women as a man and as a writer—a success that may have been trying for Lawrence. Rejected by Lawrence, Arlen was accepted by European royalty the following year with his happy marriage to Countess Atalanta Mercati, with whom he had a son and a daughter.

ARLEN'S AND SAYERS'S IDEALS FOR Newer Men and Newer Women were remarkably different. Arlen's almost exclusively female readers admired Iris Storm's character, courage, independence, and wealth, qualities very few of then could ever hope to have. But their hearts belonged to her creator because he so clearly adored women and dedicated himself to the romantic ideal of love. While Arlen's emotional men and women depended on the consuming supremacy of passion, Sayers's Wimsey and Vane were intellectuals who delighted in reason, esoteric knowledge, and clever wit. But Sayers also spoke to women who had discovered and lost some degree of financial and social independence, as well as to women who were frustrated by their inability to compete fairly with men. Wimsey could be relied on to punish evil, reward good, and, most importantly of all in a time of increasing unpredictability, restore order. Both authors repeatedly emphasized that the most important characteristic of their Newer Men and Newer Women was honesty. Popular feeling in the interwar decades was bitter about the conduct and consequences of the Great War. Leaders had dishonestly promised a quick and conclusive victory as well as a better life for the survivors and their families.

While Sayers tried to keep her personal life private, Arlen's private and public lives were inseparable from each other. He was among the most lionized men of the 1920s in both Britain and America, where, in 1927, he appeared on the cover of *Time* magazine. But Sayers's fame was more enduring. All the Wimsey novels are still in print, and her hero and heroine still appear in movies and in stage and television plays. Although Arlen continued to produce novels, short stories, essays, and plays, and although six films were based on his writings, he never again matched the popularity of *The Green Hat*. In 1941, Arlen was publicly humiliated by a Member of Parliament for not really being English enough, in spite of his patriotic anti-Nazi writings and absolute dedication to his new country. Arlen resigned from his position as public relations officer for the Midlands Region and left England. He lived on the Continent and in America with his wife and family until his death in New York in 1956. His son, Michael Arlen, became a television critic for the *New Yorker* and published award-winning memoirs.

Both Sayers and Arlen reached an enormous variety of readers all over the world. But did the Sayers mysteries or *The Green Hat* demonstrably influence individual thinking and behavior? Determining the content, substance, and meaning of an audience's response is problematic even when readers demonstrate their approval by enthusiastic loyalty to an author. Arlen gave his mostly feminine readers an emotionally opulent, romantic fantasy. We don't know whether those readers felt a passing frisson of yearning or an effective life-changing experience. Romantic fantasies are rarely useful in dealing with the complexities of everyday life. Still, in one reported incident, Joseph Stalin, in the midst of the catastrophic assault on the Soviet Union by the Nazi military forces in the 1940s, was distracted by his continuing obsession with the causes of his wife's suicide two decades earlier. He complained to his daughter, Svetlana Alliluyeva, that he blamed that "vile book" that his wife had been reading shortly before she killed herself. The book "very much in vogue at that time" was *The Green Hat*. It is far more likely that living with Stalin might have encouraged any woman to kill herself. Sayers also tried to provide escape, but she used her characters and her own experiences to explore the requirements and consequences of living a life different from what prevailing practice demanded. Whether Sayers's pragmatic advice was followed can only be imagined.

We know what Sayers and Arlen meant to say because they told us their intentions; and we can read what they said. We also know that they each had an enormous following. Arlen is no longer read, because Iris Storm and her social and cultural life clearly belong to another time and place. Although Sayers still speaks to the contested lives and choices that her characters share with us, they, too, owe their ideas, identities, and behavior to the decades between the wars. The assumptions and beliefs resonant with the readers of these best sellers occurred within the context of the ambiguous residue of the Great War. Those scars and fears were magnified by the encroaching, terrifying proximity of another European debacle. If the readers of Sayers and Arlen found them to be irrelevant in that context, would they have read them with such enthusiasm?

Fall Semester 2015

Encyclopaedia Britannica, eleventh edition.

7

Encyclopaedia Britannica

JOSEPH EPSTEIN

"Encyclopedia," in its root definition, means "circle of knowledge." Pliny the Elder (A.D. 23–79), perhaps the world's first encyclopedist, used the word to describe his *Natural History*. The circle implies all-round education, which in turn suggests everything worth knowing, hence omniscience. In 1751, under Denis Diderot and Jean d'Alembert, the famous French *Encyclopédie* began publication with roughly this ambitious intention. Seventeen years later, in Edinburgh, a printer and antiquary named William Smellie brought out the first of a three-volume set of books under the title *Encyclopaedia Britannica*, a work that would see its final print version—32,640 pages in thirty-two volumes—published in 2010. We all live now of course with that useful but not always reliable hodgepodge called *Wikipedia*.

Self-improvement is at the heart of the encyclopedic enterprise. People certified with degrees from what the world considers the best universities and colleges sometimes forget that we are all autodidacts, on our own in the endless attempt to patch over the extraordinary gaps in our knowledge. Doing so efficiently is the promise held out by an encyclopedia, which claims to provide all the world's pertinent knowledge, right there in twenty-four, twenty-nine, or thirty-two volumes, usually with a bookcase thrown in at no extra charge.

Encyclopedias and, by extension, encyclopedists can and have had their not especially hidden agendas. The French *Encyclopédie* was, in effect, a house organ for the Enlightenment; its editors wished to change the way people thought, which meant that they wanted to secularize learning, thereby striking a blow against the educational dominance of the Jesuits. The program of many lesser encyclopedias was more straightforward: to make a profit. The one encyclopedia that set out to do both, show a profit while embodying the spirit of its age, was the eleventh edition of the *Encyclopaedia Britannica* (1910–11).

The eleventh was the last great encyclopedia. Its greatness derived not alone from its contributors or its organization, but also from the spirit infusing it. This spirit was one of confidence in progress—material, scientific, artistic, and spiritual, even if not religious. The society in which the eleventh was composed and published considered itself, as Denis Boyles notes in *Everything Explained That Is Explainable* (2016), to be "the Rome to the long nineteenth-century's Greece, an era in which engineers spoke the language of visionaries. And it was English."

English the eleventh edition indubitably was, in its principal editors, in the vast majority of its contributors, in its imperialist confidence. Behind the scenes, though, the work was the inspiration of an American huckster named Horace Everett Hooper. A huckster with a difference, Hooper was also an idealist: he was wily for the public good, or at least that portion of the public intent on its own educational betterment.

In American publishing, the decades preceding the appearance of the Eleventh were marked by highbinders and sidewinders. Pirating English books was all but standard practice. (Charles Dickens, much aggrieved by these offenses when practiced upon his own books, demonstrated his grievance in his novel *Martin Chuzzlewit*, a chronicle of American operators and charlatans.) In this free-wheeling publishing atmosphere, Boyles reports, the English *Encyclopaedia Britannica* was "a very lucrative target." The encyclopedia had better sales in the United States than in England. The hunger for self-improvement among Americans made the *Britannica* fine game for publishing poachers, who served it up to their readers in revised and bogus versions. "Entries," Boyles writes, "were edited, omitted, and added at will, and sometimes without much regard for quality."

Over the years the cachet of the *Encyclopaedia Britannica* never waned; only its profits did. "The *Britannica*," Boyles writes, "had brought prestige, but not much profit, to every proprietor and publisher who had touched it since its first appearance in 1768." As the

Britannica increased in size over the years, selling it became all the more difficult. Hooper had ideas about how to change this. One of the poachers would soon become the gamekeeper.

Among the books Hooper sold in America were versions of the ninth edition of the *Britannica*. He was immensely impressed by it. Much therein was worthy of admiration. The ninth edition, brought out in twenty-five volumes between 1875 and 1889, represented a dazzling anthology of English writing. Articles ran to 40,000 words, and some to the length of small books. Among its contributors were James Bryce, Matthew Arnold, William Morris, John Stuart Mill, and Robert Louis Stevenson. (Contributors to the seventh edition included William Hazlitt, Thomas Malthus, Walter Scott, and Mill.) The ninth edition was one of the splendid achievements of the Victorian Age.

Hooper, Boyles writes, "understood that his business wasn't just selling books. It was monetizing authority." An Anglophile, Hooper took it upon himself to improve the sales of the *Britannica* in England by leashing it to that other grand English editorial institution, *The Times*. Such was the authoritativeness of *The Times* that in some foreign countries its correspondents were thought more powerful than the English ambassador. "*The Times*," Mr. Boyles writes, "was as imperishable a part of national life as the Church of England, though more widely believed." Despite its towering prestige, *The Times* was a financial loser. Hooper intervened with a plan by which the two, newspaper and encyclopedia, could each profit.

On the business side, the fortunes of *The Times* began to change when a man named Charles Moberly Bell, who had earlier been a cotton merchant and a *Times* correspondent in Egypt, became the paper's business manager and began to put its financial house in order. The idea of rescuing *The Times* through its sponsoring of a revised version of the ninth edition was Hooper's. If the newspaper would permit him to sell the old ninth edition of the *Britannica* under its auspices—in what would be called a *Times* edition—it would gain serious sums in royalties while the encyclopedia would gain allure and sales leads through its association with *The Times*.

The *Britannica* editorial offices soon thereafter moved to the top floor of the Times building at London's Printing House Square. Hooper brought aboard an advertising adept named Henry R. Haxton, a Hearst journalist of bohemian spirit who counted among his friends Ambrose Bierce, James Whistler, and Stephen Crane and who didn't mind pushing the pedal all the way down in his advertising copy. In effusive, highly colored prose, Haxton's ads suggested that people had to acquire the *Encyclopaedia Britannica* or remain forever benighted. As Boyles puts it, Haxton made it seem "that the *Britannica* was not just a book, it was a cure."

In 1903, Hooper and Haxton devised a contest called "The Times Competition," whereby readers of the newspaper were asked to answer, in essay form, questions on subjects of general information. Prizes amounting to £3,585 were offered, first among them a full four-year scholarship to Oxford or Cambridge. Haxton claimed in advertisements that those who entered the competition would acquire "Closer concentration of mind, Practice in ready reasoning, Quickness in finding facts, A new form of recreation, An invaluable fund of general information." One could not pick up the questions at the *Times* offices but had to mail in one's request. Readers wise in the ways of salesmanship will grasp that this provided an astonishing list of leads for selling the ninth edition. These were used, in the best full-court-press salesmanship, to inundate possible customers for the *Britannica* with mail and even telegrams. "From my bath, I curse you" was the reply of one such recipient of these sales tactics. But the general public response was, in Boyles's words, "immediate and overwhelming."

Some might view this as commercial genius, but to many Englishmen of the day it was American vulgarity let loose and a besmirching of the dignity of *The Times*. By such heavy-breathing advertising and promotions, Hooper and Bell, both victims of English upper-class xenophobia, withstood insults and resistance, and their methods eventually brought *The Times* out of the red. The Hooper innovation of selling the *Britannica* on the installment plan was no small help. Boyles estimates that Hooper and a business partner named Walter Montgomery Jackson cleared more than a $1 million between them, and *The Times*—measured by today's exchange rate—something like £6.5 million.

The editor of the revised ninth edition and later of the eleventh— the edition called the tenth was the ninth with nine supplemental volumes added—was a literary journalist named Hugh Chisholm. Sharing Hooper's idealism, Chisholm felt that the *Britannica* was "the best way of democratizing self-education." He coordinated the gargantuan project of the ninth edition, whose immensity entailed 1,507 contributors, a staff of 64 assistant editors, some 40,000 articles, and an index of roughly 500,000 entries, the whole weighing in at 250 pounds. Along with being a brilliant editorial manager, Chisholm was a trenchant writer. Boyles quotes from his *Britannica* entry on Lord Acton: "Lord Acton has left too little completed original work to rank among the great historians; his very learning seems to have stood in his way; he knew too much and his literary conscience was too acute for him to write easily, and his copiousness of information overloads his literary style. But he was one of the most deeply learned men of his time, and he will certainly be remembered for his influence on others."

In a highly readable style, nicely seasoned with occasional ironic touches, Boyles limns the intricate business negotiations that went into the creation of the eleventh edition. He chronicles *Britannica's* departure from *The Times* after Lord Northcliffe acquired the newspaper in 1908; its being taken up by Cambridge University until that university's Syndics found its marketing measures too garish; and its sale, in 1920, to Sears, Roebuck in the United States, which sold it chiefly through its catalogue.

Boyles provides excellent portraits of the key figures responsible for the nineteenth- and early twentieth-century editions of Britannica. His last chapter is given over to the eleventh's mishandling, owing to its having been a work of its time, of such key, and in our day supersensitive, subjects as women, African Americans, Native Americans, Asians, Arabs, and its difficulties with Catholic and Protestant readers. None of this finally diminishes the overall accomplishment that is *Encyclopaedia Britannica's* eleventh edition. Boyles ends by asserting that the ethos of progress that undergirded the eleventh was put paid to by World War I: "Even the most visionary Edwardians would never have ventured to guess that a deeply held belief in the ideology of Progress would lead eventually to the first twenty-four hours of the Battle of the Somme."

The élan of the eleventh edition was never regained. In the United States, the set was marketed chiefly by door-to-door salesmen, whose pitch was less to self-education than to the guilt of parents concerned about the social mobility of their children. Prestige, though, still clung to the encyclopedia: well into the twentieth century, the person who wrote the *Britannica* article on any given subject was thought to be the world's leading authority on that subject.

In 1943, Sears, wishing to unload the *Encyclopaedia Britannica,* donated it to the University of Chicago. Robert Hutchins, then president of the university, didn't see how an intellectual institution could also run and sell such a work, so he offered it for a derisive sum to William Benton, a former advertising man who was then his vice president for public affairs, with the university to receive a handsome royalty. At Benton's death in 1973, these royalties had amounted to $47.8 million.

Business was carried on as usual until 1968, when Benton hired Sir William Haley as the editor in chief of the *Britannica.* Haley had been a director of the *Manchester Guardian,* the director-general of the BBC, and editor in chief of *The Times*—a résumé that could have been completed in its perfection only by his having also been editor of the *Oxford English Dictionary.* I was one of Sir William's senior editors and held him in the highest esteem. A cultivated man of gravity and wide knowledge, he planned to expand the *Britannica*'s coverage and raise its literary and intellectual quality through his connections with Isaiah Berlin, Hugh Trevor-Roper, and other members of a remarkable generation of English philosophers, historians, and scientists.

The *Encyclopaedia Britannica* under Haley figured to be a splendid set of books, a rival, perhaps, to the great eleventh edition. Alas, it was not to be. Corporate politics worked against Haley, who departed the company. (When I left not long after, he wrote to me: "I am glad you have departed the Britannica; they worship different gods than we.") Robert Hutchins, the one man with influence over Benton, contrived to elevate his old sidekick Mortimer Adler to the directorship of a vastly revised *Britannica.* Once in charge Adler, a man whose high IQ was matched only by his low sensibility, twisted the set into separate volumes of longer and shorter entries, called respectively the Macropaedia and the Micropaedia, with a vast index volume called the Propaedia. The result was an intellectually tidy and not especially readable work. The great day of the *Britannica*'s distinction was done and, after the advent of the Internet, would never return. You can look it up.

Spring Semester 2016

A version of this lecture appeared in the *Wall Street Journal,* 17 June 2016.

Newsstand, New York City, 1960.

8

Current American and British Newspapers

BOISFEUILLET JONES, JR.

A common feature in the American and British newspaper industries during the twentieth century was an economic winnowing process resulting in a single strong local newspaper in each city. Even in the largest cities, secondary newspapers and downscale tabloids struggled to survive. But London has been different. It has dominated Britain in population, politics, government, commerce, finance, law, media, and culture. And London has continued to have several competing quality daily and Sunday newspapers as well as a number of tabloid papers, each occupying a somewhat different political niche and appealing to certain segments of the public.

Since the early 1900s, Britain's railway system enabled London newspapers to be distributed to outlying regions of the country. In the far larger and more decentralized United States, where a local newspaper could publish timely national news provided by the cooperatively owned Associated Press or other news services, there was no significant national newspaper distribution until after World War II. The *Wall Street Journal*, with its specialized business and financial news, used same-day mail service to build the first national delivery operation. Al Neuharth of Gannett began *USA Today* in 1982 as a national weekday newspaper aimed particularly at business travelers, for whom the easy-to-read paper was made available at airports and hotels. The *New York Times*, primarily a locally distributed newspaper, had long circulated from its plants in the New York region to eastern cities for readers who wanted a more comprehensive newspaper to supplement their local one. The *Times* had tried publishing West Coast and Paris editions, but closed them in 1964 and 1976 after five years of losses. In the 1990s, as most American newspapers cut back on news coverage for anything that was not local, the *Times* used satellite links to local newspapers' printing plants to roll out, area by area, a financially successful national edition.

The *Washington Post*—despite being the dominant newspaper in the nation's capital, with considerable coverage of politics, government, and foreign affairs—repeatedly concluded that distributing in print across the country would be unprofitable. Instead, the paper created a news service, a columnists syndicate, and other means to distribute its content through hundreds of newspapers and media outlets. Locally, the *Post* was read not only by official Washington but also by a much larger number of ordinary metropolitan-area adults. In the early 1990s, over half of them read the *Post* on weekdays, and three-quarters read it on Sundays. The largest *Post* advertisers, such as department stores and grocers, wanted to reach this mass local audience and had no interest in advertising outside the Washington area. If an advertiser wanted to reach nearby Baltimore, it would take out an ad in the *Baltimore Sun*. By contrast, the *Times* reached an elite audience in New York, about one-fifth of adults. These well-educated and upper-income readers attracted advertisers selling high-end products and services. The advertisers could reach some of the same segment of readers around the country through the *Times*' national edition.

The *Times* and the *Post* for fifty years have been the leading national newspapers in the sense that their reporting tended to set the daily agenda for coverage and discussion by television networks and other media on American political matters and issues. In recent decades, the *Wall Street Journal* also has contributed regularly to the national dialogue, as have the Washington bureaus of the *Los Angeles Times* and the McClatchy (formerly Knight-Ridder) newspapers. But the overall number of Washington-based newspaper reporters has declined, while the press corps from digital and niche publishers like Politico has grown. In Britain, the leading quality daily national newspapers are the *Guardian, The Times* (of London), and the *Telegraph*—and their sister Sunday newspapers. In addition to competing with one another, they have operated in the looming presence of the nonpartisan BBC and its sizable news-reporting capacity.

In both countries, the national newspapers' special role continues for the moment, but their resources and impact have diminished in the new digital world. Like all general-interest newspapers, they built their businesses around the ability to deliver a large daily package of content. A print newspaper was the only way someone each morning could access a large amount of timely news, sports, commentary, reviews, event schedules, crosswords, advertising, and much else. The whole bundle of features attracted readers for different reasons. Advertising-rich parts of the newspaper subsidized other parts and mostly paid for the journalism. But the Internet, and particularly the World Wide Web after 1994, enabled new businesses using new tools for communicating and distributing information to "unbundle" newspapers and disrupt their business model. Multiple websites could easily and cheaply provide the specific information anyone wanted at any time for no or minimal cost. Young people who grew up with computers and, later, smartphones never developed the habit of reading a print newspaper. Newspapers' websites did not save them as news sites and blogs proliferated and as many digital users stopped seeking packaged news and instead got what they wanted from news aggregators or, later, from Facebook and other social media.

By 2005, when high-speed broadband Internet service had become widely accessible in urban areas, the Web's impact on newspapers intensified at a startling rate. Declines in paid print circulation accelerated, dropping almost by half for newspapers—including national newspapers—in the United States and Britain during the next decade. The Web's more immediate and larger impact was on newspapers' advertising. It had generally represented about 80 percent of revenue for American newspapers and for British regional and local ones, and about 50 percent for the British nationals.

The most profitable part of newspapers' advertising revenue was classified advertising—the listings of local jobs, cars, homes, apartments, and miscellaneous merchandise. These franchises were lost to free and easily searched specialized websites such as Hot Jobs, Auto.com, and Craigslist. In the United States, newspaper classified advertising revenue dropped from $17 billion to $5 billion between 2006 and 2012. The disappearance of classified marketplaces in newspapers also meant the loss of readers who often bought the paper mainly to check the classifieds. In Britain, the regional newspapers, not the national newspapers in London, had the bulk of classifieds, and they have suffered greatly. The national papers' loss in revenue came more from the decline in other advertising and in circulation.

Newspapers have built high levels of digital readership, but the advertising revenue generated by it has not come close to compensating for newspapers' loss of print ad revenue. Total newspaper advertising, print and digital, has decreased in each of last ten years. In the United States, print advertising between 2006 and 2012 dropped from $47 billion to $19 billion, while digital advertising increased only slightly, from $2.7 billion to $3.5 billion. Declines at British newspapers have followed the same pattern.

Rates for Web advertising have been low because of the abundant choices and targeted traffic streams available to advertisers. Google and Facebook have obtained about half the revenue. With their huge number of users and data about their habits and interests, Google and Facebook can offer personalized advertising to advertisers of any size through numerous options, including targeted textual and video advertising on mobile devices. In addition, digital news readers bothered by slow-loading ads and intrusive cookies increasingly use ad-blocking tools. Newspapers in turn have increasingly accepted native, or sponsored, advertising, which avoids ad blockers because it is embedded in the news body. If newspapers (and other Web producers) fail to disclose clearly to readers that an advertiser is providing and paying for sponsored content, they risk losing the trust of readers who feel deceived.

To help offset the large loss of ad revenue, newspapers rapidly increased the sales price of print editions. Using price-sensitivity analysis, newspapers were willing to accept the loss of some buyers and readers if it provided an immediate overall gain in circulation revenue. In the long term, the extra decline in readership has meant less pull for advertisers and ultimately a decline in ad revenue. The *Washington Post* is a stark example. Its daily single-copy price stayed at 25¢ until 2002; in early 2016, the daily price was $2.00. Prices for Sunday and for home delivery subscribers—who represent most of the circulation at the *Post* and other American newspapers—have also increased sharply in the last fifteen years. In January 2016, a single copy of the *New York Times* cost $2.50 on weekdays and Saturday, and $5 on Sunday in the New York area. In Britain, circulation price increases have followed the same pattern, but not so sharply among the national newspapers, which have significant single-copy sales and compete with one another. The *Guardian*'s daily cover price rose to £1.80 in 2015, the *Daily Telegraph* is £1.40, and *The Times* is £1.20. Their sister Sunday newspapers are more expensive. The downscale tabloid newspapers are about half the cost.

The other way for newspapers to make significant new revenue has been to charge viewers for digital news. The *Wall Street Jour-*

nal and the *Financial Times*, with their essential finance and business content, had immediate success with paid sites. Most general-interest newspapers were initially reluctant to charge, concerned that they would lose digital viewers. An exception was the *Arkansas Democrat-Gazette*, where the publisher, Walter Hussmann, in 2002 stopped providing unlimited free digital access to nonsubscribers of the print paper. His goal was to retain as much print circulation, and therefore print revenue, as possible, even at the cost of Web traffic and revenue. And indeed, print circulation losses in Little Rock were less than in comparable midsize newspapers with free websites. In 2009, the journalist-entrepreneur Steve Brill cofounded Journalism Online, a business that helped hundreds of newspapers charge for digital content in a gradual way.

In 2011 the *New York Times* and then more newspapers introduced metered pay systems, which go into effect for nonsubscribers after they view, say, ten articles for free during a month. Its system avoids suppressing the flow of large numbers of visitors, who can still gain free access through social media, search engines, and blogs—and who eventually might become digital subscribers. In 2015, the *Times* had well over a million digital-only paying subscribers. In Britain, the *Telegraph* was an early user of a metered pay system. *The Times* adopted a more restrictive pay wall in 2010, while the *Guardian* still has no pay wall.

The *Washington Post* was a latecomer to a pay system. With print circulation that is almost totally local and Web traffic that is over 90 percent national and international, the *Post* in 2014 installed a metered system with different options for digital-only subscribers. The more expensive option includes local news. Like the *Times*, the *Post* can still attract a large funnel of visitors by using a number of means to allow and encourage people to see *Post* content for free. Pay systems evolve over years, and newspapers continue to look closely at their own and everyone else's systems as media use changes, advertising revenue continues to dwindle, and reliance on digital subscriber revenue grows. The *New York Times* in 2015 made more revenue from print and online circulation than from total advertising, and the *Post*'s print and online circulation revenue approached 40 percent.

Even with diminished revenues, the print editions of the American and British national newspapers still provide most of the revenue to carry the business and pay for quality journalism as the digital transformation continues. Their prospects for success may depend on their owners' ability and commitment to persevere during this difficult transition period of dependence on the disrupted print business.

THE LATE *WASHINGTON POST* EDITOR Ben Bradlee said that what it takes to make a good editor is to have a good owner. Certainly, the publishers Katharine Graham and her son Don Graham gave him newsroom autonomy, room to do aggressive reporting, and ample resources to build a large and talented staff. They steadfastly backed him for twenty-seven years—including during difficult times such as the government's lawsuit to stop publication of the *Pentagon Papers*, threats during the early days of Watergate, and the fallout from Janet Cooke's Pulitzer Prize–winning fabricated article, "Jimmy's World." But Bradlee also meant that business acumen and resources were necessary to succeed. After World War II, he had worked at a small prize-winning start-up Sunday newspaper in Manchester, New Hampshire, for two years, until business realities forced the owner to sell to the entrenched *Union-Leader*. Bradlee started as a reporter at the *Post* in 1948, when the newspaper was losing money and was one of four dailies in town.

Fig. 8.1. Katharine Graham, publisher of the *Washington Post*, 1963–79. Photo by Dan Farber. Courtesy of the *Washington Post*.

The *Post*'s owner then was Eugene Meyer, who had bought it in 1933 at a bankruptcy sale. Meyer had no experience in newspapers. He had made a fortune in finance by the time he was forty, then served for twenty years in five successive administrations as a dollar-a-year head of federal finance programs. Meyer threw himself into the *Post* full-time, made some early mistakes, but invested steadily to build the business and to improve the paper's news and editorial quality. In his first ten years, circulation more than tripled. For twenty years, throughout the Great Depression and later, he funded substantial annual losses. To protect the newspaper, he and his son-in-law and successor, Philip Graham, bought two television stations in the early 1950s to strengthen and diversify the company. In 1954, Graham engineered the purchase of the other quality morning paper in Washington, the *Times-Herald*.

The merger made the *Post* viable and left the *Evening Star* as the only other large newspaper. The *Star* was a highly profitable newspaper with a strong news staff, but it had the bad luck of being an afternoon newspaper, so it had to compete with nightly television news as well as with the morning *Post* and its enlarged circulation from the *Times-Herald* merger. The *Star* closed in 1981 and left the *Post* as the only sizable daily newspaper in the nation's capital.

When Phil Graham died in 1963, his widow, Katharine, rejected offers to buy the newspaper and became publisher herself to keep it in the family. She strengthened the newspaper and, to gain access to capital, took the company public in 1971 through a structure with two classes of stock that maintained family control. She overcame the press union's vandalism and strike in 1975–76. Her lawyers won a seminal antitrust suit that upheld the newspaper's reliable and effective circulation system. She hired Bradlee as editor and expanded funding for the newsroom. She brought Warren Buffett and other business leaders onto the board of directors.

Her son, Don Graham, worked at the company for more than forty years, including twenty-one as publisher and twenty-one as CEO of the parent company. He built the *Post* into one of the strongest major newspapers in the country, and he did it while approving news budgets that far exceeded those of papers in similarly sized metropolitan areas. The company also invested heavily on the digital news side and, as Web competition took its annual toll on revenue, cut costs at the newspaper where possible. But in 2013, he and his niece, then-publisher Katharine Weymouth, saw no path to a continued profitable future unless they were willing to either significantly diminish the newsroom and editorial quality or have the

relatively small parent company subsidize the newspaper, to the det-
riment of public shareholders.

Hard as it was, Don Graham looked for a suitable wealthy buyer
who shared his family's values about supporting independent journalism. He wound up selling the newspaper to the billionaire and
technology whiz Jeff Bezos. Like Don Graham's grandfather, Bezos
had no newspaper experience; he bought the *Post* to support the
journalism rather than to advance his own business or political
interests. And he could easily buy and support the newspaper for
many years without debt or obligations to shareholders. At Amazon,
Bezos was willing to forgo short-term profits patiently for the sake
of the long term. He was obsessed with providing the best possible
customer experience and believed in constant research and testing.
The *Post* staff was stunned to learn that the Graham family newspaper would be sold after eighty years of ownership. But Don Graham was so respected and trusted that the common reaction was, "If
Don thinks this is the best way for the *Post* to thrive, then so do I."[1]

Bezos so far has lived up to expectations. He has maintained and
supported the news and editorial staff. He has invested in digital
development, adding fifty new Web-savvy reporters and fifty engineers to the newsroom in one year. He is in effect making the paper
a news and technology company that adapts constantly, particularly
in social media. The *Post* lately has rated among the top tier of online global news organizations in unique U.S. visitors to the site and
mobile apps, surpassing the *New York Times* in October 2015. It is a
statistic that does not reflect revenue or level of engagement, but is
an important indicator of an expanding base of frequent readers.

THE SULZBERGER FAMILY, WITH THE SAME intense motivation as
the Grahams to protect their newspaper, occupy a special place in
newspaper history for maintaining the viability and quality of the
New York Times under family ownership for 120 years. Adolph Ochs
scrambled to purchase it out of receivership in 1896, shepherded
the newspaper to prominence during almost forty years as publisher, and left it as a viable business when he died in 1935. Ochs's
only child, Iphigene, and her husband, Arthur Hays Sulzberger,
publisher from 1935 to 1961, passed their sense of a public trust to
maintain the newspaper's independence and preeminence along to
their children and their descendants, who with determination continue to control and manage the newspaper.

The Sulzbergers took long-term measures to secure the business
strength of the newspaper. Its last remaining quality competitor,
the *New York Herald Tribune*, grew out of the merger between the

Herald and the *Tribune* in 1926. It had outstanding writers and was widely admired for its journalism. But under the ownership of the Reid family, it did not have the resources and commitment necessary to match the *New York Times* in circulation and growth under Arthur Hays Sulzberger. Weakened, the *Herald Tribune*, under the new owner, John Hay Whitney, folded in 1966 following prolonged labor strikes.

Under Sulzberger's son, Arthur Ochs Sulzberger, publisher between 1963 and 1992, the *Times* constructed new production plants, overhauled its circulation system, avoided debilitating strikes by agreeing to expensive long-term contracts with its unions, and created new lifestyle and culture features in the paper to attract revenue. The *Times* became a public company, with the family-owned B shares put in a trust that controlled the company. Under Arthur O. Sulzberger, Jr., the *Times* rolled out its successful national print edition and invested heavily in digital enterprises. When the deep recession began after the 2008 financial crisis, the *Times* found itself overextended and financially strapped. It sold off other businesses and stopped paying dividends. It cut costs widely but also soon resumed investment in its newsroom and digital products. In 2016, a family-run process began deciding on Arthur Jr.'s successor as publisher from among three next-generation contenders, including his son, Arthur Gregg Sulzberger.

Unlike the *New York Times* and the *Washington Post*, the *Los Angeles Times* has suffered from unsteady ownership. It rose into the ranks of the nation's leading quality newspapers under Otis Chandler, the fourth-generation Chandler publisher, in the period 1960–80. But Chandler family disagreements and management missteps in the late 1990s led to the sale of the *Times* and the rest of the Times Mirror media empire to the Chicago-based Tribune Company in 2000. Burdened by the huge new debt, the company ordered cost-cutting measures at its newspapers, which were still profitable (without the debt service). The *Times'* newsroom resisted, and three successive editors and publishers quit.

Matters became worse when the struggling Tribune Company in 2007 agreed to go private in a heavily leveraged sale to an employee stock ownership plan under the control of the Chicago real estate developer Sam Zell. Within a year, the Tribune Company filed for bankruptcy protection and did not emerge from bankruptcy for four years, until 2012. The new owners, investment fund managers, split the assets into two publicly traded companies. The newspapers became Tribune Publishing, and the more profitable broadcast properties became Tribune Media.

Fig. 8.2. Arthur Ochs Sulzberger, Jr., publisher of the *New York Times*, 1992–.

During this prolonged period of corporate uncertainty, the *Los Angeles Times* received varying directives from Chicago headquarters on strategy and focus for the news staff. The *Times'* print circulation has dropped about as much as that of the *Washington Post*. Its newsroom has decreased to about 450 people, compared to about 700 at the *Post* and 1,300 at the *New York Times*, but still contains a talented staff and is much larger than newsrooms in other major cities. Its digital audience, while growing, is about half as large as those of the *New York Times* and the *Washington Post*. It is uncertain whether the controlling owners will expect a short-term return on investment, sell one or more newspapers to wealthy individuals or groups, or patiently pursue a strategy that uses the value of its journalism.

In Britain, the *Guardian*, the smallest of the three major quality national newspapers, is positioned on the mainstream liberal left and is owned by the Scott Trust. The trust was created in 1936 and endowed in the 1940s by the son of the longtime editor and owner to secure in perpetuity the newspaper's financial and editorial independence. Once known as the *Manchester Guardian*, it dropped "Manchester" in 1959 and moved to London in 1964 to compete as a national newspaper.

The *Guardian*'s news operations have had the benefit of two accomplished editors, Alastair Hetherington and Alan Rusbridger, each serving for over twenty years, and of freedom from the burdens of debt or shareholder pressure for profits. The Scott Trust endowment increased to £800 million after selling its interest in the Auto-Trader advertising business in 2014 and the *Manchester Evening News* and other local newspapers to the Trinity Mirror regional chain in 2010. Rusbridger, chairman of the Scott Trust in 2015, says the endowment will give the *Guardian* leeway to handle the transition to the digital world. He compares it to the advantage that the BBC has with its public funding, and that other newspapers have with subsidies from their parent corporations or wealthy individual owners. Like *The Economist* and the *Financial Times*, the *Guardian* has aggressively expanded internationally, with digital editions in the United States and Australia. Two-thirds of the *Guardian*'s digital traffic now comes from outside Britain. Along with the *Daily Mail*—but with far more original journalism—it is in the top tier of digital English-language newspapers for audience size. Rusbridger advocates for the open flow of news on the Web, and the *Guardian*'s websites are free and open-source. The *Guardian* does charge for mobile applications and offers paid premium services as well as monthly and yearly membership programs.

The *Guardian*'s nonprofit ownership and endowment, while advantageous, will not ensure success or survival indefinitely. Its print circulation has declined more rapidly than that of the newspapers without unlimited free digital access. It has had large operating losses in recent years, rising to £40 million in 2015. Acknowledging that the newspaper must operate sustainably, the new editor and the business CEO have announced plans that include significant cost cuts in staff and other expenses over the next three years. Conversion to nonprofit status is not a practical solution for most newspapers. The *Philadelphia Inquirer*, after struggling through bankruptcy and different owners, in 2014 landed an owner who in 2015 donated the paper to the Philadelphia Foundation with an endowment and a public-benefit mission of quality journalism for the community. Such a conversion takes a willing donor—something difficult to achieve when a newspaper has value and there are multiple owners or shareholders in a publicly traded company.

Rupert Murdoch, the son of an Australian newspaper magnate,

Fig. 8.3. Alan Rusbridger, editor-in-chief of the *Guardian* (1995–2105), 2013. Photo by Dan Chung, *Guardian*.

bought two British tabloids in the late 1960s and then *The Times* in 1981. Roy Thompson's media company sold the venerable newspaper after a debilitating, prolonged strike. Thompson, a Canadian who had made a fortune by buying small newspapers in Canada and the United States, had acquired *The Times* from members of the Astor family in 1967. Among British national newspapers, *The Times* has occupied a middle, somewhat Conservative-leaning position on the political spectrum, with an orientation toward the legal and professional ranks.

Murdoch's ownership has not been without controversy. From the outset, there were complaints about interference with newsroom autonomy. In 1986 management successfully opened a plant with new technology in Wapping despite a yearlong violent strike and secondary boycotts by the printers' unions, which bitterly lost their stranglehold over the Murdoch newspaper group. In 2011 a phone-hacking scandal caused Murdoch's News Corp to close the *News of the World* tabloid.

Yet critics today acknowledge that Murdoch is in some ways a romantic about newspapers and has absorbed losses at *The Times* to maintain its newsroom. In 2008, News Corp purchased the *Wall Street Journal* with an eye-popping $5 billion unsolicited bid for the Bancroft-family-controlled Dow Jones Company, and has supported its newsroom's budget even as News Corp wrote down the value of the purchase to $2.8 billion.

Rupert Murdoch is in his mideighties. His sons Laughlan and James serve as operating heads of News Corp's newspapers as well as of the very profitable 20th Century Fox broadcasting and cable TV businesses, which have been split off into another Murdoch-controlled public company. Perhaps the sons, Laughlan in particular, will have their father's commitment to the newspapers in the Internet age, but it is an open question.

Questions also exist about the future of the *Telegraph*, the privately owned Conservative and Euroskeptic national paper. It is in the strongest financial position among Britain's quality newspapers: still profitable, and with the highest print circulation and a large

Fig. 8.4. Rupert Murdoch, owner of *The Times*, 1981. Photo by Judah Passow.

digital audience. For almost sixty years the Berry family was the principal owner. Under Michael Berry, Lord Hartwell, publisher from 1954 to 1986, the *Daily Telegraph* established its position as the largest-selling and most comprehensive newspaper. When he retired in 1986, the newspaper was sold to Hollinger International. In 2004, David and Frederick Barclay bought the newspaper from Hollinger after the forced departure of Hollinger's disgraced leader, Conrad Black. The twin Barclay brothers are billionaires whose commercial holdings include hotels, casinos, breweries, and real estate.

There have been periodic questions of editorial interference in behalf of advertisers. There were six editors in eleven years after the 2004 purchase, a time when a steady hand could have helped guide the newsroom through the digital transition. The Barclay brothers are over eighty, and David Barclay's son, Aidan, has for years quietly overseen the businesses while the veteran newspaperman Murdoch MacLennan has been CEO of the *Telegraph*. There has been no indication what the Barclays' commitment to the *Telegraph* will be as business conditions in the industry continue to deteriorate. For the moment, the *Telegraph* is relatively well positioned in print and online.

How LONG WILL NEWSPAPERS in the United States and Britain continue to publish in print? Circulation decline continues. Print readers today represent a more loyal core—though an aging one. Newspapers have been using their assets to build new revenue streams, such as by selling data and marketing services, holding conferences, and providing printing and delivery operations. But the hard fact remains that advertising and overall revenue continue to shrink, and below a certain level the revenue will not support the costs of printing and delivering a daily newspaper. The *Christian Science Monitor* converted from a national daily newspaper to a weekly magazine in 2008. The Russian billionaire Evgeny Lebedev may soon tire of paying the inevitable losses of the print version of the *Independent*, whose circulation in Britain fell to 60,000 in 2015.

Some newspapers, notably the *Times-Picayune* in New Orleans and other Newhouse papers in Cleveland and Portland, Oregon, in 2015 shifted resources aggressively to daily digital coverage and ceased print editions except on higher-revenue days of the week such as Wednesdays, Fridays, and Sundays. Negative reaction in New Orleans was strong, and success is not certain. A leading analyst of the newspaper industry recently wrote that it will probably be five or ten years before most newspapers begin to phase out print on the daily side, but that even then the Sunday print edition, with its lucrative preprinted advertising inserts, will continue. The near-term outlook for many small newspapers appears better, because there are fewer alternatives to them for advertisers and for readers seeking local news and other local information. Over half of local newspaper readers rely on only the print edition for local news.

Will it matter how long print newspapers last? It certainly does at present, because the print side still makes most of the revenue that supports what remains of the journalism. The impact of severe cutbacks in newsroom staff over the last decade—about 40 percent, or 20,000, lost in the United States, and 8,000 in Britain—can be readily observed in the decline of coverage of local government, courts, and schools by many chain-owned local newspapers in both countries. Nevertheless, newspapers continue to provide most of the original news gathering on matters of public interest. Beat reporting can lead to important investigative projects, explanatory reporting, and news analysis. Newspapers that are sufficiently strong and independent can perform the watchdog's role of holding officials accountable for their actions and of deterring questionable conduct. Whistleblowers and other sources rely on newspapers to report their revelations and protect their anonymity if necessary.

Articles in print newspapers can still focus public attention on important matters. What is printed in prominent positions on the front page reflects the judgment of experienced editors on what information is important and what is adequately supported as factual. Newspapers, particularly in the United States, self-police longstanding journalistic ethics and standards that lend them an authoritative voice not extended to many digital-only news sites. Other major news organizations, such as the Associated Press, the BBC, and many broadcasters, share newspapers' aspirations to maintain accuracy and fairness, although public trust in all media has declined as the partisan political divide has intensified and people increasingly use only media that reinforce their views.

It will still matter whether newspapers' values endure after newspapers have fully transformed into digital news organizations. They already bear the pressures associated with multimedia platforms, interactivity, traffic optimization, and constant change. Facebook was founded in 2004, and within a decade digital users were obtaining more news from social media than from websites. The iPhone was launched in 2007, and within a decade digital users were obtaining more news from mobile devices than from desktop computers. Newspapers with valued content are now building substantial revenue through varieties of paid digital subscriptions, and perhaps their best chance of thriving in the long term will be by investing in the kinds of quality journalism that people want and cannot adequately get elsewhere for free. Any such approach will require patient owners who do not aim to maximize profits or sacrifice journalistic values.

Spring Semester 2016

1. Paul Fahri, *Washington Post*, 5 Aug. 2013; Alexander Matthews, MSNBC.com, 6 Aug. 2013.

Secret Intelligence Services (MI6) Building, Vauxhall Cross, London. Photo by Laurie Nevay. New Central Intelligence Agency headquarters, Langley, Virginia. CIA website.

9

The Anglo-American Special Relationship in Intelligence

JOHN PRADOS

Vietnam's national day is 2 September. As it happens, on 2 September 1945, British-Indian troops under General Douglas C. Gracey landed to restore colonial prerogatives to French authorities in Saigon, while in Hanoi officers of the Office of Strategic Services (OSS), an American intelligence agency, stood alongside Vietnamese communist cadres at the ceremonies establishing the Democratic Republic of Vietnam. Without putting too sharp a point on this, the situation was evocative of the Anglo-American relationship in intelligence as it emerged from World War II. The British and Americans were "cousins," as the relationship became known in intelligence parlance: often friends, but sometimes in competition, and at moments even suspicious of each other.

In truth, the OSS, as America's first (semi-)independent intelligence agency, had learned much by apprenticing with British cousins like the Secret Intelligence Service (MI6), the Security Service (MI5), or the Special Operations Executive, a covert action unit. Britain had experienced, standing services for both intelligence and counterespionage functions that dated at least to 1909, before World War I—and some might trace them as far back as Queen Elizabeth I. A good basis for cooperation also existed. The chief of the coordination unit that the British set up in the United States, Sir William Stephenson, enjoyed a warm friendship with the head of the OSS, General William Donovan. At the national level, Donovan had good relations with, and access to, President Franklin D. Roosevelt; the British spy chieftain, Sir Stewart Menzies, enjoyed similar access to Prime Minister Winston Churchill. Plus, the United States and United Kingdom were allied.

There were other reasons for continued unity in the march into the post-war world. A main one, of course, was that the British government had adopted a foreign policy of preserving a special relationship with the United States. London considered this among its most important interests. With British economic contraction in the war's aftermath, London's desire to benefit from American money and resources figured early on, and later the British services had an even stronger desire to use U.S. assets in their special operations. Meanwhile, cooperation in some kinds of intelligence work—notably, radio intelligence—had never ceased and was only further fortified by wartime agreements such as BRUSA (Britain–United States of America) and its successors. When, in 1947, the Americans returned to the field, for the first time creating a full-fledged peacetime intelligence entity, the Central Intelligence Agency (CIA), many officials on both sides of the ocean were the same people who had been partners during the recent global war. There were friendships and camaraderie to build on. On the American side, specific reasons added to the attractions of the British connection. For one thing, President Harry Truman wanted the CIA to get up to speed quickly, and British expertise could help in that. For another, with far-flung possessions spanning the globe, Britain had bases almost anywhere that Washington wanted to act. Equally important, the British services were already involved in many of the places where the CIA wanted to get into the game.

Conversely, dynamics amounting to centrifugal forces sometimes drove the allies apart. British and American interests were not always identical. In 1945 and after, U.S. foreign policy, which, before the war, had limited its scope largely to Latin America and the Pacific rim, took a trajectory toward the global concerns of a superpower. This development was the obverse of London's perspective of diminishing horizons. At each stage—the British pullback from Greece and Turkey in 1947, the ending of the Raj in India and Pakistan that same year, the independence of many commonwealth countries in the following decades, the withdrawal from east of Suez in 1967—Britain attempted to preserve some modicum of its previous power while newly emergent nations clamored for U.S. assistance. MI5 typically tutored the special branches and security services of the new nations. MI6 tried to keep watch on them. Winston Churchill had famously declared that he had not become the king's first minister to preside over the dissolution of the British Empire, but prevailing conditions made that evolution a reality, though mostly to the embarrassment of Clement Attlee. In any case, London's efforts to preserve its colonial interests were the most discordant element in post-war Anglo-American intelligence relations.

Those differences figured in CIA officers' opinions of the cousins. Joseph Burkholder Smith, a political action specialist who rose to the upper-middle ranks in the American spy agency, recorded that colleagues mostly exhibited two views of the British services. In one, CIA spooks acclaimed their cousins as the most sagacious spies in the business. In the other, they regarded the British as supercilious snobs who denigrated the Americans as upstarts and fought for British colonial interests. In the opinion of Ray Cline, a CIA man who reached the top rank, technology developments inevitably relegated the British to the second rank. The advent of spy satellites, especially, led Cline to observe that only tradition prompted U.S. intelligence to believe it should continue to share with Great Britain.

THIS VIEW OVERSIMPLIFIES A VERY IMPORTANT symbiotic relationship, which has indeed waxed and waned over time but continues to be of great importance today, seven decades after the end of World War II. Regardless of the technological environment, there have always been reasons why the cousins have kept up their relations—and those connections have been of key importance to both. What follows re-examines the special relationship in two ways: one by looking at broad types of intelligence activities—what CIA mavens like to call "disciplines"—and the other by surveying a range of particular operations over the sweep of post-war history.

Since Ray Cline attributed the British fall from grace to technology, a good place to begin might be technical collection. Technical collection—what Richard Helms once called the "machine spies"—has been popular all around because it is a spy technique that allows one to *plan* budget outlays and compare expenses with results. Within the British spy community, the Government Communications Headquarters (GCHQ), the British equivalent of the Americans' code-breaking National Security Agency (NSA), has always been the foremost spy service measured by budget and personnel. And even in the age of increased sophistication at the NSA, the link with GCHQ has afforded Washington additional resources for coverage it cannot manage, plus access to a range of scientific and code-breaking talent that would otherwise be denied to the United States.

Meanwhile, London without doubt benefits from the fruits of the NSA's communications vacuum cleaner. The UKUSA agreement has replaced the old BRUSA one and its supplements, and today unites not only the cousins but also Australia, Canada, and New Zealand.

Some historic cases demonstrate the benefits of intelligence sharing. First off, Hong Kong's station at Little Sai Wan was a featured outpost overlooking the People's Republic of China. Under UKUSA, both U.S. and Australian code breakers were stationed with the British there. During the Chinese Civil War and the Korean War, the British station offered the best place to keep watch on Mao Zedong. American intelligence records for 1950 contain a series of weekly reports on Soviet bloc military developments, among them the movement of Chinese armies from the southwestern part of that country to the positions from which Beijing intervened in the Korean War. In an age before satellites, that reporting could only have come from radio intercepts. Similarly, during the Vietnam War, signals intelligence (or "SIGINT," as it has become known) from Hong Kong provided a window into North Vietnamese communications as well as Chinese assistance to Hanoi.

As with the SIGINT, there are places the British were the technology experts who gave the U.S. its key information. In overhead reconnaissance, until the CIA developed its U-2 aircraft, the British Royal Air Force was the *only* one flying photographic missions into the Soviet Union. The first spy plane photos of the Soviets' medium-range ballistic missile (MRBM) test site at Kapustin Yar in Ukraine came from the cousins in 1953, several years before the U-2. American analysts became aware during the 1950s that the MRBMs had a significant launch impediment—the hours-long interval required to fuel them—data developed from the interpretation of British photographs. When the U-2 came online, the British were offered the opportunity to base some of the planes in their country and have British pilots train on the aircraft. London, no doubt terrified of those same Russian MRBMs, initially rejected the offer, but later, under Harold Macmillan, moved to cooperate.

Once spy satellites were put in place, a ground station at Alice Springs in the Australian outback was absolutely vital to controlling the spacecraft and downloading their images during a whole segment of Earth orbits. Here the United States relied on British political clout—in 1975, Prime Minister Gough Whitlam moved to review Australia's entire relationship with U.S. intelligence, threatening the station at Alice Springs. Washington prevailed upon London to have its governor-general for the Commonwealth of Australia revoke his approval of the cabinet. London effectively engineered a coup overthrowing the Australian government to benefit U.S. intelligence.

So much for the machine spies. How about on-the-ground espionage? For one thing, confirmation of the Russians' need to fuel their MRBMs eventually came when the CIA obtained a copy of the Soviet technical manual pertaining to the rockets. That manual came from a spy—Colonel Oleg Penkovskiy—who had been recruited by and was being run by MI6. The same manual proved crucial to the CIA in verifying the existence of Soviet missile bases in Cuba in 1962. Penkovskiy had first offered his services to the CIA, but was rejected. That pattern prevailed in several other espionage cases. The former Russian spy agency librarian Vasili Mitrokhin, whose archive of documents salvaged from Soviet spy records is the most valuable repository of true Russian spy material, faced rejection from the CIA station in Riga, Latvia. His archive would have been lost but for MI6. Probably the most valuable spy of the later stage of the Cold War, Oleg Gordievsky, also was an MI6 recruit. A frequent modus operandi emerged between the cousins. The British would recruit and run an agent whom the CIA would equip, in an operation the Americans would finance. Partly this came about because MI6 could operate more easily in some places than the Americans, but it was also because the British were adept at recruiting spies. They ran somewhere between forty and sixty major agents during the Cold War years. There were places, including Hanoi and Beijing, and even Moscow for a time, where for many years MI6 had stations but the CIA none, making the cousins the exclusive avenue by which the CIA could accomplish certain missions. Refuting Ray Cline's denigration of the special relationship, some of these situations endured long into the satellite age.

One important feature of the CIA's activity was covert operations. Here MI6 already held the lead. By working with East Germans and infiltrating the Baltic States, the British were engaged in places where the CIA wanted to go. The Americans' early covert operations into Ukraine, Russia, and the Baltics took lessons from the British and made use of some of their contacts. MI6 organized its operations by region, each supervised by an officer termed a "controller." The CIA's operations directorate soon had regional divisions under chiefs. The CIA then went further, creating divisions or staffs for functional purposes such as paramilitary and psychological operations, international organizations, and so on. MI6 did not go there. But the cousins engaged in joint covert operations, starting with one in Albania in the early 1950s.

As they had in other contexts, the British offered the use of bases that made CIA covert operations possible. With the Albania project just mentioned, much of the training for CIA operatives to be sent into the country took place in Malta, a British dependency. When the CIA moved in the late 1950s to overthrow the Indonesian leader Sukarno, British Singapore became the closest base to the scene of the action. For decades, Hong Kong remained the CIA's window into the People's Republic of China. During the Vietnam War, certain operations into Cambodia were mounted from Hong Kong. As late as 1983, when the CIA wanted to operate around the British Caribbean island of Grenada, its base was on Trinidad, another former British dependency. The cousins' bases were vital to CIA activities.

In one area, counterespionage, the special relationship caused damage on both sides of the Atlantic. In 1951, the British diplomats Guy Burgess and Donald Maclean defected to Russia, followed by the British spy Kim Philby in 1963. This exposed a "Cambridge ring" of Russian spies that went back to the 1930s and implicated both British and American counterspies who had failed to detect the penetrations. The CIA's James Angleton, whom Philby had fooled, began a witch hunt for Soviet "moles" that had purportedly undermined CIA spying on Russia for nearly two decades. Under the spell of the Soviet defector Anatoli Golitsyn, Angleton gained access to British files and then pointed accusatory fingers at Her Majesty's agency personnel. On another occasion, he prepared a memorandum accusing Prime Minister Harold Wilson of being a spy for the Russians. While authentic Soviet spies were uncovered in the U.S. Air Force, in the NSA, and among Americans serving at NATO headquarters, none of Angleton's fantasized enemies was real, and many skilled CIA officers had their careers ruined.

For the British, discovery of the Cambridge ring led to a similar witch hunt. Was there a "fourth man"? A fifth? The royal art historian Anthony Blunt and the former GCHQ, MI6, and Treasury official John Cairncross were revealed as members of the ring. But accusations roiled the water all around, and Angleton's suspicions fueled those of the British counterspy Peter Wright. Scandals such as that which engulfed the defense minister John Profumo in the early 1960s churned the water even more. Accusations aimed as high as Sir Roger Hollis, who headed MI6 from 1956 to 1965. The "Fluency" investigation cleared Hollis after interviewing more than fifty officers, including Hollis himself, twice. In the area of counter-intelligence, it might have been better for the cousins if their intelligence relations had been less intimate.

In one domain, intelligence analysis, it might be argued that each side taught the other. Consider intelligence work as a cycle that includes the acquisition of information, its interpretation, its embodiment in reports, and officials' ability to enjoy the fruits of this process. Both the United States and Britain provide for such an intelligence cycle, but each has a different system. In British practice, the data acquired are disseminated to a Cabinet Committee, where a unit known as the Joint Intelligence Committee (JIC) crafts the analyses, which are then circulated to officials. This is a considerable job—in the early 1990s, the British government estimated the volume of annual reporting at roughly 40,000 items, one-third from MI6, the remainder from GCHQ. In the American system, information is analyzed before the reports are disseminated. Indeed, reports are considered to be "finished intelligence." Where this function used to be entirely reserved to CIA, it is now distributed between that agency and the Office of the Director of National Intelligence (ODNI), which is responsible for the most authoritative reports, called National Intelligence Estimates (NIEs). The NIEs are American equivalents of the JIC appreciations.

The character of the cycle is important because intelligence officers worry about their relevance to policy makers. In the American system, CIA and ODNI officers lack direct knowledge of what information, in what form, is most useful to policy makers. They end up hosting seminars, conducting polls, or collecting questions to determine interests. In the British system, because the JIC exists within the Cabinet Office, the policy makers are already represented among its ranks. On the other hand, opportunities for generating intelligence to please are magnified in the British system, where the people doing the appreciations are already aware of what answers their bosses want to hear.

ANOTHER WAY TO APPROACH THE QUESTION of what utility the special relationship in intelligence has had for each nation is to briefly survey a series of historical cases stretching back to the early days of the alliance. The Albania operation, which MI6 code-named "Valuable" but the CIA knew as "BG/FIEND," is a clear starting point. This operation started with Kim Philby in Washington as MI6 liaison to the CIA, representing it on committees coordinating the covert operation, and perfectly situated to betray every move to Soviet intelligence. Philby lost that post after the Burgess and Maclean defections, but the truth is that the Albanian communists' state apparatus was so deeply implanted that they pretty much had the country wired for sound. The British made their infiltrations by sea, the CIA favored aircraft, and each cousin had its favorites among Albanian exile groups, who provided the recruits. This inability to adopt a unitary policy became one early lesson of the joint operations.

Southeast Asia during the early 1950s was another front where the cousins did a lot together. The British were fighting a counterinsurgency war in Malaya. The Americans supported the French in Indochina and later moved toward taking their own stand in Vietnam. Maurice Oldfield, who finished his career as MI6 chief from 1973 to 1978, was serving a tour in Singapore then, and he took the position that there was a coordinated communist threat to be met by coordinated Western action. The British commissioner-general for Southeast Asia, Malcolm MacDonald, agreed. The CIA officer Joseph B. Smith first met the cousins in Singapore, where he and the Brits cooperated on propaganda operations, planting articles suggesting Red Chinese aggression and other lurid things. In Bangkok, the MI6 station chief, Michael Wrigley, an Oldfield acolyte, partnered well with the CIA's "Red" Jantzen. It was the Foreign Office, not the cousins, that was the obstacle.

By far the most effective of the early joint operations was "TP/AJAX" in Iran, where MI6 and the CIA teamed up to overthrow the parliamentary government of Mohammed Musaddiq and hand power to the Shah of Iran. The fear was that Musaddiq was susceptible to communist control. In addition, the Anglo-Iranian Oil Company (a forerunner of BP) was unhappy because the Iranians had demanded a greater share of its profits and then, frustrated at the company's intransigence, had nationalized oil production. London took up its cause. In Washington, the Truman administration had attempted to mediate the situation, but when Dwight D. Eisenhower became president in 1953, he decided on a more active role after seeing intelligence estimates that (mistakenly) cast Iran as moving into the communist camp. MI6 and CIA officers met in Beirut to plan the operation. The British did not want to be seen to be involved. Instead, the CIA's Kermit Roosevelt took action, using MI6 communications channels and British-recruited agent networks. It started out badly but was saved when Roosevelt succeeded in getting portions of the Iranian military to go over to the Shah and occupy Musaddiq's residence on 19 August 1953. The prime minister surrendered the next day. Clearly, the British cousins would never have succeeded in this ploy without the CIA.

A few years later the shoe was on the other foot. American intelligence liaison officers in London noticed their British counterparts becoming increasingly distant. The moment, delicate for British diplomacy, featured another nationalization, this time the Egyptians effectively taking over the Suez Canal, which Britain had been operating and protecting. Prime Minister Anthony Eden became increasingly strident in his claims against Egyptian leader Gamal Nasser, and plotted with France, angry with Nasser because

Fig. 9.1. Kermit Roosevelt, 1926. Library of Congress Prints and Photographs Division, npcc.27526.

of the Egyptians' support for Algerian revolutionaries fighting for their independence. Britain and France enlisted Israel in a scheme to justify their takeover of the canal—Israel would attack Egypt in the Sinai and drive toward canal, whereupon Britain and France would intervene, pretending to separate the warring parties. The United States, kept in the dark about all this, tried to mediate, organizing talks among countries that used the canal, and attempting other diplomatic approaches. The CIA's warning specialists, suspecting an imminent crisis, alerted Eisenhower. Israel attacked on 29 October 1956. Seeking more information, the president ordered a U-2 spy plane to fly over the area and obtain new photographs. In CIA lore, this flight was overhead, above Egyptian air bases, just as Anglo-French bombers blasted them. Suez provides an example of the special relationship in hard times.

By 1960, when the Belgian Congo had achieved independence, the cousins had repaired their relations. Here was a case where the CIA and MI6 were operating in the same country with similar but not identical goals. The Congolese premier, Patrice Lumumba, had aroused American ire. Plotting his demise, the CIA sent its station chief, Lawrence Devlin, weapons, poisons, and instructions to get rid of Lumumba. The British cousins had posted Daphne Parks as MI6 representative in the Congo, and she proceeded to build amicable relations with Lumumba. Parks cooperated with Devlin but refused to participate in any plot. Devlin, by his own account, was also loath to have anything to do with murdering Lumumba. Both were upstaged by Belgian spies, who used a Congolese political faction to arrest Lumumba and then kill him. Parks, incidentally, continued working alongside the CIA for several years, and later became MI6 station chief in Hanoi, reporting intelligence that helped the United States in the Vietnam war.

A semi-delicate moment in the special relationship came in British Guiana. From 1961 through 1964, Washington, convinced that Guianese leader Cheddi Jagan was a communist or a fellow traveler, was determined to prevent his becoming leader of an independent Guiana. British authorities appear to have wavered on the scheme, at times making room for a CIA operation, sometimes opposing it. Available evidence suggests that London never told the cousins to desist, and it never instructed British authorities in Guiana to obstruct CIA activities. The Americans conducted a political action in Guiana, organizing parties to oppose Jagan, creating labor disputes and political unrest to discredit him or force his party into compromising situations. The British helped the CIA by adopting a proportional-representation electoral system that posed the greatest possible obstacle to Jagan's political party in the pre-independence vote. Jagan's party received the highest tally in the December 1964 poll, but it could not form a majority in the legislature.

London appears to have had misgivings after its experience in British Guiana. For a considerable time, the cousins seem to have stopped cooperating on covert operations.

Meanwhile, the British had an experience from which the Americans could have benefited. This came during the troubles in Northern Ireland and involved the interrogation of prisoners, which the American cousins have found especially controversial in the war on terror. The Joint Intelligence Committee in 1965 issued a memorandum governing interrogation techniques, and it came to be considered the bible for people in the field. But in Northern Ireland in 1970, during a period of high tension, interrogators abandoned their bible. A scandal followed. British security officers resorted to some of the same methods ("walling," noise, stress positions) that Americans later employed against suspected terrorists, incurring criminal jeopardy. In the British case, press revelations exposed the torture.

Investigations followed, at first within the security services, then by the JIC, then by government commissions and Parliament. At each turn, the British government expected the inquiries to silence the controversy. Instead, nothing stilled the roiling political waters. In the mid-1970s, the British government was forced to pay damages to IRA victims. British accounts maintain that London warned Washington on this very point in the war on terror. The CIA did not listen. British security officers were enjoined from participating in CIA actions. Worse yet, the British cousins, despite their warnings and refusals to collaborate in the interrogations, were nevertheless implicated in the Binyam Mohamed case and others and forced to pay restitution. They remain under a cloud. (Mohamed is an Ethiopian national and British resident who was interrogated in Morocco and then held in the Guantanamo Bay military prison for five years without being charged.)

This was not the only time American action or inaction adversely affected the British government. The clearest case must be the Falklands War of 1982, when Argentina, which had disputed British sovereignty over those South Atlantic islands since the nineteenth century, invaded them. British intelligence had been contracting for some time—a kind of counterpart to withdrawal east of Suez—and that was true for Latin America as well. By 1982, the MI6 station in Buenos Aires was the sole remnant of a once-vibrant network. The British had some coverage of Argentina, but because their Buenos Aires unit had to cover the entire continent, plus the virtual instantaneous character of the Argentine decision for war (and lack of any visible mobilization), the British were put in American hands. At the time, the United States was an ally of Argentina. In fact, the Reagan administration depended on Argentine intelligence to front for the CIA with the Nicaraguan contras. That left Washington in a quandary about supplying any warning to London of the threat to the Falklands. The American cousins kept their silence. British authorities had difficulty believing that U.S. satellites and spy planes, NSA SIGINT, and American embassies in the region had all found nothing, not to mention CIA assets in Argentina or Argentine intelligence officers working with the CIA. The Falklands wound remained an irritant in the intelligence special relationship.

Despite misgivings, during this period and throughout the 1980s, MI6 went ahead giving the CIA an assist in its biggest secret war yet, the struggle of Islamic mujahedeen against the Soviet occupiers in Afghanistan. The British contracted retired or former members of its special warfare community to serve as field hands in the secret war. The British could do things the Americans could not—

Pakistani rules kept the CIA, for the most part, from crossing into Afghanistan, but no such prohibitions applied to the British. All the secret services had their favorites among the Afghan resistance groups, and the British championed Ahmed Shah Massoud, whose rebel band dominated the Panshir Valley in the northeastern corner of the country. Fast-forward more than a decade: the Massoud forces became the backbone of the Northern Alliance, the key Afghan allies who gave the Americans entry into the country. In fact, the assassination of Massoud by Al Qaeda operatives on the eve of the 9/11 attacks enraged the fighters he had led and made them even more enthusiastic about enlisting with the CIA. The British cousins' discovery of the Northern Alliance was a gift to the Americans.

Another gift, one much more appreciated by President George W. Bush but, in fact, much less helpful to the shared interest of the Anglo-American alliance, came in 2002–3 with the British intelligence reporting on Iraq, particularly regarding alleged Iraqi weapons of mass destruction (WMDs). The British reporting became very important to President Bush in building the support he needed to invade Iraq. Prime Minister Tony Blair comes out of the Iraq War story bearing most of the British blame, but the country's intelligence services marched right behind him. The GCHQ helped the Americans monitor communications of United Nations delegations as part of an attempt to secure a UN resolution authorizing the use of force against Iraq. MI6 agent networks acquired no more than thin data on Iraqi weapons. The Joint Intelligence Committee made elaborate constructions upon the thin data. It also assumed that the absence of contravention amounted to proof of the existence of Iraqi WMDs. John Scarlett, the first JIC head to come from the intelligence agencies rather than the government bureaucracy, should have known better. He not only failed to protect the JIC against such faulty methodology, but also exchanged notes and drafts with the American cousins on making the British version of the Iraq report more hard-hitting (and thus exaggerated) than it should have been, permitted Blair's office to further manipulate the text, and, with the war on—and investigators actively seeking proof on the ground of the claims made in prewar intelligence reports—lobbied for certain prewar WMD claims to be graded as accurate even though no evidence for them had been found.

THE ANGLO-AMERICAN SPECIAL RELATIONSHIP continues. It has survived now for seven decades. This survey shows that both sides have had a range of parallel, even if not identical, interests. With

Fig. 9.2. Sir John Scarlett, 2011. Chatham House.

the diminution of British imperial interests over time, the degree of parallelism in the intelligence area has grown. The survey also shows that the British services have continued to be useful to the U.S. intelligence community even in the high-tech age of modern espionage. London's people can operate in places where Americans cannot, do things better in some respects, and provide another source of technical and creative expertise to apply to problems that defy easy solution. The British government certainly benefits from access to the raw intelligence obtained by the Americans from their sources, whether agents or machine spies. And the vastly greater scale of U.S. intelligence collection affords the British data of a scope they could not otherwise match. In spite of blackouts occasioned by the foreign policies of one side or the other, or setbacks in intelligence sharing attributable to counterintelligence doubts, analytical disputes, or questions regarding the cousins' intelligence methods, the alliance had sustained its broader cooperation. On both sides of the pond, spies have had reason to credit the special intelligence relationship.

Guy Burgess, 1950. Getty Images.

10

The Quest for Stalin's Englishman: Guy Burgess

ANDREW LOWNIE

In November 1979 Anthony Blunt was exposed as the fourth member of the Cambridge spy ring after Kim Philby, Donald Maclean, and Guy Burgess. I had just left school and was about to go to the very university where the four men had been recruited as undergraduates by the Russians. Almost every week there seemed to be new revelations in the newspapers of Cambridge spies, such as John Cairncross and Leo Long, until the Cambridge ring quickly appeared to number more like fifty than five. Why had these privileged young men agreed to work for a country they hardly knew and a system that even then was known to be totalitarian? How had they been recruited? What damage had they done? Were there still undiscovered recruits?

So began a fascination with the Cambridge spies that has lasted to this day. In 1984, while at Cambridge, I organized a symposium on the subject with Professor Christopher Andrew, Britain's leading historian on British intelligence and one of my tutors. Other contributors included Andrew Boyle, whose book *The Climate of Treason* had revealed Blunt's treachery; Robert Cecil, who was writing a book on his Cambridge contemporary and Foreign Office colleague Donald Maclean; Chapman Pincher, the author of several books on the Cambridge spy ring; and John Costello, who was writing a biography of Anthony Blunt.

Costello asked me to help research his book, so at a time when I should I have been revising for my Finals, I was interviewing distinguished elderly gentleman in retirement in the Home Counties. In 1984 the generation that had been at Cambridge in the thirties were in their mid-seventies, and many were prepared to talk, especially to a Cambridge undergraduate. I wined and dined spies, such as Michael Straight, and those who had been involved in the investigations, such as Arthur Martin from MI5 and Nicholas Elliott from MI6. I talked to the brothers of Guy Burgess and Donald Maclean and interviewed on tape contemporaries such as Noel Annan and Stuart Hampshire and Burgess's boyfriend Jack Hewit, who supplied his own unpublished account of their relationship.

Costello's book *The Mask of Treachery* was published in 1988, and I then decided to write a book on Guy Burgess, to me the most appealing and enigmatic of the Cambridge spies, who had not yet had a biography. The quest for Stalin's Englishman had started.

It has been a long journey that has taken me from elderly all-male parties in Tangier to interviewing KGB generals in Moscow, from weeks spent in archives all over Britain, and America to clashes with the FBI, CIA, Foreign Office, and Cabinet Office as I campaigned to secure release of documents under Freedom of Information legislation.

An early breakthrough, after an advertisement in the *Spectator,* was to meet Peter Pollock, who wrote in February 1998: "I certainly know and could tell you more about Guy Burgess than any one still alive, or probably even dead, excepting his mother or Anthony Blunt." Pollock had been the love of Burgess's life. They had met in 1937 and been lovers and then close friends until Burgess's death in 1963. He had never spoken before. I jumped on a plane to Tangier, where he happily answered a series of questions, including Burgess's sexual preference in a homosexual relationship.

Peter casually mentioned he had left some of Burgess's letters and drawings in my room. Many of the drawings turned out to be by a former lodger of theirs, Francis Bacon, and shortly afterward found their way to the Tate, but the Burgess letters, even though undated and reliant on postmarks when envelopes had been kept, were fascinating, humanizing the spy and giving a strong sense of his circle of friends—many of them previously not connected with him, such as Michael Redgrave, Lucian Freud, Winston Churchill's niece Clarissa, Frederick Ashton—and lovers such as the writer James Pope Hennessy.

Submissions to the literary agency that I run have over the years yielded a few gems, including the memoirs of a female diplomatic colleague, a woman who claimed to have seen him in his final days in Britain, and a man whom Burgess had tried to seduce on the boat to America in 1950. A chance discussion at a dinner with one of Churchill's former secretaries revealed that Churchill had been alerted within twenty-four hours of their departure, contradicting the official version that no one knew until after the weekend they fled.

Burgess's close friend Goronwy Rees wrote a very insightful study of Burgess, *A Chapter of Accidents* (1972). I found the original script in the Welsh National archives in Aberystwyth. No one had looked at it since being deposited, but it was full of wonderful material not in the published version, including confirmation that Burgess had seduced Donald Maclean at Cambridge.

Quite often, I realized my interviewees were not telling me all they knew. Steven Runciman, when interviewed in the 1990s, claimed he had hardly known Burgess. Twenty years later I took on representation of his literary estate and found photo albums of holidays they had had together. Put in touch with Runciman's biographer, I discovered the two men had met almost every day when Burgess was at Cambridge, and were probably lovers.

Given Burgess's reputation as a promiscuous homosexual and traitor, many close to him in his life subsequently distanced themselves. Letters were destroyed or certainly not made available. Burgess did keep letters in an old guitar case—for blackmail rather than sentimental purposes—but these disappeared into the MI5 archives after his disappearance in 1951. His letters to his mother were thrown into her grave, but happily were copied by MI5 and are now in The National Archives.

Intelligence history has its particular challenges. By its nature, it is secret, so records are not kept or, if so, rarely released. Those who work in intelligence sign confidentiality agreements that forbid them from talking about their work, and even when allowed to, they are reluctant to discuss it with outsiders. The researcher always has to be careful of what is said. Do they really know what happened? As in any debriefing, is one simply being told what one wants to hear? Is a disinformation game going on—a particular trait of the Russians.

In spite of the challenges, I managed to interview over a hundred people who knew Burgess and had never spoken before, to look at private papers no one else had consulted, and, under FOIA legislation, to force governments to open up secret archives. The result, I hope, does justice to a man often dismissed as a joke figure, showing him to have been generous and also selfish, a brilliant man with a glittering career ahead who threw it, and all he loved about Britain, aside for a cause, only to end his life in a lonely tragicomic exile in

Russia. Guy Burgess was in many ways a patriot and very British, and yet he never expressed any regrets about betraying his country and his friends. To the end of his life, he remained a fascinating paradox—Stalin's Englishman.

In October 1955, a damage assessment memorandum for the Joint Chiefs of Staff concluded:

- Burgess and Maclean were Soviet agents for many years prior to their defection. They were apparently protected from exposure and dismissal for a long time by other highly placed officials of the British government, particularly the Foreign Office.
- Maclean had access to practically all high-level plans and policy information that were Joint US/UK/Canada projects. As Code Room Supervisor, he naturally had access to all the UK diplomatic codes and ciphers as well as the opportunity to scan all incoming and outgoing communications.
- In the fields of US/UK/Canada planning on Atomic Energy, US/UK post-war planning and policy in Europe and all by-product information up to the date of defection undoubtedly reached Soviet hands. Probably via the Soviet embassy in London.
- All UK and possibly some US diplomatic codes and ciphers in existence prior to 25 May 1951 are in possession of the Soviets and of no further use.
- Insofar as US security implications are concerned it would appear that very nearly all US/UK high level planning information prior to 25 May 1951 must be considered compromised . . . It may be more appropriate to assume total compromise as of the defection date.

Maclean's devastating impact was clear, but Burgess's treachery was less apparent. The following year the Senate Subcommittee on Internal Security looked again at the Burgess and Maclean case. It interviewed many of the key participants, including Maclean's sister Harriet Sheers, looking, in particular, at whether either diplomat had affected the war in Korea through his revelations.

A note from the State Department, as part of the evidence, concluded, "The Department has also failed to bring to light any information which would justify it in stating that developments affecting the security of the United States could be traced to Burgess during the period of approximately nine months when he served as second secretary of the British Embassy in Washington," and "There is no information in the Department's records which would indicate that Burgess, in his position in the Far Eastern Department of the British Foreign Office in 1948, furnished information valuable to the Chinese communists and injurious to the United States."

We know some of the material that Burgess passed to the Russians, and that it was so extensive that much of it was never even translated—the Russian agent Kislytsin talked about Burgess bringing out suitcases of documents, and at one point Burgess requested he be supplied with a suitcase. But we know only what the Russians have chosen to share in authorized books such as *Deadly Illusions* (1993) and *The Crown Jewels* (1999), fascinating accounts that nonetheless have to be treated carefully, since the Russian authorities often had another agenda. There are certainly still shelves of material on the Cambridge spy ring that have not been released. What we do know, according to *The Crown Jewels,* is that from 1941 to 1945 Burgess passed 4,604 documents to Moscow Centre. These documents included, among much else, telegraphic communications between the Foreign Office and its posts abroad, position papers, and minutes of the Cabinet and Chiefs of the Imperial General Staff.

But even when we know what documentation was taken, we don't know who saw it, when, and what they did with the material. The irony is that the more explosive the material, the less likely it was to be trusted, since Stalin and his cohorts couldn't believe that it wasn't a plant. Also, if it didn't fit in with Soviet assumptions, then it was ignored. Much of the material that Burgess supplied, out of practical necessity for security reasons, came in oral briefings, which could easily be misinterpreted as it was passed on.

What could Burgess have passed to the Russians? Clearly, anything he drafted himself, but also anything that came across his desk or he asked to see. In particular, as Hector McNeil's private secretary and as a Far East expert, he would have seen very important and secret documents, especially crucial during the Four Powers conferences, when the British negotiating position would have been known to the Soviets during the conferences themselves. He was known to work late and on weekends, and had access to secret safes, but even plain texts of enciphered cables were useful for code-breaking efforts. We can certainly surmise that he passed information about the post-war peace conferences and founding meetings of the United Nations, NATO, and, the OECD, plans for the reconstruction of post-war Germany, and the immediate negotiating positions at conferences such as that creating the Brussels Treaty.

Guy Burgess was also a magnificent manipulator of people and trader in gossip. He was highly social and almost always out at dinners and night clubs—usually paid for by his expense account or by others. In the Foreign Office, he is remembered for always attending the group tea at four and popping in and out of other people's offices. He knew how to extract material through charm, provocation, his powers of argument and knowledge, and, when required, blackmail. Here was a man who supposedly kept every love letter in case it could be useful and who was happy to lend his flat for assignations. People liked him and confided in him, and Burgess took every advantage. As Goronwy Rees noted, "Guy possessed an appalling fund of information to the discredit of numerous persons in this country. Collecting it was one of his private hobbies; it was a native instinct in him and it was done primarily, I think, for purposes of gossip and private amusement; but I believe . . . it constitutes a formidable weapon of pressure and blackmail."

Tom Wylie, Dennis Proctor, and Fred Warner may not have been Soviet agents, but they might as well have been as they showed Burgess the interesting papers that crossed their desk. One can only speculate at the information he may have gleaned from his friends in intelligence, Guy Liddell and David Footman, on their weekly visits to the music hall. And there was always the excuse at various moments that Burgess was working in the cause of anti-fascism, that the Russians were our allies, or that it was for some hush-hush British organization.

Apart from actual documents, he could provide lists of agents when he worked for MI6 and MI5, he could interpret policy and human nature, and he could provide insights into character that might allow others to exert pressure on a particular individual. Rees later wrote:

> The very existence of a secret service was for Guy a challenge to curiosity and certainly he showed a persistent determination to penetrate its secrets which had nothing to do with his official duties. It is quite certain that during the period after the war, both in London and in Washington, he acquired a remarkable knowledge for one in his position, both of the personalities and of the working of the security services . . . What is difficult to exaggerate is the amount of information which he had acquired about the machinery and methods of our security services, their organisation, and the names and positions of those who worked in them.

Indeed the very word "secret" was like a call to battle for Burgess, a challenge that he never failed to accept; he hunted out secrets like a hound after truffles.

He was also an agent of influence, most notably in the BBC and during his time on Far East affairs, where he helped shape British policy to recognize Communist China when America refused to, but also later in Moscow while working on Soviet disinformation. Then there were all the agents he was responsible for recruiting—

Anthony Blunt, John Cairncross, Michael Straight—and the agents they in turn recruited and all the information they supplied to the Russians. And these are just the agents we know about.

One of the most damaging legacies was the defection itself, which undermined Anglo-American intelligence cooperation at least until 1955, and public respect for the institutions of government, including Parliament and the Foreign Office. It also bequeathed a culture of suspicion and mistrust within the Security Services that was still being played out half a century after the 1951 flight.

Burgess was the first of the Cambridge spies to die, and history has not been kind to him, with a succession of books depicting him as some sort of tragicomic figure who achieved very little. But to the intelligence professionals, he is seen as the major figure in the group. Yuri Modin was later to write, "The real leader was Burgess. He held the group together, infused it with his energy and led it into battle, so to speak. In the 1930s, at the very start, it was he who took the initiatives and the risks, dragging the others along in his wake. He was the moral leader of the group," adding, "He was the most outstanding and educated among all the five."

Sergei Kondrashev, a KGB general who worked with Burgess on disinformation measures, agreed. Asked who was the most important of the Cambridge spies, he immediately replied, "Burgess. Definitely." It has been assumed that Burgess's most damaging period was the four years he spent in the inner sanctum of the Foreign Office, as private secretary to the deputy Foreign Secretary, but Kondrashev revealed that in Russian eyes, "One of the most important periods of his service was just before the German War," when Burgess was acting as middleman between the British and French in the crucial days immediately preceding the Second World War. It is a view shared by the doyen of spy writers, Nigel West: "Anthony told me that Guy Burgess was the genius in the network, the key man. He was the person everybody had to go to for instruction, help and advice. Guy was always in touch with the Russians and could make decisions and could counsel other people."

The question that continues to baffle writers and intelligence professionals alike is, why did Burgess do it? Why did he agree to work for a foreign power, of which he knew little, as a student, and continue to serve it until his death some thirty years later? Why did this apparently most British of figures leave behind all the things he most cherished, such as the Reform Club, gossip, his circle of lovers and friends, and his mother, to whom he was devoted, for a lonely exile in Stalinist Russia?

Burgess was a product of his generation. Had he been born a

few years earlier or later, his life would have taken a very different course, but he came from a generation politicized during the early 1930s that felt it needed to stop theorizing and do something, even if this call to action took many forms and led a few to beat a path to Moscow. David Haden Guest went to work with the Young Communist League in Battersea, and John Cornford to serve the party among the Birmingham working class, before both died in the Spanish Civil War.

For Burgess, serving the Communist Party in Battersea or Birmingham was less attractive than trying to shape political events at the highest level. It played back to his school-day fascination with Alfred Thayer Mahan's theories of great power blocs and Marxist teachings. Burgess needed a moral purpose, to do something positive in the struggle against fascism, and at a vulnerable point in his life, the Russians provided the opportunity.

Writing to Harold Nicolson in 1962, he quoted Stendhal's "The Pistol Shot in the Theatre" on the importance of timing in shaping political and personal decisions: "You were born too early to be hit by this at the age at which one acts, & the intelligentsia of the 40s and 50s were both too late. I was of the generation of the pistol shot in the 30s. I notice the intellectuals of the 60s, the young at Aldermaston, have again been hit by the continuing fusillade. I notice this with pleasure, one greets others getting into the same boat; and with sorrow that they don't know how rough the crossing is."

He refused to believe that his God had failed him, as it had Arthur Koestler, Stephen Spender, and the other fellow travelers. Like Catholics in the reign of Elizabeth working for the victory of Spain, or indeed the sleepers of Islam now, there was a certainty in the correctness of the choice. It was, as Graham Greene wrote of Philby, "the logical fanaticism of a man who, having once found a faith, is not going to lose it because of the injustices or cruelties inflicted by erring human instruments."

Burgess was guided by a strong sense of history, which he then misread. Goronwy Rees wrote, "The truth is that Guy, in his sober moments, had a power of historical generalisation which is one of the rarest intellectual faculties, and which gave conversation with him on political subjects a unique charm and fascination. It was a power which was, I think, completely native and instinctive to him. It might have made him a great historian; instead it made him a communist."

Just as the nineteenth century had belonged to the British Empire, Burgess felt the twentieth century would belong to Russia. George Weidenfeld, at one of Baroness Budberg's cocktail parties, remembered how Burgess accused him of "sitting on the fence" by supporting a pro-European policy for Britain. "There is no such thing as a European policy," he pontificated. "You've either got to choose America or Russia. People may have their own view which to choose, but Europe is something wishy-washy that simply does not exist."

In Graham Greene's *The Confidential Agent,* a character says, "You choose your side once and for all—of course, it may be the wrong side. Only history can tell that." The same can be said of Burgess.

No account of Burgess's life can be written without an understanding of the intellectual maelstrom of the 1930s, especially among the young and impressionable. In *An Englishman Abroad* (1983), Burgess is asked why he became a spy. "At the time it seemed the right thing to do," he replied. For Burgess and others, their conversion had strong political roots, but most fellow members of the Cambridge cells did not spy for the Russians and indeed lost their communist fervor in 1939 with the Nazi-Soviet Pact, in 1956 with the invasion of Hungary, or simply because they had to get on with the business of earning a living.

So why did Burgess stay the course? Partly because, having picked his football team, he loyally stuck with it through thick and thin, capable of all sorts of intellectual somersaults to keep in step with the changing situation. He stayed because he was flattered to feel that he had a real chance to affect events, and from a perverted form of imperialism: having witnessed the death of one empire, he decided to attach himself to another which he felt less materialistic. He also stayed because the Russians wouldn't let him stop and because he enjoyed his clandestine role, hunting with both the hare and the hounds.

Burgess was a spoiled child, indulged by his mother and with an absent father—a characteristic of several of the Cambridge ring—and he had never been given boundaries. His mother, who refused to set them, seemed to be grateful to first Dartmouth and eventually the Soviet Union for so doing. Without a strong moral compass, he was vulnerable to the blandishments of the highly sophisticated Soviet recruitment techniques, which offered excitement and a sense of worth. The Soviets recognized his desire for clandestine danger in his private life, but also his guilt and desire for some sort of redemption, and simply utilized it for their own ends.

The Apostles proved to be fertile recruitment ground, because the society drew men attracted by secrecy, apparent higher loyalties, and a feeling of superiority. Burgess was perhaps a classic example of his acquaintance Cyril Connolly's theory of arrested development, a Peter Pan figure who never grew up. Connolly noted that "the child whose craving for love is unsatisfied, whose desire for power is thwarted or whose innate sense of justice is warped . . . eventually may try to become a revolutionary or a dictator." Service to the Soviet Union gave Burgess a cause after he had failed with many of his other ambitions. A sense of purpose, a new beginning after rejection, the opportunity to create a heroic role for himself.

Guy Burgess wanted to be someone and shape events. Knowing he would not make it as a Cambridge don or high-flying mandarin, the role offered by the Russians seemed attractive. Malcom Muggeridge, a shrewd judge of character, reviewing the Tom Driberg biography noted "the vanity, snobbishness, romanticism, weakness masquerading as defiance, retreat from reality somehow made to seem an advance upon it, which constitute him. One senses the influences which played upon him, the perky, half-baked longing somehow to be someone."

Part of the fascination with Burgess is his complexity and paradoxes. No figure could have been more British and establishment with his Eton and Cambridge education, membership in London clubs, expensive clothes, love of British literature, hunting scenes on the walls of his flat, and final wish to be buried in Britain. But this was only one part of him, and any analysis of his character and motivation needs to be aware of his second world—with the romance of Russian music and literature and his respect for the ruthlessness of its history and political system.

Spies live double lives, sometimes out of necessity, but generally from choice. Burgess wasn't torn between his various lives; they existed in parallel and even together. Marching with the hunger marchers, he wore his Pitt Club scarf and Old Etonian tie, just in case such protective clothing was required. The order of Britain and the wild danger of Russia were simply the yin and yang of his personality.

Burgess was not unaware of the purges in the 1930s, the failure of collectivization, the labor camps, and so on. After all, he lectured on the evils of communism at the Foreign Office summer schools and made his reputation as a British propagandist against the Soviet Union, notably in the Information Research Department. But though an intelligent man, he was also politically naïve—a not uncommon combination—and he simply chose to ignore what did not suit him. Any change, such as the Nazi-Soviet Pact, could instantly be explained away in view of the bigger picture.

He had learned to compartmentalize his life and feelings as a child, and he carried this through into adulthood. Like an actor, he played each part as required, but he was a Janus. To his close friends, and in particular women, he was kind, loyal, stimulating company, a good conversationalist, thoughtful, and charming. Miriam Rothschild remembered, "He had slightly protruding top teeth (like a baby thumb-sucker) which made him youthful-looking and appealing. And he was always in sort of high spirits—like a school girl." Rosamond Lehmann felt he "was not only brilliant, but very affectionate and warm-hearted . . . I was very fond of him."

Yet from Stanley Christopherson at Lockers Park—"He wasn't the kind of boy I wanted as a friend. He wasn't quite right"—to over thirty years later, there were those who were repelled by him. Margaret Anstee, a young female colleague in the Foreign Office, thought him "extremely repulsive. He was rather greasy and dirty. He was always telling awful dirty jokes." Brian Sewell, who was eighteen when he met Burgess, remembered that "he had egg on his tie, tobacco on his breath, and wandering hands; I might have been glad of such hands of a boy of my own age, but not his and the accompanying odours—not even the strawberry milk shakes that he was inclined to buy me could compensate for those." John Waterlow put it simply, "I don't think Burgess had any real warmth of character."

Harold Nicolson could see both sides of Burgess's character and his conflicted personality: "He publicly announced his sympathies with communism and yet he heartily disliked the Russians . . . When Burgess was sober he was charming, jolly, and a magnificent talker. When he was drunk, he drooled foolish nonsense. He was a kind man, and despite his weaknesses, I don't think he could do anything dishonourable or mean. But he was so terribly impetuous."

You don't want to betray if you belong. It is all relative, but Burgess never felt he belonged. He was the outsider. At Lockers Park the fathers seemed more distinguished, at Eton he resented his failure to make Pop, at Cambridge the Etonians didn't want anything to do with him, in the Foreign Office he wasn't taken as seriously as he would have liked. Small slights grew into larger resentments, and betrayal was an easy revenge. Espionage was simply another instrument in his social revolt, another gesture of self-assertion.

His homosexuality could have been a factor in feeling like an outsider, but it strangely wasn't, because on that score he felt no sense of shame. Robert Cecil, who knew him, noticed, "He had no particular wish to change the law on homosexuality; so long as he succeeded in defying it, the risk involved gave an added frisson to his exploits." And frisson was part of the attraction of first communism and then his spying, which, as one newspaper put it, provided "a gesture of rebellion, an intellectual excitement; an outlet for his sense of adventure and love of mischief."

Spies have to be good liars and even fantasists, not least for self-protection, but for Burgess, deceit was integral to his life, from his sexual activities to his political allegiances. As Andrew Boyle noted, "Truth for Guy would always be a moving target, but the ability to dazzle friends and casual acquaintances with the lurid glare of his fantasies consistently prevented them from finding him out."

Guy Burgess sought power, and realizing that he was unable to achieve that overtly, he chose to do so covertly. He enjoyed intrigue and secrets, for they were his currency in exerting power and controlling people. Goronwy Rees recalled, "He liked to know, or pretend to know, what no one else knew, he liked to surprise one with information about matters that were no concern of his, derived from sources which he could not, or would not, reveal; the trouble was that one could never be sure whether the ultimate source was not his own imagination."

There was, too, a moral vacuum. His BBC colleague John Green remembered, "He had literally no principles at all. None at all . . ." For Steven Runciman, "It was a wasted life. There was a solid core missing . . . *épater le bourgeois.* That's what really started him off."

Burgess would, of course, not have seen his life as one of failure, hypocrisy, and deceit. Just as his Huguenot ancestors had chosen to start a new life abroad, he too had put his political principles ahead of his personal wishes. He did not see himself as having betrayed his homeland, but as a Soviet agent who had nobly served his adopted country.

Fall Semester 2016

Anthony Blunt, 1962. Getty Images.

11

John Banville's *The Untouchable*

STEVEN ISENBERG

John Banville's *The Untouchable* (1997) gives imaginative life to what Lord Annan, then Provost of King's College, Cambridge, described as "the long-running inquest upon the culture, morality, and patriotism of intellectuals" brought about by the "saga of the Cambridge spies." The artistry of the novel is, indeed, no less captivating than the reality from which it draws—the double life of Anthony Blunt, who juggled the intense secrecy of a spy with the public stature of a leading art historian.

In his recent memoir *The Pigeon Tunnel* (2016), John le Carré, once a spy and later the master of the spy novel, wrote, "Spying and the novel are made for each other. Both call for the ready eye for human transgression and the many routes to betrayal." He added, "To the creative writer, fact is raw material, not his taskmaster, but his instrument, and his job is to make it sing. Real truth lies, if anywhere, not in fact, but in nuance."

Banville's *The Untouchable* is a masterly roman à clef that demonstrates the complexities of dealing with "raw material."

In 1979, Prime Minister Margaret Thatcher revealed to Parliament that Anthony Blunt, then Surveyor of the Queen's Pictures, was the fourth man in a set to have spied for Russia. Kim Philby, Donald Maclean, and Guy Burgess had defected to Russia years earlier. Their stories had already begun to be told. All four began their illicit service to Russia in the 1930s, which W. H. Auden called "a low dishonest decade." During the Second World War, all four worked for the British secret services (either MI5, responsible for counter-espionage at home, or MI6, responsible for espionage carried out against the enemy abroad).

Facts that come from a world whose currency is duplicity, disguise, and secrets raise doubts. Miranda Carter, a fine biographer of Blunt, addresses "fundamentally unreliable sources," quoting Malcolm Muggeridge, a journalist formerly in MI6: "Diplomats and intelligence agents, in my experience, are even bigger liars than journalists, and the historians who try to reconstruct the past out of their records are, for the most part, dealing with fantasy."

Banville craftily complicates matters. Victor Maskell, the stand-in for Blunt, is the novel's narrator. He is the historian of his own life, an autobiographer. His opening chord is a confession of a "lifetime of dissembling," and his last musing concerns the fate, after his death, of "what, this memoir? this fictional memoir?" What does one call a true tale about lifelong deceit? And aren't all "true tales" embellished, wittingly or unwittingly? A spy's private testament, then, is a fiction on a fiction. "In the spy's world, as in dreams," says Maskell, "the terrain is always uncertain . . . This instability, this myriadness that the world takes on, is both the attraction and the terror of being a spy."

The Untouchable begins: " First day of a new life." Maskell has broken his rule against putting things in writing. He is seventy-two, his "old rheumy eye wild with fright." He mentions the Prime Minister, the "disgrace" of "treachery" now public. He speaks of the "jackals from the newspapers" and seizes on a word from a tabloid's front-page splash: "Exposed!—what a shiversome, naked-sounding word." It calls to mind the flashbulb photographer. Maskell cannot "recognize himself in the public version," but doesn't want "to fashion for myself yet another burnished mask." The first "burnished mask," of course, was that of an art historian: "I realize the metaphor is obvious: attribution, verification, restoration. I shall strip away layer after layer of grime—the toffee-coloured varnish and caked soot . . . until I come to the very thing itself and know it for what it is. My soul. My self."

Where did Maskell's (and Blunt's) "dissembling" begin, and why? How did the Cambridge spies, each in his own way, become convinced that their country and their class could neither defeat fascism nor build a more just society at home? In *The Missing Diplomats* (1952), published a year after Burgess and Maclean defected, Cyril Connolly, tried to explain their initial betrayal: "It was more than ten years since the end of the first world war and a new generation was growing up which found no outlet in home politics for the adventurous or altruistic impulses of the adolescent. Marxism satisfied both the rebelliousness of youth and its craving for dogma." Yet this explanation is insufficient, even for Connolly, who ultimately diagnoses in Burgess and Maclean "schizophrenic characteristics." George Steiner extends the diagnosis to Blunt in his essay "The Cleric of Treason" (1980): "Crucial as they are, neither Blunt's overt Marxism nor his freemasonry of golden lads takes us to the heart of the maze, which is the radical duplicity, the seeming schizophrenia, of the scholar-teacher of impeccable integrity and the professional deceiver and betrayer."

Banville's novel works toward "the heart of the maze," both psychologically and socio-historically. Because it was the *nation* that was betrayed, on behalf of another nation and its ideology, and because there were so many stations of this double cross — Cambridge, the Apostles, Bloomsbury, the Spanish Civil War, Moscow under Stalin, and the Second World War —*The Untouchable* is inevitably, in Banville's words, a "big public book." So how does Banville manage to get his wily, aging spy to open up and lay all the "facts"—if one may call them that—on the table?

Maskell speaks not only to the reader, but also to an interlocutor, a young woman named Serena Vandeleur. She initially comes into his house with reporters, but later confesses that she is not a reporter; she wants to write a book about him. Vandeleur is the only person who asks Maskell why he did what he did, and she keeps pressing. When Maskell says, "In my world, there are no simple questions, and precious few answers of any kind," she retorts: "There *are* simple questions; there are answers. Why did you spy for the Russians? How did you get away with it? What did you think you would achieve by betraying your country and your country's interests?" Maskell deflects: "I did not spy for the Russians . . . I spied for Europe. A *much* broader church."

Maskell's resistance is based directly on Blunt's. Sometime in the 1980s, Banville watched a documentary about the painter Poussin and Blunt, the leading scholar of his work. The opening shots came from a press conference held the day after Blunt was named as the fourth spy. Banville was struck when a camera caught Blunt unawares: "The faintest ghost of a smile passed over his face. What the smile said was: Do these people really imagine they will get anything of consequence out of me, a man who has spent decades being grilled with scant success by the best spycatchers in the land? It was at that moment that I knew I would have to base a novel on this man." To do so, he had to imagine a way to penetrate what Steiner, describing that same press conference, called "Blunt's condescension, the intact carapace of his self-esteem." Vandeleur is the key.

Banville's previous novel, *The Book of Evidence* (1989), was a proving ground for *The Untouchable*. Its narrator, the murderer Freddie Montgomery, also tells his own story and reveals his pathology. The actual ground of *The Book of Evidence* was Ireland, Banville's homeland. Blunt was the son of an English vicar, but Banville wound his spring tighter in the character of Maskell, making him the son of an Ulster Protestant bishop. Maskell became the consummate Englishman because he worked to become one. But no matter how much he succeeded, his standing was complicated by his Irish origin.

In preparation for the novel, Banville read Louis MacNeice's autobiography, *The Strings Are False* (1963). MacNeice had been a close friend of Blunt's at Marlborough College, and Banville took a bit of MacNeice's Irish life for Maskell. He gave Maskell a brother, Freddie, who cannot speak and whose howling comes from being shut within himself, a permanent infant, large in body and needing constant, tender care. (MacNeice's brother, William, had Down syndrome.) Domestic drama—the strong current of unease with his father, in life and in memory—informs and undermines Maskell's air of detachment. Without sentimentality, Banville binds Maskell in the ordinary ties of blood, even as Maskell so clearly wishes to escape them.

Banville also binds Maskell in marriage to Vivienne "Baby" Breevort, and in intense friendship to her older brother Nick. Vivienne and Nick are the children of Maskell's publisher. When accepting Maskell's proposal, Vivienne tells him that she will never love him. This is not a problem. Their marriage is to be another "burnished mask." (The wedding night of Maskell and Baby is an example of Banville at his drollest. In bed, Baby goes over a list of her former lovers, "bankers and polo players and hapless Americans." Finding out that she has married a thirty-one-year-old virgin, she says, "Poor darling, let me help you. I'm a sucker for this sort of thing.") Once Maskell discovers "his kind," in London's homosexual milieu, his wife becomes little more than a social acquaintance. And no other relationship in the novel is as subtly charged and murky as that of Maskell and Vivienne's brother Nick. These familial complexities deepen Maskell's character, inspiring empathy, even if not sympathy, for his betrayal.

How does Maskell explain his own betrayal?

Spain, the kulaks, the machinations of the Trotskyites, racial violence in the East End—how antique it all seems now, almost quaint,
and yet how seriously we took ourselves and our place on the world
stage. I often have the idea that what drove those of us who went
on to become active agents was the burden of deep—of intolerable—embarrassment that the talk-drunk thirties left us with.
The beer, the sandwiches, the sunlight on the cobbles, the aim-
less walks in shadowed lanes, the sudden, always amazing fact of
sex—a whole world of privilege and assurance, all going on, while
millions prepared to die. How could we have borne the thought of
all that and not —

    But no. It will not do. These fine sentiments will not do. I have
told myself already, I must not impose retrospective significance
on what we were and what we did. Is it that I believed in something then and now believe in nothing? Or that even then I only
believed in the belief, out of longing, out of necessity? The latter,
surely. The wave of history rolled over us, as it rolled over so many
others of our kind, leaving us quite dry.

At one point, Maskell states: "The worm in the bud is more thorough than the wind that shakes the bough. That is what the spy
knows."

If that is indeed the case, then how did the Russians plant their
worm? Banville doesn't begin with public school days, but that is
the background. In *Anthony Blunt: His Lives* (2003), Miranda Carter
writes that the British public school "offered an excellent training
in dissidence [which] inadvertently fostered a questioning and sub-
versive attitude and profound distrust of authority, necessary for any
intellectual class and vital to the manufacture of an artist, writer or
spy." Maskell took this training and applied it as a member of the
Apostles, Cambridge's elite academic conversation cluster, which
met weekly and had ties to Bloomsbury. John Maynard Keynes, a
leading light of both sets, summed up their attitude: "We repudiated
entirely customary morals, conventions and traditional wisdom."

It is at Cambridge, where dons were talent spotters for the secret
services, that Maskell meets his first Russian, Felix Hartmann. Their
conversation begins as a typical Apostolic dialogue about philosophy and art. Felix's probing moves Maskell to speak of his rejection
of "pure form" and offer his critique of Picasso's *Guernica*. Maskell
recalls this episode as his first taste of a phenomenon with which he
would later become familiar in the secret world: Felix was "going to
work on a potential recruit." Maskell savors the "brief tumescence
in the air" as the subject is changed toward the testing questions.

Of this process, Maskell says there is "nothing so tentative, nothing so thrilling, excepting, of course, certain manoeuvres in the sexual chase." Banville uses dialogue to re-create scenes from Maskell's past. The crisp, natural, individuated speech of the conversations lends the novel its internal authenticity. Recollected talk has the air of fact, as if independent of Maskell the storyteller. But this credibility is punctured by Maskell's remark: "The successful spy must be able to live authentically in each of his multiple lives." Indeed, he is a consummate actor.

A common thread runs through all the Russian handlers who figure in Maskell's spying life. While each has a different manner and effect on him, a different physical bearing and way of speaking, all reveal their own precariousness, their constant vulnerability to the whims of their bureaucratic superiors in Moscow. The handlers, purveyors of betrayal, must reckon with betrayal from their own comrades, resulting in sudden disappearances and replacements. They had a rationale for this. They were convinced, as was Maskell, that the revolution deserved allegiance toward its accomplishment, even if it may have begun in the wrong country. Britain would have been better. Indeed, even as circumstances threaten Maskell's secret life, he doesn't give any thought to defecting, especially after being told that he would never be allowed to leave Russia—even to visit the Louvre.

Maskell's Second World War experience begins in France as a security officer, along with Nick. They are eventually evacuated from Boulogne, leaving on a ship carrying tons of explosives and under fire from the shore. We later learn Nick stored this episode away because he witnessed in Maskell a certain failure of nerve, which casts a long shadow.

Once home, Nick helps Maskell find a job in MI5. It is there that Maskell gets information to pass to the Russians, including secrets from the decoding operation at Bletchley. MI5 had effectively turned German agents caught on English soil into double agents. Ironically, no one down the hall, as it were, cracked the identity of the deceivers within. The British spies were from the right families, had gone to the right schools, had the right friends—all the touchstones that vouched for loyalty. If something turned up in a man's history that indicated he might sympathize dangerously with Russia and the communist cause, it was explained away as a youthful flirtation of the thirties, before the democracies had squared themselves for the right fight.

There is a poignant moment when a young, gung-ho MI5 major, Billy Metchett, must question Maskell. Although he is thirty-five, Metchett, an Etonian, seems a schoolboy when he asks Maskell about "a trace" in Maskell's files: "It seems you were something of a Bolshie." Maskell laughs it off: "Oh that. Wasn't everyone?" Although initially startled, Billy goes with Maskell's sophisticated explanation, saying he will tell Maskell's training commander that "we've vetted you and found you stainless as a choirboy." The intelligence service of the day was without skepticism about its own; it was characterized by brass-plated naiveté and old-boy amateurism.

Throughout the novel, the Catholic novelist Querell, a Graham Greene figure, acts as a perfect foil for Maskell. He is as smoothly and smugly knowing as his counterpart, and as suspicious of Maskell's Marxism as Maskell is of Querell's Catholicism. They are two wary converts. Querell is someplace in the secret service, another member of the extended club. As the uncovering begins, it turns out that Querell had an affair with Maskell's wife. Another important difference: as a heterosexual, Querell did not run the risk of criminal prosecution, which forced homosexuals to live secretly.

Banville does not handle the spy world as a former insider; there is no operational tradecraft or jargon. Nonetheless, the portraits of Maskell and his circle are as assuredly authentic as the best of Greene and le Carré. Banville's emphasis is on Maskell's cold calculations and poise, rather than on harrowing turns of action. We see Maskell fence with his handlers over what he should be doing, dismissing some requests as silly (such as reporting on conversations by known crackpots of social standing). While he suggests shrewder moves, he is also compliant. The clandestine meetings, the messaging, the attempts to obtain secret information, are all calmly and clearly recollected, not drummed up at a pace. One standout episode concerns the seduction of foreign embassy messengers carrying secret documents on the night train to Scotland. Betrayal, impersonation, sex as entrapment, the suicide of a remorseful foreign messenger—all are set to boil at a low, steady flame.

After the end of the war, Maskell's career as art historian blossoms. In Banville's treatment, the curator's understanding of technique—of the eye, the hand, the mind, and the emotions behind paintings—are all given due emphasis. For Maskell, Poussin's painting *The Death of Seneca* is an icon of dilemma and resolution: "I saw in Poussin a paradigm of myself; the Stoical bent, the rage for calm, the unshakeable belief in the transformative power of art." The painting is like a talisman: "Art was the only thing in my life that was untainted."

Another work about Blunt, Alan Bennett's play *A Question of Attribution* (1988), casts doubt on whether even art can stand untainted.

In one scene, Blunt and the Queen discuss forgery. We can assume the Queen has been told privately of Blunt's duplicity; she comments, "So if one comes across a painting with the right background and pedigree, . . . then it must be hard, I imagine—even inconceivable—to think it is not what it claims to be." Later, when Blunt's assistant asks what they had spoken of, Blunt replies, "I was talking about art. I'm not sure she was." That Maskell is an art historian of great sophistication makes him a great vehicle for Banville's high style—an exquisite, vivacious aestheticism worthy of Nabokov, or at least of Evelyn Waugh. The raw material of Blunt gave life to Banville's Maskell, and in return, Blunt has been given a permanent, vibrant inner life.

The Untouchable is a serious novel about a spy, unconstrained by the genre of spy novel. Le Carré sees a "voluptuous" quality in the spying life. Banville does as well: "The aphrodisiac qualities of secrecy and fear" are an integral part of the novel's chemistry. Maskell comes to see the double life as a debilitating force, sapping him of moral strength and blinding him to "the actual nature of things." His high social status made him untouchable for decades, protecting him from exposure and, later, prosecution; but in the end his standing is so low that he seems to belong to the caste of untouchables. Is there really any difference? The price Maskell pays for deceit is not so much the loss of his knighthood and public grace as it is the revelation of their insignificance: "What is there to be seen behind this slender capital?" Dying of cancer, he speaks of "having lived my life in remission." What was the original disease?

Banville's novel does not press for a final judgment. The raw material at its heart divided opinions. George Steiner is on the vehement side: "What is certain is simply this. Anthony Blunt was a KGB minion whose treason over thirty years or more almost certainly did grave damage to his own country and may well have sent other men . . . to abject death. The rest is tawdry gossip." Alan Bennett, on the other hand, found it hard to work up "patriotic indignation"; Blunt seemed "condemned as much out of pique and because he fooled the Establishment as for anything that he did."

In the 1981 introduction to *The New Meaning of Treason*, Rebecca West writes that the Blunt case was hard to discuss "because the curtains have been drawn around it by a fatuous officialdom." She pressed on: "That Anthony Blunt was offered immunity from prosecution if he made a statement on his conduct and was allowed to continue as a court official was playing with fire." In the end, West calls espionage "a lout's game." This brings to mind T. S. Eliot's apt observation that the American slang expression "to double-cross" was "a useful and expressive word . . . already in decay; its original meaning of a betrayal of *both* sides is reduced to plain betrayal, which renders it superfluous."

Spring Semester 2016

A version of this lecture appeared in the *Los Angeles Review of Books,* 10 May 2017.

All Souls College, Oxford. Photo by Gary Ullah.

12

All Souls College

S. J. D. GREEN

In the summer of 1962, Anthony Sampson published *Anatomy of Britain*. Writing in response to "general bewilderment" at the loss of "national purpose," Sampson sought to diagnose Britain's faltering "modern dynamic" by exposing the "essential workings" of its body politic—"who [ran] it, how they got there, and how they [were or were not] changing." He contacted about "two hundred [important] people, in government, industry, science [and] communications and asked what they were up to." The result was a wide-ranging survey of the so-called establishment. Sampson included chapters on the Crown, Parliament and the judiciary, the civil service and the diplomatic corps. He furnished essays on the City of London and the nationalized industries. He wrote about political parties and trade unions. He was very conscious of cultural capital. Careful consideration of television and advertising was supplemented by detailed accounts of Britain's schools and universities. Finally, Sampson dissected its ancient universities. He paid particular attention to All Souls College, Oxford.

Sampson believed that All Souls was an integral part of "Britain's failing Establishment." His identification of a seemingly obscure scholarly community as part of Britain's governing institutions occasioned no surprise. Indeed, it was a contemporary cliché. In August 1958, the *Spectator* magazine challenged its readers to compose a "rhyming" ditty about "the Establishment." The winning entry began:

> *A* is for All Souls, and alike Athenaeum,
> *B* is for Bishops, it's there that you seem 'em,
> *C* is for Caste, and the Carlton and Claridges,
> *D* is for the Debs, see Debrett's for their marriages,
> *E* is for Eton, where statesmen are born,
> *F*, the FO, which they mostly adorn,

But it ended:

> *Z* is for the Zeitgeist, that threatens the lot.[1]

Sampson agreed. The establishment was doomed. That was especially so of All Souls. The college had once been a place of "truly significant influence" in British political life. Immediately before the outbreak of the Second World War, its fellows included "the Foreign Secretary, the Archbishop of Canterbury and the editor of *The Times*." These affiliations gave it "some claim to be running Britain," albeit with "disastrous results." But while All Souls still remained "prestigious," its contemporary clout was unclear. Its fellowship boasted only the minister for science, the chairman of the Atomic Energy Authority, a retired permanent secretary to the Treasury, and the Arundel Herald Extraordinary. Sampson also noted how previously "close links" with "Downing Street" and "Lambeth Palace" had become more tenuous. The present warden remained "aloof" from London society. The college's legendary "dining table" seemed "less central" to national life.

There is no evidence that Sampson ever read the writings of C. W. Brodribb. This is unsurprising. Brodribb was a factotum on the inter-war *Times*. His sole claim on posterity was a curious political treatise disguised as a bird-watching manual. *Government by Mallardry: A Study in Political Ornithology* (1932) depicted a country "governed" by neither Crown nor Cabinet, still less by "the people themselves." Instead, Britain was "led and guided" by a "peculiar flock of mallards." Those mallards were the fellows of All Souls, so called after the elusive bird that legendarily stalks its ancient quadrangles. They were the habitués of "the most exclusive society in Europe." Such separation was the product of neither ancient privilege nor new money. Its members were elected only after "the most careful scrutiny of their [intellectual] qualifications." They were presumed to possess, and also required to augment, an elevated interest in "historical, legal and constitutional studies." But theirs was no mere armchair learning. They were also "diligent travellers, familiar with all the languages and legal systems of Europe, the dominions, and America."

For these philosophers were also kings. Their dominion was the result of neither tyrannical corruption nor Machiavellian subterfuge. A far-flung empire, constituted of many peoples, required wise leadership. This demanded rule that was legitimate and responsible, but also well informed. The king-emperor furnished the first, the prime minister the second, and All Souls' Mallards, the third. Like a kind of national "rotary club raised to the nth level of efficiency," they served as an "unofficial committee [determining] the destinies of the British Empire." Brodribb refrained from naming any of its members. But he had in mind the then warden, Frederick Thesiger, 1st Viscount Chelmsford, Fellow from 1892, sometime Viceroy of India; Edward Wood, Lord Irwin (later Halifax), Fellow from 1903, Chelmsford's subcontinental successor; Sir John Simon, Fellow from 1897, Foreign Secretary to the National Government after 1931; Leo Amery, Simon's twin, Secretary for the Colonies in the previous Conservative administration; Geoffrey Dawson, Fellow from 1898, editor of *The Times* and long-standing pupil of Milner's "Kindergarten"; R. H. Brand, Fellow from 1901, principal author of South Africa's postbellum constitution and international financier extraordinaire; Lionel Curtis, Fellow from 1921, Round Tabler and presiding guru at the Institute of International Affairs (Chatham House); Reginald Coupland, Fellow from 1920, Beit Professor of the History of the British Commonwealth, later historical adviser to the Peel Commission on Palestinian partition. No doubt, Brodribb also recalled the various services performed by Colonel T. E. Lawrence, Research Fellow of All Souls, 1919–26.

Brodribb was a snob and a sycophant. But his conceit was not without insight. Its implied chronology was sound. All Souls probably was at the height of its public influence in 1932. He also understood something entirely lost on Sampson: such significance, far from being a corrupt inheritance from England's ancien régime, was the product of modernizing reform. Brodribb emphasized how it was not until the 1860s that "those Mallards had become an [important] body of birds." Only at the very end of the nineteenth century did they become "fully incorporated into all branches of public life." That was true. In 1860, a leader writer on the *Morning Advertiser* subjected All Souls to the twin tests of fairness and efficiency. He found it wanting in both: "Long before the middle of this century, a place [properly] founded for the noble purposes of religion and learning [had degenerated] into a pleasant club. The essential qualifications of the candidates were reduced to a formula—*bene nati, bene vestiti, et mediocriter docti* [well born, well dressed, and moderately learned].

The [real] examination room was not the schools but the dining
room. . . . The College was for everything but 'learning', 'a hunting box', 'a card room', 'a restaurant', 'a place of gossip'. It was the
closest of closed boroughs." Closed boroughs were finally abolished,
throughout the United Kingdom, in 1884.[2]

BUT ALL SOULS WAS TRANSFORMED. In barely one generation, it
became the most self-consciously public-spirited and academically
distinguished of Oxford's ancient colleges. That galvanizing alteration was the achievement of Sir William Anson. He was not an obvious revolutionary. Born the son of a hereditary baronet, he came
from a family long associated with the college. Educated at Eton
and Balliol, he was elected Fellow in 1867. All Souls remained his
home for the next forty-seven years. He never married. He became
the college's first secular warden, in 1881. His sister served as his
female consort. The pair was waited on by liveried servants. But ap-
pearances proved deceptive.

The University Commissioners of 1850 had discovered that nearly
three-quarters of All Souls Fellows claimed kin with its founder,
Archbishop Chichele. They concluded that most had illegitimately
exploited that relationship in order to gain advancement. New university statutes in 1854 abolished this privilege. The college rid itself
of the last of its so-called founders fifty years later. Parliamentary investigators also condemned the college's existing fellowship examination as little more than a pass-fail test. They argued that elections
to the college were ordinarily determined by extraneous, usually social and personal, criteria. University Ordinances of 1857 confined
all subsequent awards to those who had either secured a first-class
degree in Schools or won a university prize. Following a ferocious
internal debate—following, in fact, legal action brought by three
young fellows against their own college in 1864–68 for its failure to
implement those ordinances—additional procedures were imposed
to ensure the college chose those who performed most meritoriously in the fellowship examination.

Scarcely less contentious was the question of the best use of the
college itself. The commissioners proposed the suppression of half
its fellowships in order to finance ten professorships in the new subjects of Modern History and Law. The college successfully resisted
this idea, though more through financial exigency than intellectual objection. It subsequently considered countless proposals for
organic reform. Anson dreamed of creating "a college of an exceptional type, devoting itself through its professoriate and its library
to University purposes, encouraging advanced study by the endow-

ment of research, securing through a system of prize fellowships the continued interest in academic life of men engaged in professorial and public works and yet retaining its old character as a collegiate society."[3] To a remarkable extent, he succeeded.

He triumphed, in part, by working with the grain of social and political change. Perhaps the most remarkable transformation in later-Victorian England was the replacement of a "territorial" aristocracy by an "intellectual" one. Landed rule by those dynasties recounted by Lewis Namier—the Grenvilles, Pelhams, and Rockinghams—was supplanted by disinterested administration through those connections celebrated by Noel Annan—the Wedgwoods, Darwins, and Keyneses. The transition involved a thorough overhaul of England's governing and educational institutions: the civil service and the law, but also its schools and universities. Reform followed a coherent principle. According to its most explicit contemporary statement, the Northcote-Trevelyan Report on Civil Service Reform (1854), the fundamental distinction between human beings derived neither from inherited estate nor through acquired possessions but rather was the product of differentiated intellectual ability. That quality could be objectively disclosed by the proper administration of appropriate tests, that is, written public examinations. Society would be best governed when those who performed most meritoriously on these examinations were allocated its most responsible positions.

This idea gradually prevailed, and the social implications of the resulting transformation were profound. It created nothing less than a new indigenous ruling class. The access of educated persons to positions of authority ensured that modern England, unlike late nineteenth-century France—or, more spectacularly still, Tsarist Russia—largely avoided the revolutionary effusions of an "alienated intelligentsia." Anson's All Souls enthusiastically partook of this change. From 1868, College Examination Fellowships were made open to all male graduates of Oxford; they were allocated on "merit," as established by the written opinion of college examiners, subject to the (anonymous) vote of all Fellows. More pointedly still, the subjects of the examination were restricted to the new disciplines of Modern History and Law. The college even made its own competitive innovations. From 1876, it reserved the right not to fill every fellowship as places became available, but to do so only if the candidates' "intellectual qualifications" demonstrated "sufficient excellence" to "entitle" them to "that prize." Thus the mythical notion of "fellowship standard" was born.[4]

The particular purposes of English university reform were bitterly contested. One school of thought, led by Mark Pattison, rector of

Lincoln College (1861–64), was committed to transforming Albion's ancient seminary into a modern German university. It should create and disseminate knowledge, preferably in new subjects, especially the natural sciences. That meant filling it with professors. Students would remain on sufferance. The other idea was embodied by Benjamin Jowett, master of Balliol (1870–93). It has been summarized thus: "Recruit by ability. Train character. And then launch your students upon the world."[5] This notion placed little value on the utility of new learning and none whatever on the peculiar ability of professors to discover and disseminate it. Instead, it conceived of the university as a place of higher education, designed to create a public-spirited person. Its preferred pedagogic vehicle remained that of personal tuition in the classics.

Following the Selborne Commission (1877–81), Jowett's vision prevailed. Oxford became primarily a teaching university. Most of its senior appointments were concentrated in the "tutorial fellowships" of colleges. Dons taught their cleverest students "Greats," a combination of ancient philosophy and history supplemented by a smattering of modern political science and even an element of economics. Law and History became popular subjects but largely among the dullards. Science remained for "stinks"—and those who liked "bangs." Anson's genius was to appreciate that while Jowett had won, his victory was far from complete. Pattison's idea was never entirely eclipsed. In this situation, All Souls could prosper by exploiting the tension between these two visions of the university.

The fundamental precondition of that prosperity was for All Souls to remain a society without students. This curious condition emerged toward the end of the seventeenth century. Anson persuaded the Selborne Commission to make that exemption permanent by convincing the commissioners that Oxford should retain at least one college devoted to research and to high-level (that is, professorial) supervision. Thus All Souls, a society uncontaminated by the professoriate in 1850, had acquired twelve of this species by 1914. Three more were added between the wars. University Professors by then made up about one-quarter of the strength of the college. They still do. At the same time, Anson secured the indulgence of the undergraduate tutors by designing a fellowship examination that, though ostensibly limited to the subjects of Modern History and Jurisprudence, was open to Greats men too. This was achieved by supplementing the two "specialist" papers in these reserved subjects with first one "general paper" and then two slightly different "general papers," from the mid-1880s onward. These were complemented by the famous "one-word essay" after 1887. Finally, there was a translation paper, which included ancient languages. This form of examination survived, albeit with additional specialist subjects, first Philosophy, Politics, and Economics, then English, and finally Classics, into the twenty-first century. It also enabled the Greats men to compete with considerable effect. Between 1873 and 1914, more than two-thirds, or forty-three, of those elected to its Prize Fellowships had taken their sole or first degree in Literae Humaniores. A further eight grounded themselves in Classical Moderations before moving to newer academic pastures. Just nine succeeded subsequent to a B.A. in Modern History alone. Only one was similarly successful in Jurisprudence. He was Canadian.

The result was to make the All Souls Prize Fellowship both extremely difficult and highly valued. It was difficult because the statistical chances of success were low. Ordinarily, upward of twenty of the "best" men in the university competed for just two fellowships. In other colleges, the ratio was often closer to parity. It was also difficult in the sense that none was able to compete solely on the basis of what he had been taught. Thus, the All Souls Fellowship Examination became the classic test of general ability, which was increasingly prized in late-Victorian and Edwardian England. It was valued because the Prize Fellowship bestowed a stipend—not a salary—of £200 per annum on young bachelors. That was the equivalent of a reasonable middle-class family income down to 1914. This could be enjoyed for up to seven years. The college demanded nothing in return. Some took their newfound freedom lightly. Writing to his sister in the spring of 1911, six months after his election, Patrick Shaw Stewart observed that "my life increases in nothing, except expenditure."[6] Others took advantage of unexpected financial security to launch successful careers. John Simon's spectacular progress at the bar was perhaps the most striking example of such "sponsored social mobility." Many traveled. Some pursued undirected enlightenment. Others undertook political odysseys. George Nathaniel Curzon, elected in 1883, journeyed through Russia and Persia and wrote one huge book on each, the first in 1889, the second in 1892. He added a third, on the Far East, two years later. As a result, he was probably the best-informed Viceroy of India who ever lived.

But the fellowship was valued most of all because it became a rarity within the university. Selborne condemned unencumbered appointments. What had been revered as "open prizes" in one generation were reviled as "idle fellowships" in the next. The long-term effect was that by 1907, of 315 fellowships associated with the Oxford colleges, around 70 percent were either accredited as "collegiate staff" or deemed to be engaged in "university work." Conversely, nearly half of those remaining "unencumbered appointments" within the university were associated with All Souls. In this way, the college because a university-wide magnet for those seeking extra-academic avenues for fame and fortune.

Anson meant All Souls to have influence in the world. He resolved to achieve this goal by methods more reliable than merely launching men upon their careers. To that end, he continually deployed personal patronage and encouraged his protégés to do the same. He cultivated important institutional connections from and for the college. Above all, he nurtured in All Souls a peculiar kind of society that self-consciously integrated the active and the contemplative attitudes to life.

The college's patronage was conferred without shame. The results were sometimes beneficial. Hensley Henson, elected a Prize Fellow in 1884, was appointed vicar of Barking, an All Souls advowson, just four years later. His ascent passed through the chaplaincy of St. Mary's Hospital, Ilford; vicar of St. Margaret's, Westminster; canon of Westminster Abbey; and, finally, bishop of Durham from 1920 to 1938. Other careers followed similar patterns. Harry Hodson was elected a Prize Fellow in 1928. Virtually every position he subsequently held, from his election to retirement, was facilitated by the intercession of another Fellow. He was editor of the *Sunday Times* in the 1950s and 1960s.

Institutional connection was more important than personal patronage. From the moment All Souls became a prestigious society, it sought association with other similarly well-regarded public bodies. Alfred Milner's Kindergarten (a select group within the South African Civil Service) quickly attracted All Souls men such as R. H. Brand, Geoffrey Dawson, and Dougie Malcolm to the cause. That, in turn, attracted Milner's men to All Souls, notably Lionel Curtis, a Fellow after 1921. Curtis then associated the college with Chatham House and, by way of St. James's Square, with the Foreign Office. Similar sorts of connections were made at the bar and in the judiciary more widely. College contacts in the higher branches of journalism were assiduously sustained by Geoffrey Dawson, editor of *The Times* (1912–18, 1922–41).

The influence cultivated was always general. With the possible exception of the *Round Table* and imperial unity, there was no "All Souls line" on anything. It was also practical. The college was notable by its distance from the fashionable cliques of the day. The Souls accounted for just one member of Anson's College: George Curzon. Their successors, the Corrupt Coterie, contributed just two more: Raymond Asquith and Patrick Shaw Stewart. Nor were Prize

Fellows much in the moral avant-garde. There was no Bloomsbury tradition of free love at All Souls (heterosexual or homosexual). Its young Fellows practiced none of the private language of the Cambridge Apostles. In fact, they shared little in common except for membership in the same college. That was not least because they were surprisingly various in their social origins. Perhaps one-third of those elected from 1850 to 1880 were titled. Only seven of sixty-three from Anson's college were similarly elevated. True, the public schools dominated among successful candidates, though actually rather less so for the period 1878–1919 than subsequently. But this involved many schools and colleges. Compare the Apostles: over 80 percent of its number between 1870 and 1914 attended Eton. A startling 92 percent went on to Trinity (Cambridge).

Anson not only wished for All Souls to be influential. He also longed for it to remain peculiar. He achieved the latter by going against the grain of contemporary social change. Until 1881, all Oxford colleges had maintained celibacy statutes. This was not because the Victorians disapproved of sex. They understood that nothing was as effective as abstinence for inducing young men to leave otherwise agreeable billets. Selborne abolished this restriction throughout the university. That made psychologically sustainable the institutional goal of tying college fellowships to lifelong teaching obligations. Anson had no such ambition. So he brought celibacy back to All Souls by way of a discretionary bylaw. The new statutes allowed for up to twenty-one Prize Fellows in the college at any time, up to seven "Research" and three so-called Distinguished Fellows, and a theoretically unlimited number of Professorial Fellows.

Anson persuaded the University Commissioners to permit All Souls another category of fellowship: to be elected without examination, paid a fixed annual entitlement of £50, and tenable only by ex-Fellows. The idea was that these Fellows would "be of benefit to the College" by maintaining links between All Souls and the outside world and by sustaining the demographic continuity of the fellowship. Nothing in the statutes stipulated who they should be. Anson determined from the first that they should be former Prize Fellows only. Exploiting the fact that these men remained a numerical majority in the College, he forced through the necessary bylaw. Then he did something ingenious. Convention dictated that former Prize Fellows might move at the end of their seven-year terms into the "Fifty-Pounder" category by way of simple rotation. But the numerical mismatch between the number of eligible Prize Fellows and the strictly limited availability of Fifty-Pounder fellowships pointed to the possibility of invidious exclusions. Anson proposed a seemingly innocuous solution: "Fellows who married during their seven years' term should not be re-elected and that an arrangement should be made under which 'Fifty-pound' Fellows should resign their fellowship on marriage."[7] This was opposed by many professorial fellows. They feared the return of idle bachelors in another guise. So a compromise was reached. A second bylaw determined that "marriage, residence out of the United Kingdom [or] occupation which made it impossible for a former fellow to take an active part in the business of the College would make it inexpedient to elect the fellow so circumstanced."[8]

This change shaped the college for generations to come. All Souls became an exceptional college, part research institution, part think tank. It recruited the best men from within Oxford and then sent most of them out into the world. But it brought some of them back, too. Either way, it did so according to its own conventions.

CONVENTIONAL WISDOM HAS IT THAT Anson's All Souls squandered its reputation in the ignominy of appeasement. Few stated this view more forcefully than Bob Boothby, writing for the *Spectator,* in 1955: "All Souls [was] the headquarters of the establishment during the decade preceding the Second World War and it would be difficult to overestimate the damage then done to the country at that disastrous dining table."[9] But Boothby was wrong. The connection between All Souls and appeasement was a post-war invention. Cato's *Guilty Men* (1940) denounced the National Government, Big Business, and the Tory Party. It even exposed "two Mallardians" (Halifax and Simon). It never mentioned the college. Nor did All Souls appear in Claud Cockburn's condemnation of Nancy Astor's Cliveden Set (though Geoffrey Dawson did).

The reason was simple. All Souls was not the "Intellectual H.Q." of appeasement. The principal appeasers—even the Mallardians among them—did not convene in Oxford to formulate their views. Nor did they acquire these opinions from Oxford. All Souls did attempt to contribute to higher-level thinking about foreign policy after the deterioration of the international situation in 1936. But it had no discernible influence on the course of British policy down to September 1939.

This was because Anson's All Souls had already been defeated by the inexorable impact of the division of labor in society. Ronald Knox once remarked that only those who had experienced the English professions before the outbreak of the First World War could appreciate how "free" a life their fortunate beneficiaries enjoyed. He particularly highlighted the capacity to move between professions then permitted to England's most able and ambitious.[10] Anson's All Souls reveled in such amphibiousness. The range of professions it sustained was extraordinarily wide. Many of the warden's men moved back and forth between the contemplative and the active lives. Consider the case of R. H. Brand. He was an historian who taught himself economics to a level respected by Keynes. He was a private banker (Lazard's) whose public career culminated at Bretton Woods with the formation of the International Monetary Fund. He began adult life as a minor functionary in Milner's bureaucracy. He later gained Smuts's trust and served as secretary to the Transvaal delegation of South Africa's Constitutional Convention. He wrote the blueprint for the new republic almost single-handedly (age thirty). When he died, in August 1963, *The Times* remarked on the passing of a "banker, statesman . . . and philosopher." It might equally have lamented the demise of the educated English virtuoso.[11] They were killed off first by internal attack, then through a narrowing of professional possibilities, and finally by the irresistible force of modern, specialized intellectual labor.

Local dissatisfaction came to a head during the proceedings of the Asquith Commission (1919–22). E. B. Poulton, Hope Professor of Zoology, even described "the very existence of All Souls . . . as the one thing most requiring change at Oxford." Similar rhetorical flak convinced Llewellyn Woodward that "various groups in the university wanted to abolish us."[12] Anson's successors reacted to this threat in two quite different ways. Some argued for a bold departure from previous practice. Geoffrey Dawson proposed the creation of an All Souls Institute for Imperial Administration, based in the college but only tenuously related to the university. Surreptitiously, he began the process of creating it, first through the recruitment of T. E. Lawrence as a Research Fellow in 1919, followed by Curtis in 1921, interspersed with the appointment of Coupland as Beit Professor in 1920. Others suggested that the college should "appease" the university by better serving its needs. This suggested teaching fellowships at All Souls in law, history, and the social sciences. It even envisaged the creation of new research fellowships in the "physical and biological sciences." The result of such disagreement—one that, ironically, put paid to the hopes of T. S. Eliot, a candidate for a Research Fellowship at All Souls in 1925—was another compromise. This created permanent, that is, renewable, Research Fellowships in the so-called traditional college subjects (now encompassing the social sciences), together with a sufficient alteration of the examination papers to permit candidates in the new School of Philosophy, Politics and Economics to compete for the Prize Fellowships. The

first of these Research Fellows, Richard Pares, was elected in 1931.
The first PPE graduate to win a Prize Fellowship, Harry Hodson,
was elected in 1928.

These changes, taken together, wrought a little-acknowledged
revolution in the college. It went largely unacknowledged because
their short-term effect was, superficially, to strengthen the imperial element in the fellowship. Down to 1933, these included not
just Dawson, Brand, Coupland, and Curtis, but also Makins, Moon,
and Hudson. It was revolutionary because the long-term effect of
promoting three Research Fellows in short order—Pares in 1931,
A. L. Rowse in 1932, and A. H. M. Jones in 1933, allied to the impact
of electing philosophers such as Isaiah Berlin (1932), J. L. Austin
(1933), Anthony Woozley (1935), and Stuart Hampshire (1936)—was
to shift the balance of power within the college toward the academics. Between 1919 and 1927, perhaps twice as many nonacademic as
academic Fellows were elected to the college. During the ten years
leading up to the war, the numbers were roughly equal. During the
ten years after the war, the balance shifted decisively, by a factor of
two-to-one, toward orthodox academic careers.

At the same time, the range of nonacademic professions represented within the fellowship significantly narrowed. Of perhaps
thirty Fellows elected between the wars and choosing nonacademic
careers, very nearly half became lawyers, and ten more went into
either the Foreign Office or some other branch of the civil service.
Just two became politicians, two more, a publisher and a journalist. There were no churchmen and definitely no poets among them.
Moreover, in opting for such respectable occupations, most also assumed conventional lives. They moved to London, got married, and
set about advancing their careers. This allowed for less and less time
at All Souls. That was the key to the passing of Anson's All Souls.

THE ZEITGEIST CHANGED SLOWLY. As late as 1945, A. L. Rowse felt
secure enough to pen an insufferably self-satisfied portrait of the
college, suggesting inter alia that Cambridge found an equivalent,
by way of thanks for Britain's national deliverance. It never did. At
the time of Sampson's critical survey, All Souls had become an occasional player in England's establishment. That made it politically
expendable. Sir Oliver Franks, chairman of the commission set up
to investigate the state of Oxford University held in the wake of the
Robbins Report, had no hesitation in describing what remained
as "infirm of purpose."[13] It was certainly an anomalous academic
institution by that time. This was not because it was academically
undistinguished. Indeed, All Souls was the model for Princeton's

Institute for Advanced Study. The problem was that the fledgling copy quickly became the better, purer example. The irony was that the college latterly boasted not too many but too few distinguished nonacademics. At the same time, All Souls, conceived as a graduate college, was no longer unique, even in Oxford. Its rivals in this respect included Nuffield and St. Antony's, from the 1950s, and Wolfson after 1967. Survival, it seemed, pointed once more toward organic change. Why this never happened is another story.

Fall Semester 2015

1. Arcai, "The Establishment," *Spectator*, 5 Sept. 1958, p. 323.

2. Quoted in Adrian Wooldridge, "Prizes, Fellowship, and Open Competition in All Souls, c. 1850–1950," in S. J. D. Green and Peregrine Horden, eds., *All Souls and the Wider World: Statesmen, Scholars, and Adventurers, c. 1850–1950* (Oxford, 2011), p. 13.

3. H. Hensley Henson, "All Souls," in *A Memoir of the Rt. Hon. Sir William Anson* (Oxford, 1920), pp. 70–71.

4. [A]ll [S]ouls [C]ollege, [C]odrington [L]ibrary, L.R., 5.a.7., ms., cccci(g), College Meeting Minute Book, 1875–1888, College Meeting, 3 Nov. 1876.

5. Peter Hinchcliff and John Prest, "Jowett, Benjamin (1817–1893)," *Oxford Dictionary of National Biography* (Oxford, 2004), 30:761.

6. Quoted in Miles Jebb, *Patrick Shaw Stewart: An Edwardian Meteor* (Standsridge, 2010), p. 122.

7. ASC, CL, L.R., 5.a.7., ms., cccci(g), College Meeting Minute Book, 1875–1888, Stated General Meeting, 31 Oct. 1885.

8. Ibid., 14 Dec. 1885.

9. Robert Boothby, "The Establishment," *Spectator,* 7 Oct. 1955, p. 448.

10. Penelope Fitzgerald, *The Knox Brothers* (Washington, D.C., 2000), p. 265.

11. Anon., "Lord Brand: Banker and Public Servant," *The Times*, 24 Aug. 1963, p. 8.

12. E. L. Woodward, *Short Journey* (London, 1942), p. 156.

13. *University of Oxford: Report of the Commission of Enquiry*, 2 vols. (Oxford, 1966); see vol. 1, Appendix on All Souls College, esp. p. 147, para. 344.

Guglielmo Marconi and British Post Office engineers, 1897. Photo courtesy of Cardiff Council Flat Project.

13

Guglielmo Marconi and England

PAUL KENNEDY

In the bewildering and wondrously inventive first decade of the twentieth century, breakthroughs in science and technology occurred so often that it would be brash to claim that any one of them "changed the world" (which doesn't stop proponents from doing so). The Wright brothers' success in aviation in 1903 led to national air forces being created only a few years later. The automobile was becoming reliable, standardized, and produced in such numbers as to change urban landscapes. Giant transatlantic liners altered oceanic travel. Electric power was coming to houses, and oil-fueled propulsion was replacing coal-fired engines. The dreadnought battleship (1906) made all other warships obsolete, though the submarine was coming to threaten it. In both the civilian and the military realms, inventors, governments, patent lawyers, and investors all jostled to establish their place.

It was into this world that a brilliant, determined young Italian inventor named Guglielmo Marconi brought his talents and his passion to connect human beings through electric pulses (messages, voices, and, later, images) that would not require any wiring. Marconi is another example of the Victorian "self-made man"—in this case, a precocious youth fascinated by electricity and electrical wave pulses. Marconi was not one of the intellectual giants of his era, yet he was more than the mere businessman-builder of a telephone company.

Born in northern Italy to a bourgeois and cosmopolitan family, introduced early to some science professors at Bologna University, Marconi was free to experiment by himself in a sort of Benjamin Franklin way. In *Marconi* (2016), the biographer Marc Raboy, a professor at McGill University, relates how the first breakthrough occurred, sometime between the summer of 1894 and the late fall of 1895 (the conflicting accounts cited by Raboy, including Marconi's own recollections, are infuriatingly casual).

Marconi was conducting signaling experiments out of the windows of his father's Alpine vacation villa. He recalled later how the idea came to him that it ought to be possible to transmit Hertzian waves through the air—that is, without the electrical pulses that were needed to send them along land-bound telegraphic cables. Accordingly, he recruited a couple of local assistants to carry his homemade equipment and report on his experiment in "telegraphy without wires."

Sending the letter *S* in Morse code to his assistant, Mignani, on the far side of a meadow several hundred yards away was great, but not enough. What if, instead, Mignani took the receiver to the other side of the hill, out of sight of the house, and then fired a gunshot if the pulses got through? "I called my mother into the room to watch the momentous experiment. . . . I waited to give Mignani time to get to his place. Then breathlessly I tapped the key three times. . . . Then from the other side of the hill came the sound of a shot. . . . That was the moment when wireless was born."

From then on, young Marconi moved fast—in retrospect, amazingly fast—and much more swiftly than competing scientists in Europe and America. A combination of technological insight, organizational skill, and business acumen gave him, like Steve Jobs in the next century, his place in history. To the end of his life, Marconi was driven by a vision of the whole world communicating through wireless waves in the air.

But human beings live on the ground, and ground was sovereign territory. Governments dispensed patents; they claimed and awarded rights; they allocated land; and they contained armies and navies. By February 1896, with family approval and some financing, Marconi had left for England, "the country in which, owing to its large fleet, extensive coast, and large shipping interests, my invention would be most readily employed."

While that language was laconic, Raboy exhaustively yet deftly tells the tale of the next few critical years: Marconi's long stay in England, the search for funding (without losing control), the critical establishment of patents, the embrace by officials in the Brit-

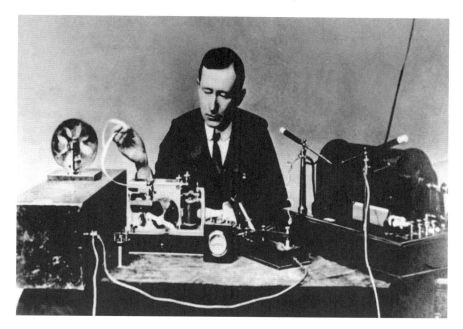

Fig. 13.1. Guglielmo Marconi and his coherer receiver (*left*) and spark-gap transmitter, 1901. *Life* magazine.

ish Post Office and Royal Navy, the ship-to-shore and ship-to-ship wireless transmissions. There is a fine chapter on the critical long-range, transatlantic experiments in 1901. These were conducted in wintry, gusty Newfoundland, whose supportive provincial government grasped almost immediately what Marconi offered: instant and vastly less expensive communication to Canada, Boston, New York, and, above all, Britain and its empire. Little wonder that such powerful entities as the (state-subsidized) Anglo-American Telegraph Co. were alarmed at this interloper. Little wonder, too, that the British, American, German, and Japanese navies scrambled to keep abreast of this magical means of communication.

In 1909, at the age of thirty-five, the Italian entrepreneur stood up proudly to receive the Nobel Prize in Physics. As Raboy unfolds his account, he makes clear the incredible extent to which the story of radio was woven into that of international politics. There is great detail here concerning Marconi's British side, which eclipsed everything else in importance for him. His speeches to learned societies and enjoyment of society life in London mixed rather amazingly with expeditions to boggy promontories in southwestern Ireland and craggy cliffs in Cornwall to supervise the erection of new stations, and with his lobbying of British MPs to try to preserve the company's monopoly (that one failed). His energy, which extended to extramarital affairs throughout his life, seems virtually boundless.

All this time, the Marconi Co. fought its many competitors, who were not just the cable firms and not just other start-up wireless companies, but also the German, American, and Japanese governments. Ironically, disasters and war helped the company on its way. When the *Titanic* was foundering in the icy North Atlantic in 1912, only its operator's desperate wireless calls caused the Cunard liner *Carpathia* to race to the scene to rescue 705 survivors. The New York press in particular went wild at the miracle of ship-to-ship radio. And when Britain went to war in 1914, Churchill at the Admiralty sent a wireless message to all the fleet: "Commence hostilities against Germany."

In retrospect, one can see Marconi's star begin to fade around this time. In war, governments wanted control of radio—radio stations, radio infrastructure, radio messages, and, if necessary, radio enterprises. The Marconi Co. and its rivals wilted, becoming junior partners of the state if they survived at all. At the same time, and more amazingly, Marconi never fully appreciated the less practical but more recognizable role of radio, in the domain of popular culture and entertainment.

Marconi's name beamed brightly once again, however, in Mussolini's Italy. The forty-year-old patriot had rushed back to Rome in 1914 as his country prepared to enter the war. Already a national icon, he was embraced by the public, the press, and politicians. As Mussolini rose, radio and fascism seemed destined for each other, and Marconi was elevated to near sainthood. It is pretty hard to figure out Marconi's real feelings about fascism, although Raboy does an extremely good job at sifting contradictory evidence. While Marconi was simply cowardly when it came to speaking out against anti-Semitism, one senses at times his growing bewilderment that the power of radio transmissions could be used not just for good but also for evil. A kind of sorcerer's apprentice shadow falls over the story.

Sadly but predictably, the more Marconi appeared as an apologist for Italian fascism, the less influence he had in his second home, Britain. In one poignant episode from early 1937, he requested seats at George VI's coronation. The reply was that, alas, Westminster Abbey was already too full. Still, perhaps Marconi wouldn't have made it. By that time, his heart attacks were more frequent, and he passed away in July 1937, at the age of sixty-three.

Raboy's book is a rock-solid, archivally based, professional work of history and surely one of the year's better biographies. It suffers, though, from being far too detailed, so the story of radio is sometimes rather eclipsed. Perhaps a book trimmed of this detail would have worked better. The invention was greater than the man. But both Marconi and his career are extraordinarily interesting because the decades in which he was at the height of his influence were also those of enormous change—the birth of the modern age. Electricity, science, nationalism, war, international business, fascism, colonialism: all claimed a place on the stage, and Marconi and his wireless ran throughout all of it.

Spring Semester 2017

A version of this lecture appeared in the *Wall Street Journal*, 9 September 2016.

Harold Nicolson, 1935. Photo by Howard Coster. © National Portrait Gallery, London.

14

Harold Nicolson and Royal Biography

JANE RIDLEY

The Round Tower, Windsor Castle, January 1949. Harold Nicolson has climbed eighty-nine cold stone stairs to reach a high room with a large gothic window. Freezing winds howl round the tower, and the small coal fire does little to counter the icy draft that rushes through the cracks in the window. He draws the curtains and crouches over a thin electric heater, wearing a greatcoat over his grey suit, a rug on his knees. The room is devoted entirely to the archive of George V, and it is kept for Nicolson's use alone. It is lined from floor to ceiling with shelves filled with closely packed canvas boxes. The boxes are labeled "A," "B," or "C" according to the subject they cover—foreign affairs, home politics, honors, and many others—and inside the boxes are files bearing a number. These numbers correspond to bound registers that lie on a table in the window. A ladder enables him to reach even the highest boxes, and by constantly consulting the register, he can make certain that not a single paper escapes him.

In addition to these official papers, Nicolson has been given the private letters. These consist of bound volumes of correspondence between King George and Queen Victoria (his grandmother), between the King and his father (Edward VII) and mother, and to his children. Only the letters to the Duke of Windsor and Queen Mary are held back. Then there is the King's diary—twenty-five fat manuscript volumes, fastened by a small lock that can be opened only by a small gold key.

Nicolson sits at his table and writes on his "tikki," as he calls his typewriter. He types his notes on separate quarto sheets, stringing them together with a "bootlace" and classifying them in separate files. He works all day, eating his sandwiches in the room to save time and avoid another climb to the top of the tower.

As the official biographer of George V, Nicolson was allowed a freedom of access unimaginable today. He is the only biographer ever to have read through the entire archive of George V. Paradoxically, however, the biography that Nicolson published set new standards for secrecy. It became the defining text of the "code of silence" observed by royal insiders, a code that still persists in a modified form today.

Nicolson's appointment came about in June 1948 when Sir Alan (Tommy) Lascelles, private secretary to George VI and Keeper of the Archives, summoned him to his room at Buckingham Palace, saying that he had a proposition to make. Lascelles was an Oxford contemporary of Nicolson, and the two men later learned French while staying at the Paris flat of the formidable Jeanne de Henaut. Thin and wiry with a scrubby moustache, a terrier-like face, and a caustic wit, Lascelles (seen recently in Netflix's *The Crown*) was the man who devised the authorized royal biography. Shrewd and sharp-witted, Lascelles was no boot-licking toady. "I have never been a dedicated 'courtier,'" he wrote, "my view of the institution of Monarchy is essentially pragmatical; I have never idealised any member of the House of Windsor, though I respect several of them."[1] Strategy rather than reverence dictated the project that he proposed to Nicolson.

That afternoon at Buckingham Palace, Lascelles explained that the King wished to commission an official life of his father, King George V. Five grandees had been consulted, and three of them suggested Nicolson. When Nicolson objected that he disliked writing biographies if he could not tell the whole truth, Lascelles replied (according to Nicolson's diary): "But it is not meant to be an ordinary biography. It is something quite different. You will be writing a book on the subject of a myth and will have to be mythological."[2]

In the edition of his father's *Diaries and Letters* that Nigel Nicolson published in 1968, this last sentence is omitted. In its place is a sentence that runs: "You will be writing a book about a very ancient national institution, and you need not descend to personalities."[3] These bland words were inserted at the request of Lascelles. When Nigel Nicolson showed him the typescript of the book, Lascelles redacted the mythological sentence. He told Nigel: "The King's private secy. mustn't be recorded as calling the Monarchy a 'myth', and

Fig. 14.1. Sir Alan Frederick "Tommy" Lascelles, 1943. Photo by Walter Stoneman. © National Portrait Gallery, London.

I'm sure I never used the word in that connection though Harold, quite likely, puts [it] into my mouth."[4]

As Lascelles explained, every scrap of paper was to be made available to Nicolson in the Round Tower. He was to be treated as a royal insider, on the strict understanding that he respected the trust confided in him and obeyed the code of secrecy. Nicolson was chosen because he was a "a highly civilised chap, who could be trusted never to make unauthorised use of anything he might read in the Archives or hear in conversation; because he was, in the obsolete jargon of that age, a gentleman," Lascelles later wrote. "For that reason, he was shown everything—even the intimate letters which I, though Keeper of the Archives, had never seen; and we all talked to him as if he was our Father Confessor."[5] In exchange, Nicolson would write a "mythological" book. He was not expected to write anything that was not true, but noted in his diary, "All that I should be expected to do was to omit things and incidents which were discreditable."[6] Silences then, but not lies.

Afterward, Nicolson discussed the pros and cons in a letter to his wife, Vita Sackville West. Against: he disliked having to write to order, he worried about the lack of charm in his subject and the things he would be forced to leave out. On the other hand, the challenge of writing such a life in a way that was "really interesting, really true" while observing the conventions of royal portraits appealed to him.[7] So did the interest of describing the function of the monarchy in the national life; both he and Vita were strong royalists.

Nicolson quickly saw that the only way to please Lascelles and the King while keeping faith with his integrity was to write about the reign rather than compose "a portrait of a dull individual." "I can see George V getting more and more symbolic and less real," he wrote.[8] "I shall have to make him a lay figure—dressed in ermine."[9]

The truth was that for all his biographer's principles and his anxiety about the reaction of his highbrow friends, Nicolson had no intention of refusing. A clubbable, affable figure, the sixty-one-year-old Nicolson was deeply entrenched in the post-war establishment. He was chair of the London Library and vice chairman of the National Trust, he dined regularly at the Beefsteak Club, he wrote a column called Marginal Comment each week in the *Spectator,* and he reviewed for the *Observer.*

Since resigning from the Foreign Office to become a writer in 1929, Nicolson had poured out a flood of books, most of them about diplomacy and his family, but he worried that his writing was "not good enough to justify myself having cut adrift from public service." In 1931 he embarked on a third career, as a politician. He flirted with Oswald Mosley, broke with him when he became a fascist, was elected a National Labour MP in 1935, and lost his seat in 1945. Hoping for a peerage from Attlee, he joined the Labour Party in 1947. In February 1948, he fought and lost the Croydon by-election for Labour, a humiliating fiasco that ended his political career.[10] Coming only a few months later, George V was a lifeline. As his sensible secretary remarked, "It is just what you need—an anchor. It will keep you busy for three years and prevent you doing silly things like Croydon."[11]

NICOLSON'S FILE OF CORRESPONDENCE with Lascelles, preserved today in the Beinecke Rare Book and Manuscript Library at Yale, reveals how closely he worked with his controller. The collaboration was smooth. "I don't think I have ever told you how deeply interested I am in this book, and how grateful I am to you for your help in the matter," Nicolson told Lascelles. "I don't think I have ever enjoyed writing a book so much."[12] From time to time, Nicolson reported progress to Lascelles. By July 1949 he had almost finished going through all the papers on the pre-accession period. "I shall then retire to the country and write the first version of that section of the book which covers the period till 1910," he told Lascelles. Mindful that this was an authorized biography, he wrote: "When I have finished these chapters, I shall then show them to you and you can decide whether they should be checked by Queen Mary before being submitted to the King."[13]

On 20 July, Nicolson typed the first sentence of chapter one: "Prince George was born." and reflected in his diary: "I gaze at the sentence in wonder, realising what a long journey I have to go before I reach his death. It is like starting in a taxi on the way to Vladivostok."[14] There can be few biographers who are not familiar with the feeling.

At Sissinghurst that summer, sitting at the simple wooden writing desk in his book-lined downstairs study, looking out over the garden that Vita and he had created and that he called m.l.w. (my life's work), Harold clattered away on his typewriter. He had perfected the skill of typing automatically while thinking of the next sentence, and he wrote very fast.[15] 3 August 1949: "Work hard all day at Chapter II and finish it." 4 August: "Begin Chapter III." 8 August: "finish Chapter III."

Nicolson claimed that George's character was "crystallized" during his years at sea, from twelve to seventeen. "As a child he was vivacious, affectionate, inclined to self-approval and thus easily discouraged." During the years of naval discipline, however, "while retaining all the impulses . . . of boyhood, he . . . soon developed a quality more forcible than ordinary manliness—a categorical sense of duty. It was this . . . which became the fly-wheel of his life." Hence the "recurrent theme" of Nicolson's biography: "the contrast between the simple straightforwardness of King George's character and the intricate political fluctuations with which he had to cope."[16]

After a month or so of this, Nicolson found himself "getting a down" on George V: "He is all right as a gay young midshipman. He may be all right as a wise old king." But the intervening period presented serious problems: "For seventeen years he did nothing at all but kill animals and stick in stamps."[17] This undermined the argument of Nicolson's book: "If my theme is 'the simple man with the categorical sense of duty' then how can one justify the fact that he could make no effort at all to prepare himself for future responsibilities."[18] Mindful of his assignment to write a mythological royal biography, Nicolson felt unable "to point out how fundamentally lazy and selfish he was during this time and make these seventeen years spent in slaughtering our feathered friends one of the 'points' in the narrative . . . I will not be allowed to 'attack' him or even to criticise except in mealy mouthed terms."[19]

Once George succeeded as king, Nicolson's theme of public duty took over. He announced the shift of gear by inserting a chapter on the constitutional role of the monarchy. The journey to Vladivostok seemed endless, however. Having coaxed his motorcar "upwards towards the summit, I find that what I thought was the top turns out only to be a little col with alp upon alp beyond."[20]

After describing the King's central role in the constitutional crisis of 1911 and the Home Rule struggle of 1914, Nicolson changed gear again with the outbreak of the First World War, when the Crown was no longer at the forefront of events. The biographer, wrote Nicolson, was faced with a problem of composition: "If he seeks to describe the war, then his principal figure will immediately fade away into the clouds of battle. If, on the other hand, he attempts to depict the King as a symbolic leader, raising his baton against a background of fleets and armies, then the focus of the picture will be incorrect." Rather than tell the story of the war, therefore, Nicolson sought to answer the question, "How, during those four dark years, was the King's influence brought to bear?"[21] Less interesting to him was the other side of that question: how did the war change the monarchy?

NICOLSON SPLIT THE BOOK INTO FOUR PARTS, and as each section was completed, it was set in galley proofs, bound, and sent to the royals to read. Queen Mary responded promptly and positively.

Fig. 14.2. Queen Mary, consort of King George V, c. 1920s. Library of Congress Prints and Photographs Division, ggbcin.31282.

Lascelles told Nicolson: "My spies at M-rlb-r-gh H--se tell me that the little foundling that you laid on its doorstep is thought to be a fine healthy child wh. will need but little correction."[22] She asked for very few changes—the most significant was a letter from Queen Alexandra describing the Kaiser as "mad and a conceited ass."[23] (This was apparently because "Queen Mary has rather a soft spot in her heart for the late Kaiser who wrote her charming letters from Doorn."[24]) George VI allowed the book to pass with barely a comment. Nicolson was asked to change only eighty-two words.

The book earned the royal nod of approval largely because of Lascelles. If Lascelles thought it was good, that was enough for the King, who was a sick man toward the end of the process and in no condition to scrutinize the proofs. Lascelles seems to have sidelined Owen Morshead, who as Royal Librarian had supervised biographers for a quarter of a century. As Keeper of the Archives, Lascelles was Morshead's manager in the hierarchy of the household. "I have a feeling that the latter is rather touchy," wrote Nicolson, "and I can only hope that he doesn't feel that I have ignored him."[25] According to Lascelles, however, Morshead was like a cat who required cosseting—stroke him continually and he is yours for keeps.

NICOLSON WAS NOT EXPECTED TO WRITE much about King George's private life because that had already been dealt with in another authorised biography—John Gore's *Personal Memoir* of King George V, published in 1941. "It shows me that I shall have to concentrate on the political side and need not mention the personal side," Nicolson wrote. "Gore has done his job very well, and I am surprised that he was allowed to say as much."[26]

The appointment of John Gore by King George VI and Queen Mary to write a memoir of George V that "will not be concerned with any of the official aspects of the reign" was announced in *The Times* on 25 October 1938. On the same day, the royal advisers released the badge of the House of the Windsor: an image of the Round Tower, where the archives are kept.

By contrast with the sociable Nicolson, Gore was a modest, retiring man who wrote a tiny, neat script. He described himself as a Crusoe and disliked London. For thirty years he contributed weekly articles to the *Telegraph,* the *Standard,* and the *Sphere:* his columns were written, said his obituarist, "without the stimulus of London chatter, but in the reflective quiet of his country home."[27] Gore was a lifelong friend of Lascelles—the two men had served in the Bedfordshire Yeomanry throughout the First World War—but Gore's biography was commissioned by Clive Wigram, Keeper of the Archives (1931–45).

Wigram was hardly a bookish figure: Gore found him "a bore and a fool." The man who directed Gore's work was Owen Morshead, whom Gore thought "very chatty and long winded."[28]

Morshead was very close to the widowed Queen Mary, and it seems likely that the project for a personal memoir of the late king originated with her. By seizing the initiative, Queen Mary doubtless hoped to preempt the critical or flippant unofficial biographers who had plagued previous monarchs. No official life was written of Queen Victoria; instead, an edition of her letters was published. The result was a gap that Lytton Strachey hastened to fill. His brilliant and irreverent *Queen Victoria* (1921) caused outrage in royal circles. George V greeted the book with an explosion of rage. "He was very angry and got quite vehement about it," said his son, the Prince of Wales (who was discovered in "roars of laughter" over the description of Queen Victoria and John Brown).[29] The palace was also caught napping in the case of Edward VII. Sidney Lee's dismissive essay in the *Dictionary of National Biography* stung the royal advisers to embark on the tortuous process of forcing Lee to recant and produce an authorized life, which eventually appeared in 1925. Even George V found Lee's two fat volumes somewhat colorless, noting that the book was "very interesting but not always quite accurate."[30]

For Queen Mary there was a pressing need to control her husband's image. The quarrel between George V and his eldest son had culminated in the crisis of the abdication. A favorable biography was one way of absolving George from blame.

To establish the King's character, Gore—or perhaps more accurately, Queen Mary and Owen Morshead—took a calculated risk. The book reveals more about the King's private life than any previous authorized royal biography had ever done. Perhaps the only comparable example is Jonathan Dimbleby's strikingly candid life of Prince Charles. As the Duke of Windsor remarked when Queen Mary criticized him for writing magazine articles about his youth: "I would submit that the personal memoir of Papa undertaken by John Gore at your and Bertie's request . . . contains far more intimate extracts from Papa's diaries and glimpses into his character and habits than I would have dared to use or thought suitable to include in the story of my early life."[31]

"Frank, simple, honest and good": that, according to Gore, was the essence of King George V.[32] His book was like that too, utterly lacking in the knowing irony and waspish wit of writers such as Lytton Strachey or James Pope-Hennessy. In spite of its intimacy, it is a eulogy. One American reviewer who regretted the absence of Strachey's caustic pen observed that "frank, simple, honest and good" added up in practice to dullness. It leaves unanswered questions, too. If George really was as Gore described, how are we to account for his success in the difficult business of being king?

There is another problem. It seems hardly credible that this simple, loving man should have been such a brute to his sons. Gore's chapter on the King's relations with his sons was cut by George VI, and instead he wrote a section about the gulf between the post-war generation and the socially conservative monarch. These pages were written to order, revised several times, and carefully vetted both by Queen Mary and the King.[33]

THE YEAR 1941 WAS NOT A GOOD ONE IN WHICH TO PUBLISH A BOOK on the family life of a dead British king. Though he won the James Tait Black prize, Gore failed to secure an American publisher, dashing his hopes that the royalties would pay for his children's school fees. Nicolson was more fortunate in his timing. Coming out in August 1952, only six months after the accession of Elizabeth II, at a high point of popularity for the monarchy, *King George V* was a literary and political event. It was saluted with leaders in *The Times* and the *Manchester Guardian*. Today, John Gore's intimate account of George's private life seems more modern, but Nicolson's formal political narrative of the reign was the biography that the public wanted in 1952. *King George V* sold 10,000 copies in two weeks. The two-page lead review in the *Times Literary Supplement* by "a cantankerous person wishing to find fault" (the anonymous reviewer was the *Times* journalist and historian A. P. Ryan) was gratifying to Nicolson, "as it shows that even a hostile critic cannot find errors of fact or faults of style and appreciation."[34]

Lascelles was delighted with Nicolson's work. He predicted that "it is gong to put you, in the judgement of today & tomorrow, in the select circle of great biographers; a relatively small circle it is, too, with a lot of knaves & charlatans milling round its periphery."[35] He told Nicolson: "It is a noble, & notable book—in every way a credit to its only begetter."[36] The truth was that the begetter of the book was Lascelles himself. Nicolson had done what he was told and written a mythological biography. "I can only say," wrote Lascelles, "that I feel sure that Lord Stamfordham would commend it—and praise can go no further."[37] These were not empty words. Stamfordham, private secretary to George V from 1911 until Stamfordham's death in 1931, was the architect of the style of monarchy that Lascelles sought to perpetuate under George VI—dutiful, effective, and discreet, operating smoothly behind the scenes. "Your saying that you think Stamfordham would have approved is a very great encouragement," replied Nicolson, "since I really regard that man as one of the wisest & most decent people of that rather disturbed period."[38]

On Nicolson's recommendation, Lascelles went on to commission Sir John Wheeler-Bennett to write an authorized biography of King George VI. Together with James Pope-Hennessy's 1959 *Queen Mary,* this trilogy of authorized biographies formed a narrative that, given the restrictions on access to the archives, "was almost impossible to contest."[39]

THE TIDAL WAVE OF PRAISE AND ACCLAIM left Nicolson strangely unmoved. "I ought to feel elated," he wrote. "But somehow I am rather indifferent and do not experience any inner feelings of self-satisfaction."[40] When someone told him that Queen Mary approved of the way he had made the King come alive, Nicolson exploded in his diary: "Good God! I have created a pure tailor's dummy, and have not tried to make him live at all, since if I did so he would appear as a stupid old bore."[41]

Very different from the tailor's dummy were the portraits that Nicolson had dashed off a quarter of a century before in *Some People,* a sparkling collection of autobiographical essays. Perhaps the funniest of the sketches is the one of Lord Curzon. Here is Nicolson on Curzon at work: "He was a sitting at his cabin table writing on loose sheets of foolscap in a huge flowing hand: his pencil dashed over the paper with incredible velocity: his lips moved: from time to time he would impatiently throw a finished sheet upon the chintz settee beside him."[42] Anyone who has struggled to read the voluminous loops of Curzon's handwriting will recognize the picture. George V himself shouted with laughter over *Some People.* By contrast, the authorial voice of Nicolson's *King George V* is stately and authoritative. There are no jokes. We are never shown the King at work, laboriously writing in his schoolboy hand, let alone taken into his bedroom.

In his time at the Foreign Office, Nicolson was trained to obey the Obligation of Secrecy, and he understood the royal code.[43] "I quite see," he wrote, "that the Royal Family feel their myth is a piece of gossamer and must not be blown upon . . . What is a relief to me is that I shall not have to do too much portraiture. I shall be able to leave all that to John Gore, who has really done it very well indeed."[44]

But the Nicolson of *Some People* was still alive, buried beneath the carapace of the official biography. "It will be fun being 'in search of George,'" wrote Nicolson, "but it will be hell writing the thing."[45] Nicolson began his researches by interviewing the surviving members of King George's household, who freely gave their views. These conversations often took place over dinner or lunch at the Beefsteak Club. He had candid talks with John Gore. Queen Mary gave him an audience, and he also spoke to the Duke of Windsor and to junior royals such as Lord Carisbrooke.

The Beefsteak conversations lifted the curtain on real life at the palace. Queen Mary was an enigma. Some said she managed her husband, but most of the courtiers whom Nicolson spoke to agreed that she was terrified of him. George's sister Princess Victoria was described as a "really wicked woman," poisoning him against his sons.[46] As for George himself, his old servants described him as stupid, ignorant, horrible, garrulous, simple, and unimaginative, but also loyal, modest, funny, and acute. None of this went into the book.

IN 1965, HAROLD NICOLSON'S SON NIGEL began work on his edition of his father's diaries. Nearing eighty, Harold was suffering from dementia, and Nigel hoped to pay for his father's care at Sissinghurst by publishing the diaries. Nigel, a man of considerable moral courage, believed in transparency. He later shocked conventional society by publishing *Portrait of a Marriage* (1973), his mother Vita Sackville West's naked account of her affair with Violet Trefusis. For Nigel, the "real interest" of the section of the diary covering the writing of the biography lay in Harold's private reactions to his study of the King, which differed markedly from what he wrote in the book.[47] Since Harold was unable to guide him, Nigel sent his typescript to be read by Tommy Lascelles, now a spry seventy-eight-year-old living at Kensington Palace.

Lascelles urged caution. He worried that publication of the diaries would violate the royal code of secrecy. People would get "the idea that the book was a false, put-up job—an elaborate pro-monarchical facade—which would be wholly unjust."[48] For Nigel Nicolson, however, what mattered his father's reputation. "My concern was that people on reading his diaries should be astonished to find that the hagiography, which is an accepted part of royal biography, should have mesmerised his mind." "When I asked you," he wrote to Lascelles, "whether the time had come to tell 'part of the truth', I meant the truth about my father's feelings, not the truth about King George."[49] It all came down to truth. In spite of observing the code of secrecy, Harold Nicolson's allegiance was to telling the truth.

Spring Semester 2017

Permission to quote from the Harold Nicolson papers at Sissinghurst and the Harold Nicolson Diaries at Balliol College was graciously given by the copyright holder, Juliet Nicolson.

1. Lascelles to Nigel Nicolson, n.d. [1967], in *King's Counsellor*, ed. Duff Hart-Davis (Phoenix, 2007), p. 432.

2. Nicolson to Vita Sackville West, 8 June 1948, Harold Nicolson Diary, Balliol College Archives.

3. Nigel Nicolson, ed., *Harold Nicolson: Diaries and Letters, 1945–1962* (Collins, 1968), p. 142.

4. Lascelles's notes for Nigel Nicolson, n.d. [1968], Lascelles Papers, CHAR [Churchill Archives Centre] LASC 8/8.

5. Lascelles to Nigel Nicolson, n.d. [1967], in *King's Counsellor*, pp. 432–33.

6. Nicolson to Vita Sackville West, 8 June 1948, Harold Nicolson Diary, Balliol College Archives; James Lees-Milne, *Harold Nicolson* (London, 1981), II, pp. 222–23.

7. Nicolson to Vita Sackville West, 8 June 1948, in *Nicolson: Diaries and Letters, 1945–1962*, pp. 142–44.

8. Nicolson to Vita Sackville West, 9 June 1948, Harold Nicolson Diary, Balliol College Archives.

9. Nicolson to Vita Sackville West, 22 July 1948, Sissinghurst Papers.

10. David Cannadine, *Aspects of Aristocracy* (London, 1994), pp. 220–35; Thomas Otte, "Harold Nicolson," *ODNB*.

11. Nicolson to Vita Sackville West, 8 June 1948.

12. Nicolson to Lascelles, 19 July 1949, Harold Nicolson Papers, Gen Mss 614, box 17, Beinecke Library, Yale.

13. Nicolson to Lascelles, 6 July 1949, in ibid.

14. Nicolson, diary entry for 17 July 1949, in *Nicolson: Diaries and Letters, 1945–1962*, p. 173.

15. Lees-Milne, *Harold Nicolson*, II, p. 283

16. Harold Nicolson, *King George the Fifth: His Life and Reign* (London, 1952), pp. 32–33.

17. Nicolson to Vita Sackville West, 17 Aug. 1949, in *Nicolson: Diaries and Letters, 1945–1962*, p. 174.

18. Harold Nicolson Diary, 16 Aug. 1949, Balliol College Archives.

19. Nicolson to Vita Sackville West, 17 Aug. 1949, Sissinghurst Papers.

20. Nicolson to Lascelles, 10 Aug. 1950, Harold Nicolson Papers, Gen Mss 614, box 17, Beinecke Library, Yale.

21. Nicolson, *King George the Fifth*, p. 248.

22. Lascelles to Nicolson, 20 Dec. 1949, Harold Nicolson Papers, Gen Mss 614, box 17, Beinecke Library, Yale.

23. Bound proof annotated by Queen Mary, I, pp. 40–41, Sissinghurst Papers.

24. Harold Nicolson Diary, 5 Jan. 1950, Balliol College Archives.

25. Nicolson to Lascelles, 28 Sept. 1951, Harold Nicolson Papers, Gen Mss 614, box 17, Beinecke Library, Yale.

26. Harold Nicolson Diary, 14 Oct. 1948, Balliol College Archives.

27. *The Times*, Gore obituary, 23 July 1983.

28. Harold Nicolson Diary, 3 Nov. 1948, Balliol College Archives.

29. Frances Donaldson, *Edward VIII* (London, 1974), p. 101.

30. John Gore, *King George V: A Personal Memoir* (London, 1941), p. 348.

31. Philip Ziegler, *King Edward VIII* (London, 1990), pp. 523–24.

32. Gore, *Personal Memoir,* p. xv.

33. Murray to Gore, 20 Nov. 1939, John Murray Archive, Acc. 13328/171 EE6, National Library of Scotland; Gore, memorandum for George VI, 14 Mar. 1940, Gore Family Papers; Gore, *Personal Memoir,* pp. 365–70.

34. Harold Nicolson Diary, 15 Aug. 1952, Balliol College Archives.

35. Lascelles to Nicolson, 2 Dec. 1952, Harold Nicolson Papers, Gen Mss 614, box 17, Beinecke Library, Yale.

36. Lascelles to Nicolson, 2 Aug. 1952, in ibid.

37. Lascelles to Nicolson, 3 Aug. 1950, in ibid.

38. Nicolson to Lascelles, 10 Aug. 1950, in ibid.

39. Andrzej Olechnowicz, "Historians and the Modern British Monarchy," in Olechnowicz, *The Monarchy and the British Nation* (Cambridge, 2007), p. 10.

40. Harold Nicolson Diary, 17 Aug. 1952, Balliol College Archives.

41. Ibid., 26 July 1951.

42. Harold Nicolson, *Some People* (Oxford, 1983), p. 145.

43. Ibid., pp. 130–31.

44. Nicolson to Vita Sackville West, 9 Sept. 1948, Sissinghurst Papers,.

45. Ibid.

46. Harold Nicolson Diary, 27 July 1949, Balliol College Archives.

47. Nigel Nicolson to Lascelles, 4 Jan. 1967, Sir Alan Lascelles Papers, CHAR LASL 8/8.

48. Lascelles to Nigel Nicolson, Jan. 1967, copy, in ibid.

49. Nigel Nicolson to Lascelles, 11 Feb. 1967, in ibid.

Herbert Butterfield, 1961. Photo by Walter Bird. © National Portrait Gallery, London.

15

Keeping an Eye on the Present: Whig History of Science

STEVEN WEINBERG

It was the Cambridge historian Herbert Butterfield who described and condemned what he called "the whig interpretation of history."[1] In a book with that title, the young Butterfield in 1931 declared, "The study of the past with one eye, so to speak, upon the present is the source of all sins and sophistries in history." He spread special scorn on those historians, including Lord Acton, who subjected the past to contemporary moral judgments, who, for instance, were unable to see the Whig Charles James Fox as anything but a savior of British liberties. Not that Butterfield was personally unwilling to make moral judgments; he just did not think it was the business of historians. According to Butterfield, a whig historian studying Catholics and Protestants in the sixteenth century feels that "some loose threads are still left hanging unless he can say which party was in the right."

Butterfield's strictures were fervently taken up by later generations of historians. Being called "whig" came to seem as terrifying to historians as being called sexist or Eurocentric or Orientalist. Nor was the history of science spared. The historian of science Bruce Hunt recalls that when he was in graduate school in the early 1980s, "whiggish" was a common term of abuse in the history of science. To avoid that charge, people turned away from telling progress stories or giving "big picture" stories of any kind, and shifted to accounts of small episodes, tightly focused in time and space.

Nevertheless, in teaching courses on the history of physics and astronomy, and then working up my lectures into a book, I have come to think that whatever one thinks of whiggery in other sorts of history, it has a rightful place in the history of science. It is clearly not possible to speak of right and wrong in the history of art or fashion, nor, I think, is it possible in the history of religion, and one can argue about whether it is possible in political history, but in scientific history we really can say who was right. According to Butterfield, "One can never say that the ultimate issue, the succeeding course of events, or the lapse of time has proved that Luther was right against the Pope or that Pitt was wrong against Charles James Fox." But we can say with complete confidence that the lapse of time has shown that, about the solar system, Copernicus was right against the adherents of Ptolemy, and Newton was right against the followers of Descartes.

Though the history of science thus has special features that make a whig interpretation useful, it has another aspect that makes the idea of keeping an eye on the present troublesome to some professional historians. Historians who have not worked as scientists may feel that they cannot match the working scientist's understanding of present science. On the other hand, it must be admitted that a scientist like myself cannot match the professional historian's mastery of source material. So who should write the history of science, historians or scientists? The answer seems to me obvious: both.

I should disclose that I have a dog, or at least a book, in this fight. In *To Explain the World: The Discovery of Modern Science* (2015), I acknowledged that "I will be coming close to the dangerous ground that is most carefully avoided by contemporary historians, of judging the past by the standards of the present." Reviews were generally favorable, but one in the *Wall Street Journal* (by a professional historian) took me to task for my attention to the present. The review was headed "The Whig Interpretation of Science."

Now, some criticisms of whiggery, by Butterfield and others, are either irrelevant to the history of science or not controversial. Certainly, we should not oversimplify or pass moral judgments, designating some past scientists as spotless heroes or infallible geniuses, and others as villains or fools. For instance, we must not gloss over Galileo's getting it all wrong in a debate over comets with the Jesuit Orazio Grassi, or Newton's fudging his calculations to achieve agreement with observations of the precession of Earth's axis. In any case, it is ideas and practices that we should hold up to present standards, not individuals. Above all, we must not imagine that our predecessors thought the way we think, only with less information.

It is Butterfield's injunction against presentism, "the study of the past with one eye, so to speak, on the present," that still represents a serious challenge to whiggish historians of science. In laying out maxims for a history of science that emphasizes its internal development, Thomas Kuhn in 1968 argued, "Insofar as possible (it is never entirely so, nor could history be written if it were), the historian should set aside the science that he knows."[2] A more uncompromising stand against using present knowledge was taken by several sociologists who studied science as a social phenomenon, including the well-known Sociology of Scientific Knowledge group at the University of Bath.

Meanwhile, whiggery in the history of science has not lacked defenders. They are found especially among those, such as Edward Harrison, Nicholas Jardine, and Ernst Mayr, who have worked as scientists. I think that this is because scientific history with an eye

Fig. 15.1. Thomas Kuhn. Photo by John Clifford Gregory.

to present knowledge is needed by scientists. We don't see our work as merely an expression of the culture of our time and place, like parliamentary democracy or Morris dancing. We see it as the latest stage in a process, extending back over millennia, of explaining the world. We derive perspective and motivation from the story of how we reached our present understanding, imperfect as that understanding remains.

Certainly, history should not ignore those influential past figures who turned out to be wrong. Otherwise, we would never be able to understand what it took to get things right. But the story makes no sense unless we recognize that some were wrong and some right, and this can be done only from the perspective of our present knowledge.

Right and wrong about what? A whig history of science that amounts just to a totting up of plus and minus scores for whatever facts that a past scientist has gotten right or wrong would not be very interesting. Much more important, it seems to me, is to trace the slow and difficult progress that has been made over the centuries in learning how to learn about the world: what sort of questions can we hope to answer, what sort of notions help us to these answers, how can we tell when an answer is correct? We can identify which historical practices set future scientists on the right path, and which old questions and methodologies had to be unlearned. This can't be done without taking account of our present understandings, painfully learned.

For an example of a whiggish judgment of the past, take the ancient fundamental question, of what substance is the world made? Much credit is often given to Democritus of Abdera, who around 400 BC proposed that matter consists of atoms, moving in the void. One of the leading universities in Greece today is named after Democritus. Yet from a modern perspective, the good guess of Democritus about atoms represented no progress in the methods of science. None of the many surviving fragments of Democritus's writings describe any observation that could suggest the existence of atoms, and there was nothing that he or anyone else in the ancient world could do with this idea to confirm that matter really does consist of atoms. Though right about matter, Democritus was wrong about how to learn about the world. In this he was not alone; no one before Aristotle seems to have understood that speculative theories about matter need to be confirmed by observation.

One's judgment of Aristotle provides a good test of one's attitude to the history of science, for Aristotle was, in a limited sense, the first scientist, and much of the subsequent history of science consisted of responses to his teaching. Aristotle argued that Earth is a sphere, not only on the theoretical grounds that this shape allows the greatest amount of the element earth to get closest to the center of the cosmos, but also on the basis of observations: the shadow of Earth on the moon during a lunar eclipse is curved, and the starry night sky changes its appearance as one travels north or south. But Aristotle's work shows no understanding that mathematics should be an important part of the study of nature. For instance, he made no attempt to use observations of the night sky at different latitudes to estimate the circumference of the Earth. His theory that the planets ride on spheres pivoted on other spheres, all with Earth at their center, agreed only qualitatively with their observed apparent motions. The failure to get quantitative agreement with observation did not bother him or many of his followers.

Mathematics began to be used constructively in scientific theories in the Hellenistic age and then in the Greek part of the Roman Empire. Around AD 150, Claudius Ptolemy put the final touches on a mathematical theory of the solar system that agreed pretty well with observation. (In the simplest version of Ptolemy's theory, planets travel along circles called epicycles, whose centers travel around larger circles that have Earth at their center.) With the benefit of present knowledge, this agreement is not surprising, because the simplest version of Ptolemy's theory gives precisely the same predictions for the apparent motions of the sun, moon, and planets as the simplest version of the later theory of Copernicus. Yet for a millennium and a half a debate persisted between followers of Ptolemy, called astronomers or mathematicians, and adherents of Aristotle, often called physicists. Ptolemy was wrong about actual motions in the solar system, but right about the need for quantitative agreement with observation.

It was one of the great achievements of the scientific revolution of the sixteenth and seventeenth centuries to work out the modern relation between mathematics and science. Mathematics was important to the Pythagoreans, but as a form of number mysticism, and to Plato, but as a model for a purely deductive science that experience has shown could never work. The modern relation between mathematics and natural science was spelled out by Christiaan Huygens in the preface to his *Treatise on Light* (1690): "There will be seen [in this book] demonstrations of those kinds which do not produce as great a certitude as those of Geometry, and which even differ much therefrom, since whereas the Geometers prove their Propositions by fixed and incontestable Principles, here the Principles are verified by the conclusions to be drawn from them; the nature of these things not allowing of this being done otherwise." The remarkable thing is not that Huygens understood this, but that, well into the seventeenth century, it still needed to be said.

Aristotle saw no need of experiment, the artificial arrangement of circumstances that are more revealing than what we encounter naturally. Presumably, he thought that there was a profound difference between the natural and the artificial, and that only the natural world was worth study. Like Plato, he thought that it was possible to understand things only when one knew their purpose. These ideas stood in the way of learning how to learn about the world.

Such judgments of Aristotle and his followers are just the sort of thing, keeping one eye on the present in studying the past, still often condemned by some historians. For instance, a distinguished historian of science, the late David Lindberg, commented, "It would be unfair and pointless to judge Aristotle's success by the degree to which he anticipated modern science (as though his goal was to answer our questions, rather than his own)." And in a revised edition of the same work: "The proper measure of a philosophical system or a scientific theory is not the degree to which it anticipated modern thought, but its degree of success in treating the philosophical and scientific problems of its own day."[3]

To me, this is nonsense. The point of science is not to answer the questions that happen to be popular in one's time, but to understand the world. Not that we know in advance what kinds of understanding are possible and satisfying. Learning this is part of the work of science. Some questions, such as "what is the world made of?" are good questions, but are asked prematurely. No one could make progress in answering this question until the advent of accurate measurements of chemical weights at the end of the eighteenth century. In the same way, the effort at the start of the twentieth century by Hendrik Lorentz and other theoretical physicists to understand the structure of the recently discovered electron was premature: no one could make progress on the electron's structure until the advent of quantum mechanics in the 1920s. Other questions, such as "what is the natural place of fire?" or "what is the purpose of the moon?" are bad in themselves, leading away from real understanding. Much of the history of science has been a matter of learning what sort of questions should and should not be asked.

I am not arguing that whig history is the only interesting sort of history of science. Even a whig historian may be interested in exploring the impact of general culture on developments in science, or vice versa, without needing to worry about the role that these developments played in the progress toward modern science. For instance, the atomic theory of Democritus offered an illustration of how the world might work without the intervention of the gods, and thereby had a great influence a century later on the Hellenistic philosopher Epicurus and later still on the Roman poet Lucretius, an influence that did not depend on whether the theory was well grounded by modern standards, which it wasn't. Likewise, you can feel the impact of the scientific revolution on general culture in the poetry of Andrew Marvell. (I am thinking particularly of his poem "The Definition of Love.") The impact also runs in the opposite direction. The sociologist Robert Merton argued that Protestantism played a major role in fostering the great scientific advances of seventeenth century England. I don't know whether that is true, but it is certainly worthy of interest.

But there is an element of whiggery even here. Why should a historian of science focus on the intellectual environment of, say, Hellenistic Greece or seventeenth-century England if it were not that something was happening then that advanced science toward the present? The history of science is not merely a tale of intellectual fashions succeeding one another without direction, but a history of progress toward truth. Though this progress was denied by Thomas Kuhn, working scientists feel it in their bones. Thus, whig history is not just one of several interesting kinds of scientific history. The evolution over many centuries of modern science is a great story, as important and interesting as anything else in the history of human civilization.

Butterfield seems to have had a sense of the legitimacy of whiggery in the history of science. In 1948 lectures at Cambridge on the history of science, he attributed an historical importance to the scientific revolution that he never granted to England's Glorious Revolution, beloved of the Whigs.[4] I found his account of the scientific revolution thoroughly whiggish, and the same impression was had by others, including A. Rupert Hall, a student of Butterfield's. Much earlier, in *The Whig Interpretation of History,* Butterfield had shown himself potentially receptive to a whig interpretation of history under some conditions. He acknowledged that if morality were "an absolute, equally binding on all places and times," then the historian "would be driven now to watch the story of men's growing consciousness of the moral order, or their gradual discovery of it." Though a devout Methodist, Butterfield did not believe that there was an absolute moral order revealed to us by history or religion or anything else. But he did not doubt that there were laws of nature, equally binding on all places and times. It is precisely the story of the growing consciousness of the laws of nature that the whig historian of physics hopes to tell, but the story cannot be told without keeping an eye on our present knowledge of this order.

Fall Semester 2016

A version of this lecture appeared in the *New York Review of Books,* 17 December 2015.

1. I follow Butterfield in capitalizing "Whig" when it refers to a political party, and leaving the *w* lowercase when referring to an intellectual tendency.

2. Thomas Kuhn, "The History of Science," in *International Encyclopedia of the Social Sciences* (New York, 1968), XIV, p. 76.

3. David C. Lindberg, *The Beginnings of Modern Science* (Chicago, 1992).

4. Herbert Butterfield, *The Origins of Modern Science* (1950; rev. edn., New York, 1957).

William T. Maud, *"A Peek at the Natives": Savage South Africa at Earl's Court. Graphic,*
24 June 1899.

16

Re-illustrating the History
of the British Empire

ANNAMARIA MOTRESCU-MAYES

The text has finally disappeared under the interpretation . . . A noble pos-terity could again misunderstand the entire past, and in so doing, per-haps, begin to make it tolerable to look at.
Friedrich Nietzsche, *Beyond Good and Evil* (1878)

It requires a significant leap of faith to assume that there are valid historical connections between a painting depicting sev-eral Caucasian women at risk of being raped, a panoply of thick tubular objects resembling burnt sugar canes, and an advertisement showing two toddlers playing with a soap bar. But when examined in the context of their specific means of production and distribu-tion, these three examples are representative of British imperial and postcolonial popular culture. Joseph Paton's painting *In Memoriam* (1858), Donald Locke's art installation *Trophies of Empire* (1972–74), and a Pears Soap advertisement made in the late 1890s show ongo-ing shifts in the visual history of the British Empire while simultane-ously challenging interpretative canons that would label such art-works as illustrations of events, beliefs, or marketing strategies.

The historian Niall Ferguson declared, in the opening address of his John Bonython lecture in 2010, "Empires on the Edge of Chaos," his fascination with Thomas Cole's *The Course of Empire* (1833–36). He said that these five large paintings are extraordinary in their de-piction of the "life cycle of an empire": the savage state, the pastoral state, the consummation of empire, the destruction of empire, and desolation. From this perspective, Cole's paintings and most other visual records representing historical events primarily function as illustrations. Indeed, historians continue to use images as factual testimonials. Ferguson did this by setting the scene for his lecture in a romanticized and predictably doomed visual historical narrative before challenging cyclical theories of historical processes and their place in the popular psyche. Most often, historians are particularly attentive to the immediate documentary merit of an image. Major publications such as *The British Empire: The Cambridge Illustrated History* (edited by P. J. Marshall, 1996), *The Oxford History of the British Empire* series (edited by Wm. Roger Louis, 1998–), *Illustrating Empire: A Visual History of British Imperialism* (edited by Ashley Jackson and David Tomkins, 2011), *Picturing the Empire: Photography and the Visualization of the British Empire* (James R. Ryan, 1997), *Visions of Empire: Patriotism, Popular Culture, and the City, 1870–1939* (Brad Beaven, 2012), *Imperialism and Popular Culture* (John M. MacKenzie, 1987), and *Exhibiting the Empire: Cultures of Display and the British Empire* (edited by John McAleer and John M. MacKenzie, 2015), to name just a few, use images as illustrations of visual constructions of British imperial narratives.

Perhaps a more rewarding method for assessing the historical relevance of imperial iconography is to consider images to be "visual manuscripts" rather than illustrations documenting British colonial culture, events, personalities, political crises, or wars. This critical perspective allows historians to explore an image not only for its immediate iconographic applicability to an historical event but also from the perspective of what the artist might have chosen to ignore or censor. This methodology offers possible answers to a core question regarding the relationship between artistic styles and ideological agendas: "Why should images be studied as reliable historical evidence, as primary research sources?"

Interpreting an image often results in either an in-depth exploration or an abrupt dismissal, a flat "no idea." Both interpretative frameworks are usually anchored in a viewer's specific visual literacy, the ability to understand complex visual conventions and to contextualize an image historically. From this perspective, visual language is like any other language: it has a distinctive "accent" (that is, cultural specificity); it develops, alters, and dies; and sometimes it is recycled within other languages. It also constantly adds to its lexicon and adjusts its grammar. For example, the racially reductive portrayal of African people in William T. Maud's *"A Peek at the Natives": Savage South Africa at Earl's Court* (1899; chapter-opening illustration) is dismissed today based on the dual assumption that it was merely representative of the late nineteenth-century popular imperial culture, and that the artist did not mean it as a caricature of his European contemporaries' racial attitudes. The image shows a Victorian family—mother holding the hand of their young son, who is dressed in a sailor costume, and father kneeling next to their daughter, who is wearing a white dress—looking at the entrance of a tent that frames the smiling faces of several African men. In the context of late nineteenth-century imperial popular culture, this image would have echoed European audiences' ideological and cultural expectations. Today, most interpretations of this image would elaborate on the intrinsic social and moral inadequacy of displaying or portraying non-European people as exotic exhibits in what the cultural historian Pascal Blanchard has justly termed "human zoos."[1]

Trophies of Empire (1972–74; plate 1), by the Guyanese artist Donald Locke, is another work that highlights some of the ways in which visual research methods can help historians decipher imperial and postcolonial representations of racial and cultural hierarchies. This artwork is exceptionally suggestive of complex racial and gender power hierarchies. At first glance, it can be described as an orderly display of black and brown cylindrical objects carefully placed in crystal, fine china, or silver chalices and candlesticks. Some of these cylindrical objects are chained to each other with metal or leather straps. The immediate and profound effect of the work on the audience establishes it as a thought-provoking "empire strikes back" visual narrative. The overriding tension in this display simultaneously bewilders the viewer and provokes interpretations that require negotiating sexual and postcolonial narratives: sadistic and emasculating stories of capture and control, implicit narratives of self-empowerment, and, finally, parodies of the all-pervading imperial fear of miscegenation.

Heralded as Locke's masterpiece, *Trophies of Empire* is an installation that fuses a particular imperial trope (non-European indigenous sexuality) with questions of trade and agricultural practices (slavery, harvesting sugar cane) and with white settlers' material culture (ornaments such as the rose glass bowl and silver jugs). The visual economy of Locke's artwork relies on his audiences reading these composite objects as phallic fetishes. With a perfect flair for metonymic effect, Locke invites us to recognize the imperial trope of colonized indigenous men, who were often portrayed as highly sexualized beings prone to dangerously crude behavior, and then to identify a more complex story line of cross-cultural, self-empowered African identities.

THE CONCEPT OF "VISUAL ECONOMY"—the interpretative frameworks within which images are evaluated, understood, and ascribed meaning and aesthetic significance—can be used to challenge conventional historical and theoretical assumptions about British colonial visual culture. See, for example, a series of small paintings made on timber boards in Tasmania in 1829–30: *Governor Arthur's Proclamation to the Aboriginal People* (plate 2). Archival records from the early 1800s indicate that indigenous Tasmanians made drawings on living tree trunks, known as dendroglyphs, to commemorate initiations or burial rites, or to mark territorial boundaries. The designs of such bark pictograms included on a few occasions representations of European oxcarts and cattle. The Tasmanian surveyor-general George Frackland noted in 1829 that he "was struck by evidence for a propensity among indigenous Tasmanians to depict events, to communicate visually."[2] Consequently, he proposed that the "real wishes" of the government and its goals for peaceful coexistence should be conveyed by similar pictorial means. The proposal was made at a time when the rapidly expanding British settlements in Van Diemen's Land (Tasmania) were being met with sustained guerrilla action by indigenous peoples in the Black War (1824–31), an ongoing conflict that led Lieutenant Governor George Arthur to declare martial law in 1828. Having secured Governor Arthur's endorsement, Frackland oversaw the production on Huon pine boards of around one hundred "proclamation boards," all representing the "cohabitation of settlers and Aboriginal people" and a common punishment for murder: hanging.[3] All hundred or so bark pictograms, of which only seven have survived, show the same sequence of events across four scenes, each drawn on a horizontal strip, as in a comic book, and each covering about a quarter of the board. The first scene depicts eight people, two races, and two genders: an indigenous man and a Caucasian man dressed identically in dark trousers and light-colored shirts, arms around each other, and each accompanied by an identical dog; two young girls, one indigenous and one Caucasian, both wearing yellow dresses; and two women, one Caucasian holding an indigenous baby, and the other an indigenous mother holding a Caucasian baby. There could hardly be a stronger example of a mirroring effect of racial and cultural equality. The second scene, drawn underneath the first vignette, shows a group of British soldiers meeting (making "first contact") with a small group of indigenous people, the latter portrayed wearing little if any clothing. The third and fourth scenes replicate the mirroring-effect narrative announced in the first scene. Life in an egalitarian society is reflected in the same punishment being meted out for the same crime: a killer being hanged, whether he used a spear or a musket to dispatch his victim. Importantly, the punitive measure is dispensed in both panels by the British military.

Art historians and conservation scientists have confirmed that these bark pictograms were probably made by convict artists using the *spolvero* technique of pricking with a pin the outlines of a drawing. The proclamation boards were attached to trees at eye level so that indigenous Tasmanians could have easy access to them—a communication strategy that shortly afterward aroused unfavorable public opinion across Van Diemen's Land. A note published in the *Hobart Colonial Times* on Friday, 5 March 1830, predicted the likely failure of the effort to achieve its goal:

> We are informed that the Government have given directions for the painting of a large number of pictures to be placed in the bush for the contemplation of the Aboriginal Inhabitants. These pictures are said to be representations of the attacks made by the black upon the white population, and in the back ground is to be seen a gallows with a black suspended; and, also the same consequence to the white man, whom in the other picture is represented as the aggressor. However praiseworthy the attempt to enlighten by any means this benighted race, we fear the causes of their hostility must be more deeply probed, or their taste as connoisseurs in paintings more clearly established, ere we can look for any beneficial result from this measure. When in the most civilized country in the world it has been found ineffective as example to hang murderers in chains, it is not to be expected a savage race will be influenced by the milder exhibition of effigy and caricature.

There are no reports whether the proclamation boards made sense to indigenous Tasmanians, who might have read the images in a manner other than left to right and top to bottom; worse, looking at the boards would have meant confronting representations of dead people—a coarse cultural blunder that violated indigenous people's avoidance practices relating to deceased members of their community.

In the absence of indigenous Tasmanian dendroglyphs, it is difficult to conclude whether there was a match or a clash between the two visual economies. Since, however, the proclamation boards were made at George Frackland's recommendation, and since he was familiar with examples of Tasmanian bark pictograms, the patterning of the proclamation boards may confirm the use of a common visual language. Ultimately, perhaps the key detail in *Governor Arthur's Proclamation to the Aboriginal People* bark paintings series is the disruptive presence of the military. Two racially and culturally

distinct communities are shown coexisting peacefully until their
first contact with European soldiers, which is followed by scenes of
killings and executions—the archetypal portrait of the savage and
pastoral stages of an empire's life cycle.

HISTORIANS OFTEN INCLUDE IMAGES in their books based on their
illustrative quality. The visual narrative is commonly highlighted
in captions that describe what the historian knew about the image
or assumed it to show. Details of architecture, landscape, and human presence can bolster the credibility of an image as a pertinent
illustration of a specific historical event. Most often, the apparent
legibility of an image masks how it was designed, distributed, and
interpreted at the time of its production. A pertinent example of
meanings clashing at the confluence of the visual narrative told by
an image and the use of the image as an illustration of a key historical event is found in Sir Joseph Noël Paton's (1821–1901) commemo-
rative painting *In Memoriam* (1858; plate 3). Reproductions of this
painting have been used many times to illustrate a crucial event during the Indian Rebellion (also known as the Indian Mutiny) of 1857.
Clustered in the center of a stone-walled basement, four women
(one is an ayah, an Indian nurse), a young girl, two toddlers, and a
baby convey recent as well as imminent agony—torn dresses, scattered gloves and hats, bare feet, strewn lace scarves, frayed clothes,
unfastened hair, cyanotic lips, and cadaverous faces—all eight characters seem frozen in a desperate, ultimate attempt to attain safety
through prayer. Moreover, the main character in Paton's painting
epitomizes the heroic British female, who defined imperial popular
culture at the time of the rebellion: holding a Bible in her left hand,
she gazes heavenward while clutching protectively the waist of a
half-undressed young woman with her right hand. A group of Scottish soldiers is shown entering the scene in the upper-left corner of
the painting, their demeanor balanced between prowling and vigilance. Their presence can be interpreted as an answer to a prayer—
the women are saved—or, less conventionally, as a sort of speech
bubble translating the women's prayers. Despite the explicit deus ex
machina visual narrative, the Highlanders' presence suggests a palpable sense of danger. They were, however, not the first men whom
Paton depicted discovering this group of distressed memsahibs.

In making *In Memoriam*, Paton chose initially to translate public horror incited by the story of what become known as the Bibighar Massacre, when Sepoys—Indian soldiers serving in the British
Army—killed over one hundred British women and children in
June 1857 at Cawnpore (Kanpur). It was not the horror of the mas-

sacre but the paralyzing terror experienced by those under siege that the painter decided to depict while evoking Christian religious rhetoric and martyrdom. Alongside the evocative title, Paton wrote a dedication—"Designed to Commemorate the Christian Heroism of the British Ladies in India during the Mutiny of 1857, and their Ultimate Deliverance by British Prowess"— and quoted Psalm 23: "Yea though I walk through the shadow of the Valley of Death, I will fear no evil, for thou art with me." When first exhibited at the Royal Academy, *In Memoriam* provoked public outrage. The critic of the *Illustrated London News* found it "too revolting for further description," adding, "It ought not to have been hung, and in justice to the hanging committee, we believe that it was not done so without considerable compunction and hesitation."[4] Yet a reviewer for the *Critic* acclaimed the painting: "[It is] one of those sacred subjects before which we stand not to criticise, but to solemnly meditate. We feel it almost a profanation to hang this picture in a show-room, it should have a chapel to itself."[5] Nevertheless, the painting was considered by many viewers at the Royal Academy in 1858 as exceedingly offensive chiefly because of a key detail in the upper-left corner of the canvas. The public's vehement indignation persuaded Paton to make some crucial visual (and historical) amendments. In the original version, "'maddened Sepoys, hot after blood," in the words of *The Times*, were bursting through the door.[6] In the revised versions, Paton painted over the Sepoys' portraits a group of Scottish soldiers—their presence indicating, by virtue of the imperial ethos, their roles as last-minute saviors of the terrified British women and children. Clearly, the mental images shared by the British public upon seeing the original version of this painting, images of white women in the grasp of indigenous soldiers, challenged long-established cultural and sexual taboos. The sense of imminent terror remains acute in the updated visual narrative, despite its having been sanitized. While the prescribed interpretation of the painting is driven by the title and agrees with the generally accepted redemptive conclusion of this traumatic historical episode, the sense of horror and looming death is not entirely canceled by the revision: the risk of being raped and killed by the Sepoys has been reassigned to the lurking and belligerent-looking Highlanders. Paton's fluctuating documentary accuracy, adjusted to match fictionalized versions of historical trauma, adds renewed controversy to the illustrative merit of his painting.

Another artist bowing to British audiences' demand for a palatable representation of imperial history befitting Victorian and late-imperial sensibilities was Felice Beato (1832–1909), who chose to painstakingly reconstruct the aftermath of a massacre for the sake of a photographic record. *Interior of the Secundra Bagh after the Slaughter of 2,000 Rebels by the 93rd Highlanders and 4th Punjab Regiment; First Attack of Sir Colin Campbell in November 1857, Lucknow* (plate 4) shows four Indian men standing or sitting among decomposing bodies and human skeletons in front of a ruined palace. It is now well known that Beato rearranged elements of the scene so that it would comport with the public's imagination of the event. But he did not change the image after the fact, as did Paton. Instead, at Beato's request, bodies of dead Sepoys were exhumed and scattered across the ground in front of the palace to give viewers a clearer sense of historical immediacy, one usually achieved when ideological and cultural expectations match convincing visual narratives.

Both Paton's painting *In Memoriam* and Beato's photograph *Interior of the Secundra Bagh* raise important questions about the methods available to historians when assessing visual domains that contribute to the study of reimagined historical, particularly imperial, collective memories. More than half a century ago, E. H. Carr announced in his George Macaulay Trevelyan Lectures, given at the University of Cambridge in 1961, "Our picture [of the immediate past] has been preselected and pre-determined for us, not so much by accident as by people who were consciously or unconsciously imbued with a particular view and thought the facts which supported that view were worth preserving."[7] Such considerations can help scholars develop a critical framework for answering such key questions as "Who has the right to speak about and on behalf of collective memories of imperial history?" "Which colonial visual tropes are best equipped for postcolonial recycling?" and "How can postcolonial iconography help rewrite imperial narratives of racial hierarchies?"

Possible answers can be found when analyzing the following two images in a framework that highlights questions of white supremacy and racial, cultural, and gender hierarchies that were often at the core of imperial civilizing programs. In particular, the theme of hygiene was used to promote colonial commercial enterprises and to commodify imperial racial stereotypes. Thus, cleanliness and whiteness were interchangeable epitomes of British (European) colonial power. The advertising of hygiene products and physical (and, by proxy, racial) purity became an imperial responsibility that was conscientiously embraced by major commercial companies such Pears Soap. For example, one Pears Soap advertisement from the late 1890s (plate 5) recalls the juxtaposed vignettes from *Governor Arthur's Proclamation to the Aboriginal People*. It shows two toddlers discovering the "miraculous" effects of skin whitening as a by-product of following basic hygiene practices. The top half of the image shows an African toddler sitting in a washtub engraved with the slogan "Matchless for the Complexion"; a Caucasian toddler, sporting a white apron, hands him a bar of soap. The bottom half of the image shows the African toddler sitting on a stool next to the washtub and looking in the small mirror held by his Caucasian friend. The new, "sanitized" image of the bather is almost complete: his entire body has acquired white skin, but his face remains black, from lack of soap use, undoubtedly. In this advertisement, the language of Victorian-era scientific racism mingles with ideas of progress and the imperial civilizing mission. A pristine white complexion was a sign of social upward mobility, high-class status, and racial supremacy. Consequently, the use of soap became an act of civic and imperial duty that eclipsed immediate sanitary, medical, or educational needs. The soap trade was promoted across the British Empire by widespread advertising campaigns that, in their rhetoric, promoted imperial ideologies of European (Caucasian) racial supremacy.

The offensive and often (inadvertent) comic effects produced by such posters advertising the imperial trade-and-civilizing mission have been recently recycled by several artists in media installations or composite artworks. Rajkamal Kahlon, for instance, reinterprets another classic Pears Soap advertisements as a caustic account of neo-imperial guilt.[8] The original colonial advertisement shows a girl teaching her younger brother how to use Pears soap for doing small loads of washing in a ceramic basin set, for his convenience, on a chair. The boy stands on a small footrest so that he can easily reach the basin. On the floor next to the chair are a jug of water and a white tablecloth. The visual narrative endorses domesticity, proper hygiene protocols, and thoughtful game-based learning. In 2012, Kahlon built on the rhetoric of this image to offer a postcolonial interpretative twist aimed at historical sanitizations of ideological narratives. She used a copy of this Pears Soap advertisement found in an issue of the *Graphic: An Illustrated Weekly Newspaper* (London) published in the late nineteenth century. After the addition of a few details in acrylic and gouache, her "advertisement" includes Osama bin Laden's decapitated head neatly resting on a plate on top of a wooden dresser, and one corner of the tablecloth on the floor is drenched in blood. Kahlon kept the original late nineteenth-century jingle used to promote Pears soap to young Victorian audiences: "This is the way we wash our hands, / Wash our hands, / Wash our hands / This is the way we wash our hands / With Pears' Soap in the morning." The unsettling satire that underwrites her recycled narrative of the original Pears Soap advertisement is a successful reminder of how imperial visual and ideological rhetoric can assist in re-evaluating British imperial cultural governance and twenty-first-century War on Terror agendas.

Comparing popular visual interpretations across time frames—for instance, in imperial and postcolonial cultures—is often as revealing as comparing divergent contemporary perspectives on a shared historical past. In *The Men Who Lost America* (2013), Andrew O'Shaughnessy challenged some of the key interpretative stereotypes still supporting common historical views of the American War of Independence. In a British Studies seminar in April 2015, O'Shaughnessy gave a brief but compelling comparison of the book covers chosen by his British and American publishers. Both include details from John Singleton Copley's life-size painting *The Siege of Gibraltar* (1783–91), but they have different, thematically driven subtitles. The U.S. edition opted for the title *The Men Who Lost America: British Leadership, the American Revolution, and the Fate of the Empire* and for a close-up of the British commander George Augustus Eliott, 1st Baron Heathfield, around whose stately equestrian portrait Copley's painting pivots (plate 6a). This cover, in O'Shaughnessy's opinion, goes against the core theme proposed in the book, and it could be interpreted as showing General Eliott in a "disdainful pose" while his subaltern stares at him distrustfully, as if saying, "Are you being serious?" A slightly different message and marketing strategy were employed by the British publisher, which chose the title *The Men Who Lost America: British Command during the Revolutionary War and the Preservation of the Empire* and an image showing the right half of Copley's painting, in which most of the British army is depicted, in O'Shaughnessy's words, as a "rugby scrum of red coats looking triumphant" (plate 6b).[9] These cropped images and subtitles reflect popular ideologies that needed to be "illustrated" for distinctive audiences, alerting them to the historical matters at hand. As a *grand finale* humorous hint, O'Shaughnessy mentioned his British publisher's verdict: "No one in Britain is interested in reading about defeat. You have to write about the victories"[10]—and the British cover image is indeed evocative of a victory, although the title announces a more complex, less laudatory historical context. In both cases, the subtitles and the carefully chosen excerpts from Copley's painting simultaneously translate and echo a dual, parallel ideological pathos: an American-centered triumphalist narrative and a diplomatically revisionist British account of the same historical event. O'Shaughnessy's short theoretical exercise in establishing a comparative framework emphasizes how important it is for historians to combine literary and visual research methods when addressing issues of national memory-building and identity-sharing modes of representation across postcolonial visual narratives.

The case studies discussed here offer just an indication of a vast amount of similarly relevant visual material and will, it is hoped, help confirm cross-disciplinary theories employed by scholars of British imperial studies when interpreting illustrations of the British Empire. This is an ongoing process of trial, error, and discovery that will ultimately test canonical interpretations of British imperial iconography. There is a long-established tradition of grappling with the multiplicity of cultural and psychological meanings generated by images and objects. In *The Principles of Psychology* (1890), William James noted, "A man has as many social selves as there are individuals who recognize him and carry an image of him in their minds."[11] When applied to British imperial studies, this truth could perhaps reveal, in a pertinent critical framework, that there are as many visual histories of the British Empire as there are scholars and audiences who visually explore it.

Fall Semester 2016

The epigraph is taken from Friedrich Nietzsche, *Beyond Good and Evil: Prelude to a Philosophy of the Future,* trans. Judith Norman, ed. Rolf-Peter Horstmann (Cambridge, 2002), p. 37.

1. The image was used as an illustration in *Exhibitions: L'Invention du Sauvage,* ed. Pascal Blanchard, Gilles Boetsch, and Nanette Jacomijn Snoep (Paris: Actes Sud, Musee du Quai Branly, 2011), p. 34.

2. Quoted in Nicholas Thomas, "Governor Arthur's Proclamation to the Aborigines," in *Artist and Empire: Facing Britain's Imperial Past,* ed. Alison Smith, David Blayney Brown, and Carol Jacobi (London: Tate Publishing, 2015), p. 177.

3. Ibid.

4. Quoted in Brian Allen, "In Memoriam," in *The Raj: India and the British, 1600–1947,* ed. C. A. Bayly (London: National Portrait Gallery Publications, 1990), p. 325.

5. Ibid.

6. Ibid.

7. E. H. Carr, *What Is History?* (1961; London: Penguin, 1990), p. 13.

8. Reproduction available on the artist's website at www.rajkamalkahlon.com/copy-of-blowback?lightbox=dataItem-ixnoa36i2.

9. Andrew O'Shaughnessy, podcast of the British Studies seminar "The Men Who Lost America", 24 Apr. 2015, http://liberalarts.utexas.edu/britishstudies/Lectures/Audio-Recordings.php.

10. Ibid.

11. William James, *The Principles of Psychology* (New York: Henry Holt, 1890), p. 294.

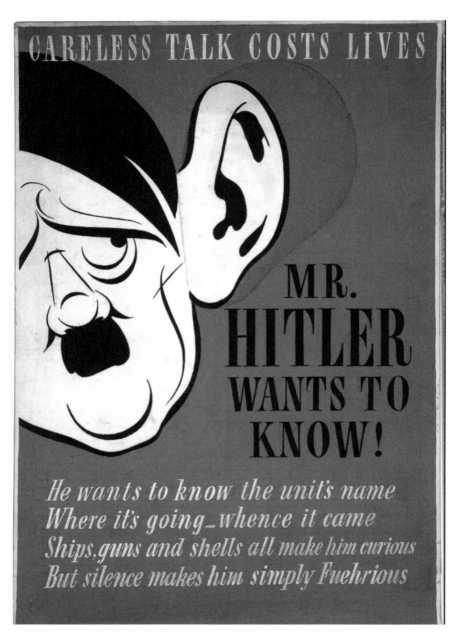

"Mr. Hitler Wants to Know!": part of the "Careless Talk Costs Lives" campaign in Britain.

17

Britain Is Your Friend: Propaganda during the Second World War

ROSEMARY HILL

In 1942, the Ministry of Food issued the Emergency Powers Defence (Food) Carrots Order. The ministry had requisitioned all carrots "grown on holdings of one acre and above" the year before, buying them at twopence per pound, and it now had a hundred thousand tons to get rid of. Before 1939 and the outbreak of war, Britain imported 70 percent of its food. Rationing was introduced in 1940, and the humble carrot, cheap and easy to grow, had many advantages. The principal difficulty was in getting people to eat them. In addition to recipes for carrot curry, carrot jam, and a nasty-sounding carrot and rutabaga juice drink called Carrolade, there were posters featuring the Ministry of Information's Doctor Carrot, an avuncular fellow in spats and a top hat carrying a medical bag labeled "vit-A." Like many wartime campaigns, it was aimed at parents, particularly mothers, with the promise of healthy food for children. The ministry also resorted to the myth that carrots make you see in the dark, an advantage during the blackouts and that, it went so far as to suggest, they were the secret of the RAF's success in nighttime raids.

The carrot campaign was one of hundreds waged throughout the war in Britain and the empire with posters, leaflets, and films. By turns advisory, exhortatory, or simply informative, they were generally more stoical than bellicose, and often humorous. David Welch's account in *Persuading the People; British Propaganda in World War Two* (2016) is based on the Central Office of Information archive in the British Library, with occasional excursions beyond it, and he considers a wide range of material. It was in the summer of 1939, when war seemed inevitable, that a propaganda strategy began to be worked out. A Chatham House report considered the possibilities and set out eighty-six ground rules. Some of them, such as the need to appeal to instinct rather than reason, and to come up with powerful slogans and repeat them relentlessly, were based on a careful reading of *Mein Kampf.* Many of the resulting catchphrases, "Make Do and Mend," "Dig for Victory," "Careless Talk Costs Lives," went into the language, though the one that is now most famous, "Keep Calm and Carry On," did not. Because that campaign was intended for use in the event of invasion, the posters were never distributed, and became widely known only when one turned up by chance in Barter Books in Northumberland in 2000.

Hitler's hints were of only limited value to Chatham House. Totalitarian states have a natural advantage in manipulating public opinion, and the British government was anxious to emphasize the difference between its own democratic constitution and the dictatorships with which it was at war. After a brief experiment with a Press and Censorship Board, the government abandoned serious efforts to control the media. Lord Reith, who was briefly minister for information, believed that the news was "the shock troops of propaganda" and that it should be as full and truthful as possible in order to be believed. This became the official position, a change of policy that left the ministry floundering, caught between press demands for information and wary defense staff refusing to give it. For some time, the department in charge of boosting public morale was, Welch points out, itself seriously demoralized. Matters improved in 1941 when Churchill's friend and fixer Brendan Bracken was put in charge. For the rest of the war, the ministry produced propaganda that for all its directness and reliance on repetition conveyed subtle messages. It was always going to be a people's war, affecting civilians as much as the military, and as Churchill warned in a speech in 1901, such wars would be "more terrible than those of kings." Coinages such as the "Home Front" and the "Kitchen Front" both acknowledged the dangers faced by the general population, and encouraged their efforts. National camaraderie was bolstered by making important figures seem ordinary—Princess Elizabeth in her Auxiliary Territorial Service uniform stripping down an engine—while ordinary people were made heroic. The fire watcher and the air-raid warden appeared on posters picked out in silhouette as guardian angels haloed by a night sky full of fire and searchlights.

Women were the specific target of numerous campaigns. As mothers and housewives, they kept the home fires burning, and according to the government pamphlet *Fifty Facts about the Women of Britain at War* (1944), in 1941–42 they picked two hundred tons of rosehips to make baby syrup. They knitted socks and, as instructed, applied "decorative patches" to holes in their families' clothes. But they were also recognized as a valuable untapped resource. Pamphlets with titles like *Eve in Overalls* urged them to take over from the men at the front as factory workers, dispatch riders, and bus drivers, and to play "the role which they deserve" in the war effort. One of the most powerful and enduring images of the war was created for this campaign. Laura Knight's oil painting *Ruby Loftus Screwing a Breech Ring*, among the largest pictures commissioned by the War Artists Advisory Committee, was shown at the Royal Academy Summer Exhibition in 1943. It was widely reproduced in newspapers, became the subject of a Paramount Newsreel, and made Ruby famous. Indeed, the propaganda aimed at getting women out of the home was so successful that after 1945 it required considerable efforts and much emphasis on the role of the "housewife" to get them to go back in again, efforts that were only ever partially successful. The Second World War, like the First, marked a permanent expansion of the possibilities open to women.

The British propaganda machine had one particular advantage over the enemy that Welch does not consider. It is surprising in such a highly illustrated book that he gives virtually no consideration to the images themselves, which owed their effectiveness in large part to the great flowering of graphic design in Britain between the wars. In 1913, Frank Pick of the newly amalgamated Underground Electric Railways Company asked the calligrapher Edward Johnston and his pupil Eric Gill to create a symbol and a typeface that would give visual identity to the unified network. The Johnston Sans lettering and red, white, and blue roundel of the London Underground marked the beginning of a golden age. As well as the precisely detailed stations, there were travel posters, which in turn influenced other kinds of advertising, notably the work commissioned by Shell Oil. By 1939, Britain had dozens of designers who knew how to convey a persuasive message in vivid and appealing imagery that was technically suitable for mass reproduction and accompanied by smart, clean lettering. One of the best was the lithographer Frank Newbould. Before the war, he supplied designs for posters encouraging people to visit Southend by rail—a scene of colorful deckchairs on the prom—or "Edgware by Tram," the latter campaign suggesting that Edgware was little changed since Dickens's day. Most popular and long remembered was the jolly fisherman being pulled along a beach by a little girl in a swimsuit over the words "Skegness is so bracing; It's quicker by rail." This graphic vocabulary translated easily into a series of war posters: "Your Britain, fight for it now." They included Alfriston Fair (a scene of swing boats and roundabouts), the South Downs, and Salisbury Cathedral, a symbol since John Constable's day of English identity enduring in the face of change.

Newbould worked as an assistant to Abram Games, one of the greatest designers of the last century, who was in charge of official posters after 1942. Games, who had produced images for London Transport and Shell in the 1930s, brought a more sternly modernist vision to his work that did not always find favor with Churchill. Games was less concerned with a bucolic past than with an idealistic future, and his images of the present, including a child with rickets, were not thought to convey a sufficiently encouraging message. By contrast, his ATS recruiting poster was altogether too encouraging, featuring such a glamorous blonde that there were worries it would attract the "wrong sort" of girl. His best designs were visual puns: a spade as a ship's prow, a vegetable garden growing into a family dinner table. The ministry's exhibition architect was another significant modernist, Misha Black, who had worked on the 1938 Modern Architectural Research Group exhibition *New Architecture*. Overall, the ministry could call on the range of British art and design at its best. Some of the strangest images were by another former London Transport artist, Walter E. Spradbery, who worked in linocut and watercolor and produced posters during the Blitz under the title "The Proud City." They were not obvious morale boosters. St Paul's surrounded by rubble could be interpreted as a symbol of defiance, but its companion, which shows the Temple Church in ruins, the oldest part all but destroyed, is dispiriting, despite the rainbow in the background. Yet it was one of the designs chosen for use abroad. With its accompanying quotation from Charles Lamb translated into Farsi, it is hard to imagine what impression it made in the Persian Gulf.

Welch observes a distinct trend in this kind of "bloody but unbowed" propaganda. Even when Britain could rely on the strength of the empire, and was indeed doing so, much of the rhetoric dwelt on standing alone. Nor, during the first years of the war, was anyone allowed to labor under the illusion that they were winning. Defeats were turned to advantage, most notably by Churchill, whose career as a broadcaster took off with the evacuation of the British Expeditionary Force from Dunkirk. Churchill appealed to those images of Metroland, seaside, and rolling downland that the war had co-opted for its own posters, promising: "We shall fight on the beaches . . . We shall fight in the fields and in the streets, we shall fight in the hills; we shall never surrender." Dunkirk and the little ships that performed the evacuation became as much a symbol of national heroism as the Battle of Britain, which was also carefully presented, Welch explains, as an exaggeratedly unequal struggle. The "few" to whom so much was owed were in fact "the world's first and only fully co-ordinated air defence system," and British aircraft production was by then greater than the Germans' by a factor of two. It seems that even a real victory had to be presented to the British as being, like Waterloo, a close-run thing.

Russia's entry into the war on the Allies' side in 1941 caused a screeching of brakes in the propaganda department. Yoked to existing mistrust of communism, the Soviet Union's pact with the Nazis had fitted an image that was easy to promote—of two brutal ideologies forming a natural alliance. Only the *Daily Worker,* which stopped criticizing Germany after the Nazi-Soviet Non-Aggression Pact in 1939, had to be suppressed by Herbert Morrison, the Home Secretary, in a rare instance of direct censorship. After 1941, it became necessary to see the Soviets as comrades in arms and to impress on the population that "Their Fight Is *Our* Fight." Stalin was transformed with only partial success into "Uncle Joe," a character who never exuded much warmth or reassurance. Welch includes an extraordinary image of the Albert Hall reconfigured as a Soviet rally, the organ obscured by a vast hammer and sickle and a headline (in Russian) reading, "Long Live the Red Army! Greetings from the British People." In 1943, Laurence Olivier, who was something of a one-man propaganda machine in the war years, helped out by starring as a Russian engineer called Ivan Kouznetsoff in the film *Demi-Paradise,* in which Kouznetsoff comes to Britain and soon settles down and makes friends.

When it came to demonizing the enemy, the approach seems to have been calibrated according to nation. Japan was unknown to most Europeans. So while detailed depictions of hand-to-hand fighting were generally avoided as being more disturbing than encouraging, Allied soldiers bayoneting combatants over the slogan "Smash the Japs" were thought to be effective. Japan could be presented as a buck-toothed bug-eyed spider whose legs spread with the rays of the rising sun to entangle Korea in its web. The Italians were, by contrast, generally fat, ridiculous, and not strikingly less appealing than Stalin. Hitler could be anything from a jolly Fougasse cartoon, eavesdropping on careless talk on the bus, to a figure like Kronos in Goya's *Saturn Devouring His Son,* with the skulls of France, Romania, Poland, Belgium, Greece, and Jugoslavia at his feet (plate 7). Yet at this darkest end of the range, where many images laid emphasis on the Nazi persecution of Christians, the Holocaust did not feature, even when the facts were known. One reason for this, Welch suggests, was that after the First World War, a population that had been fed endless stories of Hun atrocities had been disillusioned to find them exaggerated, and resented having been lied to. The other, more potent, and disturbing reason was the level of anti-Semitism in the British population. Home Intelligence Reports constantly recorded complaints about Jews controlling the black market and dodging military service. Thus, the post-war situation was the reverse of that in 1919. Only after V-E Day did the population at large begin to understand the full horror of what it had been fighting against.

Welch has a good section on propaganda for the empire, which had its own version of carrot-and-stick messages: "British Ships Guard African Shores" and "Thank You Sierra Leone" sounded the positive note. At the same time there were pamphlets explaining why German colonization would be much worse than British: "Germany would make West Africans into slaves"; "Britain is your friend and believes in progress for all." More cheerful and original were the postcards by the Egyptian cartoonist Kimon Evan Marengo, who worked as Kem. These told the story of the war in images based on the eleventh-century Iranian epic the *Shahnameh.* The three warriors who defeat the tyrant Zahhak, who is Hitler, are drawn in the style of a Persian miniature, except that on closer inspection the first has a cigar, the second a pipe, and the third a cigarette in a holder. Just recognizable as Churchill, Stalin, and Roosevelt, they have Hitler's corpse tied over the horse beside them while Goebbels is dragged along at its tail (plate 8).

Welch's survey is broad and lively; it is just a pity that he takes little interest in the imagery and the artists who created it. Not all their names can now be traced, but many can, and the style and the ethos they created says much about Britain during the war and after, when Black, Games, and some of the others went on to play an important part in designing the peace. Games created the logo of a compass with a helmeted Britannia's head for the Festival of Britain, for which Black worked on the architecture. They made good some of the promises of their propaganda as the barbed wire came off the beach at Southend and the lights went on over the Dome of Discovery.

Spring Semester 2016

Ernest Bevin, Foreign Secretary, 1945–51. *Encyclopaedia Britannica.*

18

Ernest Bevin and Palestine:
Bevingrads and Demonologies

WM. ROGER LOUIS

"Like Samson" bringing down the temple over his head to destroy the assembled Philistines, according to a critic at the time, "so Mr. Bevin, in his determination to destroy Zionism, made Britain's Palestine policy collapse into ruins."[1] The physical symbol of this failure became clear with the building of barbed-wire fences in February 1947—about halfway from the end of World War II in 1945 to the time of Israel's independence in May 1948. More precisely, it was the time when Britain handed over the Palestine issue to the United Nations. The barbed-wire enclaves were called Bevingrads, sealing off British defense zones. One of the zones in the central part of Jerusalem included the Anglo-Palestine Bank building and the central post office. The police conducted body searches of those wanting to enter the fenced areas. The British Army remained an efficient fighting force, but the Bevingrads in fact became internment camps for British soldiers and policemen, who were permitted to leave only when on duty. Ironically, the British were prisoners in the mandated territory they had ruled since World War I.

My question is, how can the era of the Labour government be reassessed to judge the extent to which Ernest Bevin can be held responsible—or for that matter, the extent to which any one person can be held accountable, from both the British and Zionist perspectives—for such a complex British catastrophe as the end of the Palestine mandate? How did the Zionists gradually shape a considered view of Bevin? What was the reaction of his colleagues in the British government to him at the time? And what of the way in which he was regarded in the wider circles of Parliament and the British public?

Above all, what was Bevin's ultimate aim? Here I take account of not only Zionist assessments at the time but also those of Bevin's critics in England, of whom Richard Crossman was foremost. Crossman was the leading British Zionist, famous as a backbencher of the Labour Party, later as leader of the House of Commons, and subsequently as editor of the *New Statesman*. He is remembered today mainly for his *Diaries of a Cabinet Minister,* which revealed the inner workings of the British government. During World War II, he served in the Allied Expeditionary Force and was one of the first British officers to enter the Dachau concentration camp in the spring of 1945. Later that same year, Bevin nominated him as a member of the Anglo-American Committee of Inquiry on Palestine. He never subsequently forgave Crossman for the "stab in the back" (Bevin's own phrase) betraying not only Bevin himself but also the Prime Minister, C. R. Attlee. Crossman became known as "the man who stabbed Ernie Bevin in the back." It is of paramount interest that he wrote later of Attlee and Bevin: "Clement Attlee and Ernest Bevin plotted to destroy the Jews in Palestine and then encouraged the Arabs to murder the lot. I fought them at the time as murderers . . . [and] for genocide."[2] Crossman wrote only a half-dozen years after the creation of the Jewish state.

During the early part of World War II, in January 1941, Chaim Weizmann and others believed that Bevin had an open mind and was favorably disposed toward the Jewish cause. Bevin was then Minister of Labour. The minutes of a meeting of the Jewish Agency in London record Weizmann as saying that "he had a great belief in Mr. Bevin who was open-minded and energetic."[3] Yet a few weeks later, Bevin had acquired a guarded attitude. He said that "personally" he would like to see the Jewish people firmly established in Palestine, but he now seemed to be preoccupied with "another important factor in the situation—the Arab factor." In view of the German danger to Egypt as well as Britain in 1941, the British, in Bevin's own words, "could not afford to do anything which might make our relations with the Arab countries more difficult."[4]

No one in the early part of the war would have guessed that Bevin would become Foreign Secretary in 1945, or that he would be

Fig. 18.1. Richard Crossman, 1936. © National Portrait Gallery, London.

remembered in England as a powerful political personality comparable to Lords Castlereagh, Palmerston, Salisbury, and Sir Edward
Grey. No one during the war could have predicted Bevin's part in
the Palestine controversy. Yet as prelude, the wartime conversations
are of interest not only because of the indications of Bevin's future
thought but also because there is evidence that the Zionist leaders
were already wary of Harold Beeley, later to become Bevin's right-
hand man. Beeley during the war worked at Chatham House under
Arnold Toynbee (who was himself a significant anti-Zionist). Beeley
was known already to have an anti-Zionist reputation, but those on
the Jewish Executive Committee debated whether it would be useful
to make contact or run the risk "antagonizing" him further. Again,
no one would have supposed that Beeley would eventually play such
a prominent part in Palestine's future—in the view of some Zionists,
a diabolical part.

There were two sets of demonologies. One was the Zionist, in
which Bevin came to rank only a few rungs below Hitler; and the
other, the British, in which, from Bevin's vantage point, the diabolical

Fig. 18.2. Chaim Weizmann, 1949. National Photograph Collection of Israel, Photography Department, Government Press Office, digital ID D670-0293.

work had been done by A. J. Balfour in 1917. Bevin is on record as saying that the Balfour Declaration was the greatest mistake in Britain's imperial history. Whenever it came up in conversation with Zionists, he would dismiss it simply as a power-politics statement made to rally Jews in Europe and America to help Britain at a critical time during the war. He probably underestimated the commitment by Balfour and others at the time to the Jewish cause, but he certainly would have been aware of the steadfast dedication of Balfour's niece, Blanche "Baffy" Dugdale, who served on the Jewish Executive Committee up to the time of the founding of the Jewish state. She moved in high circles and had contact with key politicians. As Balfour's niece, she symbolically represented the continuity of British Zionist alignment since World War I.

Under the leadership of Chaim Weizmann, Baffy Dugdale worked with Lewis Namier, the historian; Ivor Linton, who later became an Israeli diplomat; and others in the headquarters of the Jewish Executive Committee in Great Russell Street, not far from the British Museum. Baffy was Balfour's biographer as well as his niece. She is of interest moreover because of her extensive friendships with anti-Zionists and Zionists, including Walter Elliot, the Secretary of State for Scotland before World War II, who confided to Baffy secrets of the British government at the highest level. Other friends included Sir Reginald Coupland, the historian of the empire and commonwealth at Oxford. Baffy was always part of Weizmann's inner circle. Moreover, she had a lasting friendship with David Ben-Gurion despite the friction with Weizmann and their later break. With Ben-Gurion, Baffy shared a lasting interest in classical Greek literature, especially Plato. She believed that statesmanship on the model of her uncle's was essential for a unified movement for a Jewish state. She thus despaired of the factions, disagreements, and open controversies among Zionists in England, America, and Palestine. She believed that only Weizmann's intelligence and foresight could prove effective against Bevin, whom she held in warm contempt even as she recognized his authority and persistence in trying to block Zionist aims in Palestine.

The cumulative historical knowledge of the Jewish Executive Committee in London and their friends more than matched that of officials in the Colonial Office and Foreign Office, in part because Reginald Coupland had been the mastermind of the report by the 1937 Royal Commission on Palestine, which recommended partition. The breadth of Coupland's cultural and religious as well as historical knowledge was clear on every page of the report. The other historical document on which everyone focused attention was the famous (or infamous) White Paper of 1939, which severely limited the immigration of Jews to Palestine at the time of their greatest need, and proposed an Arab-Jewish state in which the Jews would always be a minority. The White Paper acquired notoriety for, among other reasons, Ben-Gurion's famous exclamation, "We shall fight the War as if there was no White Paper, and the White Paper, as if there was no War." Yet whenever the White Paper was mentioned in Zionist discussions with Ernest Bevin, he would simply dismiss it, invariably saying that he wanted to find a solution to post-1945 problems, not those from 1939.

Bevin was the architect of Britain's post-war Palestine policy. He dominated the Cabinet of the Labour government. The power of his intellect as well as his domineering manner was well conveyed by Roy Jenkins when he wrote that the Prime Minister, usually a stern taskmaster, allowed Bevin to have his way in Cabinet discussions but denied the privilege to anyone else. Once when the drift of discussion seemed to be going in the opposite direction from his own views, Bevin interrupted and said, "That won't do Prime Minister. . .

it don't fit in with my policy." Jenkins goes on to describe how Bevin "stopped the engine in its tracks, lifted it up, and put it back facing the other direction."[5] No one else could have done it. The core of his thought on Palestine was that the solution to the problems arising from the Holocaust should be resolved by reintegrating the Jews into European society rather than encouraging mass immigration to Palestine. In the post-Holocaust circumstances of 1945, such a view from the Jewish perspective was unspeakable. There were from the outset two virtually irreconcilable positions.

Churchill referred to Bevin as "a working class John Bull." As patriots, the two shared common characteristics. Churchill was a Zionist, though his commitment varied. He was well disposed toward Weizmann. During the war, he set up a highly secret committee to further the Zionist cause. But toward the end of the war, everything changed. One of Churchill's close friends was Lord Moyne, who held the position of Minister Resident in the Middle East. In November 1944, he was assassinated by the Jewish militant group Lehi, known to the British as the Stern Gang. Churchill's attitude toward a possible Jewish state changed immediately. He became less than lukewarm in support of the Zionist cause. To Weizmann, the assassination was a catastrophe. Churchill had lent invaluable support. But he now became more critical of Bevin, deploring the loss of British "blood and treasure," just as Bevin became emotionally distraught when speaking of British working-class soldiers in Palestine. "I cannot bear *English Tommies* being killed . . . They belong to my class. They are my people."

Bevin at first was confident that he could resolve the Palestine problem, making the extravagant statement that he would pin his career on it. He acquiesced in the American proposal for a Committee of Inquiry, in the belief that it would conclude that Palestine was essentially an Arab country. It would be a country in which Jews and Arabs could eventually live in harmony, though with the Jews as a permanent minority. There would be Jewish and Arab provinces in a federal structure. Instead, the committee recommended not only partition but also the immediate admission of 100,000 Jews, as President Harry S. Truman had already proposed. Bevin and Attlee believed that Crossman as a member of committee had played a critical part in tilting the commission toward a solution at absolute variance with British interests in the Middle East.

BEVIN'S GENERAL AIM, AS DISTINCT from his ideas about Palestine, was to develop the Middle East and Africa in a way that would to enable Britain to remain one of the Big Three with the United

States and the Soviet Union. With the support of the Arab states, the Middle East would replace India as Britain's source of strength, especially in oil. Britain could fend off the danger of the United States reducing Britain to the status of a vassal. American economic assistance was vital to post-war recovery, but on this point there was no love lost between the two countries. To achieve their aims, the British would have to do no less than reconstruct the British Empire on the basis of equal partnership between the British and the Arabs. Palestine was the stumbling block. It led Bevin to say to Weizmann that if the Jews wanted a fight, they could have one. In response to Bevin's first major speech in Parliament on Palestine, Weizmann called it "brutal, vulgar and anti-Semitic." At another time, Bevin uttered his unfortunate phrase about the Jews wanting to get to the head of the queue. Weizmann parried with a comment that was emotionally moving: Jews had held high priority in the queues leading to the crematoria of Auschwitz and Treblinka.

By the autumn and fall of 1945, the first stage of Zionist demonology had crystallized. Yet there was still considerable speculation about Bevin's personality and his general ideas about Palestine. The Zionists believed him to be ignorant, incoherent, and perhaps a captive of what was called the "Foreign Office Gestapo." The perception of Bevin as illiterate and confused was a misconception. With his working-class background, he was certainly not as articulate as the leaders of the Zionist movement or the Foreign Office officials who had gone to Oxford or Cambridge. Yet he not only mastered his briefs. He also had his own independent and original ideas. He once commented, without bragging but simply making a point, that he was one in a million—but it did not prevent him from making errors of judgment. One was his statement that he knew why President Truman insisted on the admission of 100,000 Jews to Palestine: it was because there were already too many of them in New York. There was an element of black humor and occasional bursts of anger, though his loss of temper was usually exaggerated.

Palestine was not one of Bevin's priorities, nor did he want it to be. But in July 1946 he faced the blowing up of the King David Hotel. From the British vantage point, it was a major act of terrorism, though of course one man's terrorist is another's freedom fighter. Chaim Weizmann responded immediately by saying that it represented a catastrophe and would have incalculable effects on the British military and civilian administration in Palestine well as on the government in London. He was certainly right. Almost immediately, General Evelyn Barker, the officer commanding in Palestine, declared that British troops were to have no social relations with the Jewish community and, in a famous comment, said that "*We will be punishing the Jews in a way the race dislikes as much as any, by striking at their pockets and showing our contempt of them.*" On the Zionist side, Weizmann for one believed that the King David explosion signified that the movement for a Jewish state was spiraling into "violence and gangsterism."

In December 1946, Weizmann was replaced by David Ben-Gurion, a development regarded by the British as carrying with it yet more activism and probable terrorism. Bevin was already thinking that a solution might be found at the United Nations. The rationale was that the moral and political authority of the U.N. would strengthen the British position, assuming that the majority of the fifty-seven members would recognize that Palestine was essentially an Arab country and that any lasting solution would have to be acceptable to the Arabs.

In February 1947—the same month as the building of the barbed-wire Bevingrads—Bevin announced in Parliament that Britain would look to the United Nations. Curiously enough, both the British and the Zionists were optimistic. Harold Beeley calculated that the Arab states would support a proposal for a strengthened British trusteeship regime and, with it, the plan for a binational state. Weizmann, with reduced institutional authority but still with immense influence, believed that the Zionist cause at the U.N. might emerge triumphant. One development seemed especially encouraging. Sumner Welles, who had served as Roosevelt's Under-Secretary of State until 1942, volunteered to help. He had long experience in Latin America and knew personally many of the ambassadors to the United Nations. The mobilizing of the Latin American delegates in November 1947 was one of the essential reasons for the eventual vote in favor of partition.

February 1947 was a point of climax. Bevin had to take decisions against the background of the great emotional debate about India, the collapse of new defense arrangement with Egypt, a sense of impending economic disaster in Britain, and one of the worst winters in British history. At one point during a meeting with a Zionist delegation, the lights in the Foreign Office went out, but Bevin said, not to worry, "we have the Israe*lites* with us." He argued the case relentlessly in the discussions of the Cabinet. He emphasized the repercussions of partition on the Arab states. The loss of Arab goodwill would mean the elimination of British influence from the Middle East to the advantage of Russia, which in turn would weaken the position of Britain and the British Commonwealth in the world.

There was also the dimension of the United Nations, where a

showdown could not be avoided, because of the indeterminate status of the mandate in international law. Bevin and, most particularly, Harold Beeley, who prepared the detailed case, did not want to be held responsible in Arab eyes for a policy of partition. By taking the question to the U.N., the British would appear to assume an impartial position while in fact allowing the pro-Arab majority of the General Assembly to decide the issue for them, or so they hoped.

As late as February 1947, despite renewed outbreaks of terrorism and virtual civil war, Bevin considered but rejected, with a ring of confidence, the possibility of evacuation. He did not wish to leave the Arabs, the Jews, the Americans, and the United Nations, he said, stewing in their own juices. Striking a note of defiance, Bevin said that the British would go to the U.N. to rally support, *not* to surrender the mandate.

Against the background of a rising danger of anti-Jewish sentiment in England because of terrorist attacks on British troops, and increasingly virulent anti-British sentiment in New York, the tension between the British and the Zionists reached new heights. In July 1947, the Irgun hanged two British sergeants and placed booby traps on their bodies. They became martyrs. Bevin told the U.S. Secretary of State, General George Marshall, that the executions would never be forgotten, and that "anti-Jewish feeling in England now was greater than it had been in a hundred years." The Zionists also had symbolic figures, and they appealed to a much greater public conscience. In the same month, British authorities turned away some 4,500 Jewish refugees aboard the *Exodus*. In one of his "black rages," Bevin decided "to teach the Jews a lesson." The passengers aboard the *Exodus* would be returned to their port of embarkation in France. As it transpired, the Jews refused to disembark. Bevin, blundering from one position to another, wound up sending the survivors of the Nazi murder camps back to Germany.

When the members of the U.N. Special Committee on Palestine visited Palestine in the summer of 1947, they found the British community in a stage of siege. Wives and children had been evacuated. The number of British police and military forces, together with contingents of the Arab Legion, rivaled the symbolic figure of the 100,000 Jewish refugees who were still interned in European displaced person camps. The U.N. committee observed the Bevingrads, where British personnel were bivouacked behind barbed wire. One-tenth of the armed forces of the entire British Empire occupied a territory the size of Wales.

There was one soldier for every eighteen inhabitants in the country, or, as one observer calculated, one for every city block.

The drain on the economy for military upkeep alone amounted to close to £40 million a year to an England still on wartime rations. Churchill directed questions to Bevin in Parliament: "There is the manpower of at least 100,000 men in Palestine who might well be at home strengthening our depleted industry. What are they doing there? What good are we getting out of it?" When Britain moved into a severe economic crisis in 1947, a broad consensus of public, parliamentary, and Cabinet opinion held that military withdrawal was an economic as well as a political and ethical imperative.

The general crystallization of British sentiment in favor of withdrawal did not necessarily contradict the Foreign Office's hope, Harold Beeley's hope in particular, of preserving Britain's political and strategic position by relying on probable action by the United Nations. This was a rational and, indeed, ingenious calculation, as the Zionists at the time recognized. It was based on the assumption that even biased or obtuse observers would not endorse partition, because the creation of a Jewish state would precipitate full-scale civil war—in fact, an international war.

Bevin assumed that the Soviet Union and the United States on this issue, as on others, would gravitate into opposite camps. He hoped that the United Nations would support an independent binational state in which Jewish rights would be guaranteed and the promise of a national home more or less fulfilled. As it turned out, the British merely reconfirmed that the United Nations did not operate on British rational assumptions.

The struggle for the Jewish state, as Bevin was beginning to discover, was fueled not only by a sense of historical necessity in the wake of the Holocaust, but also by genuine humanitarian sentiment as well as worldwide animosity to British imperialism. Anticolonialism, as it has been traditionally understood, was a conspicuous force in the summer and autumn of 1947. The opportunity to disrupt the British Empire in the Middle East certainly helps explain Soviet motivation. All these developments triggered the British decision in September 1947 to evacuate.

In England, a certain current of public protest was guided by Richard Crossman, who was then assistant editor of the *New Statesman* as well as a Member of Parliament. He expressed revulsion against suppressing a people who had suffered unspeakable atrocities under the Nazis. All this was occurring when the British feared the impending collapse of their economy. Decisions on Palestine were being made during a time of underlying economic anxiety, which thus provides a key to the mood of September 1947. By then, even Bevin had concluded that the only way to resolve the international, local, and metropolitan tensions was to evacuate Palestine—evacuation pure and simple.

In the critical Cabinet meeting, Bevin reemphasized that Palestine was a heavy drain on British resources and was creating a dangerous spirit of anti-Semitism in Britain. He believed that the date for the withdrawal of British administration and British forces should be announced as soon as possible. Only by imposing a definite time limit would there be any hope of forcing the Arabs and Jews to make arrangements for their own political future, as had been proved in the analogous case of India. The Indian solution thus played a prominent part in the decision and was duly applied to Palestine, with similar bloody results, only on a smaller scale.

After September 1947, the influence of the British diminished. They stayed on for some eight months, until the expiration of the mandate at midnight on 14–15 May 1948. When the Union Jack was hauled down for the last time in Jerusalem, there were memorable episodes, such as the singing of "Auld Lang Syne" as well as "God Save the King." But the termination of the mandate from Ernest Bevin's point of view was only part of the story. The paramount aim was to remain on good terms with the Arabs as well as the Americans. The British could not do so as long as Palestine continued to poison the atmosphere. Arab nationalism, frustrated in Palestine, could not be appeased. It was the American failure, in Bevin's eyes, to curb militant Zionism that was at the heart of the trouble.

BEFORE THE HISTORIC VOTE by the United Nations in favor of partition on 9 November 1947, Ernest Bevin wrote a letter in which he expressed the belief that the Jewish state would eventually become communist: "Partition would suit them [the Russians] as a principle . . . Stalin would have no compunction at all in exploiting these nationalities to achieve his object by means of a whole series which Russia could control." On another occasion, Bevin used the phrase "international Jewry," with its connotation of conspiracy, as an explanation of what had gone wrong. He reinforced his belief that the Jews might be fitting into Stalin's plan for eventually absorbing Jewish Palestine into the system of Soviet satellites. His ideas on this subject were not idiosyncratic. British apprehensions about the Jews and communism can be traced to the time of the Russian Revolution in 1917. Stereotyped ideas, absurd as they may seem in retrospect, help explain Bevin's attitude toward the Zionists in 1947–48. Later, during the 1948 war, Czechoslovakia supplied arms and ammunition to the Jews. British intelligence reports indicated that refugees from Eastern Europe included indoctrinated communists. Bevin's attitude and his suspicions, though misguided in retrospect, were at least comprehensible.

He tried to influence other territorial outcomes of the struggle on two occasions. In early 1948 he encouraged King Abdullah of Jordan to take over most of "Arab Palestine." He said, "It seems to obvious thing to do," and then repeated to Abdullah, "It seems the obvious thing to do, but do not go and invade the areas allotted to the Jews' under the United Nations partition plan." His plan consisted of reducing the Jewish part of Palestine to a rump state, which would at least be acceptable, he hoped, to the Arabs. Again, an understandable hope, but also, once again, a miscalculation of the Arab response.

On the eve of the Arab-Israeli war of 1948–49, no one, including Bevin, anticipated the extent of the Arab collapse and the Israeli victory. The British associated themselves with the Arab cause as one that would be ultimately compatible with their own sense of purpose and mission in the Middle East. During the course of the war, Bevin became convinced that a grave injustice was being perpetrated because of U.S. support of the Israelis. The Americans were responsible for the creation of a "gangster state" headed, in the words of a prominent Foreign Office official, by "an utterly unscrupulous set of leaders." Bevin had to recognize that the Israelis held frontiers that they had the military capability to defend. He believed that the United States would refuse to rein in militant Zionism, but he could not neglect the overriding importance of retaining American goodwill. The only way to prevent Israel from establishing its own frontiers would be by British intervention, which Parliament and public world not tolerate.

Bevin's exasperation can be summed up in his own words about the American attitude toward the new state, which continued to build up in the course of the war of 1948–49: "Let there be an Israel and to hell with the consequences"—and "peace at any price, and Jewish expansion whatever the consequences."[6]

What about Richard Crossman's allegation that Bevin and Attlee plotted to destroy the Jews in Palestine and encourage the Arabs to murder the lot? Crossman actually used the word "genocide." There is no evidence for any of this. It reflects on Crossman himself, his enjoyment in stirring up controversy for the sake of controversy, shock for the sake of shock. Crossman was Britain's pre-eminent Zionist, but this episode reflects poorly on him.

In recent years my assessment of Bevin has shifted, in part because of the cumulative evidence of his anti-Jewish attitude. Some of his closest associates believed he had crossed the line. The Under-Secretary at the Foreign Office wrote in May 1948, the day or so after Israeli independence:

> I must make a note about Ernest's anti-Semitism, which has come out increasingly sharply these past few weeks, with the appalling crisis in Palestine. There is no doubt, to my mind, that Ernest [Bevin] detests Jews. . . . He says they taught Hitler the technique of terror—and were even now paralleling the Nazis in Palestine. They were preachers of violence and war—What could you expect [in Palestine]?

Bevin uttered such thoughts when he was angry. But, again, there is no evidence along the lines suggested by Richard Crossman. I do not believe that Bevin as an anti-Semite. But he said many things that made others think that he was. He was simply—passionately—anti-Zionist.

How does one square the circle with Bevin, who created the North Atlantic alliance, who stands as one of the great Foreign Secretaries in British history, and who was beloved in the Foreign Office? Or Clement Attlee saying late in life that the man he missed most was Ernest Bevin, a man of integrity and principle?

In the case of Palestine, I believe it helps to remember that the positions of Bevin and Weizmann were irreconcilable. It took time for both of them to realize that there could be no compromise, but they entirely understood each other. Bevin was committed to maintaining as much friendship with the Arab states as possible. Palestine was the barrier. Thus his frustration and anger.

Weizmann, Ben-Gurion, and others knew that Bevin would keep the Jewish state as small as possible in order to make is acceptable to the Arabs. Thus his agreement with King Abdullah that Jordan should invade Palestine and occupy all areas that were not heavily populated by Jews. It was clear that Bevin would go as far as he could to keep Israel reduced to a rump state, a small territory along the shore of the Mediterranean.

Weizmann believed that by the spring and summer of 1948, Bevin had descended from being anti-Jewish to becoming an anti-Semite. Bevin believed that the new state of Israel was ruled by a set of anti-British gangsters calling themselves Zionists or Israelis. These are judgments engraved in history. At least we now have the historical perspective to understand them. The outcome was a triumph for Weizmann and Ben-Gurion, but on the British side there was a divided outlook. It was a defeat for Bevin and his view that the Jews should be reintegrated into Europe rather than allowed to create a state in the Middle East. On the other hand, it was a victory for the ghost of A. J. Balfour and his niece Baffy, who lived to the very day of Israeli independence.

Spring Semester 2017

1. Arthur Koestler, *Promise and Fulfillment: Palestine, 1917–1949* (London, 1949).

2. Janet Morgan, ed., *The Backbench Diaries of Richard Crossman* (London, 1981), p. 326.

3. Minutes of the Jewish Agency Executive Meeting, 8 Jan. 1941, Weizmann Archive.

4. "Report of Interview with The Right Hon. Ernest Bevin," Secret, 28 Jan. 1941, Weizmann Archive.

5. Roy Jenkins, *Nine Men of Power* (London, 1974), p. 68.

6. Bevin to Franks (draft), 3 Feb. 1949, FO 371/75337.

Mahmoud Abu Al-Fath, Egyptian journalist, politician, and businessman. *Al Ahram Weekly Online.*

19

Britain's Egyptian Allies
and the Suez Crisis

BARNABY CROWCROFT

In the short, unhappy life of America's imperial moment in the
Middle East, in the opening years of this century, the figure of
Ahmad Chalabi remains one of the bitterest memories. Chalabi
had been an almost fifty-year exile from Iraq, forced from the country following the 1958 revolution against its Hashemite monarchy. A
Western-educated banker and politician, Chalabi was a man driven
throughout his career by a single overriding goal, to change the regime in Iraq. In the obituaries crowing over his death, in November 2015, he was the "archetype of the shady exile on the payroll of
foreign powers." He was a "masterful manipulator" who duped an
inexperienced and hubristic American president into a disastrous
intervention in the cauldron of the Middle East. He was, as a biographer titled his life, "the man who pushed America to war."[1]

In the aftermath of the venture that marked the end of Britain's
rather longer imperial moment in the Middle East, in the late 1950s,
some British officials wrote in a remarkably similar vein about a remarkably similar-sounding figure. Mahmoud Abu Al-Fath was a
veteran Egyptian journalist, businessman, and politician. Following the revolution that overthrew Egypt's monarchy, in 1952, he was
also a prominent globe-trotting exile. He was a man of charm and
intelligence, and in the course of a long and varied life, he amassed
a great deal of money and lived in considerable style. He was the

friend of the conservative Right of the British political establishment, and for some years sent letters and analyses of Egyptian politics to both Britain's prime minister and the American president.

At the height of the crisis over Egyptian President Gamal Abdel Nasser's nationalization of the Suez Canal, in August 1956, Abu Al-Fath informed both Western leaders that whatever the current picture prevailing in world media and public opinion, "Egyptians had a different perspective." "They view the Suez crisis," he wrote, "as an unexpected, blessed event, which might cause their liberation from Nasser's dictatorship, and save the Arab world from communism." The British saber rattling and military buildup, he said, was neither ill advised nor an overreaction; it was actually having an excellent impact in Egypt. It had inspired all opponents of Nasser to come out into the open for the first time, in anticipation of the approaching end of his political career. A forceful response in the months to come would "encourage all good elements, not only in Egypt, but throughout the Middle East."[2] Through the summer of 1956, Abu Al-Fath lobbied, cajoled, implored, and eventually persuaded. He was, a British diplomat in the Cairo embassy wrote, bitterly, after the episode's dramatic denouement, "an unprincipled filibuster"; a man "willing to cooperate with anyone irrespective of ability, affiliation or character" in the pursuit of his own ends, which were "largely financial."[3] Mahmoud Abu Al-Fath was the man who pushed Britain to war in 1956.

The Suez crisis is one of the best-trodden patches of post-war British history. In addition to day-by-day accounts of the crisis and the ensuing invasion of Egypt, we have wide-ranging studies of Suez and, for example, the mass media, the intelligence services, the civil service, the universities, and even cartoonists. We know about its impact on the United Nations, the Commonwealth, Europe, the special relationship, and the Cold War. The experiences of the United States, Israel, and France in the crisis have likewise been the subject of extensive scholarly investigation and revision. Keith Kyle, someone who did much to uncover some of the Suez Crisis's most persistent mysteries, concluded some two decades ago: "There is not much that is not known by now about what happened at Suez."[4]

For all this, we continue to know remarkably little about the experience of the country that was at the heart of the whole affair: Egypt. Egyptian archives for the period of the crisis are not open. The standard works of reference on the event in Egypt, moreover, remain those written by President Nasser's speechwriter and confidant, Mohamed Heikal. It is therefore perhaps unsurprising that the conventional account of Egypt's experience of the crisis, sixty years on, remains largely that which was provided by the Egyptian leadership at the time. This version portrayed the Suez crisis as a pivotal step in Egypt's long-standing struggle for national independence. It was the moment when President Nasser "personally embodied his country's identity" and rallied nationalist resistance against attempted imperialist domination. Nasser's leadership in the crisis "restored the dignity" and the "lost pride" of "individual Arabs everywhere" after decades of foreign rule and humiliation. Suez was the moment when Egypt finally avenged the crimes of generations of British colonialism. In such a context, Mahmoud Abu Al-Fath seems an incongruous figure indeed. We may even be inclined to conclude—as did an Egyptian state prosecutor summing up in a show trial of some of Abu Al-Fath's acquaintances a year after the crisis—that Egyptians who plotted against Nasser were simply "imperialist agents and hirelings" involved in a "conspiracy against Egypt."[5]

The problem with this account, however, is that over the past decade, a growing body of evidence has suggested that Mahmoud Abu Al-Fath was just one of a surprisingly wide range of Egyptian participants in the genesis of the Suez crisis. The Egyptians involved in a "conspiracy against Egypt" seem to have included a broad spectrum of people: politicians, businessmen, journalists, civil servants, religious activists, military officers, and members of Egypt's royal family in exile. Indeed, the range and diversity of these participants has increasingly prompted the question of what on earth they were doing, to end up ranged against the Arab world's most charismatic national leader and at least tacitly on the side of the "West's leading colonialist," Anthony Eden. Are we looking at the case of dozens of self-serving and unprincipled Chalabi-like figures? What we are to make of Britain's "Egyptian allies" in the Suez crisis?

THE SUEZ CRISIS BEGAN WHEN President Gamal Abdel Nasser nationalized the Suez Canal Company, on 26 July 1956. Britain's Prime Minister, Sir Anthony Eden, and much of the British government were outraged by the prospect of Egypt's military ruler controlling this strategic artery of the British Empire. American pressure and British military unpreparedness, however, prevented Eden from launching the immediate counterstrike he desired, leading to months of intense diplomatic activity in search of a negotiated international settlement. When Nasser rejected any international arrangement for the future of the canal, Eden was left under increasing domestic pressure to achieve a result by force, even as the permissive climate for military action receded. In October, Eden's French counterpart, Guy Mollet, proposed that a secret agreement be reached with Israel whereby Israeli forces would invade the Sinai Peninsula, justifying an Anglo-French police action to separate the two forces and protect the canal. This collusion enabled Britain to launch the military campaign that its armed forces had now been long preparing, on 1 November. But this "Tripartite Aggression," as it became known in the Arab world, took place in circumstances that few had imagined in July, and with results that even fewer could have foreseen.

From the outset of the Suez crisis, the underlying British aim was what we would now call "regime change." In the first meeting of the inner war cabinet, the Egypt Committee, the day after the nationalization, it was agreed that while Britain's "ultimate purpose" was to restore the canal to international control, its "immediate objective" was to "bring about the overthrow of the present Egyptian government." Or as Eden put it to President Eisenhower, "the removal of Nasser and the installation in Egypt of a regime less hostile to the West."[6] The British government and armed forces were equally adamant that there was no possibility of Britain acting as an occupying force in Egypt following an invasion, something inconceivable in the changed world of the 1950s. Egypt had to be restored to Egyptian control within a matter of days. The ability to find a willing and able successor government to step in was therefore a linchpin to the success of the Suez operation from the beginning.

This dimension of the crisis has been one of its most enduring mysteries and has left the historiography with something of a puzzle. Despite knowing that the military action was always about regime change in Egypt, we have been considerably in the dark about what exactly was envisaged in its place. For many, the regime change element of the crisis has been a central charge for the almost criminal irresponsibility of Eden's leadership: the Prime Minister simply "wanted Nasser murdered," as one of his junior ministers later wrote, did not want an alternative government in Egypt, and really did not "give a damn if there [was] anarchy and chaos" in the country after Nasser's demise.[7]

The post-war planning process for the Suez operation and the prospective new regime in post-Nasser Egypt was, without doubt, a shambolic affair. A number of studies have shown how this element of the post-war planning was effectively outsourced to a collection of British political mavericks, such as the Conservative Member of Parliament Julian Amery and other Tory diehards with one foot in the secret services, who used their personal contacts to link up British officials with the anti-Nasser Egyptian opposition forces. As a senior MI6 operative caustically recalled of the process, former

World War II special operatives flocked into Whitehall with news of plots and conspiracies, all "rather too puffy of face and corpulent of body to play wistful roles," but who nonetheless enjoyed the chance to share old war stories and sport their DSOs, MCs, and Croix de Guerre: "The play not the reality was the thing."[8] The post-war planning for the Suez crisis has therefore taken on the air of comic opera rather than that of serious and meaningful planning for a major political-military intervention. There really was no serious alternative to Nasser.

The records, however, suggest another way of interpreting all this. The inattention to this dimension of the operation reflected not crisis or desperation in the British establishment, but confidence. There was no "blueprint" for a post-Nasser government by design, not by inability, because senior officials specifically forbade its creation. The chief architects of the Suez operation perceived there to be so many options in Egypt that there was no need to limit Britain's ability to respond to events on the ground, and because if word got around that Britain was favoring one candidate, that man's position would be considerably undermined as the imperialist stooge installed at the point of British bayonets. Invasion planners nonetheless engaged with a broad-based successor administration that included discontented elements from across the Egyptian political spectrum, including the military. In such a setting, rather than study the intrigues of British spymasters, cloak-and-dagger operatives, and maverick political figures—exciting as these are—the answer to this long-standing puzzle of the Suez crisis lies in Egypt, and among the members of the Egyptian opposition.

BY THE END OF THE SUMMER OF 1956, the British Prime Minister had quite good reason to be confident in the prospects of a post-Nasser regime in Egypt, because he by then had in his pocket assurances from the emissaries of the three most prominent living nationalist political figures in Egypt. All these figures could lay claim to significant mass-mobilizing power and, as Eden knew only too well, proud track records of anti-British nationalist politics. And their communications both encouraged British action to overthrow Nasser and indicated the willingness of each figure to work in a post-Nasser successor government.

The first of Britain's most prominent allies in Egypt in 1956 was the popular hero of the 1952 revolution and Egypt's first president, General Mohammed Naguib. General Naguib was an icon in the last years of the Egyptian monarchy as a war hero and reputed defender of the armed forces against the king, and he then became the figurehead of the military coup of July 1952, which had otherwise been led by largely unknown junior officers. As Egypt's first president through 1953 and 1954, he oversaw many of the revolution's early reforms aimed at taking apart Egypt's old monarchical order. But by the summer of 1956, Naguib had been imprisoned for almost two years after making a dramatic break with the new regime less than eighteen months after the revolution. Famously claiming that his "military honor" prevented him from further collaboration with the revolutionary regime, since Colonel Nasser was turning Egypt into a personal dictatorship and police state, he joined with leaders from Egypt's old parliamentary parties in public demonstrations for the restoration of Egypt's constitution, the return of the army to its barracks, and the reintroduction of civilian rule. But since Nasser and his circle exercised control over the security services, the hard-liners in the Revolutionary Command Council were able to isolate Naguib's supporters in the military, seize control of the capital, and detain the president. Even kept away from the public eye, however, Naguib remained a powerful popular symbol in Egypt in 1956, and was described by the British government's Egyptian contacts as someone who could rally around him the Egyptian army and a significant section of the mass public. And the Egyptian leader who had once talked of "cleansing the Nile of British imperialist filth" was, after a few years of Nasser's rule, prepared to cooperate with Britain in order to cleanse Egypt of its revolutionary regime.[9]

Alongside former president Naguib was the second major figure of Egypt's nationalist movement, one of perhaps even greater political stature, the five-time former prime minister Mustafa Al-Nahhas. Nahhas was a consummate figure of the ancien régime: a wealthy pasha who collaborated with Britain during World War II. But he stood at the head of Egypt's greatest national political party, the Wafd, which had been at the forefront of the struggle against Britain since Egypt's earlier revolution of 1919. Nahhas was an early and bitter enemy of the military regime following its suspension of the constitution and political parties. He was arrested, banned from public life, and, following his public support for Naguib's attempted counter-coup of 1954, held under house arrest, where he would remain for the rest of his life. Nahhas was an old man by the time of the Suez crisis, and though he continued to direct the Wafd party apparatus from house arrest, he was reportedly uninterested in personally assuming power. But he was eager to "redeem his reputation . . . even through an act of sacrifice"; and his emissaries spoke to British contacts in London of his expectations that in the course of

Fig. 19.1. Generals Gamal Abdel Nasser and Mohammed Naguib, 23 July 1954. Bibliotheca Alexandrina.

a military intervention, he could be broken out of his house arrest to dramatically appear at Friday prayers at one of Cairo's large mosques and initiate the mass demonstrations that would mark the end of the regime.[10] In 1956, Nahhas was perceived by friends and enemies alike to retain a potentially decisive personal influence and popular power as Egypt's senior statesman.

The third major Egyptian political leader among Britain's Egyptian allies, and perhaps the most unexpected, was the supreme guide of the Society of Muslim Brothers, Hassan Al-Hudaybi. Hudaybi had been a supporter of the 1952 revolution against the monarchy, but he too had dramatically fallen out with the new military regime. In the crisis of 1954, he closely associated himself with President Naguib and placed the Muslim Brotherhood behind the effort to restore civilian and parliamentary rule—accusing Nasser of creating a "military dictatorship . . . to replace the tyranny of Farouk."[11] Months later, Hudaybi found himself detained and imprisoned for alleged involvement in an assassination plot against Nasser, and was eventually joined by 10,000–20,000 members of his movement. In the summer of 1956, through the intermediaries of the brother-hood's leaders in exile, Hudaybi placed the movement behind the Egyptian opposition's efforts to rid Egypt of the Nasser regime. The brotherhood, he claimed, would be content to become the country's "official opposition" in a reconstituted successor state.

These three major Egyptian nationalist figures were the most prominent of the political leaders who now appear to have been be-hind the Suez operation, or were in some way connected with the covert Anglo-Egyptian planning. Dozens of other figures are im-plicated in British documents, and many more were subsequently identified in a wave of arrests in Egypt that followed the failed Anglo-French intervention. Seen in this context in 1956, Mahmoud Abu Al-Fath looked less like a filibuster than a facilitator of a rare all-party coalition. It was a remarkable moment of unity among Egypt's historically querulous opposition. "Unlike the Bourbons," as Julian Amery summed up the situation to Britain's foreign minister, months before the intervention began, "the Egyptian opposition have learned from experience."[12]

So why did all these once-prominent figures on the Egyptian national scene take such a unexpected position during the Suez crisis? All of Britain's Egyptian allies in 1956 viewed the political practices of "Nasser's new Egypt" not as the culmination of some long-running struggle for national dignity but as policies entirely at variance with the achievements of Egypt's longer nationalist strug-gle against Britain. In their correspondence and publications, many laid stress on their place in a political struggle that had achieved Egypt's sovereign independence, its system of parliamentary govern-ment, and the most advanced legal system, free press, and political culture in the Arab world. All these had entirely disappeared follow-ing the revolution.

Throughout intelligence reports of antigovernment dissent and in opposition propaganda, the phrase "police state" recurs frequently as the principal criticism of the emerging Nasserist regime. By the time of the Suez crisis, all the principal opposition figures had been victims of these forces. In the course of 1955, the security state had routed the three great bastions of Egypt's liberal political life: the media and newspapers, in April, the legal profession, in July, and the universities, in September. Even senior Egyptian government of-ficials expressed contempt for this turn to military autocracy; as the Egyptian governor of the Suez Canal Zone told an American diplo-mat in 1956, "All twenty-two million of us live in a huge concentra-tion camp."[13]

For many nationalist intellectuals, it was the continuation of personal military rule in Egypt that was unthinkable. Mahmoud Abu Al-Fath's propaganda writings of the mid-1950s often conveyed a sense of disbelief at what he perceived to be the new ideology constructed in support of the regime. This doctrine, he wrote, "which Nasser himself proclaims," that "the Egyptian people . . . are not yet fit for a parliamentary system" and needed "the tutelage of ten inexperienced [and] ignorant young colonels," constituted the real offense to Egypt's national dignity.[14] These differences connected also with Egypt's stance in international affairs. The anti-Nasser opposition forces downplayed the anti-Western posture of the new regime, frequently expressing shock at how Nasser had succeeded in barely two years in completely isolating Egypt from its main trading partners and sources of international aid while progressively guiding the country away from its former geopolitical partners and toward the Soviet Union.

THE EMERGING CONSENSUS ABOUT the broad-based Egyptian successor government that British agents had readied to overthrow President Nasser during the summer of 1956 radically overturns earlier conclusions. The claims made by Britain's Egyptian allies about Nasser's unsteady domestic position contrast so radically with established interpretations of the period that Chalabi's ghost again beckons. Could this, too, be merely the wishful thinking of would-be allies? Were Egypt's other nationalists merely a figure of the British imagination?

American officials in Egypt in the mid-1950s were notably better informed than their discredited British counterparts, and the American president, Dwight D. Eisenhower, was openly and now famously critical of Anthony Eden's favored policy toward Nasser following the nationalization of the Suez Canal. This was not, however, the result of differences over the political stability of Nasser's Egypt. In fact, by 1956 reports from U.S. diplomats in the country were pointing to a view remarkably similar to those of Britain's Egyptian informants. Nasser's regime, these officials were reluctantly concluding in 1956, had been "unable to generate any significant popular following." It had established no effective political organization and was faced with an "almost total absence of active support for Nasser among the civilian population." The regime was—in the American view—simply a "narrow military autocracy" based "almost entirely" upon the support of the younger officer group, and kept in place by a firm control of the regime's security services. The regime's enemies, meanwhile, were judged to be widespread, united, regrouping, and rearming throughout the country, and they enjoyed a considerable popular, though clandestine, following.

This largely forgotten American view of Nasser's Egypt in 1956 seems to have had considerable traction in Washington. President Eisenhower, for one, seems to have been convinced of the seriousness of Eden's analysis, though not his proposed solution. Files newly come to light reveal that Eisenhower, in the midst of Secretary of State John Foster Dulles's Suez peace diplomacy, commissioned a covert operation in August to bring about the "disposal" of Nasser "as quickly as possible" in collaboration with the British. This program—code-named Operation MASK—would "use covert means to mobilize the necessary internal political opposition to bring about his actual removal."[15] The prospect of an international conflict in the Middle East to bring down the Egyptian regime was not simply unprincipled, in the American view, but also unnecessary. Nasser of Egypt could in 1957 go the same way as Mohammad Musaddiq of Iran in 1953 and Jacobo Arbenz of Guatemala in 1954.

This emerging picture of post-revolutionary Egypt points toward the striking conclusion that it was Nasser's weakness, not his strength, that seemed to precipitate both the Suez crisis and the resort to military force that followed. Are these, then, the "Egyptian origins of the Suez crisis"? And might one therefore also conclude that the British Prime Minister's action in the Suez crisis was characteristic not so much of his madness, drug addiction, failing doctors, or faulty bile duct, as of his accurate assessment of the strategic situation in Egypt and the Middle East?

The new studies and reviews that appeared in 2016, on the sixtieth anniversary of the Suez crisis, strongly agreed that the answer is no. Britain's Prime Minister, Anthony Eden, was condemned for his "moral bankruptcy" and "inept duplicity," and his leadership through the Suez affair described as "reckless," "sick," "deranged," and "criminal."[16] The story of Britain's Egyptian allies in the Suez crisis can do little to ameliorate this prevailing image. Despite Eden's later rhetorical claim to a career defined by his philosophical opposition to dictators, from Mussolini to Nasser, his action in 1956 resembled a cynical adoption of the language of emancipation placed in the service of the exercise of power. No expressions of sympathy for his Egyptian allies' cause—or the fate to which he quickly abandoned them—appeared in Eden's later accounting of the crisis or seems to exist among his personal papers. Britain's economic and strategic position, and his personal political one, were clearly his preeminent concerns.

With hindsight, however, Eden's analysis of the geopolitical situation facing Britain in the Middle East in 1956 and of the threat posed by nationalization of the canal seems rather more astute. The Middle East in 1956 was a region largely under Western influence, with little in the way of left-leaning governments and almost no Soviet "footprint." Fifteen years later, the picture was completely transformed. Egypt, Syria, Iraq, South Yemen, Algeria, Libya, and Sudan were led by left-leaning governments, and some were Soviet satellites, hosting Soviet military advisers, forces, or military bases. The transformation in Egypt's position was striking. By the late 1960s, Cairo was being guarded by a Soviet garrison, the Egyptian intervention in Yemen was underpinned by the Soviet air force, and the country's economy was almost entirely dependent on foreign aid. In 1971 the great bastion of Western influence in the Middle East, the Kingdom of Jordan, was almost overthrown; and to complete the symbolism, India, the leading member of the British Commonwealth of Nations, signed a twenty-year Treaty of Friendship with the Soviet Union that same year. The domino theory at the heart of Cold War politics is now largely discredited as an interpretation of strategic dynamics in the nonaligned world. But the Suez crisis and the Middle East in 1956 seem to present the one place where it was rightfully invoked, and by Anthony Eden. This too, however, ultimately seems yet another mark against him. The one thing more likely to start these dominos falling than Nasser's successful nationalization of the canal was a botched Anglo-French intervention—resulting in both powers' international humiliation by the spectacular display of the United States and the Soviet Union joining hands in the United Nations to attack the colonial powers. Eden's subsequent breakdown and departure from the scene, to recuperate at the Jamaican estate of the creator of James Bond, merely completed the doleful picture.

The role of the U.S. president in the Suez crisis remains the subject of polarized debate. Two former U.S. secretaries of state, one Democrat and one Republican, reached striking and incisive conclusions on both President Eisenhower's action in 1956 and its strategic consequences, which deserve to be better known.

Eisenhower's National Security Council was notably divided over the British reaction to the challenge posed by Nasser. Those ardently opposed to Nasser were led by the Chairman of the Joint Chiefs of Staff, Admiral Radford; those opposed to Britain and France included the Under Secretary of State, Herbert Hoover, Jr.; and John Foster Dulles seemed to float between both extremes. The president decisively intervened in late October 1956 when he got wind of what Britain and France were up to. At a meeting of key members of the NSC, Eisenhower announced that while he appreciated the strength of Anglo-French feeling on this issue—a position he had repeatedly stressed since the nationalization—"nothing justifies double-crossing us."[17] Dean Acheson wrote to former president Harry Truman around the same time, complaining about what he regarded as Eisenhower's consistent modus operandi. "[The school integration crisis in] Little Rock has again shown us," he said, that "we are struck with a President who fiddles ineffectively [in a crisis] until a personal affront drives him to take unexpectedly drastic action."[18] This characterization captures Eisenhower's reaction through the summer of 1956 very well.

The strategic consequences of Eisenhower's response to the Suez crisis seem more obvious. The administration's effort to place the United States in the vanguard of the anticolonial struggle proved impossible to fulfill. For all his heroic neutrality in 1956, Eisenhower was fated to leave office with openly anti-American regimes in power in Cairo, Damascus, and Baghdad. To Henry Kissinger, the longer-term impact of Suez was written on a global rather than a merely Middle Eastern canvas. In a passage buried in a volume of his vast memoirs, Henry Kissinger reflected on why he had become such a vociferous critic of the Eisenhower administration in the late 1950s, which had come to a head over the Suez crisis. "I had always believed," he wrote,

> it essential to reduce the scope of Soviet adventurist policies in the Middle East. For this reason the United States performance in the Suez crisis of 1956 had struck me as deplorable . . . [and] mishandled. Whatever one's view of the wisdom of the British and French military action, I was convinced that we would pay heavily in the years ahead for our short-sighted playing to the gallery. I did not think that manhandling our closest allies would achieve the lasting gratitude of Nasser or those who admired him; on the contrary, he would probably be confirmed in a course fundamentally inimical to Western interests.

He added that the consequences of the U.S. response would fall not only on the combatant nations.

> The moderate regimes buttressed by British power and prestige, especially in Iraq, were likely to be weakened if not doomed by what they could only see as our siding with the radical elements exemplified by Nasser. Britain and France, their self-confidence and sense of global relevance shattered, would hasten to shed their remaining international responsibilities. The realities of power would then impel us to fill the resulting vacuum in the Middle East and east of Suez and so take on our own shoulders all the moral onus of difficult geopolitical decisions.[19]

1. Jonathan Steele, "Obituary: Ahmad Chalabi," *Guardian,* 4 Nov. 2015; Aram Roston, *The Man Who Pushed America to War: The Extraordinary Life, Adventures and Obsessions of Ahmad Chalabi* (New York, 2008).
2. Mahmoud Abul Fath, "Note for an American Friend," 10 Sept. 1956, Julian Amery Papers (AMEJ), Churchill Archives Centre, Cambridge University; Ref. 1/2/71.
3. Trefor Evans, "Leading Personalities in Egypt," 23 Apr. 1957; FO 371/125410, JE 1012/1.
4. Keith Kyle, "To Suez with Tears," in W. R. Louis, ed., *Still More Adventures with Britannia* (London, 2002) p. 277.
5. Cited in Barnaby Crowcroft, "Egypt's Other Nationalists and the Suez Crisis of 1956," *Historical Journal,* 59, 1 (2016), p. 258.
6. Eden to Eisenhower, 5 Aug. 1956, in Peter Boyle, ed., *The Eden–Eisenhower Correspondence, 1955–1957* (Chapel Hill, 2005), pp. 158–59.
7. Anthony Nutting, *No End of a Lesson: The Story of Suez* (London, 1967), p. 35.
8. George Kennedy Young, *Who Is My Liege: A Study of Loyalty and Betrayal in Our Time* (London, 1972), p. 79.
9. Phrase from Selwyn Lloyd, *Suez 1956: A Personal Account* (London, 1978), p. 12.
10. Cited in Crowcroft, "Egypt's Other Nationalists," pp. 271.
11. Ibid., p. 272.
12. Julian Amery to Selwyn Lloyd, 16 May 1956, AMEJ 1/2/37.
13. Cited in Crowcroft, "Egypt's Other Nationalists," p. 263.
14. Ibid., p. 284.
15. This operation was first detailed by Hugh Wilford in *America's Great Game: The CIA's Secret Arabists and the Shaping of the Modern Middle East* (New York, 2013).
16. See, for example, Nigel Jones, "*Blood and Sand* Comprehensively Destroys What's Left of Anthony Eden's Reputation; And Anthony Blair Should Have Paid More Attention," *Spectator,* 1 Oct. 2016.
17. MemCon, President Eisenhower, Secretary Dulles, Admiral Radford, and Herbert Hoover, 29 Oct. 1956, John Foster Dulles Papers, White House Memorandum Series, box 4, Dwight D. Eisenhower Library, Abilene, Kansas.
18. Acheson to Truman, 8 Oct. 1957, in David McCullough, ed., *Affection and Trust: The Personal Correspondence of Harry S. Truman and Dean Acheson, 1953–1971* (New York, 2010).
19. Henry Kissinger, *The White House Years* (New York, 1988), p. 417.

Jamal al-Husayni, president of the Palestine Arab Delegation to the League of Nations, c. 1930s. Central Zionist Archives.

20

Limitless Violence in Palestine

CAROLINE ELKINS

In the spring of 1939, as war clouds gathered over Europe and countless Jews sought safe passage from the continent's eastern reaches to the promised land of Palestine, Jamal al-Husayni, president of the Palestine Arab Delegation to the League of Nations, was cloistered within Geneva's Hotel Victoria. In his mind's eye were reams of firsthand accounts offering evidence of humiliations, torture, and widespread, indiscriminate destruction. He begged the league's Permanent Mandates Commission to investigate the horrors unfolding not under the Third Reich's elongating shadow, but rather beneath that of Britain's liberal imperialist regime in Palestine.

It was in this sliver of a mandated territory—no bigger than Belgium or Wales—that the league, under Article 22 of its Covenant, had bestowed upon Britain a "sacred trust of civilisation" to promote the "well-being and development" of Palestine's inhabitants.[1] Yet for al-Husayni, there was little sacred or trustworthy about British rule. Born into one of Jerusalem's most influential and politically connected families, the middle-aged, mustached Arab diplomat with piercingly alert eyes had spent nearly his entire adult life under Britain's imperial thumb. During the inter-war years, al-Husayni had become a quietly important player in the debacle unfolding in Palestine. He crisscrossed the mandated territory and the broader Middle East, the United States, and Europe, where he was known, even in British circles, for his pragmatism and conciliatory approach when addressing Palestine's spiraling civil and colonial violence, and the triangulated intractability of Anglo, Arab, and Jewish relations, particularly around the question of expanding Jewish immigration and land purchases.

By the time al-Husayni found himself in the Hotel Victoria, unremitting violence had racked his homeland for some three years. The Arab Revolt, as it was known, ignited as a general strike in April 1936 and then spread throughout much of the territory's rural areas. Britain's response was nothing short of draconian. From the get-go, Arab politicians, as well as European missionaries, local colonial officials, residents of Palestine, and military and police personnel, documented Britain's repressive measures, which were targeted primarily at the Palestinian Arab population. Accounts of torture and humiliation, murder, and systemized suffering were privately brought to Britain's successive high commissioners in Palestine as well as to the War and Colonial Offices.

Denials emerged as the official response—denials that had been well rehearsed in previous imperial dramas. According to myriad British officials, the lies and exaggerations were the handiwork of Arab propagandists, fueled in part by the opportunistic inveigling of Europe's rising fascist tide, which sought to discredit the good name of Britain and its empire. Prime Minister Neville Chamberlain's Cabinet went so far as to dismiss the flow of allegations from Palestine as "absolutely baseless" and declared "the character of the British soldier is too well known to require vindication."[2]

Still, al-Husayni persisted. Drawing on his international reputation and mindful of the flow of accusations piling upon his desk, the diplomat went to the League of Nations. "British troops," he asserted, "have adopted increasing measures of repression and terrorisation against the Arabs of Palestine who stand to defend their country." Gesturing to the situation's gravity through historical analogy, he continued: "Such atrocities of the dark ages, to which the human race, nowadays, look back with disgust and horror, of torturing men during criminal investigation and assaulting peaceful people and destroying their properties wholesale when peacefully lying within their homes are actions that have daily been perpetrated in the Holy Land during the greater part of the last three years." Among other excesses, al-Husayni described the "scorching" of body parts with "hot iron rods," "severe beating with lashes," the "pulling out [of] nails and scorching the skin under them by special appliances," and the "pulling of the sexual organs." He detailed the British forces' widespread ransacking and looting of homes, summary executions, disappearances, the denial of food and water to innocent civilians, the rape of women and girls, and the destruction of livestock. The diplomat then reminded the league that "if the Mandatory [power of Britain] is innocent of these excesses then our demand for a neutral enquiry should be welcomed by all concerned"[3]

Stretching back before the Victorian era, conceptions of brown and black subjects, justifications for—even the necessity of—violence, and moral claims to a superior civilization created a tapestry of ideas that found expression in colonial administrations, imperial security forces, legal scaffoldings, and policies of divide and rule that created civil wars and left them in imperialism's wake, as well as nationalist conceptions of Britain and the benevolent myths that belied them. So, too, did they find expression in the league's Permanent Mandates Commission, which was as much a reflection of liberal imperialism's agenda as it was an oversight agent for its alleged transgressions.

The extension of Britain's global power and domination in the nineteenth century brought with it history-defining debates about universal principles, free markets, the protection of property, the rule of law, and, importantly, who was and was not entitled to the rights and responsibilities of citizenship. Beginning in the early nineteenth century, liberal thought evolved in Europe and intersected with the rise of empires. The mutually constitutive relationship between liberalism and imperialism had profound consequences for British conceptions of liberty, progress, and governance, both at home and abroad.

Defining much of British thought was the categorical assumption that a parochial Western liberalism, intrinsically universal, belonged to all people worldwide. Yet there were deep contradictions in the liberal imperial project—contradictions that were increasingly understood through a racial lens. John Stuart Mill juxtaposed civilization and barbarism to create new ideological idioms. He advocated for a progressive notion of citizenship and a narrative of human development that was intimately bound with Britain's civilizing mission. Good government in the empire had to be adjusted to local "stages of civilization," and Mill advocated a paternalistic form of despotism to tutor the empire's children. According to Mill, "a civilized government, to be really advantageous to [subject populations], will require to be in a considerable degree despotic: one over which they do not themselves exercise control, and which imposes a great amount of forcible restraint upon their actions."[4] In effect, England had a right, even a responsibility, to rule despotically to reform the barbarous populations of the world.

A series of violent events in the empire hardened notions of imperial subjects and their rights. The civilizing mission, despite its rhetorical staying power, was greatly eviscerated and replaced with moral disillusionment and a disavowal of liberalism's capability to transform backward peoples, at least in part. It was replaced by a British imperial rule that, while still projecting its moral claims of the civilizing mission, accentuated and codified difference, and countenanced the threat and deployment of forms of violence. The Indian Rebellion of 1857 followed by the Morant Bay Rebellion in Jamaica and with it the Governor Eyre crisis precipitated this volte-face. The Anglo-imperial pendulum swung in the conservative direction, with the likes of Thomas Carlyle and James Fitzjames Stephen leveraging the moment to further authoritarian views on imperial rule. For his part, Stephen was relentless, asserting an unapologetic racial superiority and advocating absolute rule in the colonies and, with it, the necessity of coercion. As far as Mill's beloved rule of law was concerned, Stephen did not hedge: "Force is an absolutely essential element of all law whatever. Indeed law is nothing but regulated force subjected to particular conditions and directed toward particular objects."[5]

In retrospect, the "liberal" in Britain's liberal authoritarianism was often difficult to discern. Initial acts of conquest gave way in the twentieth century to elaborate legal codes, the proliferation of police and security forces, circumscriptions on free-market economies for the colonized, and administrative apparatuses that marginalized and oppressed entire populations while fueling racial and ethnic divisions within and between them. The lived realities of Britain's burden in the empire were vastly different from the nation's self-representations, grounded as they were in an historical consciousness that was equally as deft at collective erasure and creating approbatory versions of the nation's past as it was in disseminating these ideas.

The paradox between the lived imperial experiences of the colonized and the laudatory claims of Britain's civilizing mission can be traced to the conjoined nineteenth-century birth of modern liberalism and imperialism. Together, they were shaped in an era when national interests were inextricable from the growth and spread of capitalism. A dominant narrative of universal human emancipation, equality, rights, and the civilizing mission materialized simultaneously with a suppressed underside of repression as expressed in evolutionary thought, racism, class, and sexism, among other things.

In the decades ahead, these paradoxes were thrown into relief time and again through episodic eruptions of large-scale violence in the empire. Violent measures and practices of suppression were increasingly honed and exported from one hot spot to the next. Some of Britain's most illustrious political and military leaders cut their teeth in the empire and circulated through Britain's colonial possessions. Much of the violence they deployed was understood at home through the liberal authoritarian lens, though colonial violence unfolding in plain view increasingly relied for cover on liberalism's justificatory powers of paternal beneficence as well as its twinned abilities to obfuscate while ostensibly illuminating its behavior in empire.

Racial and cultural differences became institutionalized at every level of executive, legislative, and judicial rule in the British Empire. It is scarcely surprising that military doctrine also reflected the "rule of colonial difference" pervading British discourse, practices, and institutions at home and in the empire. As Britain dealt with small imperial wars and other eruptions of violence, its military increasingly considered the best ways to deal with so-called recalcitrant natives, often termed terrorists. In turn, these practices became part of the broader institutionalization of violence. They were best captured in the work of Colonel Charles Callwell, a graduate of the Royal Military Academy and veteran of several nineteenth-century imperial wars. His *Small Wars: Their Principles and Practices*—originally written in 1896 and updated after he served as a staff officer and commander in the South African War—became the starting point for nearly all counterinsurgency theorists and practitioners, even down to the present day. Callwell's expansive work synthesized not only Britain's countless military engagements throughout the empire, but also drew lessons from French, Spanish, American, and Russian campaigns. Together, these reference points supported not only the perceived short-term effectiveness of unbridled force, but also liberal imperialism's framework for such repressive measures.

For Callwell, when European troops were engaged in wars against "uncivilised" and "savage" populations, as opposed to civilized armies, a different set of rules were needed. Callwell pointed to the "moral force of civilisation" underwriting European superiority, and the need to teach "savage" peoples "a lesson which they will not forget."[6] When endorsing total destruction of the enemy, Callwell emphasized the "moral effect" that brutality wrought upon "uncivilised" populations. Furthermore, as Callwell summarized: "[The] object is not only to prove to the opposing force unmistakably which is the stronger, but also to inflict punishment on those who have taken up arms." He emphasized how "[the] enemy must be made to feel a moral inferiority throughout . . . [Fanatics and savages] must be thoroughly brought to book and cowed or they will rise again."[7]

In the years ahead, legal and political frameworks evolved that reflected and accommodated liberal authoritarianism's punitive violence—a punitive violence that Callwell had so clearly articulated. As Callwell highlights, once conventional warfare methods were jettisoned, "it is then that the regular troops are forced to resort to cattle lifting and village burning and that the war assumes an aspect which may shock the humanitarian."[8] In the intersection between the legal and political, government by consent came increasingly to define England, Scotland, and Wales in the nineteenth century, whereas order was imposed on Ireland, for example, through a series of Insurrection Acts, Habeas Corpus Suspension Acts, and deployments of martial law. When these were not sufficient, Coercion Acts were introduced, with measures to control arms, provide for special systems of trial, and criminalize oath taking, among other things. Significantly for Ireland and other parts of the empire, little under the Coercion Acts conferring emergency-like powers could be questioned in a court of law. At the time, the jurist and constitutionalist theorist Albert Dicey made clear that the Coercion Acts were fully incompatible with the rule of law and the ideals of civil liberties, stating: "In principle . . . thoroughly vicious . . . [it] in effect gave the Irish executive an unlimited power of arrest; it established in them a despotic government . . . [It] could not be made permanent, and applied to the whole United Kingdom without depriving every citizen of security for his person freedom."[9] Ultimately, the acts became the precursors for legal codes that transferred repressive powers to civilian authorities who, in turn, could declare a state of emergency.

IN PALESTINE IN THE 1930s, the British government undertook a series of steps that consolidated decades of legalized lawlessness into a set of emergency powers that would become *the* model for future counterinsurgency campaigns. In the wake of the Wailing Wall violence in the late 1920s, and the Permanent Mandates Commission's noteworthy chastening of Britain's lack of coercive will, the Palestine (Defence) Order in Council, passed in 1931, conferred on the high commissioner a set of powers that exceeded any similar legislation to date. Based on earlier codes in Ireland and India, the Order in Council empowered the high commissioner to declare a state of emergency and, with it, to issue and amend regulations. The Order in Council lay unpublished until the 1936 general strike and, with it, the start of the Arab Revolt. High Commissioner Arthur Wauchope declared a state of emergency in Palestine and issued the first of a series of emergency regulations and amending orders on the 19 April 1936. These included authorization to take possession of buildings and essential items; the control of transport, firearms, telecommunications, and shipping; press regulation and censorship; arrests without warrants; detention without trial; deportation; the power to demolish buildings, including villages and homes; and the imposition of the death penalty for discharging firearms and sabotaging phone and rail lines.

Still, the military wanted more legal coverage to unleash an all-out assault. Their man in charge, Air Vice-Marshal Richard Peirse, and his successor, Lieutenant-General John Greer Dill, believed the emergency regulations were inadequate, particularly those regarding the punitive destruction of property and the unleashing of reprisals, which had been permissible in Ireland. That the Collective Responsibility and Punishment Ordinances had been on the books in Palestine since the mid-1920s seemed to matter little; nor did the recently enacted Collective Fines Ordinance. Peirse wanted martial law, though after the Colonial Office's legal minds in London fretted, it was determined that martial law would, in fact, be too restrictive on the military and the punitive actions of its soldiers, since the civil courts were still sitting in Palestine and could well challenge repressive military actions. In martial law's place came the Palestine Martial Law (Defence) Order in Council of 26 September 1936 and subsequently a new Palestine (Defence) Order in Council on 18 March 1937. Section 6 (1) stated that the high commissioner "may make such Regulations . . . as appear to him in his unfettered discretion to be necessary or expedient for securing the public safety, the defence of Palestine, the maintenance of public order and the suppression of mutiny, rebellion and riot, and for maintaining supplies and services essential to the life of the community."[10] Statutory martial law was put into effect.

The War Office gave its field officers and soldiers a wide berth in defining and implementing the use of force. Building on Callwell's earlier and highly influential work, Major General Sir Charles Gwynn's *Imperial Policing* helped shape how British soldiers conducted themselves "in aid of the civil power" when fighting colonial wars, which Gwynn and many others understood to be as much policing operations as they were military ones.[11] As for the military, its norms had been codified under the *Manual of Military Law* in 1929, and the relevant portions—"Notes on Imperial Policing" and "Duties in the Aid of the Civil Power"—were reproduced for the troops in pocket form for easy reference while on the front lines. The manual stated, "The existence of an armed insurrection would justify the use of any degree of force necessary effectually to meet and cope with the insurrection"; it loosely defined "collective punishments," "reprisals," and "retributions"—all of which could well "inflict suffering upon innocent individuals . . . [and were] indispensible as a last resort."[12] The coupling of the military's code of conduct and the extraordinary civil-emergency measures offering legal coverage meant that Britain's troops, along with the local police force, operated virtually without restraint or fear of prosecution. As a steady stream of complaints and accounts of atrocities piled up on the desk of Palestine's chief secretary and those of officials in London's Colonial and War Offices, almost nothing, legally, was required to be done. In the few cases in which prosecutions took place, acquittals were more the norm than the exception.

In the years before the Arab Revolt, there was already in place what was known as a "Black and Tan" culture, which the British government had consciously imported to the mandatory territory. Churchill hand-selected his good friend Charles Tudor, who had led the Black and Tans and Auxiliaries in Ireland and who, despite the resounding critiques of the Black and Tan methods during the Irish War, would take them, and the men who had unleashed them, to Palestine. There a similar mentality and set of practices unfolded. The former Black and Tan Douglas Duff recalled in his memoir: "In 1922, we regarded 'the lesser breeds without the law' differently than is the case today. Mentally, I suppose, we were still living in the great days of Empire; our attitude was that of Britons of the Diamond Jubilee era, to us all non-Europeans were 'wogs' and Western non-Britons only slightly more worthy."[13] Over ten years later, Tudor and Duff were gone from the Mandate, but the Black and Tan culture was not. Instead, when the Arab Revolt could not be suppressed, the destruction of civilian society, along with the insurgents, became the overriding objective, both on paper and in practice. A military and administrative complex appeared, one that had been forming in previous small wars but was in clear view in late-1930s Palestine and later moved, sometimes with the same actors, from one imperial war to another. Under the emergency regulations in Palestine, effective power shifted to the military command, which was in charge of all security forces. The high commissioner—at this point, Harold MacMichael—had, in practice, only nominal control, and that was precisely the point of the emergency regulations.

When the British could not regain the initiative and suppress the Arab Revolt, the military's General Staff report was clear: "In the long run the adoption of repressive measures from the very start will probably be both the most expedient and the most humane way of restoring peace."[14] To this end, after a cease-fire collapsed with the publication of the Peel Report in 1937, a host of experienced operatives were brought in, forming the backbone of the complex. They included Arthur Bomber Harris—who was part of Churchill's cadre that developed air control in Iraq, and he brought these methods with him to Palestine where he repeated the oft-heard refrain of the "moral effect" of bombing. In the case of the mandate, he wrote: "We must (and under such circumstances can) make up for a lack of numbers by using rougher methods with the rebels than we dare do in peace. One 250 lb or 500 lb [bomb] in each village that speaks out of turn within a few minutes or hours of having so spoken; or the complete blotting out of a few selected haunts, *pour encourager les autres.*"[15]

Sir Charles Tegart and David Petrie, the future head of MI5, were brought in to clean up Palestine's police force and bring the methods that Tegart, in particular, had honed for decades as head of the Intelligence Branch of the India Colonial Police force in Bengal. There, he was linked to the tortures that took place at the Andaman Island prison, and as one underling casually noted, he was "not beyond circumventing the law to achieve results."[16] Like Harris, Tegart was renowned and adored by his men, who repeatedly said how much they wished to emulate the Man of Iron, as he was known. Tegart introduced to Palestine the famed Tegart Wall, which was useless, and the Tegart Forts. He also brought methods of interrogation that were set up in the Arab Investigation Center as well as in the forts themselves. There, according to one colonial official, "selected police officers were to be trained in the gentle art of the 'third degree,' for use on Arabs until they 'spilled the beans,' as it was termed in criminal circles."[17] After he submitted his report on a host of police force recommendations, Tegart became the special liaison officer between the police and the military, working closely with Harris, as well as General Officers Commanding Archibald Wavell and Robert Haining.

Major General Bernard Montgomery, like Harris, had honed his skills in the empire, and when referring to the Irish War, he minced no words as far as his approach: "I think I regarded all civilians as 'Shinners' [members of Sinn Féin]. . . My own view is that to win a war of this sort, you must be ruthless."[18] The term "ruthless" permeates Monty's directives; the private archives of missionaries and European observers at the time; the memoirs of soldiers, administrators, and police officers; and interviews with the same. Account after account of the atomization of villages, tortures, senseless killings, humiliations, and the like pervade the record. When recounting why they engaged in such behavior, soldiers and police officers offered multiple reasons: boredom, fear, anger. Some marveled at their own ability, as they would say, to "go bezerk." Horrific acts were described casually and encoded within in a racial and cultural framework. Arthur Lane, a young soldier, inadvertently confirmed the cascading effects of an imperial despotism that Edmund Burke had cautioned against over a century earlier: "In those days, I don't know, you was a young warrior and it was excitement. And you was, I don't know, you was supreme, you was in charge, you was in control, you had the power. And this is what it was all about, you know, being the soldier, you had the power to do things, and you did it."[19]

At the same time, it was occasionally difficult to tell, even for local officials, who was on which side of the Arab divide. The peace bands, or peace gangs, as local officials called them in Palestine, were armed groups loyal to the al-Husanyi family's rivals, the Nashashibi family. Together with a colonial-groomed leader, Fakhri Abd al-Hadi, these peace bands unleashed terror on the countryside. In fact, British intelligence in Damascus had trained Fakhri, and after consultation with Tegart, he was brought into Palestine to help do Britain's bidding. Fakhri rightly earned his nickname, the "Butcher." He and his forces were most effective in the final mop-ups of the villages—which had been divided into "good" and "bad" categories, much as Tegart and others had done in India. There was also the evolution of Jewish supernumeraries, some of whom were instrumental in Orde Wingate's Special Night Squads, a third force.

Regardless of how many arrows al-Husanyi had in his quiver of imperial recrimination, he was no match for Chaim Weizmann, the head of the World Zionist Organization, and his uncanny political skills, or for the liberal imperial ethos that infused the League of Nations on the eve of the Second World War. Together with the unflagging efforts of Weizmann promoting the Zionist cause, a set of overdetermined conditions, rooted in liberal imperialism's norms, hung over Geneva, at least insofar as the Arabs were concerned. Perhaps even al-Husanyi knew his letter was at best a symbolic gesture, written as much for the historical record as for effecting change within the league's chambers and the war-torn countryside of Palestine. In fact, the Permanent Mandates Commission had already dismissed similar petitions that concerned Arabs had filed, including allegations of the use of poison gas and of British forces behaving "in a manner inconsistent with their duty to maintain public security and protect life and property.[20] The Zionist lobby—together with the commission's unwavering position that Britain had failed in upholding the original terms of the mandate and had not been re-pressive enough—meant any further appeal for a "neutral enquiry," even from the likes of Jamal al-Husanyi, would fall on deaf ears.

In the end, al-Husanyi never received a response. Germany in-vaded Poland on 1 September 1939, and the world war that had been looming over events in Palestine erupted. Britain, so long beholden to the league's inflexible policies—embedded as they were in the terms of the original Balfour Declaration—broke ranks before the Permanent Mandates Commission's wartime demise and instituted a pro-British approach that belied Anglo maneuvers elsewhere in the empire. It was a move that the league, and its refusal to recon-sider the original terms of the mandate, had hamstrung for years.

Wielding their newfound imperial free agency in Palestine, Brit-ish officials were, in fact, poised to sacrifice their Zionist allies on the altar of strategic necessity. Arab states were needed for wartime support, and the Jews could hardly jettison Britain in the face of Hitler's lethal anti-Semitic policies. When the dust settled over the corpses and broken bodies and minds of Palestine's fellaheen popu-lation, Britain reversed its policies in favor of Arab demands, which in the context of September 1939 were aligned with British inter-ests. London issued the White Paper of 1939, and with it declared that 75,000 further Jewish immigrants would be allowed into Pales-tine, after which point all entries would be subject to Arab consent. Moreover, the White Paper imagined, within a decade, the creation of a unitary state in Palestine. Such hubristic imperial maneuvering overlooked the unintended consequences of cultivating and arming situational allies, like the Jews, in the Arab Revolt's context of le-galized lawlessness and the unprecedented consolidation of norms honed elsewhere in the empire, whether in the air, on unconven-tional battlefields, in domestic spheres, in the hand-to-mind combat of interrogations, or on the floor of Parliament and in the Cabinet's smoke-filled rooms. The Arab Revolt proved a crucial turning point in imperial convergences, and its political coda ensured another Palestinian war in the years to come. This time Weizmann, the well-trained Jewish supernumeraries, and the Zionist network of support and intelligence gathering would not be on Britain's side. But first, Britain had an even bigger war to fight, and one where empire-tested forms of warfare would be brought home to the metropole and to battlefields and interrogation centers in Europe and beyond before being re-exported to the empire, where His Majesty's Forces would first face the Zionists in Palestine in the immediate post-war years, followed by a series of wars with both anticolonial and civil dimensions in Malaya, Kenya, Cyprus, and elsewhere—wars that would witness the norms of violence matured in the Arab Revolt repeating themselves over and again in rural and urban landscapes across the empire.

Spring Semester 2017

1. *The Covenant of the League of Nations,* Article 22 (Boston, 1929); League of Nations, *An Interim Report on the Civil Administration of Palestine, during the period 1st July, 1920–30 June, 1921,* part I, "The Condition of Palestine After the War," 30 July 1921.

2. G. D. Roseway to C. G. L. Syers, memorandum, 12 Jan. 1939, TNA, WO 32/4562.

3. Jamaal Husseini, president, Palestine Arab Delegation, to His Excellency, the President of the Permanent Mandates Commission, 12 June 1939, TNA, WO/32/4562.

4. Mill, *Considerations on Representative Government* (London, 1861), p. 4.

5. James Fitzjames Stephen, *Liberty, Equality, Fraternity,* ed. Stuart D. Warner (Indianapolis, 1993), p. 111.

6. C. W. Callwell, *Small Wars: Their Principles and Practices* (Lincoln, 1996), p. 102.

7. Ibid., pp. 41, 72, 148.

8. Ibid., p. 40.

9. A. V. Dicey, *The Case against Home Rule* (London, 1886), p. 117.

10. Quoted in A. W. Brian Simpson, *Human Rights and the End of Empire: Britain and the Genesis of the European Convention* (Oxford, 2001), p. 86.

11. Charles W. Gwynn, *Imperial Policing* (London, 1934).

12. *Manual of Military Law* (London, 1929), pp. 103, 255.

13. Douglas V. Duff, *Bailing with a Teaspoon* (London, 1953), p. 46.

14. "Military Lessons of the Arab Rebellion in Palestine, 1936," 166, TNA, WO 191/70.

15. Harris to AVM Nichol, memorandum, 5 Sept. 1938, TNA, AIR 23/765.

16. Quoted in Michael Silvestri, "'An Irishman Is Specially Suited to Be a Policeman': Sir Charles Tegart and Revolutionary Terrorism in Bengal," *History Ireland,* 8, 4 (Winter 2000), p. 43.

17. Edward Keith-Roach, *Pasha of Jerusalem: Memoirs of a District Commissioner under the British Mandate* (London, 1994), p. 191.

18. William Sheehan, *British Voices from the Irish War of Independence 1918–1921: The Words of British Servicemen Who Were There* (West Link Park, Ireland, 2005), p. 151.

19. Arthur Lane, interview, accession 10295, Sound Archive, Imperial War Museum.

20. For example, Permanent Mandates Commission, *Minutes,* 32nd (Extraordinary) Session, 30 July to 18 Aug. 1937, Annex 4, pp. 211–18.

Six to Sixteen: A Story for Girls (1876), by Juliana Horatia Ewing. Rudyard Kipling, c. 1872.

Plate 1. Donald Locke, *Trophies of Empire*, 1972–74. Digital image T14319 © Tate, London.

Plate 2. *Governor Arthur's Proclamation to the Aboriginal People*, 1829–30.

Plate 3. Joseph Noël Paton, *In Memoriam*, 1858. Private collection.

Plate 4. Felice Beato, *Interior of the Secundra Bagh after the Slaughter of 2,000 Rebels by the 93rd Highlanders and 4th Punjab Regiment; First Attack of Sir Colin Campbell in November 1857, Lucknow*, 1858. © British Library.

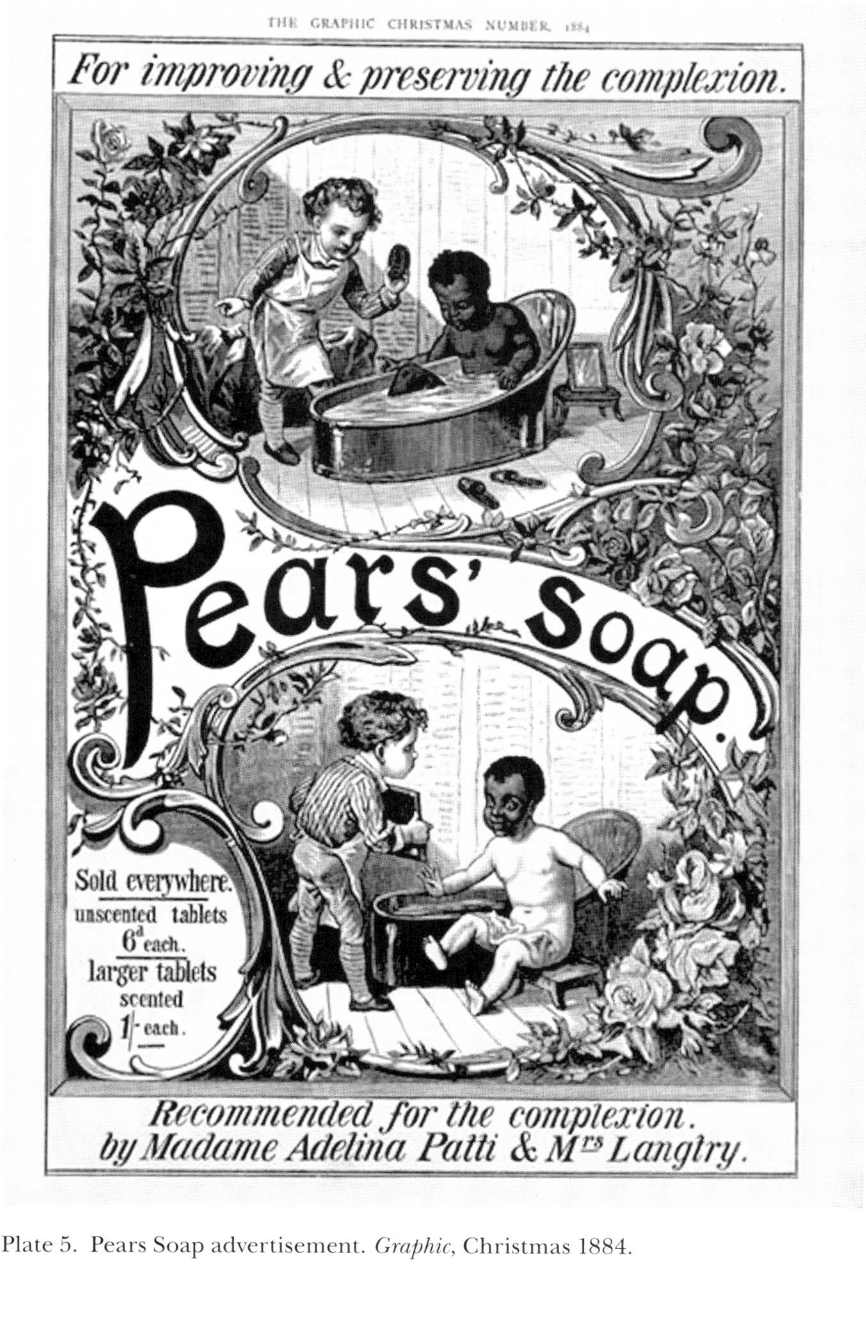

Plate 5. Pears Soap advertisement. *Graphic*, Christmas 1884.

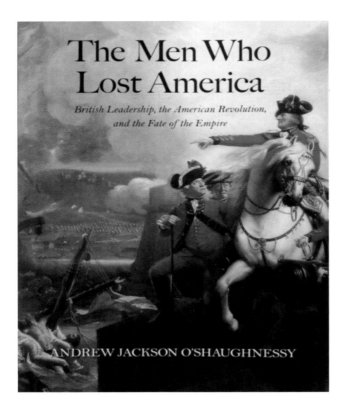

Plate 6. Different details from John Singleton Copley's *The Siege of Gibraltar* (1783–91) were used for the American (*top*) and British book jackets of *The Men Who Lost America* (2013), by Andrew O'Shaughnessy.

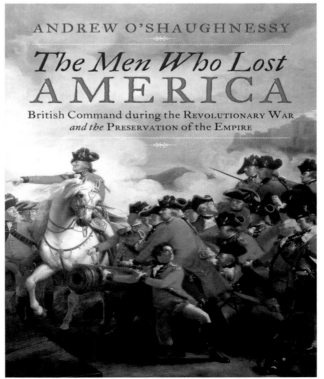

Plate 7. "Maneater," 1941–42, modeled on Francisco Goya's *Saturn Devouring His Son* (c. 1819–23). © IWM (Art.IWM PST 0176).

Plate 8. Kimon Evan Marengo, *The Arrival of the Promised Warriors, Churchill, Stalin, and Roosevelt, Led by the Symbol of Iranian National Liberation, Kaveh*, 1942. © Estate of Kimon Evan Marengo.

21

Rudyard Kipling and Mrs. Ewing

MICHAEL HOLROYD

Rudyard Kipling was born in Bombay at the end of 1865. Like many children whose parents lived and worked in India, he was sent "home" at the age of six or seven to be properly educated in England. This was to be a most unhappy period of his life, at a school he called the "House of Desolation." He hardly saw his family and did not tell them of his loneliness and the bullying he suffered. It was not until 1936, the year before he died, that he wrote an autobiography that made public the humiliation he had endured. *Something of Myself* was posthumously published the following year and criticized for containing, in fact, very little of himself, the original text having been severely edited under the guidance of his wife so as to omit any material that might be damaging.

But Kipling makes very clear his wretched time at school. He never forgot the lack of kind words spoken to him. "I was regularly beaten," he wrote. His only escape lay in reading books—until the deprivation of reading was added to his punishments. He became half blind, had a nervous breakdown, and saw mysterious shadows of things that were not there. He gradually learned to avoid this calculated torture by telling lies, which were what the adults wanted to hear and which, he later thought, became the foundation of his writing. He created a new world in which his old enemies were turned, not into friends exactly, but powerful moral and political allies. The fatal compromise of liberalism, he came to believe, led inevitably to bloodshed.

In the opening chapter of *Something of Myself,* Kipling refers to a novel called *Six to Sixteen* by Mrs. Ewing. "I owe more in circuitous ways to that tale than I can tell," he wrote. Juliana Horatia Ewing had inherited her literary talent from her mother, the writer and editor Margaret Gatty, who soon saw that her daughter was to "go far beyond me." Juliana's demanding and sometimes tyrannical father, the Reverend Alfred Gatty, was not in favor of her marriage to Major Alexander Ewing. He worked in the British Army's pay department, but the question was, how much did he get paid himself? The answer was, too little—at least that was what her father thought. But in *Six to Sixteen,* his daughter strongly opposes the belief that "money's the great thing in this world." Though her father was not a bishop and her husband not a general, they provided Mrs. Ewing with a modestly respectable place in society. Her trouble was ill health. She was unable eventually to travel abroad with her husband, and for the sake of the air and the water she went to Bath—where she died in her midforties.

Kipling did not tell readers of his autobiography the full title of Mrs. Ewing's influential novel. *Six to Sixteen* had a surprising subtitle: *A Story for Girls.* So what, in circuitous ways, did he owe to this story for girls?

Mrs. Ewing is usually described as a late Victorian children's writer —she has a major entry in Daniel Hahn's *Oxford Companion to Children's Literature* (2015). But her "story for girls" is a novel for young adults. It is presented as an autobiography written by Margaret Vandaleur, whose early years, like Kipling's, were passed in India. "The first six years of my life were spent chiefly with my Ayah", she writes.

> I loved her very dearly. I kissed and fondled her dark cheeks as gladly as if they had been fair and ruddy, and oftener than I touched my mother's . . . My most intimate friends were of the Ayah's complexion . . . I have forgotten the language of my early childhood, but its tones had a familiar sound; those dark bright faces were like the faces of old friends, and my heart beat for a minute, as one is moved by some remembrance of an old home.

The story is told by an orphan, Margaret's parents having died from cholera and fever when their daughter was five or six. Kipling's parents had not died while he was that age, but it felt as if they were dead when they left him to the mortification of an English school and returned to India. Mrs. Ewing describes the educational management of young girls in England during their "awkward years" as being designed to make them "feel stronger and happier." She introduces us to the schoolmistress, who is "at once bland and solid," which seems to produce "a favourable impression on parents and guardians." Moreover, "being stout, and between fifty and sixty years old, she was often described as 'motherly.'" But the children soon discover that she is neither just nor truthful. She "seemed to break promises, tell lies, open letters, pry into drawers and boxes, and listen at keyholes, from the highest sense of duty." Though she prides herself on keeping the children "under supervision," she never notices that one of Margaret's school friends is seriously ill. "I feel there has been culpable neglect," she says mournfully when the doctor arrives to take the patient away to hospital. But the doctor corrects her. The neglect sprang "from the best motives," he explains, but adds, "I have known too many cases in which the ill-results have been life-long, and some in which they have been rapidly fatal." In short, such schools were as harmful as prisons that released into the world inmates who had become more dangerous than when they were admitted.

What Kipling learned from this "autobiography" was that English schools for girls were as unpleasant and dangerous as boys' schools. Mrs. Ewing's stories for girls were the very opposite of Lord Chesterfield's letters to his son, which warned upper-class people against laughter because it occasioned "a shocking distortion of the face." Mrs. Ewing, who had a natural sense of humor, intended her readers to laugh, and it is very difficult not to do so when reading many of her pages.

In the novel, a close friend of Margaret's tells her that certain vices such as cheating, lying, gluttony, petty gossip, and malicious mischief making are confined to the lower orders. But Margaret replies that she learned otherwise as a small child in India: "I have heard polished gentlemen lie, at a pinch, like the proverbial pickpocket, and pretty ladies fib as well as servant girls . . . Customers cheat as much as shopkeepers, but I do think that many people who ought to 'know better' seem to forget that their honour as well as their interest is concerned in every bargain."

Rudyard Kipling first read Mrs. Ewing's novel when he was very young. Her early pages set in India mirrored his own happiness at home there. He reread it during his school years in England, remembering it almost word for word over fifty years later when he was writing his autobiography. "I knew it, as I know it still, almost by heart," he wrote. "Here was a history of real people and real things." Mrs. Ewing's novel helped him survive when he was a schoolboy and may have come to his aid in later days of dejection. But after he returned to India and became a successful writer, he found himself in the "unmeasurable gulf that lies between two races."

By the time he won the Nobel Prize in Literature in 1907, he was well known as the private soldiers' poet and had achieved fame for beating the drum on behalf of the British Empire. The British had indeed done some good work in India: extending the Indian railways and canals and establishing the first adequate forest service. Although the East India Company was there to trade and make a profit, it also reorganized the Public Works Department, brought in civil servants, and created a just legal system. The company invested in education, too, and thus many Indians spoke excellent English and played enjoyable cricket (though no Englishman believed that an Indian eleven would ever get the better of the English team).

But none of this greatly appealed to Kipling—indeed, he came to question it. While spreading their own version of culture through India, many of the British maintained a sense of superiority. There was a lack of generosity among them, an authoritarianism leading to acts of cruelty. "An' if you treat a nigger to a dose of cleanin'-rod / 'E's like to show you everything 'e owns," wrote the young Kipling in "Loot."

But as he told the Irish writer John Stewart Collis later in his life, he did not believe that the British traveled abroad in order to create empires. On the contrary, they simply traveled, as do all people who live on islands, to explore more of the world. Among them, he admitted, were some adventurous, well-armed traders who arrived on the east coast of India. They found themselves in a land of warring tribes and soon observed that wherever the British travelers pitched their tents, there was safety. You could go to bed without fear and wake up in peace. There was nothing more tranquilizing than a few guns. This handful of well-armed British voyagers eventually spread their influence over the whole country, and to their surprise, the English found themselves in possession of a subcontinent.

So what happened? What went wrong? Collis copied down what Kipling said, and was to publish it in *An Irishman's England* (1937). Nothing need have gone wrong, Kipling explained, if only a lot of busybodies had not insisted on "democratizing and elevating the people. They must be given a vote, they must be educated and all the rest of it . . . And now we see the result."

Kipling's circuitous journey from the heart of Mrs. Ewing's novel to such a belief seems contrary to his international reputation as a great drumbeater for the empire. He was, as it were, two people. At different ages and in special circumstances, he seemed to become his own enemy, challenging and suppressing in private what he

wrote for the public and revealing what he put aside when addressing readers with his usual confidence.

Spring Semester 2016

A version of this lecture appeared in the *Times Literary Supplement*, 10 August 2016.

David Livingstone, 1864.

22

The British Empire:
Ramshackle or Rampaging?

JOHN M. MACKENZIE

Few adjectives describe the British Empire better than "protean," and the diversity and scale of that empire ensure that it does indeed appear to take on all sorts of different shapes. Precisely because there were several British empires, in chronological, thematic, and geographic terms, its history continues to be written from a variety of perspectives, though focusing on limited themes. Some historians have suggested that the British Empire was so ramshackle that its influence was minimal, both in its power and authority overseas and in its cultural effects in Britain. Others have argued that the transformations wrought by the empire were extensive, that from the point of view of social, environmental, economic, and cultural history, the global effects were very considerable. But whatever else can be said about the British Empire, the fact is that it has continued to be a major source of historical fascination, reflected in the extraordinarily extensive number of books published on its historical impact. For example, the Manchester University Press's Studies in Imperialism series, founded in 1984, has surprisingly reached (in 2017) over 140 volumes. In addition, many distinguished works in British imperial history have come from other publishers during the same period. Moreover, more popular works by television pundits, journalists, politicians, and others continue to pour from the presses. It can now truly be said that it is incredibly difficult for one person to keep abreast of all of this: specialization may be even more essential. Some may offer a counsel of despair, that a fully comprehensive history of the British Empire has become impossible. But excessive specialization leads to a particular focus, and such a slanted view can well have ideological import. Basically, historical perspectives break down into the political, military, administrative, economic, environmental, and cultural. The political economy of empire has been by far the most popular, but such an approach increasingly needs to be informed by developments in environmental and cultural history.

It may well be argued that a full understanding of the British Empire can be gleaned only from making connections across centuries and continents, as well as among disciplines and theoretical and analytical positions. As is well known (and laying aside postcolonial theory, subaltern studies, and other significant developments), we have recently passed through a number of years in which approaches based on the concept of the British World have been explored. This movement arose from the notion that imperial history had for too long concentrated on the so-called dependent empire, upon India as well as African and other colonies. The focus was pulled back to the territories of settlement, to patterns of migration, and to aspects of the transnational social, economic, and cultural features of the empire. This was done in the interest of putting together an overall imperial history out of the shattering of the empire's past into the nationalist components inspired by decolonization. A renewed focus on the territories of white settlement was also in the interest of escaping from a time-expired view of the empire as a set of forces that radiated out from the so-called metropole to the periphery. Instead, the empire in its practice was constantly transformed by a dynamic process of reciprocal exchanges. Moreover, its character and influences were transmitted among colonies as well as from the outer limits to the center. In addition, the empire of settlement and the so-called dependent empire should be placed within one frame, from the point of view of indigenous peoples and imperial personnel, as well as of economics, cultural exchanges, and indeed the nonwhite migrant patterns of the later nineteenth century, which were desperately blocked by policies of white Canada, Australia, and New Zealand. The empire was, in effect, formed out of a series of moving metropoles. The British Empire had many capitals, not just London.

James Belich's book *Replenishing the Earth* (2009) was significant in bringing back continuity into the study of the empire, forming ideas that span the centuries from the seventeenth to the twentieth.

It crucially switched the focus from policies to people. His threefold progression from incremental colonization to explosive colonization to re-colonization has been subject to critique, particularly the third of these, but nonetheless they are exceptionally stimulating. And of course his comparison of American and British Wests—with the British territories of settlement dramatically relocated, for conceptual purposes, into the Atlantic, is intriguing, as is his throwing in of the Russian East and the French "West" in North Africa. He has demonstrated the further frightening fact that the historian can fully understand modern empires only by escaping from a purely Anglophone world and adopting comparative perspectives. Moreover, and most importantly, Belich has replaced the ramshackle with the rampaging, suggesting that the British Empire did indeed have dramatically transforming effects. However much explosive colonization happened in fits and starts—with Belich's impressive analysis of the relationship between the economic booms and busts of the nineteenth and twentieth centuries, and the flows of European migrants and the dramatic occupation of lands in the Americas, Australasia, and, to a lesser extent, South Africa—still the overall effect was entirely revolutionary. And "explosive" and "rampaging" neatly describe the dispossession of indigenous peoples and the dramatic growth of infrastructures and associated towns and cities. This has helped uncover some crucial elements that have to be fed into the history of the empire. They are continuity, intellectual history, material remains, and the environment.

Taking first the question of continuity, we can now find continuity in ideas about the empire, however much they significantly mutated over time. There is no question that we need a major work that will chart, over a longer period, the development of such intellectual grappling with empire. David Armitage has argued in *The Ideological Origins of the British Empire* (2000) that in the seventeenth century, British state building and empire building went hand in hand. This constitutes, in different and more sophisticated ways, a return to the vision of Sir John Seeley that the extension of dominion within the British and Hibernian isles was the necessary precursor of empire. Thus, the United Kingdom was indeed "constituted" by the empire. A highly suggestive book by Sarah Irving, *Natural Science and the Origins of the British Empire* (2008), has further demonstrated that the leading philosophers and scientists of the seventeenth century had the empire very much in mind as they framed their ideas within the theological contexts of the age.

From Francis Bacon to John Locke and the founders of the Royal Society, the connection between travel, exploration, and the collection of knowledge was firmly established. The emergence of the search for worldwide information, a new and all-encompassing global eye, was seen as the re-creation of dominion over nature after its loss at the time of the biblical Fall. Bacon was skeptical about colonies and the possibility of violence over indigenous peoples, but his successors were less so. Locke was secretary of the Council of Trade and Foreign Plantations, invested in the Royal Africa Company, was one of the eleven Bahamas Adventurers, and helped draft the Fundamental Constitutions of Carolina in 1669. Robert Boyle held shares in the East India and Hudson Bay Companies. Both had complex relationships with the empire and its colonies, but both saw the re-establishment of dominion over nature and the scientific study of the natural world as one of the justifications for the establishment of colonies. For Irving, these leading figures constitute the intellectual foundations of empire. Moreover, the origins of modern museums, as well as science, can be found in such explorations of the empire. John Tradescant the younger, whose natural collections (together with his father's) formed the basis of the Ashmolean museum in Oxford (opened in the 1680s), collected in Virginia three times between the 1630s and 1650s. Later, Sir Hans Sloane, whose collections effectively formed the origins of the British Museum (opened in 1759), spent time in Jamaica gathering the materials of his great assemblage. Museums, science, and the empire were indeed closely intertwined and continued to be so into the nineteenth and twentieth centuries.

The work of Armitage and Irving needs to be debated and extended. Moving forward into the eighteenth century, we surely need a great deal more discussion of the relationship between the Enlightenment and the British Empire. In *Christian Missions and the Enlightenment* (2001), Brian Stanley argues that missionary ideas constituted a reaction to the Enlightenment, but were also influenced by it. Russell Berman's *Enlightenment and Empire: Colonial Discourses in German Culture* (1998) and Gordon Stewart's *Journeys to Empire: Enlightenment, Imperialism, and the British Encounter with Tibet, 1774–1904* (2009) concentrate (in significant ways) on travel accounts and observations of other cultures in relating exploration to colonial relations. Still, we require more treatment of the wider connections between intellectual debate and imperial policy and ideologies.

Of course the great eighteenth-century intellectual flowering of the Enlightenment was a Europe-wide phenomenon, and its ideas were often contradictory. It is clear, however, that important concepts relating to empire can be found embedded in it, perhaps notably in the Scottish Enlightenment. The historical writings of

William Robertson are important here, covering Charles V and the Spanish Empire, the English in America, and older attitudes toward India, suggesting that the Scottish Enlightenment was at least partly based on a new Scottish global awareness through the experience of empire. Robertson's framing of the fourfold stadial theory, bringing social and economic ideas together into a quasi-evolutionary conceptualization of human history, was to be highly influential in the nineteenth century. Robertson is well served by *William Robertson and the Expansion of the British Empire* (2011), edited by Stewart J. Brown, but it awaits incorporation into imperial history. Further, as Richard Drayton shows in *Nature's Government: Science, Imperial Britain, and the "Improvement of the World"* (2000), notions from the scientific revolution fed into government policy, not least in the colonies, including a concern with surveys between the 1740s and 1790s. Cook's voyages, connected with Sir Joseph Banks and the Royal Society, constituted a vital turning point here. They were part of a wider picture, and some of the same ideas were still feeding through in the official funding of Livingstone's Zambezi expedition, starting in 1858. On the other hand, Adam Smith has often been depicted as an anti-imperial philosopher and economist, but his devastating critique of mercantilism led to free-trade ideas that permeated both imperial and anti-imperial ideas of the subsequent century.

Moreover, in the eighteenth century there developed, particularly through Edward Gibbon, a fascination with the Roman Empire that was to infuse British education over the next two centuries, not least in proposing the great dichotomy between imperial civilization and alleged barbarian savagery, which became central, albeit in complex ways, to imperial ethnic ideas in the era of pseudo-scientific racism associated with "high imperialism." The Scottish philosopher and historian Adam Ferguson also considered the history of Rome (though in different ways) for the lessons it offered the present. For him, the main dilemma for the British was whether liberty and the empire could be reconciled, a concern that was to activate many intellectuals over the succeeding century. The eighteenth century might also be seen as the source of ideas of humanitarian imperialism, through Edmund Burke, the later abolition movement, and the development of the evangelical missionary thrust, with all its initial idealistic optimism. Any prospectus for a work on the relationship between these great schools of intellectual ideas and the empire would continue into the high point of theorization of the British Empire in the nineteenth century, with Zachary and Thomas Babington Macaulay, James and John Stuart Mill, John Ruskin, Seeley, James Anthony Froude, Halford Mackinder, and others. We should remember that political events and policy making all took place within this maelstrom of ideas.

Such intellectual movements contain great complexities and contradictions, but the key point is that the proponents of a somewhat minimal empire either never take such ideas into account or seem to suggest that they are somehow irrelevant, a position surely hard to sustain. The key point is that the significant intellectual movements of these three centuries do not just touch upon the empire: the empire invariably stands at the center of their deliberations. Moreover, from the scientific revolution onward, the sciences were similarly inseparably bound up not just with colonies as a freely available laboratory, but also with the empire as a key point of contact among continents and peoples. The origins of many modern sciences, of vital developments in medicine, philology, environmental concerns, and above all anthropology and geography, not just in the case of Britain, but for other European states too, were all embedded in the whole project of imperialism. The course of the development of their ideas would have been different if they had been based purely on travel accounts in exotic lands. Empire was not just an enabler, but also a system of ideas central to the conceptual development of these disciplines. And it is in this area that we find the European empires, as well as the American, cooperating with one another in the nineteenth and twentieth centuries. We have, perhaps, been far too obsessed with empires as a source of tension and conflict. They could also be a zone of joint ideas and practices, a significant field that is examined in works such as *Encounters of Empires: Imperial Co-operation and Transfer,* edited by Volker Barth and Roland Cvetkovski (2015).

The other worrying thing about the "minimal empire" approach is that it fails to take into full consideration the material remains or environmental consequences of empire. It is indeed through the surviving physical presence and environmental outcomes of the empire that we can gain insights into its true nature and power. This can be illustrated by sending down "test cores" into different continents and wholly differing periods. It is surely the case that explosive and rampaging happenings can be identified even outside Belich's booms in the nineteenth century. Islands are always a special case, but still they are highly instructive. Botanists, environmentalists, and historians interested in forestry and desiccation theories are fascinated by them. If we take the case of Barbados in the Lesser Antilles, we find that the English began to colonize it from 1627. Within twenty years, its endemic tree cover had been destroyed, and the Spanish and Portuguese had already virtually wiped out or removed its indigenous inhabitants. By the 1640s, the island had been totally converted to sugar production, with all the attendant consequences, environmental and human, including the importation of slave labor. That sounds more like rampaging than ramshackle empire—and well ahead of Belich's period of explosive colonization. By midcentury, Barbados was England's most valuable colony. Elsewhere in the Caribbean, sugar economies produced equally dramatic effects on the environments and social composition of islands, while surviving military remains, such as the many colonial fortresses to be seen in Antigua, St. Kitts, and elsewhere, indicate the militarization of the landscape and the considerable competition among imperial powers. These examples of dramatic change can be duplicated by many more in the seventeenth century. Closer to Britain, the Scottish settlement of Ulster, again with massive environmental, social, cultural, and religious consequences, was another example of explosive empire dating from Elizabethan times. Again empire was constituting Britain.

Another example of imperial transformation comes from the nineteenth century, and it demonstrates the manner in which ramshackle could coexist with rampaging. As is well known, the main thrust of Livingstone's Zambezi expedition of 1858–64 was redirected from the Zambezi, where he had been confronted by the impassable power of the Kabra Bassa rapids, to the Shire River as a possible route into the region of Lake Nyasa, now Lake Malawi, which he partially explored. His ambitions became increasingly focused on what he saw as the need to outflank the Portuguese. So far as he was concerned, they not only were culpably implicated in the East African slave trade, but also constituted a barrier to the progress of Christianity and commerce into the interior. He wanted to establish there an "island of white" of colonists and traders who would trade with the local Africans, inspiring a cash-cropping revolution in the growing of cotton, sugar, and indigo, and connecting the region with the international economy. His ideas were hopelessly optimistic and idealistic, and British politicians came to disown him. But after initial tragedies, his death inspired Scottish missionaries to head for the interior, and eventually, the combined forces of Cecil Rhodes and his British South Africa Company, the Scottish public, and the press persuaded the highly skeptical government of Lord Salisbury to declare a protectorate, with Rhodes financing a minimal administration. This was certainly ramshackle empire on the cheap. Yet within two or three years of the arrival on the scene of the commissioner Sir Harry Johnston in 1891, chieftaincies had been overwhelmed, a severe hut tax designed to flush out African labor had been imposed, and land had been alienated to white settlers. Thus, paradoxically, a shoestring, ramshackle administration rapidly created a rampaging imperial outcome whose striking transformations marked the future direction of the British colony of Nyasaland and the independent country of Malawi down to the present. Here, "ramshackle" meant that there was no possibility of delay. British power had to be established by a series of quick blows. And not the least of those transformations was dramatic environmental change. Malawi constitutes an acute case, but such examples of environmental change with incalculable consequences for indigenous peoples can be found around the British Empire. Most oral researchers in Africa are well aware of the manner in which Africans allude to the dramatic environmental changes of their lifetimes. Reversing the gaze is always essential.

THE FACT OF THE MATTER IS THAT the view from above, in political and administrative history, offers a poor route into an understanding of what empire and imperialism were really like. Two things are apparent: reluctant politicians influenced the course of imperial expansion and—as in the case of Lord Salisbury and Malawi—were often reactive rather than active. But that does not suggest that the results were any less imperialistic. Thus, the British Empire never seemed to be reluctant, ramshackle, or lacking in authority or control for some of its principal victims. But we must feed in two caveats. The reach of imperial law was often restricted (for example, in game law). Some Africans and Asians lived out their lives in comparative isolation, though ultimately always influenced by imperial policies, not least in the area of property and land law (this was particularly true of settler territories). Sometimes Indians and Africans saw the British government and people in the metropolis (however impractically) as principled liberals capable of saving them from local administrators or oppressive settlers. Botswana offers a good example. Three chiefs, Khama, Sebele, and Bathoen, appealed to London in 1895 to save them from either Rhodes's British South Africa Company or the encroaching whites from across the border in the Transvaal. They succeeded, and their intervention resulted in a compromise with Northern Bechuanaland, now Botswana, being declared a protectorate free of settler power. The other so-called High Commission territories of Basutoland (Lesotho) and Swaziland succeeded in escaping incorporation into white-run South Africa. Elsewhere, Africans were doomed to disappointment, as was the celebrated delegation from the African National Congress that visited Britain in 1909 to try to persuade the British to protect blacks from the rampaging whites of the pending Union of South Africa. In Malawi, Africans failed to escape from the Central African Federation of 1953, but their 1959 revolt and connections with pressure groups in the United Kingdom helped secure the breakup of that federation barely ten years later. The indigenous peoples of the empire, the ones who felt the violence and dispossession of rampaging empire most acutely, often assumed, sometimes impractically, that the imperial center had genuine power and turned to it for help. Sometimes they discovered that the empire was indeed ramshackle, a construction prey to a range of pressure groups and complex political processes. The important point is that the imperial center, "settlerdom," and "capitalism," while often in tension, were not antithetical. They were merely arms of the same imperial phenomenon, responding to the pressures of different constituencies while pursuing a variety of objectives essentially within the same frame of empire.

Thus, it is a truism that there were indeed different types of empire all coexisting under the same flag. But whether the imperial divisions were acquired by private enterprise (which had to receive charters or grants from the Crown), by decentralized forms of activity, by "men on the spot," by unstable or turbulent frontiers, by ambitious settler expansion, or even by missionary or public pressure surely does not make the processes any less imperial. The celebrated book *Imperialism: The Story and Significance of a Political Word, 1840–1960* (1964), by Richard Koebner and H. D. Schmidt, is a valuable piece of scholarship, but the result can be regrettable. Some seem to imagine that if the word was not used, the phenomenon somehow did not exist. The fact of the matter is that modern empire, in its various forms, was in a process of evolution from at least the sixteenth century, subsequently passing through a sequence of identifiable phases. But the effects were always the same: the imposition of rule on one people by another. If there was, in the standard definition of empire, a ruling center and a dominated periphery, there could also have been multiple centers with their own peripheries. They also set about the proselytization of others into the culture of the center, and it is these aspects of the imperial culture that are most likely to survive.

Although it has been suggested that the British Empire was neither as centralized nor as autocratic as the Roman, it was certainly just as militarized, and it was equally homogeneous from a cultural point of view. Just as the Roman Empire was recognizably Roman throughout its provinces, so the British Empire was unmistakably British, whether in the so-called dependent empire, the Indian

Empire, or the settler dominions. The cultural recognition factors included the English language and its variants, building styles, residential arrangements, infrastructures, literary understanding and transmission, provincial political and administrative systems, legal provisions and punishments, artistic fashions, ceremonies, religious observances, military organization, weaponry and uniforms, the deployment of mercenaries, approaches to hunting, and other aspects of the environment. As is well represented by the British fascination with the Roman Empire and repeated references to it, the British generally thought (and indeed hoped) that their empire was rather like the Roman, although of course these similarities carried warnings, negative as well as positive lessons. Archaeology, concentrating as it does on material remains, has highlighted the common culture of ancient empires like Rome. Yet the British Empire has seldom been subjected to a similar study.

The fact that a full-scale and integrated cultural history of the British Empire has never been written has tended to obscure the extent to which Britishness was transmitted through a whole range of phenomena—including the Christian churches and missions, schools, universities, social and cultural clubs, administrative offices, legal and financial institutions, urban planning, and street furniture such as statuary and monuments. Edward Said's influential work *Culture and Imperialism* (1993) is focused in different ways. A future cultural history should deal with the "archaeology" of the material remains of empire as well as the transmission of visual, musical, and dramatic arts, many of them bound up with a global intellectual dispersal that remains strikingly influential, though modified in modern times. The remarkable enlargement of the bourgeois sphere needs to be studied in detail. This produced the extraordinary dissemination of institutions such as libraries, art galleries, museums, theatres, racecourses, botanical and other gardens, bandstands, and much else. Class as well as racial analyses will be crucial to this, as will be "rational recreation," sports (very important), and many aspects of the ceremonial (some surviving in independent countries). It would have to embrace such phenomena as clothing and the presentation of the body, interior design, concepts of gentility, and the notion of precise and disciplined timekeeping. In more modern times, European and American influences may have appeared, particularly in the dominions, but the cultural evidence of relative imperial homogeneity would seem to be almost overwhelming. The trajectory of such cultural dispersals, together with the intellectual, social, and racial ideas that bound them all together, would have to be examined, in its various forms, from the seventeenth and eighteenth centuries to the twentieth, with the influence of these cultural characteristics developing with imperial rule itself.

Notions of imperial discipline were applied to place as well as to time, as in the environmental field, where we need to examine environmental change, state forests, game reserves, national parks, irrigation schemes, and the like, as well as urban parks and gardens, including the domestic. Anyone who travels extensively in the former British Empire cannot fail to be struck by the physical, visual, and other elements that provide a sense of Britishness, even if modified by locality, climate, and period. The material remains of the empire constitute evidence of a powerful culture that in all its ramifications looks more rampaging than ramshackle. Thus, it is essential that imperial historians recognize fields outside politics, administration, diplomacy, and economic affairs. There is an increasing wealth of monographs covering some of these, but we need to draw them together into an overall pattern. The really difficult task is to link these cultural and intellectual dimensions with their economic wellsprings. To take but one example: however much India, in seventy years of independence, has sought to create a distinctively Indian culture, its cities (particularly the coastal ones, the former imperial presidency capitals of Kolkata, Mumbai, and Chennai) continue to maintain a strongly British cultural character, still rooted in their economic roles.

Why is it important that such a cultural history of the British Empire should be written? The reason is surely that it may well be in the histories of ideas, science, religious encounters, environmental issues, all forms of cultural diffusion and syncretism, that the true and longer-lasting legacy of the British Empire may reside. Many of these are reflected in the powerful material presence of the empire, and all have to be related to the economic and social forces that spawned them. Surveying these may, moreover, help us escape from the skeptical school that I have described elsewhere as "Empire Lite." After all, does it really matter to Africans, Asians, West Indians, First Nations people, Aborigines, Maoris, and others whether the British Empire was ramshackle, was created by default rather than by design, or was full of compromises and controversies? What clearly matters to them are the vast changes wrought by it—for good or ill—in their environments, social relationships, economic circumstances, cultural and material contexts. On the other hand, we must never discount the extent to which that cultural diffusion has been subjected to all sorts of syncretic influences and has thus been adopted, adapted, and incorporated into indigenous cultures. This form of cultural history is equally about crossovers and hybrid inter-connections. Thus, indigenous peoples are central to such a study. Historians have to grapple with the worlds of imaginative recon-structions in the reactions of real people, many reflected in post-colonial literatures by novelists, playwrights, and poets, which can offer significant insights taking us beyond any number of complex historical writings.

The British Empire was indeed an immensely complex affair. It was a very big thing with a myriad of local consequences, happen-ing (in different places) over four centuries. A full understanding requires an understanding of the myriad as well as the big. This discursive contribution has ranged widely to illustrate the complexi-ties and the formidable challenges, suggesting that we should place more emphasis on product, not process, on the cultural and envi-ronmental economy in addition to, or as informed by, the political economy, on continuities and comparative insights, global issues, and above all on reversing the gaze. We must break down barriers, the barriers among disciplines that create a disabling compartmen-talization, as well as the barriers between the perspectives of domi-nant and subordinate people. While we await the writing of this new form of imperial history, we can at least say that the question of a rampaging or ramshackle British Empire requires a sophisticated and nuanced answer. As the Malawi example illustrates, the ram-shackle nature of the empire, a lack of resources that would have enabled a slower, controlled approach, could lead precisely to ram-paging methods. Ramshackle and rampaging are intertwined. But despite that, the notion that the complexities of the British Empire somehow reduced its capacity for transformational power is surely misplaced. Particularly when viewed from below, that empire had tremendous environmental, economic, social, and cultural results that remain all around us.

Fall Semester 2016

A version of this article appeared in the *Journal of Imperial and Common-wealth History*, 23, 1 (Mar. 2015), pp. 99–124. Material is reprinted by per-mission of the publisher, Taylor & Francis Ltd.

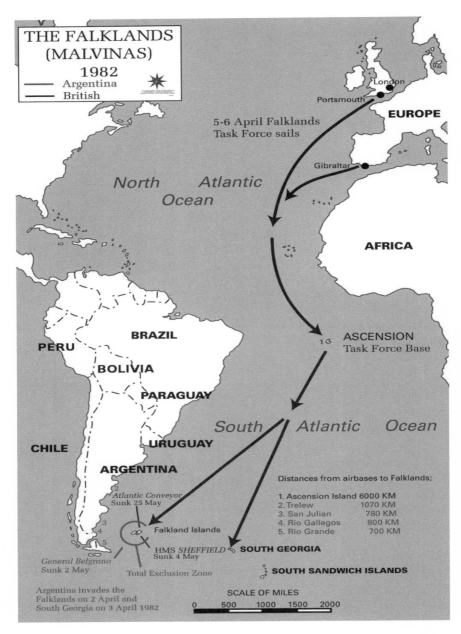

Falklands Campaign, distance to bases, 1982. Department of History, U.S. Military Academy.

23

The Falklands Conflict:
A Worm's-Eye View

SARAH BEAVER

This is not a serious academic account of the Falklands conflict. It is a few very personal and selective recollections and
reflections, checked against information now in the public
domain, based on my experience as a very junior civil servant in the
Ministry of Defence Main Building in Whitehall during the 1982
Falklands War. I finally visited the Falklands in 2007, coincidentally
at the time when members of the South Atlantic Medal Association were visiting to commemorate the twenty-fifth anniversary of
the war.

It was very moving to see the wreaths, the cemeteries, and the
memorials to those who had lost their lives in the conflict, and to
meet and hear the stories of the returning veterans, several of whom
had been seriously injured or had suffered, and continued to suffer,
from post-traumatic stress disorder, of which we are now far more
aware than previously. It was also heartening, and indeed deeply
gratifying, to see the real warmth of the welcome the returning veterans received from the Falkland Islanders, who hosted them all in
their own homes. As was clear from my discussions and negotiations
with members of the Falklands Islands government, the Falkland
Islanders remain acutely conscious of the sacrifice and cost of the
campaign to Britain, and are as committed as ever to the continuation of British sovereignty.

Unlike most of our more recent military activities in Afghanistan, Iraq, Libya, and elsewhere, where the outcome of our military operations and engagement has been far less satisfactory, with a deeply problematic legacy, the 1982 Falklands campaign was a relatively straightforward and limited engagement in which, despite immense military challenges, our immediate political and military objectives—the defeat and removal of the Argentine invaders and the restoration of self-government to the Falkland Islanders—were achieved in a few weeks.

At the time of Operation CORPORATE, the code name for the operation to recover the Falkland Islands and repossess other South Atlantic territories following the Argentine landings on South Georgia in late March 1982 and invasion of the Falkland Islands on 2 April, Northwood was a NATO and UK naval headquarters also commanding the British strategic deterrent. It was from Northwood that the whole operation was commanded. It was not until the 1990s that Britain established a joint headquarters there for the command of all joint overseas operations and subsequently developed dedicated facilities for this. Whereas there is now, deep under the Ministry of Defence in Whitehall, a secure bunker equipped with all the latest technology and communications equipment necessary for the management and coordination of government efforts in the event of crisis, back in 1982 the Defence Situation Centre in which we worked was a very basic facility.

At the time, I had no experience of how the services organized themselves outside Whitehall and very little relevant experience of operational matters. I had joined the department just two years earlier and, as an administration trainee, worked under the tutelage of a principal who critically scrutinized my drafts before they were sent off to the typing pool in the nether regions of the building, from which they would emerge two or three days later if you were lucky. In an emergency, we had to rely on the good offices of the head of division's personal assistant.

We had no access to computers until about six weeks before the invasion of the Falklands. The extremely user-unfriendly machine quickly proved itself to be far more trouble than it was worth. There was no sign of even a typewriter in the cell I was to occupy for Operation CORPORATE; all my notes and briefings for ministers and senior officials were handwritten. We did have access to a photocopier in an adjacent cell, and the typing pool had recently acquired a word processor.

When not on watch duty at the Defence Situation Centre, I joined colleagues in DS 11, the defense secretariat with the policy responsibility for the operation, drafting letters to members of the public by revising and redrafting each morning a set of numbered paragraphs intended to be incorporated as appropriate into the literally hundreds of replies that were sent out in response to the bulging sacks of pubic correspondence received each day. The letters reflected the full range of public opinion on the Falklands War, a political and national crisis in Britain, where public opinion was fanned by both the scale and extent of British losses and casualties in a very short period of time. Although the BBC and certain newspapers, to the fury of others, took a measured and critical approach, much of the popular press coverage was extraordinarily jingoistic. We received some shocking letters, including some suggesting that we should simply drop nuclear bombs on Buenos Aires. But we also had to prepare responses to letters from bereaved parents of casualties, challenging the accuracy of either the Prime Minister's initial condolence letter or that of the commanding officer who had sought to comfort the relatives with a somewhat glossed account of the relevant incident. We did our best, but as we quickly learned, no words are likely to satisfy a grieving parent.

Secure speech facilities continue to be a challenge in any operating environment, but the lack of access to usable secure speech communication facilities was a particular frustration and difficulty in 1982. When giving evidence later to the House of Commons Defence Committee inquiry into the handling of the media during the conflict, Sir Frank Cooper, the permanent secretary for the Defence Ministry, spoke of the excellent communications with the Foreign Office: "We have direct communications with them. Everybody knows everybody very well. We have got tubes which can send papers in one direction and another, television which goes from one building to another." They may have had all that in key offices on the sixth floor of the Main Building, where the permanent secretary, the senior military, and ministers had their offices, but we did not have ready access to such facilities on the fourth floor or in the tenth-floor turret in which DS 11 had its offices. I had to walk or, more typically, run down the long corridors of the Main Building and, since the lifts were painfully slow, up and down the stairs to deliver messages and papers to the sixth and tenth floors as well as the ground-floor Press Office. The pace was hectic, and I remember falling asleep from sheer exhaustion while unlocking my bike at the end of a sixteen- or seventeen-hour shift.

There was, admittedly, a cubicle off our room equipped with a secure telephone, but it could not process ordinary women's voices, and you can imagine the difficulties of the military-style conversation

Fig. 23.1. Prime Minister Margaret Thatcher with British troops in the Falklands, 1983.

of one-way speech (typically while contending with the sound of a vacuum cleaner operated by the late-night cleaners) growling down a very crackly line to our permanent representative to the UN or his staff. One of the lessons learned from the campaign was that we needed a secure telephone system that was more amenable to women's voices.

As the desk officer, I received the occasional open-line telephone call from the Prime Minister's office to inquire whether media reports of actions taking place in the South Atlantic were true and, if so, why was the Prime Minister not being kept informed. At one stage, Downing Street wanted a secure telephone link installed so that the Prime Minister could be kept briefed on immediate operational developments. But Defence Secretary John Nott, possibly protective his own position, which at times seemed somewhat marginal in a short military campaign during which the War Cabinet, chaired by the Prime Minister, met at least daily, was unenthusiastic.

BUT THAT IS TO JUMP AHEAD. At the time of the Argentine invasion of the Falklands and the Royal Marines' surrender at Port Stanley on Friday, 2 April 1982, my colleagues had, like the rest of the nation, watched and listened with fascinated horror to the news. While vaguely aware from undergraduate days that the Falkland Islands were named after the 5th Viscount Falkland, they had not been, until the last few weeks, the subject of my or much national attention or interest. The general thought of my naval colleagues, to whose adjacent offices we migrated that Friday morning, was that it was inconceivable that we would or could seek to recover them. They were nearly 8,000 miles away, and it was 3,800 miles from the Falklands to the nearest British military airfield, on Ascension Island.

But Mrs. Thatcher, strongly encouraged by the First Sea Lord, Sir Henry Leach, took a different view. Following late-night decisions and an announcement to a packed House of Commons on Saturday, a task force of some 28,000 men and over 100 ships was assembled and sent to recover the Falkland Islands. There was nevertheless

Fig. 23.2. Admiral Sir Henry Leach, First Sea Lord during the Falklands campaign.

Fig. 23.3. HMS *Sheffield* in the Indian Ocean, February 1982. Photo by Nathalmad.

a sense throughout the conflict that this was an almost unreal situation. As losses and casualties on both sides became an almost daily occurrence, many of us never entirely lost our sense of disbelief at the situation in which we found ourselves or that so many lives were being lost for such a distant overseas dependent territory that was not of strategic importance to Britain.

I moved to the Defence Situation Centre. It became the Whitehall center for the operation on 4 May, the day that HMS *Sheffield,* a destroyer, was hit by an Exocet missile fired by the Argentine Air Force, resulting in the death of nineteen crew members, the first of what were eventually to be some 255 British military casualties. I joined a roster of three other civilians taking turns on nominally twelve-hour shifts, but normally far longer, because we needed the extra manpower. We shared a small room with three military colleagues and some military clerks, who retrieved and sorted the constant stream of purple-inked signals from the racks of signal machines along one side of the room and allocated them as they thought appropriate to the civilian desk officer or our colleagues: a naval officer (a former captain of *HMS Endurance);* a former commander of the small Royal Marine contingent (thirty to forty men) that until the invasion had been Britain's sole military asset on the islands; and a RAF colleague. Around the other three walls were maps and my colleagues' photos from their service in the Falklands, visual clues to the completely unfamiliar terrain and territory with which we were intensely engaged.

My service colleagues' personal knowledge and experience of the Falklands and military matters in general was vital in interpreting the signals we received, some surprisingly immediate and compelling. I remember vividly the signal reporting that HMS *Coventry*, a destroyer, had capsized and sunk just twenty minutes after being hit on 25 May; my naval colleague said that it was inevitable there would be substantial casualties. (In the event, 19 crew members were killed and 30 injured, out of a complement of 287.) Not long afterward, we received the signal "Exocet detected 28 NMS." Just a few minutes later came the signal reporting that the *Atlantic Conveyor*, a ship taken up from trade and still carrying Chinook helicopters, a key asset, had been hit—and lost.

I never had a clear description of my role as civilian duty officer— we generally took on anything. One night I had to track down an arms dealer, who was eventually found in a hotel room with someone who was clearly not his wife, because he was thought to be in possession of some mines of the type being laid by the Argentines, whose fusing mechanism we needed urgently to understand. Another night, in an unsuccessful attempt to feed the tabloids' appetite for human-interest stories, I was tasked with arranging for a donation of cream to be delivered during the night to RAF Lyneham, to accompany a Kentish farmer's gift of his strawberry crop for the *Sheffield* survivors when they reached Ascension Island. I got the cream, but the donor was adamant there should be no publicity, because it had had substantial business in Argentina. I also kept my eyes and ears open for relevant information. One morning, noticing that the intelligence brief made no mention of the fact that some arms shipments for Argentina were possibly passing through Heathrow that day, I alerted the permanent secretary. This was time-critical information on which he did not hesitate to act.

But once the main urgent operational matters had been dealt with, my core task when on overnight duty was to prepare the morning brief (in manuscript) for the secretary of state and the permanent secretary, whose morning meeting I would then attend. On daytime shifts, I had to keep senior political figures and civilian colleagues briefed on all key operational and other developments that were reported via the Defence Situation Centre, assist the press office with the preparation of news releases, and so forth. With the five-hour time difference between Britain and the Falklands, much operational activity in the South Atlantic took place in the London evenings.

On 25 May, when we lost *HMS Coventry* and the *Atlantic Conveyor,* it was a very difficult night, the subject of severe criticism then and later regarding how the media were handled. Essentially, the navy, with a major recovery effort in progress, was anxious not to put further lives at risk by the disclosure of any information that might prejudice the rescue. The secretary of state was due to be interviewed for the ten o'clock television news, and as he departed for the ITN studio, I met him in the corridor and had to report the loss of the *Atlantic Conveyor* and explain to him the operational implications. On the news that night, there was reference to a destroyer being "in difficulty" in the South Atlantic, but as required by the navy, the ship was not named, so hundreds of naval families were kept in anxious suspense till the next day, not knowing whether their family member was involved.

The navy was by nature very secretive. The night of 14 June, when the Argentines surrendered to General Moore—Commander, Land Forces, Falklands Islands—at Port Stanley was a case in point. It had been a difficult day on the ground and in London. There had been intense fighting as our forces approached Stanley, and although we certainly knew by then that it was a matter of when, not if, our forces would prevail, the atmosphere was extremely tense. We were anxious not just about our own military forces, but also about the risk of civilian casualties. We had little confidence that the Argentines would advertise and respect the safe haven that, through the International Red Cross, we had designated around Christ Church Cathedral.

Early in the evening, I was asked for advice on what to do if the Argentines offered a cease-fire. I went up to the sixth floor for guidance and was summoned into Sir Frank Cooper's office, where he was drinking what looked like a strong whisky. He instructed me to put out on the Press Association tapes urgently a message along the lines of "British military commanders at any level have the power to accept the surrender of the enemy," "surrender" being the key word, no mention of "cease-fire." His response seemed odd and, to my mind, did not really answer the question, so although I relayed the instruction to the deputy head of public relations, who was emerging from the secretary of state's offices, it was only when Sir Frank came out and reminded us that he wanted this out on the tapes immediately that he actually went off to do his bidding. The secretary of state's private secretary, who overheard all this, clearly shared our misgivings. He alerted the secretary of state, who told me to rescind the instruction.

This took a bit of time, since the Press Office was on the ground floor. When I finally got back into the DSC, I walked through the navy cell and noticed a naval commander quickly turn over a signal that he was reading. I walked over, picked it up, and read something along the lines of "white flags are flying over Stanley." I borrowed it, made a few photocopies, and ran up to the sixth floor to deliver it to the offices of the secretary of state, the permanent secretary, and service chiefs, whose heavy oak doors, normally firmly closed, all miraculously opened to receive it as they heard me running down the corridor.

The Thatcher archives contain her notes for the historic short announcement that she was to make in the House of Commons at 10:22 that evening. The notes begin: "MOD 9 p.m. From Northwood," suggesting she was perhaps drawing on a telephone call from the Defence Ministry.[1] Her formal statement included the following: "They are reported to be flying white flags over Port Stanley. Our troops have been ordered not to fire except in self-defence. Talks are now in progress . . . about the surrender of the Argentine forces on East and West Falkland. I shall report further to the House tomorrow." I note from Lawrence Freedman's carefully researched *Official History* of the campaign that the British commanders had heard reports that the Argentines had hoisted a white flag, but at that point they could not actually see one. Nevertheless, as Freedman observes, it was a striking image, and negotiations over a cease-fire had been authorized.[2]

OF COURSE, I SHARED THE GENERAL PRIDE in what our forces accomplished. But rather than jubilation, I simply recall a feeling of immense relief that the fighting was over, that we had avoided major civilian casualties in Port Stanley, where the entire population was being held as hostages, and that there would be no more casualties on either side. But if the hostilities were over, the work was certainly not. Until early the next year, I was to continue to work on Falklands-related matters, which continued to generate an enormous amount of public and parliamentary interest as work began on a number of inquiries.

The first ones concluded rather quickly and straightforwardly, but were by no means the final word. It was difficult to make sense of the scraps of often contradictory information on which we had to draw to answer the hundreds of parliamentary questions to which, as civil servants, we had to prepare the draft replies. I dreaded the calls we sometimes received from behind the Speaker's chair in the House of Commons when the Prime Minister was preparing to field questions in the chamber and was either challenging the accuracy of our briefing notes or wanting us to be more specific than we could be.

An issue that had caused serious controversy from the start of the conflict was the Defence Ministry's provision of information to the public and its handling of the media. It was only after intense political lobbying that the number of journalists taken to the South Atlantic was increased progressively from none to twenty-nine, and they faced very real challenges and frustrations in getting their reports back to Britain. Quite apart from the question of what information could be disclosed and whether there was consistency on this between operational commanders, the ministry, and other government departments—a just about impossible challenge—the quantity of signal traffic or voice transmissions from the South Atlantic was very severely constrained. There was very limited satellite coverage of the South Atlantic, and media reports at one stage accounted for over 30 percent of the aircraft carrier HMS _Invincible's_ communications. Journalists were eventually restricted to just 700 words of copy a day. But many of the embarked journalists felt aggrieved and frustrated at the controls placed on them and were very critical of press or information officers whose task it was to "mind" them and vet their text. There was no live television coverage; all film had had to be transported physically back to the UK by sea, and after the landings, transporting the film back to the ships was a further challenge. Independent Television News reported delays of eighteen to twenty-three days before its footage was broadcast. For the journalists, this was at once a huge opportunity but also enormously frustrating and challenging. The media's own behavior through the conflict was also the subject of much critical comment and debate.

So although there was a clear feeling in Whitehall that it would be premature for Parliament to conduct a detailed investigation into the conduct of the operation while the information was still very confused and incomplete or operationally sensitive, even before the Argentine surrender it was announced that the House of Commons Defence Committee would conduct an inquiry on "The handling of public and press information during the Falklands conflict." Since the Defence Ministry's Press Office was evidently struggling with it, I was tasked with pulling together the ministry's memorandum, which had to be submitted in short order in answer to the series of questions that the committee clerk had tabled.

From the outset, I knew this was a minefield. I was very aware of the media complaints and criticisms and also knew from my work in the DSC that there were serious tensions within the Press Office, particularly between the military and civilian elements within it. But I became fully aware of some of the wider government dynamics at play only when I discovered in the National Archives a fascinating file of papers from Downing Street now available to the public.

Two of the questions we were required to address in the memorandum was "How does the Ministry of Defence Information organisation fit in with the overall Government Information Service? . . . What were the respective roles of MoD, CoI [Central Office of Information, the government's marketing and information office], FCO [Foreign and Commonwealth Office] and the Prime Minister's office in this context?" The committee clerk had also written to Clive Whitmore, the Prime Minister's principal private secretary, inviting his comments in particular "on the arrangements for the co-ordination in the Government Information Services."

From the Prime Minister's files, it was clear that there was huge nervousness about this. On 8 July 1982, Robert Armstrong, the Cabinet secretary, told Clive Whitmore that he knew of "no precedents for members of the Prime Minister's office to give or giving evidence to a Select Committee." He hoped that they would succeed in refusing to allow private secretaries to give evidence, on the "well-established ground that a Private Secretary is no more than an arm or emanation of his Minister and transactions between Ministers and their Private Secretaries are privileged."[3] But he feared that they would not be successful in resisting a request for Bernard Ingham, the chief press secretary, to give evidence. The Defence Committee chairman was particularly interested in his co-ordinating role and had pointed out at a "non-meeting" that the memorandum submitted by the Ministry of Defence had referred to No 10's "co-ordinating effort." Whitmore also reported speaking to Sir Frank Cooper and asking him to "make clear that our so-called co-ordinating function consisted for practical purposes of no more than your holding a daily meeting to ensure that you, the Foreign and Commonwealth Office and the Ministry of Defence were all aware of the latest political and military situation before you talked to your respective clients."

My drafting—for I suspect it was mine—was evidently causing problems at the highest levels! I do recall being somewhat perplexed at Sir Frank's evidence session in front of the committee on 21 July. He was subjected to some close questioning about the use of the word "co-ordinated" and whether other government departments would "subscribe wholeheartedly" to the Defence Ministry memo-randum's contents. I now appreciate the pressure he was under when he confirmed that he was "pretty confident" that they would, that Downing Street and the Foreign Office had seen the memo-randum but "might have individual glosses on it," and "that it might have been better phrased"; when asked why the other departments or himself had not deleted the word, he explained that while he accepted responsibility for it, he was away in Brussels at the time.[4] It is clear from the Prime Minister files that Bernard Ingham, who was summoned to give evidence to the committee in November, was very unhappy with Sir Frank's oral evidence. Further discrepan-cies of view about the coordinating role or otherwise of Number 10 emerged when John Nott, the Defence Secretary, gave evidence in November, with Sir Frank Cooper appearing for a second time. The committee's final report reflected its appreciation of some of the difficulties involved, but commented on the conflicting evidence from witnesses and found the "overwhelming impression of a lack of co-ordination" in Whitehall, particularly at the ministerial level, "extremely disturbing." Another issue that the committee was keen to probe was whether during an off-the-record briefing immediately before the main landings of troops and equipment in San Carlos Water, Sir Frank had deliberately misled the press by telling them that there would be "no D-Day type landing." He admitted to the committee that he had not "unveiled the whole truth" and, having it in his mind that a D-Day-type invasion was an opposed landing and that the whole aim of the operation was an unopposed landing, that he had briefed the journalists that he did not expect that type of in-vasion.[5] In its final report, the committee considered that "his con-duct was fully justified by the circumstances" and that "the credibil-ity of the Ministry's off the record briefings need not have suffered lasting damage."[6] But when Jim Meacham of *The Economist* gave evi-dence to the committee, he said that Sir Frank's explanation had been "disingenuous"; they had been told that there were all sorts of things going on all over the islands, and that they could expect to see more of the small raids such as had taken place at Pebble Island. He added that the briefing had been recorded both on tape and in shorthand, prompting the committee to ask for copies.

    That comment caused enormous problems in the Ministry of De-fence and for me. There was first the issue whether it was appro-priate for the records of an off-the-record briefing to be released, but of more immediate concern from my perspective was that the Press Office was unable to locate all the relevant tapes. A commercial company had been engaged to record the briefings, but when we replayed them, the tape ended midsentence at what seemed to be the critical stage of the briefing. Despite spending many hours listening to a pile of reel-to-reel tapes in case they had accidentally been mislabeled or over-recorded, I never found the rest. I recall that the language used by Sir Frank and the journalists was remarkably colorful, not at all what you would expect to hear from a permanent secretary or from respected national news correspondents. Of necessity, we eventually had to adopt a policy of providing selected (and also expurgated) excerpts to the committee.

From this distance, this and many of the other awkward questions that arose from the committee's inquiry and evidence sessions seem like a mighty storm in a very small teacup. But at the time, they certainly preoccupied me and the top of the office.

The committee published its report, complete with a number of recommendations, in December. Early the next year, I moved to another post. The report contained a number of recommendations for the future, most of which the government accepted, but implementation was more difficult. As more recent actors know only too well, there will always be tension between the media, the military, and government, particularly in times of war.

For the Falklands War, the bottom line was that this was a successful operation militarily and politically. For the Falkland Islanders, toward which successive British governments had demonstrated at best equivocal commitment, the war marked a turning point in their history and development. No longer were they an almost forgotten British Dependent (now Overseas) Territory. Ensuring their ongoing security required the ability to support and reinforce rapidly the massively increased military presence on the islands, which resulted in the construction of the Mount Pleasant airfield, from which the RAF operates weekly flights to Britain via Ascension Island. It is also well used by the Falkland Islanders and other visitors. The economy, previously overwhelmingly dependent on sheep farming, has diversified to include the sale of fishing rights, oil exploration, and tourism, bringing relative prosperity to the islanders. That one of the Falklands Islands government's key priorities later appeared to be to secure more appropriate check-in arrangements at RAF Brize Norton for business-class travelers on military flights to Port Stanley was testament to that.

The costs of the enduring military commitment on our considerably reduced armed forces are, however, rather more problematic, since there are many more immediate threats to Britain's security.

Ultimately there will need to be an agreement with Argentina ensuring the Falklands' peace and security, but for the moment, the prospects are bleak.

As Margaret Thatcher knew, the survival of her government was at stake when the Falklands were invaded. While opinions remain strongly divided on Thatcher and her domestic and European policies—and by the end of her eleven years as Prime Minister, I was as impatient as anyone to see her departure from Downing Street—she still commands and deserves respect for her courageous leadership in time of crisis.

Spring Semester 2017

1. *Official Record,* col. 700, 14 June 1982.

2. Lawrence Freedman, *The Official History of the Falklands Campaign* (London, 2007 edn.), II, p. 657.

3. The files are PREM-19-1883, National Archives.

4. House of Commons, First Report from the Defence Committee, Session 1982–83, *The Handling of the Press and Public Information during the Falklands Conflict* (London, Dec. 1982), 2 vols.

5. House of Commons, First Report from the Defence Committee, Session 1982–83, I, question 40.

6. Ibid., p. xiv.

"I will be with you, whatever": George W. Bush and Tony Blair, 8 April 2003. © Nick Danziger, Contact Press Images.

24

How to "Fix" a War: Tony Blair and Iraq

GEOFFREY WHEATCROFT

Ow did it happen? By now it is effortless to say that the invasion of Iraq in 2003 by American and British forces was the most disastrous—and disgraceful—such intervention of our time. It is also well-nigh pointless to say so: how many people reading this would disagree? For Americans, Iraq is their worst foreign calamity since Vietnam (although far more citizens of each country were killed than were Americans); for the British, it is the worst at least since Suez, in 1956, though really much worse on every score, from political dishonesty to damage to the national interest to sheer human suffering.

Although skeptics wondered how much more the very-long-awaited *Report of the Iraq Inquiry* by a committee chaired by Sir John Chilcot could tell us when it appeared at last in July 2016, it proved to contain a wealth of evidence and acute criticism all the weightier for its sober tone and for having the imprimatur of the official government publisher. It was a further and devastating indictment not only of Tony Blair personally but also of a whole apparatus of state and government, Cabinet, Parliament, armed forces, and, far from least, intelligence agencies.

Among its conclusions, the report says that there was no imminent threat from Saddam Hussein; that the British "chose to join the invasion of Iraq before the peaceful options for disarmament had been exhausted"; that military action "was not a last resort"; that when the United Nations weapons inspector Hans Blix said weeks before the invasion that he "had not found any weapons of mass destruction and the items that were not accounted for might not exist," Blair wanted Blix "to harden up his findings."

The report also found that deep sectarian divisions in Iraq "were exacerbated by . . . de Ba'athification and . . . demobilisation of the Iraqi army"; that Blair was warned by his diplomats and ministers of the "inadequacy of U.S. plans" for Iraq after the invasion, and of what they saw as his "inability to exert significant influence on U.S. planning"; and that "there was no collective discussion of the decision by senior Ministers," who were regularly bypassed and ignored by Blair.

And, of course, claims about Iraqi WMDs were presented by Downing Street in a way that "conveyed certainty without acknowledging the limitations of the intelligence," which is putting it generously. Chilcot stopped short of saying directly that the invasion was illegal or that Blair lied to Parliament, but he has subsequently, with understatement, said that Blair "wasn't straight" about the invasion. And his report was severe on the shameful collusion of the British intelligence agencies, and on the sinister way in which Blair's attorney general changed his opinion about the legality of the invasion.

Planning and preparations for Iraq after Saddam "were wholly inadequate," Chilcot says, and "the people of Iraq have suffered greatly." Those might seem like statements of the blindingly obvious, as does the solemn verdict that the invasion "failed to achieve the goals it had set for a new Iraq." It did more than merely fail, and not only was every reason we were given for the war falsified; every one of them has been stood on its head. Extreme violence in Iraq precipitated by the invasion metastasized into the hideous conflict in neighboring Syria and the implosion of the wider region, the exact opposite of that birth of peaceable pro-Western democracy that proponents of the invasion had insisted would come about. While Blair at his most abject still says that all these horrors were unforeseeable, Chilcot reminded us that they were not only foreseeable, but also widely foreseen.

Nor are those the only repercussions. Chilcot coyly said that "the widespread perception"—meaning the correct belief—that Downing Street distorted the intelligence about Saddam's weaponry has left a "damaging legacy," undermining trust and confidence in politicians. It is not fanciful to see the Brexit vote and the election of Donald Trump among those consequences, all part of the revulsion across the Western world against elites and establishments that were so discredited by Iraq. And so how could it have happened?

By now the war has produced an enormous literature, including several official British reports, beginning with the Hutton Report of January 2004 and the *Review of Intelligence on Weapons of Mass Destruction* the following July, after an inquiry chaired by Lord Butler, a former Cabinet secretary. While its criticism of named individuals was muted, it built up a dismal story of incompetence and official deceit.

One member of Butler's panel, which took no more than five months to hear evidence and report, was John Chilcot, a retired senior civil servant who had worked in the Home Office and with the intelligence agencies. On 15 June 2009, Gordon Brown, who had succeeded Blair as prime minister two years earlier, told Parliament that "with the last British combat troops about to return home from Iraq, now is the right time to ensure that we have a proper process in place to enable us to learn the lessons of the complex and often controversial events of the last six years," and he announced a new inquiry, chaired by Chilcot. In those two years, everything had gone wrong for Brown, from continuing violence in Iraq to financial collapse, and his plain purpose was to push the matter aside and distance himself from his predecessor.

One of the comic subplots of this unfunny story is the way that Brown, as throughout his career, always tried to avoid being associated with contentious questions or difficult decisions. "For when they reach the scene of crime—Macavity's not there!" nor James Gordon Brown if he could help it. Chilcot mentioned that Brown would sometimes send Mark Bowman, his private secretary, in his place to meetings concerned with Iraq, in the hope he could avoid personal responsibility.

So it was characteristic that when Brown first assigned Chilcot to lead the inquiry, it was to be held in camera, with as little publicity as possible. But parliamentary and public outcry put a stop to that, and Chilcot began his hearings in public view. They could all be followed, and then accessed online, and this has already been made use of by Peter Oborne for *Not the Chilcot Report* (2016), a concise assessment, carefully sourced, that appeared before the report itself, and by Tom Bower, whose *Broken Vows: Tony Blair; The Tragedy of Power* (2016) is a full-dress assault on every part of Blair's record. That includes a hair-raising account of his wildly profitable financial career since leaving office, but the book's most startling contribution to the Iraq debate is the number of attributed quotations from former very senior government officials who belatedly criticize Blair and a war that, it must be remembered, he had begun by ignoring all professional advice from anyone who knew anything at all about the subject. A Foreign Office authority on Iraq who pleaded with him that, from every previous experience, the invasion would likely be fraught and possibly calamitous was dismissed by Blair: "That's all history, Mike. This is about the future."

Over seven years, much was done to obstruct the inquiry. Sir Jeremy Heywood, the present Cabinet secretary, deplorably tried to protect Blair, and although much of what Blair wrote to Bush in the year before the war has been published, Bush's side in the correspondence has been withheld. In any case there was the ludicrous process of "Maxwellization," by which anyone criticized adversely in an official report is shown the criticisms before publication and allowed to respond. This dates back nearly fifty years to a legal challenge to such a report by the crooked publisher Robert Maxwell; that such a process should still be named after the greatest scoundrel to disfigure British public life in our time suggests that it could usefully be reexamined.

Scarcely any individual or even institutional buyer was likely to acquire the twelve printed volumes of the report, although every family of the 179 British service personnel who died in Iraq was presented with a set, for what consolation that may be, while the entire report is freely available online. Nor are many likely to read all 2.6 million words of it, but the 62,000-word executive summary is well worth reading. It illuminates once more, but very clearly, the yawning gulf between what Blair was saying publicly in the year before the war, to Parliament and even to his own Cabinet, and what he was saying in private to Bush.

Hence the anger with which the press pounced on Blair's letter to Bush on 28 July 2002: "I will be with you, whatever." It has taken some people a long time to grasp this. The story falls into place when those words are read in conjunction with the Downing Street Memo, written in the greatest secrecy five days before Blair's promise of fealty, in which Sir Richard Dearlove, the head of MI6, the Secret Intelligence Service, reported on his recent talks in Washington. "Bush wanted to remove Saddam," the memo said, "through military action, justified by the conjunction of terrorism and WMD. But *the intelligence and facts were being fixed around the policy.*" Those italicized words are the heart of the matter.

While the spread of nuclear weapons was plainly a problem, Iraq was far from the gravest threat. Sir William Ehrman, the Foreign Office director of international security in 2000–2002, told Chilcot that the nuclear programs of Iran, Libya, and North Korea were "maturing" and were "probably of greater concern than Iraq"—not to mention Pakistan, where A. Q. Khan, then nuclear program director, was operating something like a mail-order system in nuclear know-how and had supplied uranium-enriching equipment to Libya. WMDs might have been a plausible reason for invading Pakistan, just as Islamist terrorism might have been a plausible reason for invading Saudi Arabia, which had fostered al-Qaeda and from which most of the 9/11 murderers came, but for the awkward fact that Washington treats them as friendly countries. But neither made any sense at all as reasons for invading Iraq.

At the time the war began, Sir Jeremy Greenstock was British ambassador to the United Nations. He has said on BBC radio, "Hans Blix told me privately, 'I don't know that they've got them and I don't know they've not got them,'" which was the simple truth, and is perfectly congruent with Blix's saying then that his inspection regime was working and needed more time. But Blair knew that the approaching war was unwanted and unpopular in his country: a poll on 21 January 2003 found 30 percent for war, 42 percent against. Aware that he could not take a reluctant Parliament and country to war on the basis that "we don't know they've not got them," he had no choice but to dissemble and mislead.

"I wouldn't call it a lie," says Andrew Turnbull, the Cabinet secretary at the time of the invasion, quoted by Bower. "'Deception' is the right word. You can deceive without lying, by leaving a false interpretation uncorrected." Most of us would call that a distinction without a difference, but few who read Chilcot attentively will doubt that the brew of exaggeration, distortion, misrepresentation, *suggestio falsi,* and *suppressio veri* that was Blair's case for war was anything other than mendacious.

What Blair knew very well was that the Bush administration was determined to destroy Saddam, whether he possessed weapons of mass destruction or not. The purpose of the war was regime change for its own sake, even if in defiance of international law and the United Nations. And Blair's great deception—his true crime—was not his September 2002 "dossier" and all the other claims about WMDs as such, false as those claims proved to be. It was his larger case, kept up for the best part of a year, that he had not committed the country to war, when privately he had.

For the British, this was the end of a long story, from the defeat of a British army by the Turks south of Baghdad in 1916 to the creation after that war—and then pacification by bombing—of a new country called Iraq, supposedly a friendly regime with Sunni Hashemite princes ruling a Shiite majority as well as Kurds, in which respect Saddam was the Hashemites' heir. After he invaded Kuwait in 1990, the British joined the campaign to expel him, led by President Bush the Elder, but crucially with authorization by UN Security Council resolutions, and supported by Saudi Arabia as well as France, among others.

At that time, Blair was a rising politician still in his thirties and the Labour spokesman on employment. Until he was elected party leader after the sudden death of John Smith in 1994, Blair had shown no interest at all in international politics, although just before Smith died, he saw *Schindler's List.* Blair "was spellbound," he tells us, and his life was changed, though maybe not his alone. There can be no "bystanders," Blair decided: "You participate, like it or not. You take sides by inaction as much as by action . . . Whether such reactions are wise in someone charged with leading a country is another matter." Yes, it is.

After he became prime minister, in May 1997, Blair found new places to take sides. He sent British troops to restore order in Sierra Leone; he urged Western action to drive the Serbs out of Kosovo, where he was welcomed as the liberator he later thought he would be in Iraq; he tried to formulate such actions in a doctrine. One of the Chilcot panel members was Sir Lawrence Freedman, a well-known historian, who contributed to Blair's famous or notorious Chicago speech of April 1999, a speech inspired by what the jurist Philippe Sands has called "the emotional and ahistorical interventionist instincts that later led directly to the Iraq debacle."

TODAY IT IS HARD TO RECAPTURE the mood of two decades ago and the wave of adulation when Blair first entered Downing Street. Soon that adulation had washed across the Atlantic: well before the *New York Times* was writing about the "Blair Democrats," Paul Berman had called Blair "the leader of the free world." It would have gone to the head of a naturally humble man. Both Turnbull and Jonathan Powell, Blair's erstwhile chief of staff, have spoken of his "Messiah complex"—without irony, alas: he really did come to believe that he was a new redeemer of mankind.

But the crucial events took place far from London or Kosovo, in Washington in November 2000, and in New York the following September. Robin Cook was Blair's first foreign secretary and, in March 2003, the month of the invasion, the only member of the Cabinet to resign over Iraq. In his resignation speech, he rightly said that the invasion would not be taking place if Al Gore were in the White House, and so if one wanted to say who was ultimately responsible for the war, one answer would be the Supreme Court, when it frivolously awarded the 2000 election to Bush the Younger.

We know that the new administration was discussing an invasion of Iraq as soon as Bush was inaugurated, urged on by the neoconservatives who had been publicly advocating a war to destroy Saddam for years past. Just what the neocons' motives and objectives were, and those of the right-wing nationalists Dick Cheney and Donald Rumsfeld, may be debated. But one thing is certain: those motives and objectives were in no way shared by most Labour MPs or a "progressive" media in London, who were suspicious of American power and critical of Israel, who affected to revere international law, who thought that regime change as such was unlawful, and who made a cult of the virtue of the UN. To enlist their support was no easy task, but Blair was counting on the corrupt servility of his MPs as well as the supine credulity of the media, and he proved to be correct in his estimate of both.

Hence the angry bafflement of those supporters unable to contemplate the possibility that Blair might actually have had a natural affinity with Bush and the neocons, and failing also to recognize his frantic desire—somewhat at odds with the tough and decisive persona he tried to project—to be the president's best buddy: "I will be with you, whatever." And so a false account of events became almost unavoidable for him. In her great biography of her father, Lord Salisbury, Queen Victoria's last prime minister, Lady Gwendolen Cecil wrote ruthlessly of Disraeli that "he was always making use of convictions that he did not share, pursuing objects which he could not avow, manoeuvring his party into alliances which, though unobjectionable from his own standpoint, were discreditable and indefensible from theirs." That exactly describes Blair, above all over Iraq.

And yet it will not do to blame Blair alone. Among the effects of the war were a collapse of cabinet government and parliamentary government, along with what might frankly be called the corruption of the intelligence agencies. Dearlove and Sir John Scarlett, head of the Joint Intelligence Committee, colluded with Downing Street to "fix the facts," and Peter Goldsmith, the attorney general, just as patently changed under pressure his previous advice that the invasion might be of dubious legality.

Since then, Dearlove has been the head of a Cambridge college and is now chairman of an insurance company. Scarlett was knighted and promoted to succeed Dearlove as head of MI6 after the invasion and is now adviser to an investment bank. Goldsmith works for the American law firm Debevoise and Plimpton. Whatever the fate of the Iraqis, the officials responsible for their plight have not suffered greatly.

Nor was Iraq the finest hour of the media, on either side of the Atlantic. The morning after Chilcot was published, the front pages of London newspapers shouted "Weapons of Mass Deception" (*Sun*), "Shamed Blair: I'm Sorry But I'd Do It Again" (*Daily Express*), "Blair Is World's Worst Terrorist" (*Daily Star*), "A Monster of Delusion" (*Daily Mail*), and "Blair's Private War" (*The Times*). You would never guess from this chorus of outrage that those newspapers all supported the war at the time, as of course did almost all the America media, with the exception of that unlikely pair, the Knight-Ridder chain and the *New York Review of Books*.

Sorriest of all were the liberal papers, the *Guardian* and its Sunday counterpart, the *Observer*. While the *Observer* fell completely for Blair and his war, the *Guardian* was more hesitant. And yet a week before the invasion, it said editorially, and almost inexplicably, "But there is one thing Mr. Blair cannot be accused of: he may be wrong on Iraq, badly wrong, but he has never been less than honest." No hindsight is needed to see how utterly mistaken those words were—or to point out that the two papers had the right response ready-made, from what they had said about Suez in November 1956.

"It is wrong on every count—moral, military and political," said the *Manchester Guardian* (as it still was). "To recover from the disaster will take years—if indeed it is ever possible." More eloquent still was the *Observer*, with what is perhaps the single most famous editorial sentence to appear in a London paper in my lifetime, penned as British troops went ashore at Suez by David Astor himself, the paper's owner-editor: "We had not realized that our government was capable of such folly and such crookedness."

Apart from sharing the view that a stable democracy could be created in Iraq, Blair thought it was his duty to support Washington in principle, and that he was Bush's guide as well as his friend. As early as March 2002, he told Labour MPs "very privately" that "my strategy is to get alongside the Americans and try to shape what is to be done." He endlessly repeated this, to his Cabinet (without telling them that he had committed the country to war) and to favored journalists, some of whom swallowed it. When the invasion began, the commentator and military historian Max Hastings wrote in the *Daily Mail* that "Tony Blair has taken a brave decision, that the only hope of influencing American behavior is to share in American actions."

All this displayed the kind of personal and national vanity that afflicts prime ministers, stemming from Churchill's "special relationship" and Harold Macmillan's even more pernicious image of "Greeks to their Romans." These have been the grand illusions of British policy ever since: the belief that the two countries have a "special" affinity, and that the worldly-wise English can tutor and restrain the energetic but backward Americans. Successive prime ministers have failed to grasp the simple truths that the Americans neither want nor need such guidance, that the United States is a sovereign country whose interests and objectives may or may not co-incide with British interests and objectives, and that like any other great power in history, it will pursue them with small regard for the interests of its supposed friends, let alone its avowed enemies.

Before long, Hastings saw the error of his ways, renouncing the war and denouncing Blair. As much to the point, he has more re-cently, and very truly, written that "the notion of a 'special relation-ship' was invented for reasons of political expediency by Winston Churchill, who then became the first of many prime ministers to discover it to be a myth." It was just as much a myth for Blair, who "overestimated his ability to influence US decisions on Iraq," Chilcot said, and in any case, Anglo-American friendship can "bear the weight of honest disagreement" and "does not require uncondi-tional support where our interest or judgments differ."

One might add that among every other perverse consequence, Iraq actually damaged Anglo-American relations, by lowering the British military in American esteem. The U.S. Army was deeply un-impressed by its ally's performance, with one general saying that the final ignominious British withdrawal from Basra could be seen only as a defeat.

That leaves Blair. His public attempt to answer Chilcot on the day the report appeared was excruciating. Haggard, and incoherent, he seemed dimly aware that his reputation had collapsed and that he is now more despised and ill regarded than any other modern prime minister. Any public intervention by him now can only have the op-posite effect, as in the summer of 2015 when, every time he begged Labour members not to vote for the aging leftist Jeremy Corbyn as party leader, he further ensured Corbyn's triumph. Not that there is any need to feel pity for him: he feels quite enough himself, be-moaning "the demonic rabble tearing at my limbs," which words may make others think sourly of those Iraqi men, women, and chil-dren whose limbs really were torn apart.

His life now is hugely lucrative but hideous to behold. Blair roams the world like the Flying Dutchman, with an estimated £25 million worth of properties and a large fortune, including benefits from a Wall Street bank and a Swiss finance company, sundry Gulf sheiks and the president-for-life of Kazakhstan. He doubtless justifies to himself his work for Nursultan Nazarbayev, whose Kazakh regime has been strongly condemned by human rights organizations, in the same strange antinomian way in which he justified how he took us into the Iraq war: whatever he does must be virtuous because he does it.

Long after those distant years of triumph, the truth about Blair finally becomes clear. He believed himself to be a great leader and redeemer; some of the weirder passages in his memoir—"I felt a growing inner sense of belief, almost of destiny . . . I was alone"— suggest an almost clinically delusional personality; and of course he did something shameful or even wicked in Iraq. And yet in the end, Tony Blair isn't a messiah or a madman or a monster. He is a mediocrity. He might have made an adequate prime minister in ordinary days, but in our strange and testing times, he was hopelessly out of his depth. Now we are left with the consequences.

Fall Semester 2016

A version of this lecture appeared in the *New York Review of Books,* 13 October 2016

Bus advertising for the Leave and Remain campaigns, 2016.

25

Seeking a Role: Britain after Brexit

KENNETH O. MORGAN

Euroskepticism in modern Britain is a by-product of the Second World War. It has been the most decisive and divisive element in our recent history. The war was fundamental to the British psyche. It was "our finest hour," distinguished by Churchill's iconic speeches and new heroes such as Dame Vera Lynn, "the forces' sweetheart," who became a centenarian in March 2017. V-E Day in particular was a monument to patriotic unity, whereas France had to contend with its memories of Vichy and the Resistance. On Christmas Day, the Queen's annual televised message, full of peace and goodwill, was invariably followed by wartime films celebrating our defeat of the Germans, the sinking the *Graf Spee,* and the like. The Europe referendum on 23 June 2016 had Boris Johnson comparing the European Union with the Nazi occupation of Europe, and the victory of Brexit with the escape from Colditz. He was rewarded by becoming Foreign Secretary.

But 1945 was a legend of a very specific kind. It symbolized Britain fighting alone. The Battle of Britain in 1940 (notwithstanding the Polish and Czech pilots who flew with the RAF) was central to it. Dunkirk (seen in France as a betrayal) was a retreat from Europe hailed as a triumph. Victory in the war was not associated with our European allies but rather seen as a rescue of defeated or collaborationist continentals from occupation. After the war, Britain's destiny was linked with the Anglo-American alliance—the Labour

Fig. 25.1. Boris Johnson, mayor of London, 2008–16.

government under Attlee endorsed the "special relationship," a unique myth, reaching its climax with Sir Oliver Franks as ambassador in Washington in 1948–52. The Commonwealth was also of great importance after 1945, through trade and the sterling area. By contrast, no great effort was made to give a lead in Europe. British ministers refused to participate in the Schuman Plan for a multinational coal, iron, and steel community.

Throughout the fifties, little changed. Churchill's inspiring speeches, delivered while in opposition, endorsed a united Europe in some form but led to nothing. The old man manifestly did not want to be part of a European super-state. The British government remained aloof from Continental moves to develop a union. Foreign Office officials ridiculed the 1955 conference in Messina as reflecting "eruptions in Sicily." Britain, humiliatingly defeated in the Suez invasion in 1956, nevertheless steered well clear of the Treaty of Rome the following year.[1] In 1962 at West Point, the former US secretary of state Dean Acheson spoke scathingly of Britain losing an empire but still seeking a role.

It all changed in the sixties, more specifically, in the first two weeks of July 1966. Ironically, this was a time of national celebration when England won the football World Cup, providentially defeating the West Germans in the final. The continuing weakness of the British balance of payments and the pound helped undermine a previous mood of self-confidence in the fifties, especially in relation to the economy. It ended with the devaluation of the pound in November 1967, regarded as a national humiliation. It also confirmed the end of the empire, with a refusal to send troops to Vietnam and the withdrawal of British forces from east of Suez, notably from Singapore. At home, there was the first sign of the possible breakup of the United Kingdom with a Welsh nationalist (Plaid Cymru) victory in the Carmarthen by-election (14 July) and soon after a Scottish Nationalist triumph at Hamilton. Most crucially of all, there was a profound change of policy toward Europe. Harold Macmillan mounted a first attempt to join the EU, followed by Labour's Harold Wilson in 1967. Even though both were rebuffed by President de Gaulle's veto, European membership remained on Britain's public agenda. The good relationship of Edward Heath with de Gaulle's successor, Georges Pompidou, marked a decisive change, and in 1972–73 the British Parliament strongly backed their country becoming a member of the Common Market.

But there were profound divisions over this decision in both Labour and Conservative ranks. Wilson, Prime Minister again in 1974, decided to resolve those of Labour by turning to a referendum, the first such in British history. This was preceded by a so-called renegotiation skillfully conducted by Foreign Secretary James Callaghan, which he described as "negotiating for success."[2] In the referendum campaign in the summer of 1975, the link with Europe was hailed by government, opposition, and business as a guarantee of prosperity and peace—wartime memories were still fresh then. Wilson handled the discussions with much skill and kept his distance from the formal debate, as did Callaghan, another skeptic. There was limited use of what was called in 2015 "Project Fear," though much reference to Britain being "the sick man of Europe." Arguments over invasions of British sovereignty were seldom heard. Platforms were shared by supporters and opponents of joining Europe—Heath and Roy Jenkins, Michael Foot and Enoch Powell. Business and the bulk of the Conservative Party were strongly pro-Europe. There was, significantly, no emphasis on the Jean Monnet–type idea of an ever-closer union, but much on economic revival after membership. But the resounding victory of the pro-Europeans, by a two-to-one majority, seemed to settle the issue forever. Margaret Thatcher campaigned for Europe; James Callaghan became far more pro-European as premier from 1976 through his strong relationship with his fellow Social Democrat, Germany's Helmut Schmidt, and even contemplated a monetary union. Harold Wilson could reflect with satisfaction that Europe had not split his party.

But the debate was very far from over. Popular hostility to an unelected, bureaucratic European Commission remained. There was endless popular humor about European directives on the shape of bananas and cucumbers. The British parties increasingly changed sides. Labour, previously hostile to the European Common Market as a capitalist club, campaigned in 1983 to leave it—no bowing to the sacrosanct verdict of the people there. But Labour then swung to supporting European membership under the leadership of the formerly Euroskeptic Neil Kinnock. Michael Foot, even more Euroskeptic, became pro-European in his old age, partly through his links with Continental socialists in Portugal and Greece. Kinnock later actually became an EU Commissioner in Brussels. The trade unions swung round massively after a spirited socialist address by Jacques Delors—"frère Jacques"—at their Congress in Brighton in 1988. Labour now saw Europe as embodying the progressive ideals of the Social Chapter, which became part of the Maastricht Treaty, with its rights for workers and women, and a minimum wage, the cherished ambition of Keir Hardie and the pioneers before 1914.

Conversely, Delors's rhetoric had a very different impact on the Conservatives. Even though Mrs. Thatcher worked reasonably well with Brussels, and importantly devised the European single market in 1986, she and most grassroots Tories reacted strongly against the Brighton speech. For Delors had also talked up the central controlling role of the EU and forecast that 80 percent of legislation would now come from Brussels. There was also mention of a common currency: Thatcher's 1988 Bruges speech illustrated the new impetus to Euroskepticism. It was a mood that haunted John Major's government from Maastricht in 1992 onward. It challenged every Conservative leader from Major to Cameron. There was a growing sense of hostility to an alien, controlling European authority as a threat to British parliamentary sovereignty, plus growing arguments over the admission of refugees and asylum seekers and the way in which the European Court of Human Rights had begun to check decisions of Parliament and the British government. It was a theme much associated with Theresa May, Home Secretary in the Cameron government after 2010.

This linked up, in a somewhat confused way, with another disturbing feature, unknown for many centuries—English nationalism. It was stimulated by the influence acquired by the devolved Celtic nations, especially Scotland, through the formula-driven Treasury block grant and excessive political influence through the "West Lothian question," at the expense of England, where four-fifths of the population lived. Devolution and Europe appeared to be interlinked—undermining the country within and without. English nationalism thus began to find a stronger, increasingly Euro-skeptic, voice. When the UK Independence Party (UKIP) emerged as the voice of Europhobia after 2000, it was in England, especially in wealthy southern England, that it first found its major voice.

The growing Europhobia of people in England (and later in previously Europhile Wales) was in many respects baffling. In very many ways, the UK had found its own perfect formula. It was in and out of Europe at the same time. It fully retained its sovereignty while being a contributor to EU policy making. Some British institutions—notably the universities—became heavily involved with their European counterparts and flourished through collaborative research projects and student exchanges. In the general elections of 2001, 2005, and even 2010, Europe, while a continuing divisive factor among the Tory grassroots, was not a great point of argument between the party leaders. UKIP, and its anti-immigrant leader Nigel Farage, seemed at most a noisy minority on the fringes of politics.

Then in 2004 there came a new, highly provocative ingredient— further mass immigration. As several new countries from eastern Europe joined the EU, transforming its original core, there was a massive influx into Britain of immigrants from the new entrant countries, which had a dramatic impact on many areas. At least 700,000 Poles who came to Britain seeking jobs settled there, as did many Hungarians, Lithuanians, and others. This aroused much hostility, not only in comfortable southern England, where relatively few immigrants settled, but also in industrial areas in the north of England and the Midlands, where complaints mounted at the way immigrants were able to acquire jobs and houses and to make much use of health and other social services at the supposed expense of the native inhabitants. The new visitors from eastern Europe were white, mainly Christians, and less of a culture shock than immigrants from, say, Muslim countries of the Middle East. They worked hard and dutifully paid their taxes. But they aroused even more racist passion. Farage expended ignorant fury at Romanians in particular, most of whom he claimed, quite wrongly, were unemployed or criminals or both.

The main protests were located almost entirely in a group of right-wing critics in the Conservative Party, some of whom, such as

Fig. 25.2. David Cameron, Prime Minister (2010–16), May 2010. Crown copyright.

Iain Duncan-Smith or John Redwood, had once been the so-called bastards who challenged John Major in the nineties. When David Cameron formed a coalition in 2010, they turned their fire on the pro-European Liberal Democrat ministers and their leader, Nick Clegg, but also on Cameron personally. In his 2013 Bloomberg speech in London, Cameron was compelled to talk of repatriation and renegotiation and to promise an early referendum on membership of the EU. After the general election of 2015, with its narrow Conservative victory, Euroskeptic pressure was almost overwhelming. Cameron now promised his troops that that they would have their chance in 2016 even if he would not back them. He appeared buoyed up by victories in the voting-reform referendum in 2011 and, narrowly, in the Scottish referendum in 2014. He was in a confident, indeed an overconfident, mood that he could carry the vote a third time. The polls had long suggested that while the Brexit supporters made all the noise, the silent majority would wish to remain in Europe. But few, let alone the Euroskeptic-sounding Cameron, tried to elaborate the case for staying in and its benefits. With its bureaucratic approach and democratic deficit, a closer, stronger Europe

was too dangerous a topic. Pro-European passion, let alone idealism, were absent.

The referendum was held on 23 June 2016. The campaign that
preceded it was contemptible. There was little debate, but much of
what the Trump people in the U.S. presidential election called "alternative facts" or "post-truth." There was serial lying from Brexit
partisans, including over the total of immigrants or the claim (later
disavowed by Boris Johnson) that Brexit would release £350 million
a week for the National Health Service. The tabloid press, notably
the *Daily Mail,* the *Daily Express,* and the *Sun,* was very one-sided and
used intimidatory language (for example, "enemies of the people").[3]
The passion was all on the Leave side, notably over the figures for
immigration: the Brexit battle bus featured a large picture, subti-
tled "Breaking Point," of a long queue of immigrants trying to get
in—in fact, they were people trying to cross the Croatia-Slovenia
border. Cameron's low-key campaign received no help at all from
Labour, which was expected to provide mass support for Remain.
Jeremy Corbyn, Labour's elderly, newly elected Marxist leader, was

Fig. 25.3. Jeremy Corbyn, Labour leader, 2017. Chatham House.

in reality a Leave supporter, despite paying lip service to the cause that most Labour voters backed. The minority Liberal Democrats were seldom in evidence. The impetus all came from Leave partisans, who fought a negative campaign with great success, notably Boris Johnson and Michael Gove. Labour voters seemed to hold back, perhaps believing it to be mainly an argument between the Tories. And against expectations, Leave won the victory, 51.9 percent against 48.1 percent, determining the course of British history for decades to come.

WHY THE ARGUMENTS FROM STRONGER IN, the chief Remain organization, fell on such unfertile ground is a major problem. At first, the Remainers, notably the Chancellor, George Osborne, pushed the fear aspect hard, as officials like the Governor of the Bank of England and members of the International Monetary Fund prophesied the doom and disaster that could follow. Osborne forecast that Britain would enter into a recession. These claims were simply not believed by a people who had suffered years of severe austerity under the previous regime. As in Scotland, many people refused to believe in Project Fear. The European idea was presented in negative terms, and the economic aspect of the argument was soon disposed of. Among other factors, it could be argued that the EU was very poor at advertising its achievements. Much of its largesse went unheralded and unrecognized.

Alongside that, a visit by President Obama made no impact. He failed to show his usual sensitivity: his references to Britain falling to "the back of the queue" in seeking aid from the United States created a disagreeable sense of dependence that jarred with a British audience. Boris Johnson countered that Obama was "half-Kenyan" (and thus an anti-British colonial) anyway, plus alleging that he had removed the almost sacred bust of Winston Churchill, icon of the "special relationship," from the Oval Office.

Security issues did not play well either. Talk of the work of MI5 and MI6 suffering difficulties through reduced international cooperation with other police forces in warding off terrorist threats had scant impact, as did references to defense through NATO. Arguments about protecting world peace did not carry the same weight as in 1975 when they were made by politicians such as Edward Heath, William Whitelaw, and Denis Healey, who had once fought bravely on the beaches of Normandy or Anzio. Older voters, the core of the Brexiters, now discounted distant memories of the war years.

By contrast, immigration certainly gave huge impetus to the argument, all of it on the Leave side. Cameron appeared to have brought back scant solace on the social benefit front from Brussels in this connection, and the Leave campaign, from Johnson downward, employed racist terminology and images: Johnson untruthfully forecast a mass incursion of Turkish migrants. It was ignored that non-EU countries like Norway had a greater influx of immigrants than did Britain; so were the opportunities for hundreds of thousands of British ex-pats to work or simply live in Continental Europe. It could be claimed that cooperation with France and others on border control actually helped keep immigration numbers down. Anti-immigrant feeling reached a horrific climax just before polling day when Jo Cox, a young pro-Remain Labour MP, was murdered in her Yorkshire constituency by a perverted Scotsman sympathetic to Britain First and the Ku Klux Klan. It was assumed that this barbarity would temper the worst of the racist hysteria, but this never happened.

Finally, the rhetoric focused on "getting back control," the belief that the sovereignty of Parliament and the British rule of law were being fundamentally threatened by alien European institutions, the Commissions, the Parliament, and the Court of Human Rights. Johnson wound up a debate at the end of the campaign by shouting that a leave vote would be Britain's Independence Day. The voters gave a mass affirmative response.

Viewed as a whole, the main interest in the referendum campaign is sociological and cultural rather than political. It unveiled divisions and fractures in a changing, anxious people. The major political and social rift was no longer one of class, between Left and Right, or workers and bosses. It was rather between open and closed. There was a world of difference between poorer, traditionally Labour-voting industrial communities in Tyneside and a London suburb like Lambeth, which voted 79 percent for Remain, second only to Gibraltar. There was a profound skein of divisions between old and young (the younger the age group, the more strongly Remain), educated versus nongraduates, urban or suburban versus rural, house owners versus renting tenants, the English regions versus London (also other major cities such as Manchester, Birmingham, Liverpool, and Bristol, where middle-class graduates and multiethnic communities were numerous), Scotland versus England and Wales (which showed a remarkable swing to UKIP). More generally, as in the American rust belt later that November, there were large communities that felt they were lagging behind, being betrayed, with their falling living standards, underpaid jobs, and decreasing life expectations, and who falsely blamed Europe for it. They ranged from stagnant South Wales and Durham ex-mining villages to depressed seaside resorts.

More generally, English nationalism was an angry giant roused, sometimes, to racist violence.

The poll results were a surprise. The opinion polls, often wrong, had suggested a movement to Remain in the later weeks, but Brexit campaigners, rightly, knew better. Remain lost in large measure because the anticipated Labour vote for Remain did not happen—only 65 percent of Labour voters voted Remain, while 161 Labour-held constituencies swung to back Leave. Most Conservatives were emphatically anti-European and pro-Leave, even though the Leave campaign was compromised by Conservatives' anxiety to steer clear of UKIP and to fight their own corner. Many Leavers, such as Farage, were apparently surprised by their victory. The strongest Leave vote came from older middle-class people in rural and residential areas in southern England. There was a strong anti-European, anti-immigrant reaction in areas such as the northeast and northwest of England, where there were very few immigrants. On the other hand, these areas were heavily dependent on the European connection, as with Nissan car workers in Sunderland and steelworkers in Port Talbot. Scotland voted heavily (62 percent) for Remain, as, to a lesser extent, did Northern Ireland, whereas Wales, one of the surprises, was more strongly pro-Leave than was England. The poll, at 72 percent, should have been stronger to help Remain. One feature was the importance of the 2.8 million voters who had never voted for anything before. They were overwhelmingly Leavers, apparently hostile to a supposed metropolitan elite.

The possible outcomes of what was manifestly an event of profound historical significance will be revealed over the years and decades to come. The economy will clearly go through years of uncertainty and probably suffer a slowdown as Britain moves out of the single market, where most of its trade was conducted. At the time of the 2017 general election, Britain's record for economic growth was much the worst of the G7, and domestic inflation also rose sharply after the Brexit vote. Over 40 percent of British exports had gone to European customers, who would now impose tariffs on them, but only 2 percent to American markets. This cast serious doubt on Theresa May's claim that a trade deal with the United States could counter losses in Europe. The City of London, crucial to Britain's prosperity—almost four-fifths of the national economy is based on services—was threatened with an alarming loss of jobs and business in banking to Frankfurt, Paris, or perhaps New York. Despite the Bank of England's further £60 billion of "quantitative easing," investment, hiring, and turnover will likely be weakened. Britain was

Fig. 25.4. Theresa May, Prime Minister (2016–), March 2017. Photo by Jay Allen. Crown copyright.

touted by May as becoming a very different low-cost, low-wage, low-tax country, an unappealing prospect.

Politics were already being turned upside down. Europe will haunt our parties for years to come. Negotiations with twenty-seven other sovereign nations, mostly angry at Britain's departure, are likely to be prolonged, tense, and difficult. Labour under Corbyn's leadership seemed totally destabilized, with an anti-European leader set against a strongly pro-European front bench and parliamentary party. The failure of Labour even to challenge the Brexit decision in the Commons was especially demoralizing. Hope had to rest on the unelected House of Lords. A serious by-election loss for Labour in Copeland in Cumbria (23 February 2017) was the first victory by a governing party over the opposition since 1982, confirming a long spiral of Labour decline. On the other hand, Labour did manage to defeat UKIP's right-wing president in Stoke-on-Trent, an old industrial stronghold dominated by Leave sentiment, which suggested a serious crisis for these extremist anti-Europeans. The Conservatives had their divisions, too, but less starkly so. Theresa May seemed dominated by issues of party control, illustrated by the primacy she gave immigration and the free movement of peoples in the Brexit negotiations. She was anxious to avoid the historic fate of her predecessor, David Cameron. While Lord North in 1783 had lost the American colonies, Cameron had bid farewell to Europe and, conceivably, Scotland as well.

Constitutionally, Brexit opened up many key issues, including the major role of the courts under our unwritten constitution. It was after judicial review, after a private prosecution, that first the High Court of Justice and then the Supreme Court declared for parliamentary sovereignty in triggering Article 50 and their other judgments. This should have pleased the Leave campaign, since it was precisely what they had argued for, against the dictatorial power of Brussels. Instead, distinguished judges were denounced in a *Daily Mail* headline, Nazi style, as "enemies of the people," guilty, in the eyes of the tabloid *Sun,* of "national betrayal," along with civil servants, university vice-chancellors, business leaders, and other traitors. The rule of law and judicial review had acted in the absence of a codified written constitution, the proud possession of Americans, the French, and almost all other peoples. Although the referendum result was an apparent blow on behalf of popular sovereignty, it was rather parliamentary sovereignty that had been vindicated. In the long term, the big winners were John Pym, John Hampden, and those who stood up to an overbearing king in 1642.

It was generally recognized that the referendum had a critical significance for Scotland, whose overwhelming Nationalist majority and first minister, Nicola Sturgeon, complained with reason that they were being forced out of Europe by English votes, and were being further excluded by the Supreme Court from participation in the Brexit settlement The independence issue was thus reignited. Whether another Scottish referendum would inevitably follow was less clear—the support for it had been mildly shaken by the fall in the price for Scottish oil and troubles in the financial services. Sturgeon could not afford to lose twice. In the June 2017 general election, the Scottish National Party lost significant support; its total of seats slumped from 56 to 35 as Scottish Conservatives, under the dynamic leader Ruth Davidson, made striking advances. But the issue of the separation of Scotland and the consequent breakup of the United Kingdom remained a central issue, even if less imminent than before.

Northern Ireland could also enter a troubled period. It voted Remain by a clear margin, mainly through Catholic Nationalist voters enthusiastic about union with the Republic to the South, but with some Unionist support as well. Life under the EU had been generally satisfactory to most people in the North of Ireland, both those favoring a united island and those bound in sympathy to English sentiment. The dangerous issue of the border with the South was now opened up, the question being of what it would consist, whether the old regime of border posts, police surveillance, and customs posts were to re-emerge, with all the resultant physical hazards. Significantly, the Brexit vote resulted in a rush for southern Irish passports. Difficult issues were now being opened up, perhaps the long-held ideal of a united Irish nation, perhaps a renewed phase of violence and the end of the "peace process."

Socially, the prospects were highly unclear. Theresa May delivered a New Year's message in January 2017 conveying a sense of unity and reconciliation, but with a "hard Brexit," accompanied by falling living standards, social conflict seemed a more likely prospect. One leading Conservative spoke of "blood on the streets." It was not clear how ongoing disputes between classes, generations, and regions would play out. The immediate prospect was a deep gulf between the two sides. Hopes of post-referendum reconciliation seemed unlikely when challenged by widespread hostility, even violence, toward immigrants and foreigners—for instance, attacks on Poles for doing nothing more offensive than speaking Polish in the street. The future prospects for EU citizens from overseas were uncertain, and an issue on which the government refused to offer any words of support either to them or to Britons living abroad. Whether, in spite of all the racist bitterness during the referendum, there would be much reduction in the annual EU immigration into Britain of around 335,000 (or a net figure of 180,000) was very doubtful. The think tank Global Future pointed out that 22 percent of EU immigrants were professionals and a further 25 percent worked in skilled occupations, whose expertise would be essential, for instance, in the health service. The further 56 percent who were unskilled included many seasonal workers, for instance, in agriculture, horticulture, and tourism, and others in vital services such as transport and construction. In a world of globalization, the inward movement of peoples might not slow down significantly after all. Indeed, British business broadly welcomed it.

Then post-Brexit Britain assumed a completely different aspect after the sensational results of the 8 June general election. Called by Theresa May, so she said, to shore up her political authority before the European negotiations later that month, there was a strong swing to Labour, which gained its strongest share of the vote since Attlee. This destroyed the Conservatives' majority in the Commons entirely and left them dependent on a distinctly shaky pact with the tiny sectarian Democratic Unionist party in Ulster, a supporter of Brexit but a moderate one that did not wish to harden the borders with the Irish Republic. Strikingly, a general election that May announced would be focused on Brexit was marked by very little discussion of the issue, not even of immigration. May was unwilling to debate any details of the issues, and Jeremy Corbyn, the Labour leader with Leave sympathies, preferred to steer the campaign toward more congenial issues such as health and education. The anti-European UKIP collapsed, and won no seats at all. Instead, Remainers in many parts of England and Wales swung strongly to Labour, showing more interest in issues of welfare policy and public services. The Conservatives fared particularly badly in cities, where the voters, especially university students in places like Oxford, Cambridge, Canterbury, Reading, and Sheffield, exacted revenge for the referendum. The only area of Conservative advance was in Scotland, where unionist sentiment was strongly pro-Europe. It looked as if the saga of contradictory British views toward a more united Europe had taken a dramatic and unforeseen turn. A softer Brexit settlement now emerged as a real prospect.

WORLDWIDE, HOW WOULD A POST-BREXIT Britain be regarded? Long before 23 June 2016, Britain seemed to be an apprehensive and introspective country. The implications of an extreme change in such areas as defense, security, environmental policy, energy, and social and educational "soft power" would surely be considerable. Britain also demonstrated, through UKIP and nonpolitical groups, ugly signs of the nationalist, populist movements emerging in France, the Netherlands, Germany, Austria, and other countries. Political scientists spoke of political transformation, the rise of new forms of populism, and "identity politics" among marginalized national and ethnic groups. The similarity has often been noted, sometimes superficially so, to Trump's election in the United States and the success of his nativist "America First" appeal. But the prospect of a meeting of minds across the Atlantic, perhaps a rekindled special relationship, as hinted at by the Trump-May talks in Washington, seems very remote. Trump, after all, while he backed Brexit, is an aggressive nationalist and protectionist of paranoid inclinations from whom the United Kingdom differs on numerous moral and political issues. Symbolically, Trump's state visit to Britain, planned for September, was canceled. Britain, one of the world's big three at Potsdam and leader of the Commonwealth and sterling area in

1945, was now lonely and rudderless. Dean Acheson would have noted that it was still searching for a role, fifty years on.

Some historians have floated a fanciful alternative. With Europe being cast aside, some predicted a revived Churchill-like Union of the English-Speaking Peoples. After all, a hero to some of Theresa May's entourage is Joseph Chamberlain, who championed this vision at the dawn of the twentieth century. The notion has been canvassed of a new role, an alliance with the United States and the mainly English-speaking white dominions in trade, defense, and perhaps other matters This would not be the old Commonwealth, but it could provide a new, flexible "devolved network" of influence. Some have thus written of the rise of an "Anglosphere."[4] In my own judgment, such a forecast is totally incredible and has proved to be so over a century and a half, when, for instance, Australia and New Zealand have focused on being Asian or southern Pacific powers, and Canada North American. The idea of British leadership of an Anglosphere, improbable in Chamberlain's time, when the United States was led by nationalists such as Teddy Roosevelt, is derisory. Yet our angry world is now highly unpredictable. Much conventional wisdom is being overturned. It would indeed be extraordinary if, as Britain's role in Europe evaporates, somewhat late on cue the empire strikes back.

Spring Semester 2017

1. Conversation of Sir Roger Makins with Livingstone Merchant and Burke Ellrick of the U.S. State Department, 21–22 Dec. 1955 (National Archives, F371/115999), M1017/14, cited in Kenneth O. Morgan, *The People's Peace* (Oxford, 1999 edn.), p. 136.

2. Kenneth O. Morgan, *Callaghan: A Life* (Oxford, 1997), p. 421.

3. *Daily Mail,* 10 Nov. 2016, a charge directed against the High Court judges who ruled that triggering Article 50 and the terms of a Brexit settlement had to be approved by a sovereign Parliament.

4. On this, see Nick Pearce and Michael Kenny, "The Empire Strikes Back," *New Statesman,* 20–26 Jan. 2017; Duncan Bell, "Empire of the Tongue," *Prospect,* Feb. 2017.

British Studies at
the University of Texas, 1975–2017

Fall Semester 1975

Paul Scott (Novelist, London), 'The *Raj Quartet*'
Ian Donaldson (Australian National University), 'Humanistic Studies in Australia'
Fritz Fellner (Salzburg University), 'Britain and the Origins of the First World War'
Wm. Roger Louis (History), 'Churchill, Roosevelt, and the Future of Dependent Peoples during the Second World War'
Michael Holroyd (Biographer, Dublin), 'Two Biographies: Lytton Strachey and Augustus John'
Max Beloff (Buckingham College), 'Imperial Sunset'
Robin Winks (Yale University), 'British Empire-Commonwealth Studies'
Warren Roberts (HRHRC) and David Farmer (HRHRC), 'The D. H. Lawrence Editorial Project'
Harvey C. Webster (University of Louisville), 'C. P. Snow as Novelist and Philosopher'
Anthony Kirk-Greene (Oxford University), 'The Origins and Aftermath of the Nigerian Civil War'

Spring Semester 1976

Joseph Jones (English), 'World English'
William S. Livingston (Government), 'The British Legacy in Contemporary Indian Politics'
John Higley (Sociology), 'The Recent Political Crisis in Australia'
Round Table Discussion, 'Reassessments of Evelyn Waugh': Elspeth Rostow (Dean, General and Comparative Studies), Standish Meacham (History), and Alain Blayac (University of Paris)
Jo Grimond (former Leader of the Liberal Party), 'Liberal Democracy in Britain'

Round Table Discussion, 'The Impact of Hitler on British Politics': Gaines Post (History), Malcolm Macdonald (Government), and Wm. Roger Louis (History)

Round Table Discussion, 'Kipling and India': Robert Hardgrave (Government), Gail Minault (History), and Chihiro Hosoya (University of Tokyo)

Kenneth Kirkwood (Oxford University), 'The Future of Southern Africa'

C. P. Snow, 'Elite Education in England'

Hans-Peter Schwarz (Cologne University), 'The Impact of Britain on German Politics and Society since the Second World War'

B. K. Nehru (Indian High Commissioner, London), 'The Political Crisis in India'

Round Table Discussion, 'Declassification of Secret Documents: The British and American Experiences Compared': Robert A. Divine (History), Harry J. Middleton (LBJ Library), and Wm. Roger Louis (History)

Fall Semester 1976

John Farrell (English), 'Revolution and Tragedy in Victorian England'

Anthony Honoré (Oxford University), 'British Attitudes to Legal Regulation of Sex'

Alan Hill (English), 'Wordsworth and America'

Ian Nish (London School of Economics), 'Anglo-American Naval Rivalry and the End of the Anglo-Japanese Alliance'

Norman Sherry (University of Lancaster), 'Joseph Conrad and the British Empire'

Peter Edwards (Australian National University), 'Australia through American Eyes: The Second World War and the Rise of Australia as a Regional Power'

Round Table Discussion, 'Britain and the Future of Europe': David Edwards (Government), Steven Baker (Government), Malcolm Macdonald (Government), William S. Livingston (Government), and Wm. Roger Louis (History)

Michael Hurst (Oxford University), 'The British Empire in Historical Perspective: The Case of Joseph Chamberlain'

Ronald Grierson (English Banker and former Public Official), 'The Evolution of the British Economy since 1945'

Marian Kent (University of New South Wales), 'British Oil Policy between the World Wars'

Constance Babington-Smith (Cambridge University), 'The World of Rose Macaulay'

Round Table Discussion, 'Adam Smith after 200 Years': William Todd (History), Walt Rostow (History and Economics), and James McKie (Dean, Social and Behavioral Sciences)

Spring Semester 1977

Carin Green (Novelist) and Elspeth Rostow (American Studies), 'The Achievement of Virginia Woolf'

Samuel H. Beer (Professor of Government, Harvard University), 'Reflections on British Politics'

David Fieldhouse (Oxford University), 'Decolonization and the Multinational Corporations'

Gordon Craig (Stanford University), 'England and Europe on the Eve of the Second World War'

John Lehmann (British Publisher and Writer), 'Publishing under the Bombs— The Hogarth Press during World War II'

Round Table Discussion, 'The Author, His Editor, and Publisher': Philip Jones (University of Texas Press), William S. Livingston (Government), Michael Mewshaw (English), David Farmer (HRC), Roger Louis (History), and William Todd (History)

Dick Taverne (former Member of Parliament), 'The Mood of Britain: Misplaced Gloom or Blind Complacency?'

Round Table Discussion, 'The Origins of World War II in the Pacific': James B. Crowley (Yale University), Lloyd C. Gardner (Rutgers University), Akira Iriye (University of Chicago), and Wm. Roger Louis (History)

Rosemary Murray (Cambridge University), 'Higher Education in England'

Burke Judd (Zoology) and Robert Wagner (Zoology), 'Sir Cyril Burt and the Controversy over the Heritability of IQ'

Round Table Discussion, 'The Wartime Reputations of Churchill and Roosevelt: Overrated or Underrated?': Alessandra Lippucci (Government), Roger Louis (History), William S. Livingston (Government), and Walt Rostow (Economics)

Fall Semester 1977

Donald L. Weismann (Art and Art History), 'British Art in the Nineteenth Century: Turner and Constable—Precursors of French Impressionism'

Standish Meacham (History), 'Social Reform in England'

Joseph Jones, 'Recent Commonwealth Literature'

Lewis Hoffacker (former US Ambassador), 'The Katanga Crisis: British and Other Connections'

Round Table Discussion, 'The Copyright Law of 1976': James M. Treece (Law), Wm. Roger Louis (History), Warren Roberts, and Bill Todd (History)

Round Table Discussion, 'Freedom at Midnight: A Reassessment of Britain and the Partition of India Thirty Years After': Charles Heimsath (Visiting Professor of Indian History), Bob Hardgrave (Government), Thomasson Jannuzi, (Center for Asian Studies), C. P. Andrade (Comparative Studies), and William S. Livingston (Government),

Lord Fraser of Kilmorack (Conservative Party Organization), 'The Tory Tradition of British Politics'

Bernth Lindfors (English), 'Charles Dickens and the Hottentots and Zulus'

Albert Hourani (Oxford University), 'The Myth of T. E. Lawrence'

Mark Kinkead-Weekes (University of Kent) and Mara Kalnins (British Writer), 'D. H. Lawrence: Censorship and the Expression of Ideas'

J. D. B. Miller (Australian National University), 'The Collapse of the British Empire'

Round Table Discussion, 'The Best and Worst Books of 1977': Peter Green (Classics), Robert King (Dean, Social and Behavioral Sciences), William S. Livingston (Government), Bob Hardgrave (Government), Wm. Roger Louis (History), and Warren Roberts (HRHRC)

Spring Semester 1978

Round Table Discussion, 'British Decadence in the Interwar Years': Peter Green (Classics), Malcolm Macdonald (Government), and Robert Crunden (American Studies),

Round Table Discussion, 'R. Emmet Tyrrell's *Social Democracy's Failure in Britain*': Terry Quist (UT Undergraduate), Steve Baker (Government), and Wm. Roger Louis (History),

Stephen Koss (Columbia University), 'The British Press: Press Lords, Politicians, and Principles'

John House (Oxford University), 'The Rhodesian Crisis'

T. S. Dorsch (Durham University), 'Oxford in the 1930s'

Stephen Spender (English Poet and Writer), 'Britain and the Spanish Civil War'

Okot p'Bitek (Ugandan Poet), 'Idi Amin's Uganda'

David C. Goss (Australian Consul General), 'Wombats and Wivveroos'

Leon Epstein (University of Wisconsin), 'Britain and the Suez Crisis of 1956'

David Schoonover (Library Science), 'British and American Expatriates in Paris in the 1920s'

Peter Stansky (Stanford University), 'George Orwell and the Spanish Civil War'

Alexander Parker (Spanish and Portuguese), 'Reflections on the Spanish Civil War'

Norman Sherry (Lancaster University), 'Graham Greene and Latin America'

Martin Blumenson (Department of the Army), 'The Ultra Secret'

Fall Semester 1978

W. H. Morris-Jones (University of London), 'Power and Inequality in Southeast Asia'

Round Table Discussion, 'The British and the Shaping of the American Critical Mind: Edmund Wilson's *Letters on Literature and Politics*': Hartley Grattan (History), Gilbert Chase (American Studies), Bob Crunden (American Studies), and Wm. Roger Louis (History)

James Roach (Government), 'The Indian Emergency and its Aftermath'

Bill Todd (History), 'The Lives of Samuel Johnson'

Lord Hatch (British Labour Politician), 'The Labour Party and Africa'

John Kirkpatrick (HRHRC), 'Max Beerbohm'

Brian Levack (History), 'Witchcraft in England and Scotland'

M. R. Masani (Indian Writer), 'Gandhi and Gandhism'

A. W. Coates (Economics), 'The Professionalization of the British Civil Service'

John Clive (Harvard University), 'Great Historians of the Nineteenth Century'

Geoffrey Best (University of Sussex), 'Flight Path to Dresden: British Strategic Bombing in the Second World War'

Kurth Sprague (English), 'T. H. White's *Once and Future King*'

Gilbert Chase (American Studies), 'The British Musical Invasion of America'

Spring Semester 1979

Round Table Discussion, 'P. N. Furbanks's Biography of E. M. Forster': Peter Green (Classics), Alessandra Lippucci (Government), and Elspeth Rostow (LBJ School)

Round Table Discussion, 'E. M. Forster and India': Wm. Roger Louis (History), Bob Hardgrave (Government), Gail Minault (Professor of History), Peter Gran (History), and Bob King (Dean of Liberal Arts)

Paul M. Kennedy (University of East Anglia), 'The Contradiction between British Strategic Policy and Economic Policy in the Twentieth Century'

Richard Rive (Visiting Fulbright Research Fellow from South Africa), 'Olive Schreiner and the South African Nation'

Charles P. Kindleberger (Massachusetts Institute of Technology), 'Lord Zuckerman and the Second World War'

John Press (English Poet), 'English Poets and Postwar Society'

Richard Ellmann (Oxford University), 'Writing a Biography of Joyce'
Michael Finlayson (Scottish Dramatist), 'Contemporary British Theater'
Lawrence Stone (Institute for Advanced Study, Princeton), 'Family, Sex, and Marriage in England'
C. P. Snow, 'Reflections on the Two Cultures'
Theodore Zeldin (Oxford University), 'Are the British More or Less European than the French?'
David Edwards (Government), 'How United the Kingdom: Greater or Lesser Britain?'
Michael Holroyd (British Biographer), 'George Bernard Shaw'
John Wickman (Eisenhower Library), 'Eisenhower and the British'

Fall Semester 1979

Robert Palter (Philosophy), 'Reflections on British Philosophers: Locke, Hume, and the Utilitarians'
Alfred Gollin (University of California, Santa Barbara), 'Political Biography as Political History: Garvin, Milner, and Balfour'
Edward Steinhart (History), 'The Consequences of British Rule in Uganda'
Paul Sturges (Loughborough University, UK), and Dolores Donnelly (Toronto University), 'History of the National Library of Canada'
Sir Michael Tippett (British Composer), 'Moving into Aquarius'
Steven Baker (Government), 'Britain and United Nations Emergency Operations'
Maria Okila Dias (University of São Paulo), 'Intellectual Roots of Informal Imperialism: Britain and Brazil'
Alexander Parker (Spanish and Portuguese), 'Reflections on *Brideshead Revisited*'
Barry C. Higman (University of the West Indies), 'West Indian Emigrés and the British Empire'
Gaines Post (History), 'Britain and the Outbreak of the Second World War'
Karen Gould (Art and Art History), 'Medieval Manuscript Fragments and English Seventeenth-Century Collections: New Perspectives from *Fragmenta Manuscripta*'
Round Table Discussion, 'Jeanne MacKenzie's *Dickens: A Life*': John Farrell (English), Eric Poole (HRHRC) and James Bieri (English):
Joseph O. Baylen (Georgia State University), 'British Journalism in the Late Victorian and Edwardian Eras'
Peter T. Flawn (President, University of Texas), 'An Appreciation of Charles Dickens'

Spring Semester 1980

Annette Weiner (Anthropology), 'Anthropologists in New Guinea: British Interpretations and Cultural Relativism'
Bernard Richards (Oxford University), 'Conservation in the Nineteenth Century'
Thomas McGann (History), 'Britain and Argentina: An Informal Dominion?'
Mohammad Ali Jazayery (Center for Middle Eastern Studies), 'The Persian Tradition in English Literature'
C. Hartley Grattan (History) 'Twentieth-Century British Novels and the American Critical Mind'
Katherine Whitehorn (London *Observer*), 'An Insider's View of the *Observer*'
Guy Lytle (History), 'The Oxford University Press's *History of Oxford*'
C. P. Snow, 'Reflections on *The Masters*'

Harvey Webster, '*The Masters* and the Two Cultures'

Brian Blakeley (Texas Tech University), 'Women and the British Empire'

Stephen Koss (Columbia University), 'Asquith, Balfour, Milner, and the First World War'

Tony Smith (Tufts University), 'The Expansion of England: New Ideas on Controversial Themes in British Imperialism'

Stanley Ross (History), 'Britain and the Mexican Revolution'

Rowland Smith (Dalhousie University), 'The British Intellectual Left and the War, 1939–1945'

Richard Ellmann (Oxford University), 'Oscar Wilde: A Reconsideration and Problems of the Literary Biographer'

James Bill (Government), 'The United States, Britain, and the Iranian Crisis of 1953'

Fall Semester 1980

Decherd Turner (HRHRC), 'The First 1000 Days'

Wm. Roger Louis (History), 'Britain and Egypt after the Second World War'

Alistair Horne (Woodrow Wilson Center), 'Britain and the Fall of France'

Round Table Discussion, 'Literary Fraud: H. R. Trevor-Roper and the Hermit of Peking': Edward Rhodes (History), Peter Green (Classics), William Todd (History), and Wm. Roger Louis (History),

Mark Kinkead-Weekes (Kent University), 'D. H. Lawrence's *Rainbow:* Its Sense of History'

Sir John Crawford (Australian National University), 'Hartley Grattan: In Memoriam'

John Stubbs (University of Waterloo), 'The Tory View of Politics and Journalism in the Interwar Years'

Donald L. Weismann (Art and Art History), 'British Art in the Nineteenth Century'

Fran Hill (Government), 'The Legacy of British Colonialism in Tanzania'

R. W. B. Lewis (Yale University), 'What's Wrong with the Teaching of English?'

Charlene Gerry (British Publisher), 'The Revival of Fine Printing in Britain'

Peter Gran (History), 'The Islamic Response to British Capitalism'

Tina Poole (HRHRC) 'Gilbert and Sullivan's Christmas'

Spring Semester 1981

Bernard N. Darbyshire (Visiting Professor of Government and Economics), 'North Sea Oil and the British Future'

Christopher Hill (Oxford University), 'The English Civil War'

Elizabeth Heine (UT San Antonio), and Wm. Roger Louis (History), 'A Reassessment of Leonard Woolf'

Bernard Richards (Oxford University), 'D. H. Lawrence and Painting'

Miguel Gonzalez-Gerth (Spanish and Portuguese), 'Poetry Once Removed: The Resonance of English as a Second Language'

John Putnam Chalmers (HRHRC), 'English Bookbinding from Caedmon to Le Carré'

Peter Coltman (Architecture), 'The Cultural Landscapes of Britain: 2,000 Years of Blood, Sweat, Toil & Tears to Wrest a Living from this Bloody Mud'

Thomas H. Law (former Regent, University of Texas), 'The Gold Coins of the English Sovereigns'

Round Table Discussion, 'Canadian-American Economic Relations': Sidney Wein-
    traub (LBJ School), James W. McKie (Economics), and Mary Williams (Cana-
    dian Consulate, Dallas)
Amedée Turner (European Parliament), 'Integrating Britain into the European
    Community'
Muriel C. Bradbrook (Cambridge University), 'Two Poets: Kathleen Raine and
    Seamus Heaney'
Ronald Sampson (Industrial Development Department, Aberdeen), 'Scotland—
    Somewhat of a British Texas?'

Fall Semester 1981

Jerome Bump (English), 'From Texas to England: The Ancestry of Our Victorian
    Architecture'
Lord Fraser of Kilmorack, 'Leadership Styles of Tory Prime Ministers since the
    Second World War'
William Carr (University of Sheffield), 'A British Interpretation of American, Ger-
    man, and Japanese Foreign Policy 1936–1941'
Iqbal Narain (Rajasthan University, Jaipur), 'The Ups and Downs of Indian Aca-
    demic Life'
Don Etherington (HRHRC), 'The Florence Flood, 1966: The British Effort—or:
    Up to our Necks in Mud and Books'
E. V. K. Fitzgerald (Visiting Professor of Economics), 'The British University: Cri-
    sis, Confusion, and Stagnation'
Robert Crunden (American Studies), 'A Joshua for Historians: Mordecai Richter
    and Canadian Cultural Identity'
Bernth Lindfors (English), 'The Hottentot Venus and Other African Attractions
    in Nineteenth-Century England'
Chris Brookeman (London Polytechnic), 'The British Arts and Society'
Nicholas Pickwood (Freelance Book Conservator), 'The Libraries of the National
    Trust'
Kurth Sprague (English), 'John Steinbeck, Chase Horton, and the Matter of
    Britain'
Martin J. Wiener (Rice University), 'Cultural Values and Socio-Economic Behav-
    ior in Britain'
Werner Habicht (University of Würzburg), 'Shakespeare in Nineteenth-Century
    Germany'

Spring Semester 1982

Stevie Bezencenet (London College of Printing), 'Contemporary Photography in
    Britain'
Jane Marcus (English), 'Shakespeare's Sister, Beethoven's Brother: Dame Ethel
    Smyth and Virginia Woolf'
Wilson Harris (English) and Raja Rao (Philosophy), 'The Quest for Form: Britain
    and Commonwealth Perspectives'
Al Crosby (American Studies), 'The British Empire as a Product of Continental
    Drift'
Lord St. Brides (Visiting Scholar), 'The White House and Whitehall: Washington
    and Westminster'
Elizabeth Fernea (English and Middle East Studies), 'British Colonial Literature
    of the Middle East'

Maurice Evans (Actor and Producer), 'My Early Years in the Theater'
Joan Bassin (Kansas City Art Institute), 'Art and Industry in Nineteenth-Century England'
Eugene N. Borza (Pennsylvania State University), 'Sentimental British Philhellenism: Images of Greece'
Ralph Willett (University of Hull), 'The Style and Structure of British Television News'
Wm. Roger Louis (History), 'Britain and the Creation of the State of Israel'
Peter Russell (Oxford University), 'A British Historian Looks at Portuguese Historiography of the Fifteenth Century'
Rory Coker (Physics), 'Frauds, Hoaxes and Blunders in Science—a British Tradition?'
Ellen DuBois (State University of New York, Buffalo), 'Anglo-American Perspectives on the Suffragette Movement'
Donald G. Davis, Jr. (Library Science), 'Great Expectations—and a Few Illusions: Reflections on an Exchange Teaching Year in England'
Anthony Rota (Bertram Rota Ltd.), 'The Changing World of the Bookdealer'
Eisig Silberschlag (Visiting Professor of Judaic Studies), 'The Bible as the Most Popular Book in English'

Fall Semester 1982

Woodruff Smith (UT San Antonio), 'British Overseas Expansion'
The Rt. Hon. George Thomas (Speaker of the House of Commons), 'Parliamentary Democracy'
Nigel Nicolson (English Historian and Biographer), 'The English Country House as an Historical Document'
Lord St. Brides (Visiting Scholar), 'A Late Leaf of Laurel for Evelyn Waugh'
Lt. Col. Jack McNamara, USMC (Ret.), 'The Libel of Evelyn Waugh by the *Daily Express*'
James Wimsatt (English), 'Chaucer and Medieval French Manuscripts'
Christopher Whelan (Visiting Professor, UT Law School), 'Recent Developments in British Labour Law'
Brian Wearing (University of Canterbury, Christchurch), 'New Zealand: In the Pacific, but of It?'
Robert Hardgrave (Government), 'The United States and India'
James McBath (University of Southern California), 'The Evolution of *Hansard*'
Paul Fromm (University of Toronto), 'Canadian–United States Relations: Two Solitudes'
John Velz (English), 'When in Disgrace: Ganzel's Attempt to Exculpate John Payne Collier'
Wm. Roger Louis (History), 'British Origins of the Iranian Revolution'

Spring Semester 1983

Sir Ellis Waterhouse (Oxford University), 'A Comparison of British and French Painting in the Late Eighteenth Century'
E. J. L. Ride (Australian Consul General), 'Australia's Place in the World and Her Relationship with the United States'
Edward Bell (Royal Botanic Gardens, Kew), 'Kew Gardens in World History'
The Very Rev. Oliver Fiennes (Dean of Lincoln), 'The Care and Feeding of Magna Carta'

C. V. Narasimhan (former Under-Secretary of the United Nations), 'Last Days of the British Raj: A Civil Servant's View'

Warren G. Osmond, 'Sir Frederic Eggleston and the Development of Pacific Consciousness'

Richard Ellmann (Oxford University), 'Henry James among the Aesthetes'

Janet Caulkins (University of Wisconsin–Madison), 'The Poor Reputation of Cornish Knights in Medieval Literature'

Werner Habicht (University of Würzburg), 'Shakespeare and the Third Reich'

Gillian Peele (Oxford University), 'The Changing British Party System'

John Farrell (English), 'Scarlet Ribbons: Memories of Youth and Childhood in Victorian Authors'

Peter Russell (Oxford University), 'A Not So Bashful Stranger: *Don Quixote* in England, 1612–1781'

Sir Zelman Cowen (Oxford University), 'Contemporary Problems in Medicine, Law, and Ethics'

Dennis V. Lindley (Visiting Professor of Mathematics), 'Scientific Thinking in an Unscientific World'

Martin Blumenson (Department of the Army), 'General Mark Clark and the British in the Italian Campaign of World War II'

Fall Semester 1983

Anthony King (University of Essex), 'Margaret Thatcher and the Future of British Politics'

Alistair Gillespie (Canadian Minister of Energy, Mines, and Resources), 'Canadian-British Relations: Best and Worst'

Charles A. Owen, Jr. (University of Connecticut), 'The Pre-1400 Manuscripts of the *Canterbury Tales*'

Major-General (Ret.) Richard Clutterbuck (University of Exeter), 'Terrorism in Malaya'

Wayne A. Wiegand (University of Kentucky), 'British Propaganda in American Public Libraries during World War I'

Stuart Macintyre (Australian National University, Canberra), 'Australian Trade Unionism between the Wars'

Ram Joshi (Visiting Professor of History), 'Is Gandhi Relevant Today?'

Sir Denis Wright (former British Ambassador to Iran), 'Britain and the Iranian Revolution'

Andrew Horn (University of Lesotho), 'Theater and Politics in South Africa'

Philip Davies (University of Manchester), 'British Reaction to American Politics: Overt Rejection, Covert Assimilation'

H. K. Singh (Embassy of India), 'United States-Indian Relations'

Round Table Discussion, 'Two Cheers for Mountbatten: A Reassessment of Lord and Lady Mountbatten and the Partition of India': Wm. Roger Louis (History), Ram Joshi (Visiting Professor of History), and J. S. Mehta (LBJ School)

Spring Semester 1984

M. S. Venkataramani (Jawaharlal Nehru University), 'Winston Churchill and Indian Freedom'

Sir John Thompson (British Ambassador to the United Nations), 'The Falklands and Grenada in the United Nations'

Robert Farrell (Cornell University), 'Medieval Archaeology'

Allon White (University of Sussex), 'The Fiction of Early Modernism'

Round Table Discussion, 'Orwell's *Nineteen Eighty-Four*': Peter Green (Classics), Wm. Roger Louis (History), Miguel Gonzalez-Gerth (Spanish and Portuguese), Standish Meacham (History), and Sid Monas (Slavic Languages and History)

Uriel Dann (University of Tel Aviv), 'Hanover and Britain in the Time of George II'

José Ferrater-Mora (Bryn Mawr College), 'A. M. Turing and his "Universal Turing Machine"'

Rüdiger Ahrens (University of Würzburg), 'Teaching Shakespeare in German Universities'

Michael Brock (Oxford University), 'H. H. Asquith and Venetia Stanley'

Herbert Spiro (Free University of Berlin), 'What Makes the British and Americans Different from Everybody Else: The Adversary Process of the Common Law'

Nigel Bowles (University of Edinburgh), 'Reflections on Recent Developments in British Politics'

Harold Perkin (Rice University), 'The Evolution of Citizenship in Modern Britain'

Christopher Heywood (Sheffield University), '*Jane Eyre* and *Wuthering Heights*'

Dave Powers (Kennedy Library), 'JFK's Trip to Ireland, 1963'

R. W. Coats (Visiting Professor of Economics), 'John Maynard Keynes: The Man and the Economist'

David Evans (Astronomy), 'Astronomy as a British Cultural Export'

Fall Semester 1984

John Henry Faulk, 'Reflections on My Sojourns in the British Middle East'

Lord Fraser of Kilmorack, 'The Thatcher Years—and Beyond'

Michael Phillips (University of Edinburgh), 'William Blake and the Rise of the Hot Air Balloon'

Erik Stocker (HRHRC), 'A Bibliographical Detective Story: Reconstructing James Joyce's Library'

Amedée Turner (European Parliament), 'Recent Developments in the European Parliament'

Michael Hurst (Oxford University), 'Scholars versus Journalists on the English Social Classes'

Charles Alan Wright (Law), 'Reflections on Cambridge'

J. M. Winter (Cambridge University), 'Fear of Decline in Population in Britain after World War I'

Henk Wesseling (University of Leiden), 'Dutch Colonialism and the Impact on British Imperialism'

Celia Morris Eckhardt (Biographer and author of *Fannie Wright*), 'Frances Wright and *England as the Civilizer*'

Sir Oliver Wright (British Ambassador to the United States), 'British Foreign Policy—1984'

Leonard Thompson (Yale University), 'Political Mythology and the Racial Order in South Africa'

Flora Nwapa (Nigerian Novelist), 'Women in Civilian and Military Rule in Nigeria'

Richard Rose (University of Strathclyde), 'The Capacity of the Presidency in Comparative Perspective'

Spring Semester 1985

Bernard Hickey (University of Venice), 'Australian Literary Culture: Short Stories, Novels, and "Literary Journalism"'

Kenneth Hafertepe (American Studies), 'The British Foundations of the Smithsonian Castle: The Gothic Revival in Britain and America'

Rajeev Dhavan (Visiting Professor, LBJ School and Center for Asian Studies), 'Race Relations in England: Trapped Minorities and their Future'

Sir John Thompson (British Ambassador to the United Nations), 'British Techniques of Statecraft'

Philip Bobbitt (Law), 'Britain, the United States, and Reduction in Strategic Arms'

David Bevington (Drama Critic and Theater Historian), 'Maimed Rites: Interrupted Ceremony in *Hamlet*'

Standish Meacham (History), 'The Impact of the New Left History on British and American Historiography'

Iris Murdoch (Novelist and Philosopher), and John O. Bayley (Oxford University), 'Themes in English Literature and Philosophy'

John P. Chalmers (HRHRC), 'Malory Illustrated'

Thomas Metcalf (University of California, Berkeley), 'The Architecture of Empire: The British Raj in India'

Robert H. Wilson (English), 'Malory and His Readers'

Lord St. Brides, '*A Passage to India:* Better Film than Novel?'

Derek Pearsall (York University), 'Fire, Flood, and Slaughter: The Tribulations of the Medieval City of York'

E. S. Atieno Odhiambo (University of Nairobi), 'Britain and Kenya: The Mau Mau, the "Colonial State," and Dependency'

Francis Robinson (University of London), 'Indian Muslim Religious Leadership and Colonial Rule'

Charles B. MacDonald (U.S. Army), 'The British in the Battle of the Bulge'

Brian Levack (History), 'The Battle of Bosworth Field'

Kurth Sprague (English), 'The Mirrors of Malory'

Fall Semester 1985

A. P. Thornton (University of Toronto), 'Whatever Happened to the British Commonwealth?'

Michael Garibaldi Hall (History), and Elizabeth Hall (LBJ School), 'Views of Pakistan'

Ronald Steel (Visiting Professor of History), 'Walter Lippmann and the British'

Douglas H. M. Branion (Canadian Consul General), 'Political Controversy and Economic Development in Canada'

Decherd Turner and Dave Oliphant (HRHRC), 'The History of the Publications of the HRHRC'

Robert Fernea (Anthropology), 'The Controversy over Sex and Orientalism: Charles Doughty's *Arabia Deserta*'

Desley Deacon (Government), 'Her Brilliant Career: The Context of Nineteenth-Century Australian Feminism'

John Lamphear (History), 'The British Colonial "Pacification" of Kenya: A View from the Other Side'

Kingsley de Silva (University of Peradeniya, Sri Lanka), 'British Colonialism and Sri Lankan Independence'

Thomas Hatfield (Continuing Education), 'Colorado on the Cam, 1986: From "Ultra" to Archaeology, from Mr. Micawber to Mrs. Thatcher'

Carol Hanbery MacKay (English), 'The Dickens Theater'

Round Table Discussion, 'The Art of Biography: Philip Ziegler's *Mountbatten*': Ronald Brown, Jo Anne Christian, Wm. Roger Louis (History), Harry Middleton (LBJ Library), and Ronald Steel

Spring Semester 1986

Round Table Discussion, '*Out of Africa:* The Book, the Biography, and the Movie': B. J. Fernea (English and Middle Eastern Studies), Bernth Lindfors (English), and Wm. Roger Louis (History)

Robert Litwak (Woodrow Wilson Center), 'The Great Game: Russian, British, and American Strategies in Asia'

Gillian Adams Barnes (English), and Jane Manaster (Geography), 'Humphrey Carpenter's *Secret Gardens* and the Golden Age of Children's Literature'

Laurie Hergenhan (University of Queensland), 'A Yankee in Australia: The Literary and Historical Adventures of C. Hartley Grattan'

Brian Matthews (Flinders University, Adelaide), 'Australian Utopianism of the 1880s'

Richard Langhorne (Cambridge University), 'Apostles and Spies: The Generation of Treason at Cambridge between the Wars'

Ronald Robinson (Oxford University), 'The Decline and Fall of the British Empire'

William Rodgers (Social Democratic Party), 'Britain's New Three-Party System: A Permanent or Passing Phenomenon?'

John Coetzee (University of Cape Town), 'The Farm Novel in South Africa'

Ayesha Jalal, (Cambridge University), 'Jinnah and the Partition of India'

Andrew Blane (City College of New York), 'Amnesty International: From a British to an International Movement'

Anthony Rota (Antiquarian Bookseller and Publisher), 'London Pride: 1986'

Elspeth Rostow (LBJ School), 'The Withering Away of Whose State? Colonel Qaddafi's? Reflections on Nationalism at Home and Abroad, in Britain and in the Middle East'

Ray Daum (HRHRC), 'Broadway—Piccadilly!'

Fall Semester 1986

Round Table Discussion: Dean Robert King and Members of the '"Unrequired Reading List" Committee—The British Component'

Paul Sturges (Loughborough University, UK), 'Popular Libraries in Eighteenth-Century Britain'

Ian Bickerton (University of Missouri), 'Eisenhower's Middle East Policy and the End of the British Empire'

Marc Ferro (Visiting Professor of History), 'Churchill and Pétain'

David Fitzpatrick (Visiting Professor of History, Queen's University, Ontario), 'Religion and Politics in Ireland'

Adam Watson (University of Virginia), 'Our Man in Havana—or: Britain, Cuba, and the Caribbean'

Norman Rose (Hebrew University), 'Chaim Weizmann, the British, and the Creation of the State of Israel'

Elaine Thompson (American University), 'Legislatures in Canberra and Washington'

Wm. Roger Louis (History), 'Suez Thirty Years After'

Antonia Gransden (University of Nottingham), 'The Writing of Chronicles in Medieval England'

Hilary Spurling (British Biographer and Critic), 'Paul Scott's *Raj Quartet:* The Novelist as Historian'

J. D. B. Miller (Australian National University), 'A Special and Puzzling Relationship: Australia and the United States'

Janet Meisel (History), 'The Domesday Book'

Spring Semester 1987

Round Table Discussion, 'Contemporary Perspectives on Evolution': Miguel Gonzalez-Gerth (Spanish and Portuguese), Robert Fernea (Anthropology), Joe Horn (Psychology), Bruce Hunt (History), and Delbert Thiessen (Psychology)

Alistair Campbell-Dick (Strategic Technology), 'Scottish Nationalism'

Anthony Mockler (British Freelance Historian and Biographer), 'Graham Greene: The Interweaving of His Life and Fiction'

Michael Crowder (Visiting Professor of African History, Amherst College), 'The Legacy of British Colonialism in Africa'

Carin Green (Classics), 'Lovers and Defectors: Autobiography and *The Perfect Spy*'

Lord St. Brides, 'The Modern British Monarchy'

Victor Szebehely (Aerospace Engineering), 'Sir Isaac Newton'

Patrick McCaughey (National Gallery of Victoria, Melbourne), 'The Persistence of Landscape in Australian Art'

Adolf Wood (*Times Literary Supplement*), 'An Informal History of the *TLS*'

Nissan Oren (Hebrew University), 'Churchill, Truman, and Stalin: The End of the Second World War'

Sir Michael Howard (Oxford University), 'Britain and the First World War'

Sir John Graham (former British Ambassador to NATO), 'NATO: British Origins, American Security, and the Future Outlook'

Daniel Mosser (Virginia Polytechnic Institute and State University), 'The Chaucer Cardigan Manuscript'

Sir Raymond Carr (Oxford University), 'British Intellectuals and the Spanish Civil War'

Michael Wilding (University of Sydney), 'The Fatal Shore? The Convict Period in Australian Literature'

Fall Semester 1987

Round Table Discussion, 'Anthony Burgess: The Autobiography': Peter Green (Classics), Winfred Lehmann (Linguistics), Wm. Roger Louis (History), and Paul Woodruff (Philosophy)

Robert Crunden (History and American Studies), 'Ezra Pound in London'

Carol MacKay (English), and John Henry Faulk (Austin), 'J. Frank Dobie and Thackeray's Great-Granddaughter: Another Side of *A Texan in England*'

Sarvepalli Gopal (Jawaharlal Nehru University and Oxford University), 'Nehru and the British'

Robert D. King (Dean of Liberal Arts), 'T. S. Eliot'

Lord Blake (Visiting Professor of English History and Literature), 'Disraeli: Problems of the Biographer'

Alain Blayac (University of Montpellier), 'Art as Revelation: Gerard Manley Hopkins's Poetry and James Joyce's *Portrait of the Artist*'

Mary Bull (Oxford University), 'Margery Perham and Africa'

R. J. Moore (Flinders University, Adelaide), 'Paul Scott: The Novelist as Historian, and the *Raj Quartet* as History'

Ian Willison (British Library), 'New Trends in Humanities Research: The *History of the Book in Britain* Project'

The Duke of Norfolk, 'The Lion and the Unicorn: Ceremonial and the Crown'

Hans Mark (Chancellor, UT System), 'The Royal Society, the Royal Observatory, and the Development of Modern Research Laboratories'

Henry Dietz (Government), 'Sherlock Holmes: A Centennial Celebration'

Spring Semester 1988

Lord Jenkins (Oxford University), 'Changing Patterns of British Government from Asquith via Baldwin and Attlee to Mrs. Thatcher'

Lord Thomas (author of *The Spanish Civil War* and *Cuba, or the Pursuit of Freedom*), 'Britain, Spain, and Latin America'

Round Table Discussion, 'Chinua Achebe: The Man and His Works': Barbara Harlow (English), Bernth Lindfors (English), Wahneema Lubiano (English), and Robert Wren (University of Houston)

Charles Townshend (Keele University, UK), 'Britain, Ireland, and Palestine, 1918–1947'

Richard Morse (Woodrow Wilson Center), 'T. S. Eliot and Latin America'

Chinua Achebe (Nigerian Novelist), 'Anthills of the Savannah'

Tapan Raychaudhuri (Oxford University), 'The English in Bengali Eyes in the Nineteenth Century'

Lord Chitnis (Rowntree Trust and the British Refugee Council), 'British Perceptions of U.S. Policy in Central America'

Kurth Sprague (English), 'Constance White: Sex, Womanhood, and Marriage in British India'

George McGhee (former US Ambassador to Turkey and Germany), 'The Turning Point in the Cold War: Britain, the United States, and Turkey's Entry into NATO'

Robert Palter (Trinity College), 'New Light on Newton's Natural Philosophy'

J. Kenneth McDonald (CIA), 'The Decline of British Naval Power, 1918–1922'

Yvonne Cripps (Visiting Professor of Law), '"Peter and the Boys Who Cry Wolf": *Spycatcher*'

Emmanuel Ngara (University of Zimbabwe), 'African Poetry: Nationalism and Cultural Domination'

Kate Frost (English), 'Frat Rats of the Invisible College: The Wizard Earl of Northumberland and His Pre-Rosicrucian Pals'

B. Ramesh Babu (Visiting Professor of Government), 'American Foreign Policy: An Indian Dissent'

Sir Antony Ackland (British Ambassador to the United States), 'From Dubai to Madrid: Adventures in the British Foreign Service'

In the Spring Semester 1988, British Studies helped sponsor four lectures by Sir Brian Urquhart (former Under-Secretary of the United Nations) under the general title 'World Order in the Era of Decolonization.'

Fall Semester 1988

Round Table Discussion, 'Richard Ellman's *Oscar Wilde*': Peter Green (Classics), Diana Hobby (Rice University), Wm. Roger Louis (History), and Elspeth Rostow (American Studies),

Hugh Cecil (University of Leeds), 'The British First World War Novel of Experience'

Alan Knight (History), 'Britain and the Mexican Revolution'

Prosser Gifford (Former Deputy Director, Woodrow Wilson Center, Washington, DC), and Robert Frykenberg (University of Wisconsin–Madison), 'Stability in Post-Colonial British Africa: The Indian Perspective'

Joseph Dobrinski (Université Paul-Valéry), 'The Symbolism of the Artist Theme in *Lord Jim*'

Martin Stannard (University of Leicester), 'Evelyn Waugh and North America'

Lawrence Cranberg (Fellow, American Physical Society), 'The Engels-Marx Relationship and the Origins of Marxism'

N. G. L. Hammond (Bristol University), 'The British Military Mission to Greece, 1943–1944'

Barbara Harlow (English), 'A Legacy of the British Era in Egypt: Women, Writing, and Political Detention'

Sidney Monas (Slavic Languages and History), 'Thanks for the Mummery: *Finnegans Wake*, Rabelais, Bakhtin, and Verbal Carnival'

Robert Bowie (Central Intelligence Agency), 'Britain's Decision to Join the European Community'

Shirley Williams (Social Democratic Party), 'Labour Weakness and Tory Strength—or, The Strange Death of Labour England'

Bernard Richards (Oxford University), 'Ruskin's View of Turner'

John R. Clarke (Art History), 'Australian Art of the 1960s'

Round Table Discussion, 'Paul Kennedy's *The Rise and Fall of the Great Powers*': Alessandra Lipucci (Government), Wm. Roger Louis (History), Jagat Mehta (LBJ School), Sidney Monas (Slavic Languages and History), and Walt Rostow (Economics and History)

Spring Semester 1989

Brian Levack (History), 'The English Bill of Rights, 1689'

Hilary Spurling (Critic and Biographer), 'Paul Scott as Novelist: His Sense of History and the British Era in India'

Larry Carver (Humanities Program), 'Lord Rochester: The Profane Wit and the Restoration's Major Minor Poet'

Atieno Odhiambo (Rice University), 'Re-Interpreting Mau Mau'

Trevor Hartley (London School of Economics), 'The British Constitution and the European Community'

Archie Brown (Oxford University), 'Political Leadership in Britain, the Soviet Union, and the United States'

Lord Blake (Editor, *Dictionary of National Biography*), 'Churchill as Historian'

Weirui Hou (Shanghai University), 'British Literature in China'

Norman Daniel (British Council), 'Britain and the Iraqi Revolution of 1958'

Alistair Horne (Oxford University), 'The Writing of the Biography of Harold Macmillan'

M. R. D. Foot (Editor, *Gladstone Diaries*), 'The Open and Secret War, 1939–1945'

Ian Willison (former Head of the Rare Books Division, British Library), 'Editorial Theory and Practice in The History of the Book'

Neville Meaney (University of Sydney), 'The "Yellow Peril": Invasion, Scare Novels, and Australian Political Culture'

Round Table Discussion, '*The Satanic Verses*': Kurth Sprague (American Studies), Peter Green (Classics), Robert A. Fernea (Anthropology), Wm. Roger Louis (History), and Gail Minault (History and Asian Studies)

Kate Frost (English), 'John Donne, Sunspots, and the British Empire'

Lee Patterson (Duke University), 'Chaucerian Commerce'

Edmund Weiner and John Simpson (Editors of the new *OED*), 'Return to the Web of Words'

Ray Daum (HRHRC), 'Noel Coward and Cole Porter'

William B. Todd (History), 'Edmund Burke on the French Revolution'

Fall Semester 1989

D. Cameron Watt (London School of Economics), 'Britain and the Origins of the Second World War: Personalities and Politics of Appeasement'

Gary Freeman (Government), 'On the Awfulness of the English: The View from Comparative Studies'

Hans Mark (Chancellor, UT System), 'British Naval Tactics in the Second World War: The Japanese Lessons'

T. B. Millar (Menzies Centre for Australian Studies, London), 'Australia, Britain, and the United States in Historical Perspective'

Dudley Fishburn (Member of Parliament and former Editor of *The Economist*), '*The Economist*'

Lord Franks (former Ambassador in Washington), 'The "Special Relationship"'

Herbert L. Jacobson (Drama Critic and friend of Orson Welles), 'Three Score Years of Transatlantic Acting and Staging of Shakespeare'

Roy Macleod (University of Sydney) 'The "Practical Man": Myth and Metaphor in Anglo-Australian Science'

David Murray (Open University), 'Hong Kong: The Historical Context for the Transfer of Power'

Susan Napier (UT Assistant Professor of Japanese Language and Literature), 'Japanese Intellectuals Discover the British'

Dr. Karan Singh (Ambassador of India to the United States), 'Four Decades of Indian Democracy'

Paul Woodruff (Philosophy), 'George Grote and the Radical Tradition in British Scholarship'

Herbert J. Spiro (Government), 'Britain, the United States, and the Future of Germany'

Robert Lowe (*Austin American-Statesman*), '"God Rest You Merry, Gentlemen": The Curious British Cult of Sherry'

Spring Semester 1990

Thomas F. Staley (HRHRC), 'Harry Ransom, the Humanities Research Center, and the Development of Twentieth-Century Literary Research Collections'

Thomas Cable (English), 'The Rise and Decline of the English Language'

D. J. Wenden (Oxford University), 'Sir Alexander Korda and the British Film Industry'

Roger Owen (Oxford University), 'Reflections on the First Ten Years of Thatcherism'

Robert Hardgrave (Government), 'Celebrating Calcutta: The Solvyns Portraits'

Donatus Nwoga (University of Nigeria, Nsukka), 'The Intellectual Legacy of British Decolonization in Africa'

Francis Sitwell (Etonian, Seaman, and Literary Executor), 'Edith Sitwell: A Reappraisal'

Robert Vitalis (Government), 'The "New Deal" in Egypt: Britain, the United States, and the Egyptian Economy during World War II'

James Coote (Architecture), 'Prince Charles and Architecture'

Harry Eckstein (University of California, Irvine), 'British Politics and the National Health Service'

Alfred David (Indiana University), 'Chaucer and King Arthur'

Ola Rotimi (African Playwright and Theater Director), 'African Literature and the British Tongue'

Derek Brewer (Cambridge University), 'An Anthropological Study of Literature'

Neil MacCormick (University of Edinburgh), 'Stands Scotland Where She Should?'

Janice Rossen (Senior Research Fellow, HRHRC), 'Toads and Melancholy: The Poetry of Philip Larkin'

Ronald Robinson (Oxford University), 'The Decolonization of British Imperialism'

Fall Semester 1990

Round Table Discussion, 'The Crisis in the Persian Gulf': Hafez Farmayan (History), Robert Fernea (Anthropology), Wm. Roger Louis (History), and Robert Stookey (Center for Middle Eastern Studies)

John Velz (English), 'Shakespeare and Some Surrogates: An Account of the Anti-Stratfordian Heresy'

Michael H. Codd (Department of the Prime Minister and Cabinet, Government of Australia), 'The Future of the Commonwealth: An Australian View'

John Dawick (Massey University, New Zealand), 'The Perils of Paula: Young Women and Older Men in Pinero's Plays'

Gloria Fromm (University of Illinios, Chicago), 'New Windows on Modernism: The Letters of Dorothy Richardson'

David Braybrooke (Government), 'The Canadian Constitutional Crisis'

Sidney Monas (Slavic Languages and History), 'Paul Fussell and World War II'

James Fishkin (Government), 'Thought Experiments in Recent Oxford Philosophy'

Joseph Hamburger (Yale University), 'How Liberal Was John Stuart Mill?'

Richard W. Clement (University of Kansas), 'Thomas James and the Bodleian Library: The Foundations of Scholarship'

Michael Yeats (Former Chairman of the Irish Senate and only son of the poet William Butler Yeats), 'Ireland and Europe'

Round Table Discussion, 'William H. McNeill's *Arnold J. Toynbee: A Life*': Standish Meacham (Dean, Liberal Arts), Peter Green (Classics), Wm. Roger Louis (History), and Sidney Monas (Slavic Languages and History)

Jeffrey Meyers (Biographer and Professor of English, University of Colorado), 'Conrad and Jane Anderson'

Alan Frost (La Trobe University, Melbourne), 'The Explorations of Captain Cook'

Sarvepalli Gopal (Jawaharlal Nehru University), 'The First Ten Years of Indian Independence'

Round Table Discussion, 'The Best and Worst Books of 1990': Alessandra Lippucci (Government), Wm. Roger Louis (History), Tom Staley (HRHRC), Steve Weinberg (Physics), and Paul Woodruff (Philosophy)

Spring Semester 1991

David Hollway (Prime Minister's Office, Government of Australia), 'Australia and the Gulf Crisis'

Diane Kunz (Yale University), 'British Post-War Sterling Crises'

Miguel Gonzalez-Gerth (Spanish Literature and the HRHRC), 'T. E. Lawrence, Richard Aldington, and the Death of Heroes'
Robert Twombly (English), 'Religious Encounters with the Flesh in English Literature'
Alan Ryan (Princeton University), 'Bertrand Russell's Politics'
Hugh Kenner (Johns Hopkins University), 'The State of English Poetry'
Patricia Burnham (American Studies), 'Anglo-American Art and the Struggle for Artistic Independence'
Round Table Discussion, 'The Churchill Tradition': Lord Blake (former Provost of Queen's College, Oxford), Lord Jenkins (Chancellor, Oxford University), Field Marshal Lord Carver (former Chief of the Defence Staff), Sir Michael Howard (former Regius Professor, Oxford, present Lovett Professor of Military and Naval History, Yale University), with a concluding comment by Winston S. Churchill, M.P.
Woodruff Smith (UT San Antonio), 'Why Do the British Put Sugar in Their Tea?'
Peter Firchow (University of Minnesota), 'Aldous Huxley: The Poet as Centaur'
Irene Gendzier (Boston University), 'British and American Middle Eastern Policies in the 1950s: Lebanon and Kuwait; Reflections on Past Experience and the Post-War Crisis in the Gulf'
John Train (*Harvard* Magazine and *Wall Street Journal*), 'Remarkable Catchwords in the City of London and on Wall Street'
Adam Sisman (Independent Writer, London), 'A. J. P. Taylor'
Wm. Roger Louis (History), 'The Young Winston'
Adrian Mitchell (Melbourne University), 'Claiming a Voice: Recent Non-Fiction Writing in Australia'
Bruce Hevly (University of Washington), 'Stretching Things Out versus Letting Them Slide: The Natural Philosophy of Ice in Edinburgh and Cambridge in the Nineteenth Century'
Henry Dietz (Government), 'Foibles and Follies in Sherlock's Great Game: Some Excesses of Holmesian Research'

Summer 1991

Wm. Roger Louis (History), and Ronald Robinson (Oxford University), 'Harold Macmillan and the Dissolution of the British Empire'
Robert Treu (University of Wisconsin–Lacrosse), 'D. H. Lawrence and Graham Greene in Mexico'
Thomas Pinney (Pomona College), 'Kipling, India, and Imperialism'
Ronald Heiferman (Quinnipiac College), 'The Odd Couple: Winston Churchill and Chiang Kai-shek'
John Harty (Alice Lloyd College, Kentucky), 'The Movie and the Book: J. G. Ballard's *Empire of the Sun*'
A. B. Assensoh (Southern University, Baton Rouge), 'Nkrumah'
Victoria Carchidi (Emory and Henry College), 'Lawrence of Arabia on a Camel, Thank God!'
James Gump (University of California, San Diego), 'The Zulu and the Sioux: The British and American Comparative Experience with the "Noble Savage"'

Fall Semester 1991

Round Table Discussion, 'Noel Annan's *Our Age*': Peter Green (Classics), Robert D. King (Dean, Liberal Arts), Wm. Roger Louis (History), and Thomas F. Staley (HRHRC)

Christopher Heywood (Okayama University), 'Slavery, Imagination, and the Brontës'

Harold L. Smith (University of Houston, Victoria), 'Winston Churchill and Women'

Krystyna Kujawinska-Courtney (University of Lodz), 'Shakespeare and Poland'

Ewell E. Murphy, Jr. (Baker Botts, Houston), 'Cecil Rhodes and the Rhodes Scholarships'

I. N. Kimambo (University of Dar es Salaam), 'The District Officer in Tanganyika'

Hans Mark (Chancellor, UT System), 'The Pax Britannica and the Inevitable Comparison: Is There a Pax Americana? Conclusions from the Gulf War'

Richard Clutterbuck (Major-General, British Army, Ret.), 'British and American Hostages in the Middle East: Negotiating with Terrorists'

Elizabeth Hedrick (English), 'Samuel Johnson and Linguistic Propriety'

The Hon. Denis McLean (New Zealand Ambassador to the United States), 'Australia and New Zealand: The Nuisance of Nationalism'

Elizabeth Richmond (English), 'Submitting a Trifle for a Degree: Dramatic Productions at Oxford and Cambridge in the Age of Shakespeare'

Kenneth Warren, M.D. (Director for Science, Maxwell Macmillan), 'Tropical Medicine: A British Invention'

Adolf Wood (*Times Literary Supplement*), 'The Golden Age of the *Times Literary Supplement*'

Eugene Walter (Poet and Novelist), 'Unofficial Poetry: Literary London in the 1940s and 1950s'

Sidney Monas (Slavic Languages and History), 'Images of Britain in the Poetry of World War II'

St. Stephen's Madrigal Choir, 'Celebrating an English Christmas'

Spring Semester 1992

Jeremy Treglown (Critic and Author), 'Wartime Censorship and the Novel'

Toyin Falola (History), 'Nigerian Independence, 1960'

Donald S. Lamm (W.W. Norton and Company), 'Publishing English History in America'

Colin Franklin (Publisher and Historian of the Book), 'The Pleasures of Eighteenth-Century Shakespeare'

Thomas F. Staley (HRHRC), '*Fin de Siècle* Joyce: A Perspective on One Hundred Years'

Sarvepalli Gopal (Jawaharlal Nehru University), '"Drinking Tea with Treason": Halifax and Gandhi'

Michael Winship (English), 'The History of the Book: Britain's Foreign Trade in Books in the Nineteenth Century'

Richard Lariviere (Sanskrit and Asian Studies), 'British Law and Lawyers in India'

Round Table Discussion, 'A. S. Byatt's *Possession*': Janice Rossen (Visiting Scholar, HRHRC), John P. Farrell (English), and Wm. Roger Louis (History)

William H. McNeill (University of Chicago), 'Arnold Toynbee's Vision of World History'

Derek Brewer (Cambridge University), 'The Interpretation of Fairy Tales: The Implications for English Literature, Anthropology, and History'

David Bradshaw (Oxford University), 'Aldous Huxley: Eugenics and the Rational State'

Steven Weinberg (Physics), 'The British Style in Physics'

Sir David Williams (Cambridge University), 'Northern Ireland'

Summer 1992

R. A. C. Parker (Oxford University), 'Neville Chamberlain and Appeasement'

Adrian Wooldridge (Oxford University and *The Economist*), 'Reforming British Education: How It Happened and What America Can Learn'

Chris Wrigley (Nottingham University), 'A. J. P. Taylor: An English Radical and Modern Europe'

Fall Semester 1992

Round Table Discussion, 'E. M. Forster's *Howards End:* The Movie and the Book': Robert D. King (Linguistics), Wm. Roger Louis (History), Alessandra Lippucci (Government), and Thomas F. Staley (HRHRC)

Lord Skidelsky (Warwick University), 'Keynes and the Origins of the "Special Relationship"'

Sir Samuel Falle (former British Ambassador), 'Britain and the Middle East in the 1950s'

Ian MacKillop (University of Sheffield), 'We Were That Cambridge: F. R. Leavis and *Scrutiny*'

Walter Dean Burnham (Government), 'The 1992 British Elections: Four-or-Five-More Tory Years?'

Don Graham (English), 'Modern Australian Literature and the Image of America'

Richard Woolcott (former Secretary of the Australian Department of Foreign Affairs), 'Australia and the Question of Cooperation or Contention in the Pacific'

Ian Willison (1992 Wiggins Lecturer, American Antiquarian Society), 'The History of the Book in Twentieth-Century Britain and America'

Iain Sproat, (Member of Parliament), 'P. G. Wodehouse and the War'

Standish Meacham (History), 'The Crystal Palace'

Field Marshal Lord Carver (former Chief of the British Defence Staff), 'Wavell: A Reassessment'

Lesley Hall (Wellcome Institute for the History of Medicine, London), 'For Fear of Frightening the Horses: Sexology in Britain since William Acton'

Michael Fry (University of Southern California), 'Britain, the United Nations, and the Lebanon Crisis of 1958'

Brian Holden Reid (King's College, London), 'J. F. C. Fuller and the Revolution in British Military Thought'

Neil Parsons (University of London), '"Clicko," or Franz Taaibosch: A Bushman Entertainer in Britain, Jamaica, and the United States *c.* 1919–40'

John Hargreaves (Aberdeen University), 'God's Advocate: Lewis Namier and the History of Modern Europe'

Round Table Discussion, 'Robert Harris's *Fatherland*': Henry Dietz (Government), Robert D. King (Linguistics), Wm. Roger Louis (History), and Walter Wetzels (Germanic Languages)

Kevin Tierney (University of California), 'Robert Graves: An Outsider Looking In, or An Insider Who Escaped?'

Spring Semester 1993

Round Table Discussion, 'The Trollope Mystique': Janice Rossen (author of *Philip Larkin* and *The University in Modern Fiction*), Louise Weinberg (Law School), and Paul Woodruff (Plan II Honors Program and Philosophy)

Bruce Hunt (History), 'To Rule the Waves: Cable Telegraphy and British Physics in the Nineteenth Century'
Martin Wiener (Rice University), 'The Unloved State: Contemporary Political Attitudes in the Writing of Modern British History'
Elizabeth Dunn (HRHRC), 'Ralph Waldo Emerson and Ireland'
Jason Thompson (Western Kentucky University), 'Edward William Lane's "Description of Egypt"'
Sir Michael Howard (Yale University), 'Strategic Deception in the Second World War'
Gordon A. Craig (Stanford University), 'Churchill'
Round Table Discussion, 'The Indian Mathematician Ramanujan': Robert D. King (Linguistics), James W. Vick (Mathematics), and Steven Weinberg (Physics)
Martha Merritt (Government), 'From Commonwealth to Commonwealth, and from Vauxhall to *Vokzal:* Russian Borrowing from Britain'
Sidney Monas (Slavic Languages and History), 'James Joyce and Russia'
Peter Marshall (King's College, London), 'Imperial Britain and the Question of National Identity'
Michael Wheeler (Lancaster University), 'Ruskin and Gladstone'
Anthony Low (Cambridge University), 'Britain and India in the Early 1930s: The British, American, French, and Dutch Empires Compared'

Summer 1993

Alexander Pettit (University of North Texas), 'Lord Bolingbroke's *Remarks on the History of England*'
Rose Marie Burwell (Northern Illinois University), 'The British Novel and Ernest Hemingway'
Richard Patteson (Mississippi State University), 'New Writing in the West Indies'
Richard Greene (Memorial University, Newfoundland), 'The Moral Authority of Edith Sitwell'

Fall Semester 1993

Round Table Discussion, 'The British and the Shaping of the American Critical Mind—Edmund Wilson, Part II': Wm. Roger Louis (History), Elspeth Rostow (American Studies), Tom Staley (HRHRC), and Robert Crunden (History and American Studies)
Roseanne Camacho (University of Rhode Island), 'Evelyn Scott: Towards an Intellectual Biography'
Christopher Heywood (Okayama University), 'The Brontës and Slavery'
Peter Gay (Yale University), 'The Cultivation of Hatred in England'
Linda Ferreira-Buckley (English) 'England's First English Department: Rhetoric and More Rhetoric'
Janice Rossen (HRHRC), 'British University Novels'
Ian Hancock (O Yanko Le Redzosko) (Linguistics and English), 'The Gypsy Image in British Literature'
James Davies (University College of Swansea), 'Dylan Thomas'
Jeremy Lewis (London Writer and Editor), 'Who Cares about Cyril Connolly?'
Sam Jamot Brown (British Studies) and Robert D. King (Linguistics), 'Scott and the Antarctic'
Martin Trump (University of South Africa), 'Nadine Gordimer's Social and Political Vision'

Richard Clogg (University of London), 'Britain and the Origins of the Greek Civil War'

Herbert J. Spiro (United States Ambassador, Ret.), 'The Warburgs: Anglo-American and German-Jewish Bankers'

Colin Franklin (Publisher and Antiquarian Bookseller), 'Lord Chesterfield: Stylist, Connoisseur of Manners, and Specialist in Worldly Advice'

Jeffrey Segall (Charles University, Prague), 'The Making of James Joyce's Reputation'

Rhodri Jeffreys-Jones (University of Edinburgh), 'The Myth of the Iron Lady: Margaret Thatcher and World Stateswomen'

John Rumrich (English), 'Milton and Science: Gravity and the Fall'

J. D. Alsop (McMaster University), 'British Propaganda, Espionage, and Political Intrigue'

Round Table Discussion, 'The Best and the Worst Books of 1993': David Edwards (Government), Creekmore Fath (Liberal Arts Foundation), Betty Sue Flowers (English), and Sidney Monas (Slavic Languages and History)

Spring Semester 1994

Thomas F. Staley (HRHRC), 'John Rodker: Poet and Publisher of Modernism'

Martha Fehsenfeld, and Lois More Overbeck (Emory University), 'The Correspondence of Samuel Beckett'

M. R. D. Foot (Historian and Editor), 'Lessons of War on War: The Influence of 1914–1918 on 1939–1945'

Round Table Discussion, 'Requiem for Canada?': David Braybrooke (Government), Walter Dean Burnham (Government), and Robert Crunden (American Studies)

Ross Terrill (Harvard University), 'Australia and Asia in Historical Perspective'

Sir Samuel Falle (British Ambassador and High Commissioner), 'The Morning after Independence: The Legacy of the British Empire'

Deborah Lavin (University of Durham), 'Lionel Curtis: Prophet of the British Empire'

Robin W. Doughty (Geography), 'Eucalyptus: And Not a Koala in Sight'

Al Crosby (American Studies and History), 'Captain Cook and the Biological Impact on the Hawaiian Islands'

Gillian Adams (Editor, *Children's Literature Association Quarterly*), 'Beatrix Potter and Her Recent Critics'

Lord Amery, 'Churchill's Legacy'

Christa Jansohn (University of Bonn), and Peter Green (Classics), '*Lady Chatterley's Lover*'

R. A. C. Parker (Oxford University), 'Neville Chamberlain and the Coming of the Second World War'

John Velz (English), 'King Lear in Iowa: Jane Smiley's *A Thousand Acres*'

Jan Schall (University of Florida), 'British Spirit Photography'

Daniel Woolf (Dalhousie University), 'The Revolution in Historical Consciousness in England'

Fall Semester 1994

Kenneth O. Morgan (University of Wales), 'Welsh Nationalism'

Round Table Discussion, 'Michael Shelden's *Graham Greene: The Man Within*': Peter Green (Classics), Wm. Roger Louis (History), and Thomas F. Staley (HRHRC)

Robert D. King (Linguistics), 'The Secret War, 1939–1945'

Brian Boyd (University of Auckland), 'The Evolution of Shakespearean Dramatic Structure'

Lord Weatherill (former Speaker of the House of Commons), 'Thirty Years in Parliament'

Hans Mark (Aerospace Engineering), 'Churchill's Scientists'

Steven Weinberg (Physics), 'The Test of War: British Strengths and Weaknesses in World War II'

Dennis Welland (University of East Anglia), 'Wilfred Owen and the Poetry of War'

Alan Frost (La Trobe University), 'The *Bounty* Mutiny and the British Romantic Poets'

W. O. S. Sutherland (English), 'Sir Walter Scott'

Hazel Rowley (Deakin University, Melbourne), 'Christina Stead's "Other Country"'

Herman Bakvis (Dalhousie University), 'The Future of Democracy in Canada and Australia'

Peter Stansky (Stanford University), 'George Orwell and the Writing of *Nineteen Eighty-Four*'

Henry Dietz (Government), 'Sherlock Homes and Jack the Ripper'

James Coote (Architecture), 'Techniques of Illusion in British Architecture'

Round Table Discussion, 'The Best and Worst Books of 1994': Dean Burnham (Government), Alessandra Lippucci (Government), Roger Louis (History), Sidney Monas (Slavic Languages and History), and Janice Rossen (HRHRC)

Spring Semester 1995

Elizabeth Butler Cullingford (English), 'Anti-Colonial Metaphors in Contemporary Irish Literature'

Thomas M. Hatfield (Continuing Education), 'British and American Deception of the Germans in Normandy'

Gary P. Freeman (Government), 'The Politics of Race and Immigration in Britain'

Donald G. Davis, Jr. (Library and Information Science), 'The Printed Word in Sunday Schools in Nineteenth-Century England and the United States'

Brian Bremen (English), "Healing Words: The Literature of Medicine and the Medicine of Literature'

Frances Karttunen (Linguistic Research Center), and Alfred W. Crosby (American Studies and History), 'British Imperialism and Creole Languages'

Paul Lovejoy (York University, Canada), 'British Rule in Africa: A Reassessment of Nineteenth-Century Colonialism'

Carol MacKay (English), 'Creative Negativity in the Life and Work of Elizabeth Robins'

John Brokaw (Theatre and Dance), 'The Changing Stage in London, 1790–1832'

Linda Colley (Yale University), 'The Frontier in British History'

Iwan Morus (University of California, San Diego), 'Manufacturing Nature: Science, Technology, and Victorian Consumer Culture'

Brian Parker (University of Toronto), 'Jacobean Law: The Dueling Code and "A Faire Quarrel" (1617)'

Kate Frost (English), '"Jack Donne the Rake": Fooling around in the 1590s'

Mark Kinkead-Weekes (University of Kent), 'Beyond Gossip: D. H. Lawrence's Writing Life'

Summer 1995

S. P. Rosenbaum (University of Toronto), 'Leonard and Virginia Woolf at the Hogarth Press'

Maria X. Wells (HRHRC), 'A Delicate Balance: Trieste, 1945'

Kevin Tierney (University of California, Berkeley), 'Personae in Twentieth Century British Autobiography'

Fall Semester 1995

Brian Levack (History), 'Witchcraft, Possession, and the Law in Jacobean England'

Janice Rossen (HRHRC), 'The Home Front: Anglo-American Women Novelists and World War II'

Dorothy Driver (University of Cape Town), 'Olive Schreiner's Novel *From Man to Man*'

Philip Ziegler (London), 'Mountbatten Revisited'

Joanna Hitchcock (Director, University of Texas Press), 'British and American University Presses'

Samuel H. Beer (Harvard University), 'The Rise and Fall of Party Government in Britain and the United States, 1945–1995'

Richard Broinowski (Australian Ambassador to Mexico and Central America), 'Australia and Latin America'

John Grigg (London), 'Myths about the Approach to Indian Independence'

Round Table Discussion, '*Measuring the Mind* by Adrian Wooldridge and *The Bell Curve* by Richard J. Herrnstein and Charles Murray': David Edwards (Government), Sheldon Ekland-Olson (Dean of Liberal Arts), Joseph Horn (Psychology), and Robert D. King (Linguistics)

Paul Addison (University of Edinburgh), 'British Politics in the Second World War'

John Sibley Butler (Sociology), 'Emigrants of the British Empire'

Round Table Discussion, '*Carrington*': Peter Green (Classics), Robin Kilson (History), Wm. Roger Louis (History), Sidney Monas (Slavic Languages and History), and Elizabeth Richmond-Garza (English)

Spring Semester 1996

Kevin Kenny (History), 'Making Sense of the Molly Maguires'

Brigadier Michael Harbottle (British Army), 'British and American Security in the Post-Cold War'

Carol MacKay (English), 'The Singular Double Vision of Photographer Julia Margaret Cameron'

John Ramsden (University of London), '"That Will Depend on Who Writes the History": Winston Churchill as His Own Historian'

Jack P. Greene (Johns Hopkins University), 'The *British* Revolution in America'

Walter D. Wetzels (German), 'The Ideological Fallout in Germany of Two British Expeditions to Test Einstein's General Theory of Relativity'

Thomas Pinney (Pomona College), 'In Praise of Kipling'

Michael Charlesworth (Art History), 'The English Landscape Garden'

Stephen Gray (South African Novelist), 'The Dilemma of Colonial Writers with Dual Identities'

Jeremy Black (University of Durham), 'Could the British Have Won the War of American Independence?'

Dagmar Hamilton (LBJ School), 'Justice William O. Douglas and British Colonialism'

Gordon Peacock and Laura Worthen (Theatre and Dance), 'Not Always a Green and Pleasant Land: Tom Stoppard's *Arcadia*'

Bernard Crick (University of London), 'Orwell and the Business of Biography'

Geoffrey Hartman (Yale University), 'The Sympathy Paradox: Poetry, Feeling, and Modern Cultural Morality'

Dave Oliphant (HRHRC), 'Jazz and Its British Acolytes'

R. W. B. Lewis (Yale University), 'Henry James: The Victorian Scene'

Alan Spencer (Ford Motor Company), 'Balliol, Big Business, and Mad Cows'

Peter Quinn: A Discussion of His Novel, *Banished Children of Eve*

Summer1996

Martin Stannard (Leicester University), 'Biography and Textual Criticism'

Diane Kunz (Yale University), 'British Withdrawal East of Suez'

John Cell (Duke University), 'Who Ran the British Empire?'

Mark Jacobsen (U.S. Marine Corps Command and Staff College), 'The North-West Frontier'

Theodore Vestal (Oklahoma State University), 'Britain and Ethiopia'

Warren F. Kimball (Rutgers University), 'A Victorian Tory: Churchill, the Americans, and Self-Determination'

Louise B. Williams (Lehman College, City University of New York), 'British Modernism and Fascism'

Fall Semester 1996

Elizabeth Richmond-Garza (English and Comparative Literature), 'The New Gothic: Decadents for the 1990s'

Robin Kilson (History), 'The Politics of Captivity: The British State and Prisoners of War in World War I'

Sir Brian Fall (Oxford University), 'What Does Britain Expect from the European Community, the United States, and the Commonwealth?'

Wm. Roger Louis (History), 'Harold Macmillan and the Middle East Crisis of 1958'

Ian Willison (Editor, *The Cambridge History of the Book in Britain*), 'The History of the Book and the Cultural and Literary History of the English-Speaking World'

Walter L. Arnstein (University of Illinois), 'Queen Victoria's Other Island'

Noel Annan (London), '*Our Age* Revisited'

Michael Cohen (Bar-Ilan University, Tel Aviv), 'The Middle East and the Cold War: Britain, the United States, and the Soviet Union'

Reba Soffer (California State University, Northridge), 'Catholicism in England: Was it Possible to Be a Good Catholic, a Good Englishman, and a Good Historian?'

Wilson Harris (Poet and Novelist), 'The Mystery of Consciousness: Cross-Cultural Influences in the Caribbean, Britain, and the United States'

H. S. Barlow (Singapore), 'British Malaya in the late Nineteenth Century'

Donald G. Davis, Jr. (Library and Information Science), 'British Destruction of Chinese Books in the Peking Siege of 1900'

Round Table Discussion, '*Michael Collins*': Elizabeth Cullingford (English), Kevin Kenny (History), Robin Kilson (History), and Wm. Roger Louis (History)

A. G. Hopkins (Cambridge University), 'From Africa to Empire'
Austin Chapter of the Society for the Preservation and Encouragement of Barber Shop Quartet Singing in America

Spring Semester 1997

Round Table Discussion, 'T. S. Eliot and Anti-Semitism': Robert D. King (Jewish Studies), Sidney Monas (Slavic Languages and History), and Thomas F. Staley (HRHRC)
Phillip Herring (University of Wisconsin–Madison), 'Djuna Barnes and T. S. Eliot: The Story of a Friendship'
Bryan Roberts (Sociology), 'British Sociology and British Society'
Andrew Roberts (London), 'The Captains and the Kings Depart: Lord Salisbury's Skeptical Imperialism'
Colin Franklin (London), 'In a Golden Age of Publishing, 1950–1970'
Susan Pedersen (Harvard University), 'Virginia Woolf, Eleanor Rathbone, and the Problem of Appeasement'
Andrew Seaman (Saint Mary's University, Halifax, Nova Scotia), 'Thomas Raddall: A Novelist's View of Nova Scotia during the American Revolution'
Gordon Peacock (Theatre and Dance), 'Noel Coward: A Master Playwright, a Talented Actor, a Novelist and Diarist: Or a Peter Pan for the Twentieth Century?'
Roland Oliver (University of London), 'The Battle for African History, 1947–1966'
Alistair Horne (Oxford University), 'Harold Macmillan's Fading Reputation'
Richard Begam (University of Wisconsin–Madison), 'Samuel Beckett and the Debate on Humanism'
Christopher Waters (Williams College), 'Delinquents, Perverts, and the State: Psychiatry and the Homosexual Desire in the 1930s'
Sami Zubaida (University of London), 'Ernest Gellner and Islam'
Walter Dean Burnham (Government), 'Britain Votes: The 1997 General Election and Its Implications'

Fall Semester 1997

Judith Brown (Oxford University), 'Gandhi: A Victorian Gentleman'
Thomas Cable (English), 'Hearing and Revising the History of the English Language'
Round Table Discussion, 'The Death of Princess Diana': Judith Brown (Oxford), David Edwards (Government), Elizabeth Richmond-Garza (English), Anne Baade (British Studies), Alessandra Lippucci (Government), and Kevin Kenny (History)
David Hunter (Music Librarian, Fine Arts Library), 'Handel and His Patrons'
Anne Kane (Sociology), 'The Current Situation in Ireland'
James S. Fishkin (Government), 'Power and the People: The Televised Deliberative Poll in the 1997 British General Election'
Howard D. Weinbrot (University of Wisconsin–Madison), 'Jacobitism in Eighteenth-Century Britain'
J. C. Baldwin, M.D. (Houston), 'The Abdication of King Edward VIII'
Kenneth E. Carpenter (Harvard University), 'Library Revolutions Past and Present'
Akira Iriye (Harvard University), 'Britain, Japan, and the International Order after World War I'

Anthony Hobson (London), 'Reminiscences of British Authors and the Collecting of Contemporary Manuscripts'

David Killingray (University of London), 'The British in the West Indies'

Alan Knight (Oxford University), 'British Imperialism in Latin America'

Round Table Discussion, 'King Lear in Iowa: The Film *A Thousand Acres*': Linda Ferreira-Buckley (English), Elizabeth Richmond-Garza (English), Helena Woodard (English), and John Velz (English)

Timothy Lovelace (Music) and the Talisman Trio

Spring Semester 1998

Richard Ollard (Biographer and Publisher), 'A. L. Rowse: Epitome of the Twentieth Century'

Round Table Discussion, 'Arundhati Roy's *The God of Small Things*': Phillip Herring (HRHRC), Brian Trinque (Economics), Kamala Visweswaran (Anthropology), and Robert Hardgrave (Government)

Jonathan Schneer (Georgia Institute of Technology), 'London in 1900: The Imperial Metropolis'

Trevor Burnard (University of Canterbury, New Zealand), 'Rioting in Goatish Embraces: Marriage and the Failure of White Settlement in British Jamaica'

Felipe Fernández-Armesto (Oxford University), 'British Traditions in Comparative Perspective'

Michael Mann (University of California, Los Angeles), 'The Broader Significance of Labour's Landslide Victory of 1997'

Dane Kennedy (University of Nebraska), 'White Settlers in Colonial Kenya and Rhodesia'

Round Table Discussion, 'Noel Annan, Keynes, and Bloomsbury': Jamie Galbraith (LBJ School), Elspeth Rostow (LBJ School), and Walt Rostow (Economics and History)

Lisa Moore (English), 'British Studies—Lesbian Studies: A Dangerous Intimacy?'

James Gibbs (University of the West of England), 'Wole Soyinka: The Making of a Playwright'

Marilyn Butler (Oxford University), 'About the House: Jane Austen's Anthropological Eye'

R. J. Q. Adams (Texas A&M University), 'Britain and Ireland, 1912–1922'

John M. Carroll (Asian Studies), 'Nationalism and Identity in pre-1949 Hong Kong'

Round Table Discussion, 'The Irish Referendum': Anne Kane (Sociology), Kevin Kenny (History), Wm. Roger Louis (History), and Jennifer O'Conner (History)

Fall Semester 1998

Louise Hodgden Thompson (Government), 'Origins of the First World War: The Anglo-German Naval Armaments Race'

John P. Farrell (English), 'Thomas Hardy in Love'

Carol MacKay (English), 'The Multiple Conversions of Annie Besant'

Roy Foster (Oxford University), 'Yeats and Politics, 1898–1921'

Robert Olwell (History), 'British Magic Kingdoms: Imagination, Speculation, and Empire in Florida'

Sara H. Sohmer (Texas Christian University), 'The British in the South Seas: Exploitation and Trusteeship in Fiji'

Helena Woodard (English), 'Politics of Race in the Eighteenth Century: Pope and the Humanism of the Enlightenment'

D. A. Smith (Grinnell College), 'Impeachment? Parliamentary Government in Britain and France in the Nineteenth Century'

Round Table Discussion, 'The Irish Insurrection of 1798': Robert Olwell (History), Lisa Moore (English), and Kevin Kenny (History)

Robert D. King (Jewish Studies), 'The Accomplishments of Raja Rao: The Triumph of the English Language in India'

Donald G. Davis, Jr. (Library and Information Science and History), 'Religion and Empire'

A. D. Roberts (University of London), 'The Awkward Squad: African Students in American Universities before 1940'

Chaganti Vijayasree (Osmania University, Hyderabad), 'The Empire and Victorian Poetry'

Martha Deatherage (Music), 'Christmas Celebration: Vauxhall Gardens'

Spring Semester 1999

Round Table Discussion, '*Regeneration:* Pat Barker's Trilogy on the First World War': Betty Sue Flowers (English), Wm. Roger Louis (History), and Paul Woodruff (Humanities)

Alistair Campbell-Dick (Cybertime Corporation), 'The Immortal Memory of Robert Burns'

Hugh Macrae Richmond (University of California, Berkeley), 'Why Rebuild Shakespeare's Globe Theatre?'

Ralph Austen (University of Chicago), 'Britain and the Global Economy: A Post-Colonial Perspective'

Jerome Meckier (University of Kentucky), 'Aldous Huxley's American Experience'

Peter Marsh (Syracuse University), 'Joseph Chamberlain as an Entrepreneur in Politics: Writing the Life of a Businessman Turned Statesman'

Roger Adelson (Arizona State University), 'Winston Churchill and the Middle East'

Margot Finn (Emory University), 'Law, Debt, and Empire: The Calcutta Court of Conscience'

Fred M. Leventhal (Boston University), 'The Projection of Britain in America before the Second World War'

Larry Siedentop (Oxford University), 'Reassessing the Life of Isaiah Berlin'

Ross Terrill (Harvard University), 'R. H. Tawney's Vision of Fellowship'

Juliet Fleming (Cambridge University), 'The Ladies' Shakespeare'

Elizabeth Fernea (English and Middle Eastern Studies), 'The Victorian Lady Abroad: In Egypt with Sophia Poole and in Texas with Mrs. E. M. Houstoun'

Richard Schoch (University of London), 'The Respectable and the Vulgar: British Theater in the Mid-Nineteenth Century'

Ferdinand Mount (Editor, *TLS*), 'Politics and the *Times Literary Supplement*'

Fall Semester 1999

Round Table Discussion, 'The Boer War, 1899–1902': Barbara Harlow (English), John Lamphear (History), and Wm. Roger Louis (History)

Sharon Arnoult (Southwest Texas State University), 'Charles I: His Life after Death'

Kenneth O. Morgan (Oxford University), 'Lloyd George, Keir Hardie, and the Importance of the "Pro-Boers"'

Richard Cleary (Architecture), 'Walking the Walk to Talk the Talk: The Promenade in Eighteenth-Century France and England'
Keith Kyle (Journalist and Historian), 'From Suez to Kenya as Journalist and as Historian'
Malcolm Hacksley (National English Literary Museum, Grahamstown, South Africa), 'Planting a Museum, Cultivating a Literature'
Ben Pimlott (University of London), 'The Art of Writing Political Biography'
Geraldine Heng (English), 'Cannibalism, the First Crusade, and the Genesis of Medieval Romance'
A. P. Martinich (Philosophy), 'Thomas Hobbes: Lifelong and Enduring Controversies'
Round Table Discussion, 'Lyndall Gordon's *T. S. Eliot: An Imperfect Life*': Brian Bremen (English), Thomas Cable (English), Elizabeth Richmond-Garza (Comparative Literature), and Thomas F. Staley (HRHRC)
Shula Marks (University of London), 'Smuts, Race, and the Boer War'
Round Table Discussion, 'The Library of the British Museum': William B. Todd (English), Irene Owens (Library and Information Science), and Don Davis (Library and Information Science and Department of History)
Henry Dietz (Government), '*The Hound of the Baskervilles*'

Spring Semester 2000

Susan Napier (Asian Studies), 'The Cultural Phenomenon of the Harry Potter Fantasy Novels'
Round Table Discussion, '*Dutch: A Memoir of Ronald Reagan:* A Chapter in the "Special Relationship"?': Wm. Roger Louis (History), Harry Middleton (LBJ Library), and Elspeth Rostow (LBJ School)
Norman Rose (Hebrew University, Jerusalem), 'Harold Nicolson: A Curious and Colorful Life'
Charlotte Canning (Theatre and Dance), 'Feminists Perform Their Past'
John Ripley (McGill University), 'The Sound of Sociology: H. B. Tree's *Merchant of Venice*'
Sergei Horuji (Russian Academy of Sciences), 'James Joyce in Russia'
Janice Rossen (Biographer and Independent Scholar), 'Philip Toynbee'
Max Egremont (Novelist and Biographer), 'Siegfried Sassoon's War'
Paul Taylor (London School of Economics and Political Science), 'Britain and Europe'
Lord Selborne (Royal Geographical Society), 'The Royal Geographical Society: Exploration since 1830'
Craig MacKenzie (Rand Afrikaans University, Johannesburg), 'The Mythology of the Boer War: Herman Charles Bosman and the Challenge to Afrikaner Romanticism'
Peter Catterall (Institute of Contemporary British History, London), 'Reform of the House of Lords'
Bernard Porter (University of Newcastle), 'Pompous and Circumstantial: Sir Edward Elgar and the British Empire'
Craufurd D. Goodwin (Duke University), 'Roger Fry and the Debate on "Myth" in the Bloomsbury Group'
Jamie Belich (University of Auckland), 'Neo-Britains? The "West" in Nineteenth-Century Australia, New Zealand, and America'
Round Table Discussion, 'Norman Davies's *The Isles*': Sharon Arnoult (Midwestern State University, Wichita Falls), Raymond Douglas (Colgate University),

Walter Johnson (Northwestern Oklahoma State University), David Leaver (Raymond Walters College, Cincinnati), and John Cell (Duke University)

Fall Semester 2000

Round Table Discussion, 'Paul Scott, the Raj Quartet, and the Beginning of British Studies at UT': Peter Green (Classics), Robert Hardgrave (Government and Asian Studies), and Wm. Roger Louis (History)

Suman Gupta (Open University), 'T. S. Eliot as Publisher'

Jeffrey Cox (University of Iowa), 'Going Native: Missionaries in India'

Kevin Kenny (Boston College), 'Irish Nationalism: The American Dimension'

Joseph Kestner (University of Tulsa), 'Victorian Battle Art'

James E. Cronin (Boston College), 'From Old to New Labour: Politics and Society in the Forging of the "Third" Way'

Gerald Moore (Mellon Visiting Research Fellow, HRHRC), 'When Caliban Crossed the Atlantic'

Richard Howard (Shakespearean Actor, London), '"Health and Long Life to You": A Program of Irish Poetry and Prose Presented by an Englishman, with Anecdotes'

Stephen Foster (Northern Illinois University), 'Prognosis Guarded: The Probable Decolonization of the British Era in American History'

Frank Prochaska (University of London), 'Of Crowned and Uncrowned Republics: George V and the Socialists'

Robert H. Abzug (History and American Studies), 'Britain, South Africa, and the American Civil Rights Movement'

Paula Bartley (Visiting Research Fellow, HRHRC), 'Emmeline Pankhurst'

Thomas Jesus Garza (Slavic Languages), 'A British Vampire's Christmas'

Spring Semester 2001

Betty Sue Flowers (UT Distinguished Teaching Professor), 'From Robert Browning to James Bond'

Larry Carver (English), 'Feliks Topolski at the Ransom Center'

Oscar Brockett (Theatre and Dance), 'Lilian Baylis and England's National Theatres'

Linda Levy Peck (George Washington University), 'Luxury and War'

R. James Coote (Architecture), 'Architectural Revival in Britain'

Adam Roberts (Oxford University), 'Britain and the Creation of the United Nations'

Mark Southern (Germanic Studies), 'Words over Swords: Language and Tradition in Celtic Civilization'

Round Table Discussion, 'Ben Rogers's *A Life of A. J. Ayer*': David Braybrooke (Government and Philosophy), Al Martinich (History and Philosophy), David Sosa (Philosophy), and Paul Woodruff (Plan II and Philosophy)

Bartholomew Sparrow (Government), 'British and American Expansion: The Political Foundations'

Jose Harris (Oxford University), 'Writing History during the Second World War'

Charles Loft (Westminster College), 'Off the Rails? The Historic Junctions in Britain's Railway Problem'

Dan Jacobson (University of London), 'David Irving and Holocaust Denial'—Special Lecture

Dan Jacobson (University of London), 'Self-Redemption in the Victorian Novel'

George S. Christian (British Studies), 'The Comic Basis of the Victorian Novel'
Paul Taylor (London *Independent*), 'Rediscovering a Master Dramatist: J. B. Priestley'

Fall Semester 2001

Round Table Discussion, 'Ray Monk's Biography of Bertrand Russell, *The Ghost of Madness*': Al Martinich (History and Philosophy), David Sosa (Philosophy and British Studies), and Paul Woodruff (Plan II and Philosophy)
Alex Danchev (Keele University), 'The Alanbrooke Diaries'
Robert M. Worcester (LSE and Market Opinion Research International), 'Britain and the European Union'
Martha Ann Selby (Asian Studies), 'The Cultural Legacy of British Clubs: Manners, Memory, and Identity among the New Club-Wallahs in Madras'
Roger Owen (Harvard University), 'Lord Cromer and Wilfrid Blunt in Egypt'
James Loehlin (English), 'A Midsummer Night's Dream'
Jeffrey Meyers (Biographer), 'Somerset Maugham'
Elspeth Rostow (LBJ School), 'From American Studies to British Studies—And Beyond'
Nicholas Westcott (British Embassy), 'The Groundnut Scheme: Socialist Imperialism at Work in Africa'
Round Table Discussion, 'The Anglo-American Special Relationship': Gary Freeman (Government), Wm. Roger Louis (History), Elspeth Rostow (American Studies), and Michael Stoff (History)
Christopher Heywood (Sheffield University), 'The Brontës: A Personal History of Discovery and Interpretation'
James Bolger (New Zealand Ambassador and former Prime Minister), 'Whither New Zealand? Constitutional, Political, and International Quandaries'
R. J. Q. Adams (Texas A&M), 'Arthur James Balfour and Andrew Bonar Law: A Study in Contrasts'
Ferdinand Mount (Editor, *Times Literary Supplement*), 'British Culture since the Eighteenth Century: An Open Society?'
James Loehlin (English), 'A Child's Christmas in Wales'

Spring Semester 2002

Round Table Discussion, 'Adam Sisman's *Boswell's Presumptuous Task*': Samuel Baker (English), Linda Ferreira-Buckley (English), Julie Hardwick (History), and Helena Woodward (English)
A. G. Hopkins (History), 'Globalization: The British Case'
Susan Napier (Asian Studies), 'J. R. R. Tolkien and *The Lord of the Rings:* Fantasy as Retreat or Fantasy as Engagement?'
Wilfrid Prest (Adelaide University), 'South Australia's Paradise of Dissent'
Tom Palaima (Classics), 'Terence Rattigan's *Browning Version*'
Alan H. Nelson (University of California, Berkeley), 'Thoughts on Elizabethan Authorship'
Penelope Lively (London), 'Changing Perceptions of British and English Identity'
Hans Mark (Aerospace Engineering), 'The Falklands War'
David Butler (Oxford University), 'Psephology—or, the Study of British Elections'
Robert L. Hardgrave (Government), 'From West Texas to South India and British Studies'
Geoffrey Wheatcroft (London), 'The Englishness of English Sport'

Eileen Cleere (Southwestern University), 'Dirty Pictures: John Ruskin and the Victorian Sanitation of Fine Art'

Jamie Belich (Auckland University), 'A Comparison of Empire Cities: New York and London, Chicago and Melbourne'

Churchill Conference: Geoffrey Best (Oxford University), Sir Michael Howard (Oxford University), Warren Kimball (Rutgers University), Philip Ziegler (London), Wm. Roger Louis (History)

Catherine Maxwell (University of London), 'Swinburne's Poetry and Criticism'

Round Table Discussion, 'Churchill and the Churchill Conference': Rodrigo Gutierrez (History), Adrian Howkins (History), Heidi Juel (English), David McCoy (Government), Joe Moser (English), Jeff Rutherford (History), William S. Livingston (UT Senior Vice President), and Wm. Roger Louis (History)

Fall Semester 2002

James K. Galbraith (LBJ School of Public Affairs), 'The Enduring Importance of John Maynard Keynes'

Michael Green (University of Natal), 'Agatha Christie in South Africa'

Sumit Ganguly (Asian Studies), 'Kashmir: Origins and Consequences of Conflict'

Margaret MacMillan (University of Toronto), 'At the Height of His Power: Lloyd George in 1919'

Douglas Bruster (English), 'Why We Fight: *Much Ado About Nothing* and the West'

John Darwin (Oxford University), 'The Decline and Rise of the British Empire: John Gallagher as an Historian of Imperialism'

Kevin Kenny (Boston College), 'The Irish in the British Empire'

David Wallace (University of Pennsylvania), 'A Chaucerian's Tale of Surinam'

Peter Bowler (Queen's University, Belfast), 'Scientists and the Popularization of Science in Early Twentieth-Century Britain'

Bernardine Evaristo (London), 'A Feisty, Funky Girl in Roman England'

Frank Moorhouse (Australia), 'Dark Places and Grand Days'

David Cannadine (University of London), 'C. P. Snow and the Two Cultures'

Round Table Discussion, 'Edmund S. Morgan's Biography of Benjamin Franklin': Carolyn Eastman (History), Bruce Hunt (History), Wm. Roger Louis (History), Alan Tully (History)

Mark Lawrence (History), 'The Strange Silence of Cold War England: Britain and the Vietnam War'

Tom Cable (English), 'The Pleasures of Remembering Poetry'

Spring Semester 2003

Round Table Discussion, 'W. G. Sebald's *Rings of Saturn*': Brigitte Bauer (French and Italian), Sidney Monas (History and Slavic Languages), Elizabeth Richmond-Garza (English and Comparative Literature), Walter Wetzels (Germanic Studies)

Diana Davis (Geography), 'Brutes, Beasts, and Empire: A Comparative Study of the British and French Experience'

Colin Franklin (Publisher), 'Rosalind Franklin—Variously Described as "The Dark Lady of DNA" and "The Sylvia Plath of Molecular Biology"'

Sidney Monas (History and Slavic Languages), 'A Life of Irish Literature and Russian Poetry, Soviet Politics and International History'

Neville Hoad (English), 'Oscar Wilde in America'

Selina Hastings (London), 'Rosamond Lehman: Eternal Exile'

Bernard Wasserstein (Glasgow University), 'The British in Palestine: Reconsiderations'
Anne Chisholm (London), 'Frances Partridge: Last of the Bloomsberries'
Philip Morgan (Johns Hopkins University), 'The Black Experience and the British Empire'
Jeremy duQuesnay Adams (Southern Methodist University), 'Joan of Arc and the English'
Didier Lancien (University of Toulouse), 'Churchill and de Gaulle'
Avi Shlaim (Oxford University), 'The Balfour Declaration and Its Consequences'
Martin J. Wiener (Rice University), 'Murder and the Modern British Historian'
Winthrop Wetherbee (Cornell University), 'The Jewish Impact on Medieval Literature: Chaucer, Boccaccio, and Dante'
Philippa Levine (University of Southern California), 'Sex and the British Empire'

Summer 2003

Donald G. Davis, Jr. (History and the School of Information), 'Life without British Studies Is Like . . .'
Kurth Sprague (English and American Studies), 'Literature, Horses, and Scandal at UT'
David Evans (Astronomy), 'An Astronomer's Life in South Africa and Texas'
Tom Hatfield (Continuing Education), 'Not Long Enough! Half a Century at UT'

Fall Semester 2003

Richard Oram (HRHRC), 'Evelyn Waugh: Collector and Annotator'
Round Table Discussion, 'Booker Prize Winner James Kelman: Adapting a Glasgow Novel for the Texas Stage': James Kelman (Glasgow), Mia Carter (English), Kirk Lynn, and Dikran Utidjian
Simon Green (All Souls College, Oxford University), 'The Strange Death of Puritan England, 1914–1945'
Elizabeth Richmond-Garza (English and Comparative Literature), '*Measure for Measure*'
Lewis Hoffacker (U.S. Ambassador), 'From the Congo to British Studies'
A. P. Thornton (University of Toronto), 'Wars Remembered, Revisited, and Reinvented'
Deryck Schreuder (University of Western Australia), 'The Burden of the British Past in Australia'
Robert Mettlen (Finance), 'From Birmingham to British Studies'
Paul Schroeder (University of Illinois), 'The Pax Britannica and the Pax Americana: Empire, Hegemony, and the International System'
Ferdinand Mount (London), 'A Time to Dance: Anthony Powell's *Dance to the Music of Time* and the Twentieth Century in Britain'
Brian Bond (University of London), '*Oh! What a Lovely War:* History and Popular Myth in Late-Twentieth Century Britain'
Wendy Frith (Bradford College, England), 'The Speckled Monster: Lady Mary Wortley Montagu and the Battle against Smallpox'
Harry Middleton (LBJ Library), 'The Road to the White House'
Jeremy Lewis (London), 'Tobias Smollett'
Christian Smith (Austin, Texas), 'Christmas Readings'

Spring Semester 2004

Round Table Discussion, 'The Pleasures of Reading Thackeray': Carol Mackay (English), Judith Fisher (Trinity University), George Christian (British Studies)

Thomas F. Staley (HRHRC), '"Corso e Recorso:" A Journey through Academe'

Patrick O'Brien (London School of Economics), 'The Pax Britannica, American Hegemony, and the International Order, 1793–2004'

Michael Wheeler (former Director of Chawton House Library), 'England Drawn and Quartered: Cultural Crisis in the Mid-Nineteenth Century'

Walter Wetzels (Germanic Studies), 'Growing Up in Nazi Germany, and later American Adventures'

Kathleen Wilson (State University of New York, Stony Brook), 'The Colonial State and Governance in the Eighteenth Century'

Elizabeth Fernea (English and Middle Eastern Studies), 'Encounters with Imperialism'

Chris Dunton (National University of Lesotho), 'Newspapers and Colonial Rule in Africa'

Miguel Gonzalez-Gerth (Spanish and Portuguese), 'Crossing Geographical and Cultural Borders—and Finally Arriving at British Studies'

Peter Stansky (Stanford University), 'Bloomsbury in Ceylon'

Round Table Discussion, '*The Crimson Petal and the White*': John Farrell (English), Betty Sue Flowers (LBJ Library), Wm. Roger Louis (History), Paul Neimann (English)

Ann Curthoys (Australian National University), 'The Australian History Wars'

Martha Ann Selby (Asian Studies), 'Against the Grain: On Finding My Voice in India'

Steven Isenberg (UT Visiting Professor of Humanities), 'A Life in Our Times'

Summer 2004

Carol Mackay (English), 'My Own Velvet Revolution'

Erez Manela (Harvard University), 'The "Wilsonian Moment" in India and the Crisis of Empire in 1919'

Scott Lucas (Birmingham University), '"A Bright Shining Mecca": British Culture and Political Warfare in the Cold War and Beyond'

Monica Belmonte (U.S. Department of State), 'Before Things Fell Apart: The British Design for the Nigerian State'

Dan Jacobson (London), 'Philip Larkin's "Elements"'

Bernard Porter (University of Newcastle), ''Oo Let 'Em In? Asylum Seekers and Terrorists in Britain, 1850–1914'

Fall Semester 2004

Richard Drayton (Cambridge University), 'Anglo-American "Liberal" Imperialism, British Guiana, 1953–64, and the World Since September 11'

David Washbrook (Oxford University), 'Living on the Edge: Anxiety and Identity in "British" Calcutta, 1780–1930'

Joanna Hitchcock (University of Texas Press), 'An Accidental Publisher'

Alan Friedman (English), '*A Midsummer Night's Dream*'

Antony Best (London School of Economics), 'British Intellectuals and East Asia in the Inter-war Years'

John Farrell (English), 'Beating a Path from Brooklyn to Austin'
Christopher Middleton (Liberal Arts), 'Relevant to England—A Reading of Poems'
Gail Minault (History and Asian Studies), 'Growing Up Bilingual and Other (Mis) adventures in Negotiating Cultures'
Wm. Roger Louis (History), 'Escape from Oklahoma'
John Trimble (English), 'Writing with Style'
Niall Ferguson (Harvard University), 'Origins of the First World War'
James Hopkins (Southern Methodist University), 'George Orwell and the Spanish Civil War: The Case of Nikos Kazantzakis'
James Currey (London), 'Africa Writes Back: Publishing the African Writers Series at Heinemann'
Sidney Monas (History and Slavic Languages), 'A Jew's Christmas'
Geoffrey Wheatcroft (London), '"In the Advance Guard": Evelyn Waugh's Reputation'

Spring Semester 2005

Katharine Whitehorn (London), 'It Didn't *All* Start in the Sixties'
Gertrude Himmelfarb (Graduate School, City University of New York), 'The Whig Interpretation of History'
Kurt Heinzelman (English and HRHRC), 'Lord Byron and the Invention of Celebrity'
Brian Levack (History), 'Jesuits, Lawyers, and Witches'
Richard Cleary (Architecture), 'When Taste Mattered: W. J. Battle and the Architecture of the Forty Acres'
Edward I. Steinhart (Texas Tech University), 'White Hunters in British East Africa, 1895–1914'
Don Graham (English), 'The Drover's Wife: An Australian Archetype'
A. C. H. Smith, (London) 'Literary Friendship: The 40-Year Story of Tom Stoppard, B. S. Johnson, and Zulfikar Ghose'
Paul Woodruff (Philosophy and Plan II), 'A Case of Anglophilia—And Partial Recovery: Being an Account of My Life, with Special Attention to the Influence of England upon My Education'
Toyin Falola (History), 'Footprints of the Ancestors'
Robert Abzug (History) 'Confessions of an Intellectual Omnivore: The Consequences on Scholarship and Career'
Deirdre McMahon (Mary Immaculate College, University of Limerick), 'Ireland and the Empire-Commonwealth, 1918–1972'
James Coote (Architecture), 'Building with Wit: Sir Edwin Lutyens and British Architecture'
Jay Clayton (Vanderbilt University), 'The Dickens Tape: Lost and Found Sound before Recording'
Christopher Ricks (Oxford University), 'The Force of Poetry: Shakespeare and Beckett'

Summer 2005

Blair Worden (Oxford University), 'Poetry and History of the English Renaissance'
Robert Bruce Osborn (British Studies), 'The Four Lives of Robert Osborn'

Alessandra Lippucci (Government), 'Perseverance Furthers: A Self-Consuming Artifact'

William H. Cunningham (former President of the University of Texas), 'Money, Power, Politics, and Ambition'

David V. Edwards (Government), 'Friendly Persuasion in the Academy'

Elizabeth Richmond-Garza (English), 'A Punk Rocker with Eight Languages'

Richard Lariviere (Liberal Arts), 'Confessions of a Sanskritist Dean'

Fall Semester 2005

Celebration of 30th Anniversary and Publication of *Yet More Adventures with Britannia*

Robert D. King (Jewish Studies), 'T.S. Eliot Reconsidered'

Round Table Discussion, 'The London Bombings': James Galbraith (LBJ School), Elizabeth Cullingford (English), Clement Henry (Government), Wm. Roger Louis (History)

Dolora Chapelle Wojciehowski (English), 'The Erotic Uncanny in Shakespeare's *Twelfth Night*'

Karl Hagstrom Miller (History), 'Playing Pensativa: History and Music in Counterpoint'

James D. Garrison (English), 'Translating Gray's *Elegy*'

Miguel Gonzalez-Gerth (Spanish and Portuguese), 'Another Look at Orwell: The Origins of *1984*'

Round Table Discussion, 'The Imperial Closet: Gordon of Khartoum, Hector McDonald of the Boer War, and Roger Casement of Ireland': Barbara Harlow (English), Neville Hoad (English), John Thomas (HRHRC)

Guy Ortolano (Washington University, St. Louis), 'From *The Two Cultures* to *Breaking Ranks:* C.P. Snow and the Interpretation of the 1960s'

Catherine Robson (University of California, Davis), 'Poetry and Memorialization'

Round Table Discussion, 'Britain and the Jewish Century': Lauren Apter (History), Robert D. King (Jewish Studies), Sidney Monas (History and Slavic Languages)

Hans Mark (Aerospace Engineering), 'Churchill, the Anglo-Persian Oil Company, and the Origins of the Energy Crisis: From the Early 20th Century to the Present'

Randall Woods (University of Arkansas), 'LBJ and the British'

Spring Semester 2006

Richard Gray (London), 'Movie Palaces of Britain'

Samuel Baker (English), 'The Lake Poets and the War in the Mediterranean Sea'

Thomas F. Staley (HRHRC), 'Graham Greene and Evelyn Waugh'

Gary Stringer (Texas A&M), 'Love's Long Labors Coming to Fruition: The John Donne Variorum Donne'

Caroline Elkins (Harvard University), 'From Malaya to Kenya: British Colonial Violence and the End of Empire'

Grigory Kaganov (St. Petersburg), 'London in the Mouth of the Neva'

Graham Greene (London), 'A Life in Publishing'

John Davis (Oxford University), 'Evans-Pritchard: Nonetheless A Great Englishman'

Barry Gough (Wilfrid Laurier University), 'Arthur Marder and the Battles over the History of the Royal Navy'

Ivan Kreilkamp (Indiana University), '"Bags of Meat": Pet-Keeping and the Justice to Animals in Thomas Hardy'
James Wilson (History), 'Historical Memory and the Mau Mau Uprising in Colonial Kenya'
Anne Deighton (Oxford University), 'Britain after the Second World War: Losing an Empire and Finding a Place in a World of Superpowers'
Steve Isenberg (Liberal Arts), 'Auden, Forster, Larkin, and Empson'
Harriet Ritvo (MIT), 'Animals on the Edge'
Peter Quinn (New York), 'Eugenics and the Hour of the Cat'
Dan Jacobson (London), 'Kipling and South Africa'
Fall Semester 2006
Michael Charlesworth (Art and Art History) and Kurt Heinzelman (English), 'Tony Harrison's "v."'
Peter Stanley (Australian War Memorial), 'All Imaginable Excuses: Australian Deserters and the Fall of Singapore'
Selina Hastings (London), 'Somerset Maugham and "Englishness"'
James W. Vick (Mathematics), 'A Golden Century of English Mathematics'
John O. Voll (Georgetown University), 'Defining the Middle East and the Clash of Civilizations'
James Loehlin (English), 'The Afterlife of Hamlet'
Daniel Topolski (London), 'The Life and Art of Feliks Topolski'
John Darwin (Oxford University), 'The British Empire and the British World'
David Cannadine (University of London), 'Andrew Mellon and Plutocracy Across the Atlantic'
John Lonsdale (Cambridge University), 'White Settlers and Black Mau Mau in Kenya'
Kate Gartner Frost (English), 'So What's Been Done about John Donne Lately?'
John Summers (Harvard University), 'The Power Elite: C. Wright Mills and the British'
Marrack Goulding (Oxford University), 'Has it been a Success? Britain in the United Nations'
Priya Satia (Stanford University), 'The Defence of Inhumanity: British Military and Cultural Power in the Middle East'
Don Graham (English), 'Burnt Orange Britannia: A Missing Contributor!'

Spring Semester 2007

Bernard Porter (Newcastle University), 'Empire and British Culture'
Paul Sullivan (Liberal Arts Honors Program), 'The Headmaster's Shakespeare: John Garrett and British Education'
Round Table Discussion, '*The Queen*': Elizabeth Cullingford (English), Karen King (American Studies), Wm. Roger Louis (History), Bryan Roberts (Sociology)
Martin Francis (University of Cincinnati), 'Cecil Beaton's Romantic Toryism and the Symbolism of Wartime Britain'
Susan Crane (Columbia University), 'Animal Feelings and Feelings for Animals in Chaucer'
Michael Charlesworth (Art History), 'The Earl of Strafford and Wentworth Castle'
Adam Sisman (London), 'Wordsworth and Coleridge'
Jenny Mann (Cornell University), 'Shakespeare's English Rhetoric: Mingling Heroes and Hobgoblins in *A Midsummer Night's Dream*'
David Atkinson (Member of Parliament), 'Britain and World Peace in the 21st Century'

Bertram Wyatt-Brown (University of Florida), 'T. E. Lawrence, Reputation, and Honor's Decline'

Wm. Roger Louis (History), 'All Souls and Oxford in 1956: Reassessing the Meaning of the Suez Crisis'

Indivar Kamtekar (Jawaharlal Nehru University), 'India and Britain during the Second World War'

Cassandra Pybus (University of Sydney), 'William Wilberforce and the Emancipation of Slaves'

Stephen Howe (University of Bristol), 'Empire in the 21st Century English Imagination'

Geoffrey Wheatcroft (London), 'The Myth of Malicious Partition: The Cases of Ireland, India, and Palestine'

Charles Rossman (English), 'D. H. Lawrence and the "Spirit" of Mexico'

Kenneth O. Morgan (House of Lords), 'Lloyd George, the French, and the Germans'

Fall Semester 2007

R. J. Q. Adams (Texas A&M), 'A. J. Balfour's Achievement and Legacy'

Robin Doughty (Geography), 'Saving Coleridge's Endangered Albatross'

Caroline Williams (University of Texas), 'A Victorian Orientalist: John Frederick Lewis and the Artist's Discovery of Cairo'

Susan Pedersen (Columbia University), 'The Story of Frances Stevenson and David Lloyd George'

Eric S. Mallin (English), 'Macbeth and the Simple Truth'

Mark Oaten, M.P., 'How "Special" Is the Special Relationship?'

Dan Birkholz (English), 'Playboys of the West of England: Medieval Cosmopolitanism and Familial Love'

Jeremy Lewis (London), 'The Secret History of Penguin Books'

Matthew Jones (Nottingham University), 'Britain and the End of Empire in South East Asia in the Era of the Vietnam War'

Martin Wiener (Rice University), '"Who knows the Empire whom only the Empire knows?": Reconnecting British and Empire History'

Book Launch: *Penultimate Adventures with Britannia* (Follett's Intellectual Property)

Hermione Lee and Christopher Ricks (Oxford), 'The Elusive Brian Moore: His Stature in Modern Literature'

Gabriel Gorodetsky (Tel Aviv University), 'The Challenge to Churchill's Wartime Leadership by Sir Stafford Cripps (the "Red Squire")'

Helena Woodard (English), 'Black and White Christmas: The Deep South in the Eighteenth Century'

Spring Semester 2008

Round Table Discussion, 'Tim Jeal's *Stanley: The Impossible Life of Africa's Greatest Explorer*': Diana Davis (Geography), A. G. Hopkins (History), Wm. Roger Louis (History)

Elizabeth Richmond-Garza (English and Comparative Literature), 'New Year's Eve 1900: Oscar Wilde and the Masquerade of Victorian Culture'

Robert Hardgrave (Government), 'The Search for Balthazar Solvyns and an Indian Past: The Anatomy of a Research Project'

Lucy Chester (University of Colorado), 'Zionists, Indian Nationalism, and British Schizophrenia in Palestine'

Michael Brenner (University of Pittsburgh), 'Strategic and Cultural Triangulation: Britain, the United States, and Europe'

Roger Morgan (European University, Florence), 'The British "Establishment" and the Chatham House Version of World Affairs'

Jason Parker (Texas A&M), 'Wilson's Curse: Self-Determination, the Cold War, and the Challenge of Modernity in the "Third World"'

Stephen Foster (Northern Illinois University), 'The American Colonies and the Atlantic World'

A. G. Hopkins (History), 'Comparing British and American "Empires"'

James Turner (Notre Dame University), 'The Emergence of Academic Disciplines'

Dror Wahrman (Indiana University), 'Invisible Hands in the Eighteenth Century'

Narendra Singh Sarila (Prince of Sarila), 'Mountbatten and the Partition of India'

Pillarisetti Sudhir (American Historical Association), 'The Retreat of the Raj: Radicals and Reactionaries in Britain'

Keith Francis (Baylor University), 'What Did Darwin Mean in *On the Origin of Species?* An Englishman and a Frenchman Debate Evolution'

Fall Semester 2008

Round Table Discussion, 'Ted and Sylvia': (UT English), Judith Kroll, Kurt Heinzelman, Betty Sue Flowers, Tom Cable

Roby Barrett (Middle East Institute), 'The Question of Intervention in Iraq, 1958–59'

John Kerr (San Antonio), 'Cardigan Bay'

Sue Onslow (London School of Economics), 'Julian Amery: A Nineteenth-Century Relic in a Twentieth-Century World?'

John Rumrich (English), 'Reconciliation in *The Winter's Tale:* The Literary Friendship of Robert Greene and William Shakespeare'

Richard Jenkyns (Oxford), 'Conan Doyle: An Assessment beyond Sherlock Holmes'

Theresa Kelley (University of Wisconsin), 'Romantic British Culture and Botany in India'

Sir Adam Roberts (Oxford), 'After the Cold War'

Geoffrey Wheatcroft (London), 'Churchill and the Jews'

Sir Brian Harrison (Oxford), 'Prelude to the Sixties'

Eric Kaufmann (London School of Economics), 'The Orange Order in Northern Ireland'

Robert McMahon (Ohio State University), 'Dean Acheson: The Creation of a New World Order and the Problem of the British'

Mark Metzler (History), 'Eye of the Storm: London's Place in the First Great Depression, 1872–96'

James Loehlin (English), Christmas Party at the New Campus Club, reading passages from Charles Dickens, *A Christmas Carol*

Spring Semester 2009

Margaret MacMillan (Oxford University), 'The Jewel in the Crown'

Bernard Wasserstein (University of Chicago), 'Glasgow in the 1950s'

Dominic Sandbrook (London), 'The Swinging Sixties in Britain'

Karl Meyer and Shareen Brysac (New York Times and CBS), 'Inventing Iran, Inventing Iraq: The British and Americans in the Middle East'

Albert Lewis (R. L. Moore Project), 'The Bertrand Russell Collection: The One That Got Away from the HRC'
Sir David Cannadine (Institute of Historical Research, London), 'Colonial Independence'; Linda Colley (CBE, Princeton University), 'Philip Francis and the Challenge to the British Empire'
George Scott Christian (English and History), 'Origins of Scottish Nationalism: The Trial of Thomas Muir'
Discussion led by Brian Levack and Roger Louis (History), 'Trevor-Roper and Scotland'
Warren Kimball (Rutgers University), 'Churchill, Roosevelt, and Ireland'
Ferdinand Mount (London) and R. J. Q. Adams (Texas A&M), 'A. J. Balfour and his Critics'
Dan Jacobson (London), Betty Sue Flowers (LBJ Library), and Tom Staley (HRHRC), Tribute to Betty Sue Flowers—'Hardy and Eliot'
John Darwin (Nuffield College, Oxford), 'Britain's Global Empire'
Saul Dubow (Sussex University), 'Sir Keith Hancock and the Question of Race'
Weslie Janeway (Cambridge), 'Darwin's Cookbook'
Julian Barnes, Barbara Harlow, Miguel Gonzalez-Gerth, 'Such, Such Was Eric Blair'
Cassandra Pybus (Visiting Fellow, UT Institute of Historical Studies), 'If you were regular black…': Slavery, Miscegenation, and Racial Anxiety in Britain'

Fall Semester 2009

Peter Green (Classics), 'The Devil in Kingsley Amis'
John Farrell (English), 'Forgiving Emily Brontë'
Samuel Baker (English), 'Wedgwood Gothic'
Louise Weinberg (Law), 'Gilbert and Sullivan: The Curios Persistence of Savoyards'
Elizabeth Richmond-Garza (English), 'Love in a Time of Terror: King Lear and the Potential for Consolation'
John Rumrich (English), 'John Milton and the Embodied Word'
Round Table Discussion, 'Effective Teaching': Tom Cable (English), David Leal (Government), Lisa Moore (English), Bob Woodberry (Sociology)'
James M. Vaughn (History and British Studies), 'The Decline and Fall of Whig Imperialism, 1756–1783'
Round Table Discussion, 'Bloomsbury': Betty Sue Flowers (English), Wm. Roger Louis (History), Lisa Moore (English), David Sosa (Philosophy)
Sir Harold Evans, 'Murder Most Foul'
Peter Cain (Sheffield Hallam University), 'The Radical Critique of Colonialism'
John Gooch (Leeds University), 'Pyrrhic Victory? England and the Great War'
Maya Jasanoff (Harvard University), 'The British Side of the American Revolution'
Maeve Cooney (British Studies), Christmas Party at the Littlefield Home, reading O. Henry's 'The Gift of the Magi'

Spring Semester 2010

Thomas Jesus Garza (UT Language Center), 'The British Vampire's Slavic Roots'
Marilyn Young (New York University), 'The British and Vietnam'

Daniel Howe (University of California at Los Angeles), 'What Hath God Wrought'

Roberta Rubenstein (American University), 'Virginia Woolf and the Russians'

Samuel R. Williamson (University of the South at Sewanee), 'The Possibility of Civil War over Ireland in 1914'

Steve Pincus (Yale), 'The First Modern Revolution: Reappraising the Glorious Events of 1688'

Selina Hastings (London), 'Somerset Maugham: A Life Under Cover'

Eugene Rogan (Oxford), 'Modern History through Arab Eyes'

T. M. Devine (University of Edinburgh), 'Did Slavery Make Scotland Great?'

Phillip Herring (University of Wisconsin–Madison), 'A Journey through James Joyce's *Ulysses*'

Alison Bashford (Harvard), 'Australia and the World Population Problem, 1918–1954'

Berny Sèbe (Birmingham University), 'French and British Colonial Heroes in Africa'

J. L. Berry (Austin, Texas), 'The Post-Twilight of the British Empire on the Zambian Copper Belt'

Bernard Porter (University of Newcastle), 'The Myth of Goths and Vandals in British Architecture'

Fall Semester 2010

Jonathan Schneer (Georgia Institute of Technology), 'The Balfour Declaration'

Larry Carver (Liberal Arts Honors Program), 'Reacting to the Past: How I Came to Love Teaching Edmund Burke'

Thomas Pinney (Pomona College), 'Kipling and America'

Donna Kornhaber (English), 'Accident and Artistry in *The Third Man*'

Doug Bruster (English), 'Rating *A Midsummer Night's Dream*'

Peter Stansky (Stanford University), 'Julian Bell: From Bloomsbury to Spain'

Crawford Young (University of Wisconsin, Madison), 'The British Empire and Comparative Decolonization'

Jeffrey Cox (University of Iowa), 'From the Kingdom of God to the Third World'

Roberta Rubenstein (American University), 'Approaching the Golden Anniversary: Dorris Lessing's *The Golden Notebook*'

Kenneth O. Morgan (House of Lords), 'Aneurin Bevan: Pragmatist and Prophet of the Old Left'

Robert Vitalis (University of Pennsylvania), 'From the Persian Gulf to the Gulf of Mexico: What We Know About BP'

James Curran (Sydney University), 'The Great Age of Confusion: Australia in the Wake of Empire'

Archie Brown (St Antony's College, Oxford), 'Margaret Thatcher and the End of the Cold War'

Phyllis Lassner (Northwestern University), 'The End of Empire in the Middle East and the Literary Imagination'

Spring Semester 2011

Tillman Nechtman (Skidmore College), 'Nabobs: Empire and the Politics of National Identity in Eighteenth-Century Britain'

Brian Levak (History), 'Demonic Possession in Early Modern Britain'

David Kornhaber (English), 'George Bernard Shaw: Modernist'

Lisa L. Moore (English), 'Sister Arts: The Erotics of Lesbian Landscape'

Bartholomew Sparrow (Government), 'Brent Scowcroft, Mrs. Thatcher, and National Security'
Philip Bobbitt (Law School and LBJ School), 'The Special Relationship'
Deborah Harkness (UCLA), 'Fiction and the Archives: The Art and Craft of the Historian'
Peter Clarke (Trinity Hall, Cambridge), 'The English-Speaking Peoples'
A. G. Hopkins (History), 'The United States, 1783–1861: Britain's Honorary Dominion?'
Reba Soffer (California State University at Northridge), 'Intellectual History, Life, and Fiction'
Joanna Lewis (London School of Economics), 'Harold Macmillan and the Wind of Change'
Andrew Lycett (London), 'Arthur Conan Doyle and Rudyard Kipling'
Geoffrey Wheatcroft (London), 'The Grand Illusion: Britain and the United States'
Priscilla Roberts (University of Hong Kong), 'Henry James and the Erosion of British Power'
John Higley (Government), 'Degeneration of Ruling Elites? Recent American and British Elites'

Fall Semester 2011

Round Table Discussion, 'The Oxford of Maurice Bowra and Hugh Trevor Roper': Paul Woodruff (Philosophy), Wm. Roger Louis (History), and David Leal (Government),
Marian Barber (UT Austin), 'The Scots, Irish, English, and Welsh in the Making of Texas'
Geoffrey Davis (University of Aachen), 'The Territory of My Imagination: Rediscovering Dan Jacobson's South Africa'
Nadja Durbach (University of Utah), 'Poverty, Politics, and Roast Beef: Poor Relief and the Nation in Early Nineteenth-Century Britain'
Leonard Barkan (Princeton University), 'What's for Dinner on a Desert Island: Feast and Famine in *The Tempest*'
Lindsey Schell (University Libraries), 'The Royal Wedding and the Making of a Modern Princess'
Laurence Raw (Baskent University), 'Shakespeare and Home Front during World War II'
Sir Brian Harrison (Oxford University), 'Surprising Resilience: Historians of British Conservatism since 1945'
Troy Bickham (Texas A&M), 'A New Grand Transatlantic Drama: Britain and the Anglo-American War of 1812'
Eli P. Cox III (Marketing), 'The Betrayal of Adam Smith'
Nicholas Rogers (York University), 'Crime, Punishment, and Governance in Eighteenth-Century Britain'
Donald Lamm (WW Norton and Company), 'The History of Oxford University Press'
Al Martinich (History and Government), 'Locke and the Limits of Toleration'

Spring Semester 2012

Philippa Levine (Chair), John Berry (Austin), Donna Kornhaber (English), Wm. Roger Louis (History), Elizabeth Richmond-Garza (English), '*The Iron Lady*'

Brian Cowan (McGill University), 'Henry Sacheverell and the Cult of Eighteenth-Century Personalities'

Ronald Heiferman (Quinnipiac University), 'Churchill, Roosevelt, and China'

Jeremi Suri (History and LBJ School), 'British Imperialism and American Nation-Building'

Susan Napier (Tufts University), 'Harry Potter and the Fantastic Journey'

Andrew Roberts (School of Oriental and African Studies), 'Poetry, Anthology, and Criticism: Michael Roberts and the BBC'

Michael Charlesworth (Art History), 'Derek Jarman and British Films: Paintings, Poetry, and Prose'

John Voll (Georgetown University), 'Britain and Islam in the Twentieth Century'

Sheldon Garon (Princeton University), 'Anglo-Japanese Cultural Relations, 1868–1950'

Anand Yang (University of Washington, Seattle), 'Convicts in British India'

George Bernard (University of Southampton), 'Editing the *English Historical Review*'

Selina Todd (St. Hilda's College, Oxford), 'The Problem Family in Postwar Britain'

Christine Krueger (Marquette University), 'The Victorian Historian Mary Anne Everett Green'

Jeremy Lewis (London), 'David Astor and the Observer'

Michael Winship (English), 'Napoleon Comes to America: The Publishing of Sir Walter Scott's *Life of Napoleon Buonaparte* (1827)'

Adam Sisman (London), 'Writing the Biographies of A. J. P. Taylor and Hugh Trevor-Roper'

Fall Semester 2012

Donna Kornhaber (English), 'Charlie Chaplin's Forgotten Feature: A Countess from Hong Kong'

Tom Palaima (Classics), 'The War Poems of Robert Graves'

Rosemary Hill (All Souls College, Oxford), 'Prince Albert'

Sucheta Mahajan (Jawaharlal Nehru University), 'Independence and Partition of India Reassessed'

Richard Davenport-Hines (London), 'Ivy Compton-Burnett'

Albert Beveridge III (Johns Hopkins), 'The Rise, Fall, and Revival of Anthony Trollope'

Philip Stern (Duke University), 'The Evolution of the City of Bombay'

Betty Smocovitis (University of Florida), 'Rhapsody on a Darwinian Theme'

Jad Adams (University of London), 'Tony Benn: The Making of a British Radical'

Steve Isenberg (Quondam Executive Director of PEN), 'Fathers and Sons: Edmund Gosse and J. R. Ackerley'

Paul Levy (*Wall Street Journal*), 'Lytton Strachey'

William Janeway (New York), 'Beyond Keynesianism: Maynard Keynes and the Good Life'

Dan Raff (Wharton School of Business), 'The Ancient University Presses Make Up Their Minds'

David Leal (Government), 'Method and Irrationality in the Traditions of Sherlock Holmes'

Spring Semester 2013

Kariann Yokata (University of Colorado, Denver), 'Unbecoming British? The Place of Post-Colonial Americans in the British Empire'

Brian Levack (History), 'The British Imperial State in the Eighteenth Century'

Anne Chisholm (London), 'Dora Carrington and the Bloomsbury Circle'

James Banner (Washington, D.C.), 'Academics, Intellectuals, and Popular History'

Selina Hastings (London), 'The Red Earl'

John Spurling (London), 'Sir Edmund Gibson and the British Raj'

Hilary Spurling (London), 'Pearl Buck and China'

Janine Barchas (English), 'Jane Austen between the Covers'

Wm. Roger Louis (History and British Studies), 'The History of Oxford University Press, 1896–1970'

Sir Christopher Bayly (Cambridge), 'Distant Connections: India and Australia in the Colonial Era'

Philip Waller (Oxford), 'Writers, Readers, and Reputations'

Jordanna Bailkin (University of Washington), 'Unsettled: Refugee Camps in Britain'

Geoffrey Wheatcroft (London), 'Assessing Margaret Thatcher'

Daniel Baugh (Cornell University), 'France and the British State and Empire, 1680–1940'

Richard Carwardine (Oxford), 'Lincoln and Emancipation: the British and International Consequences'

Fall Semester 2013

Henry Dietz (Government) 'British Sea Power and Napoleon in the Novels of Patrick O'Brian'

Christopher Benfey (Mount Holyoke College), 'The Myth of Tarzan'

Stephen Brooke (York University, Toronto), 'Photography and the Working Class in the 1950s'

Aram Bakshian (Washington, D.C.), '*The Economist*'

David Cressy (George III Professor of History, Ohio State), 'Gypsies and Cultural Tradition'

Stephen Weinberg (Josey Regental Chair of Science), 'The Last Magician: Isaac Newton'

James Scott (UT Statistics), 'Isaac Newton and the Birth of Money'

Lara Kriegel (Indiana University), 'Who Blew the Bugle? The Charge of the Light Brigade and the Legacy of the Crimean War'

Benjamin Gregg (Government), 'The Stasi and Secret Files'

Douglas Bruster (English), 'Shakespeare and Othello'

Miguel Gonzalez-Gerth (Founding Member of British Studies), 'Ian McEwan's Novels: Sex, Espionage, and Literature'

Allen MacDuffie, 'Dickens and Energy'

Walter Wetzels (Founding Member of British Studies), 'The Bombing of German Cities during the Second World War'

Spring Semester 2014

William S. Cunningham (UT Past President), 'Money, Power, Politics—and British Studies—at UT'

Michael Anderson (Government), 'Britain's Pacific Relations'
Rosemary Hill (London), 'Bloomsbury's Memoir Club'
Benjamin Brower (History), 'The Muslim Pilgrimage'
Margaret Jacobs (University of Nebraska), 'White Mother to a Dark Race'
Diana Solomon (Simon Fraser University), 'Seduction and Rape in Shakespeare'
Michael Stoff (History), 'Wilfred Burchett's "Warning to the World": An Australian War Correspondent Rewrites the Atomic Bomb Narrative'
Arthur Nicholson (San Antonio), 'Former Naval Person: Winston Churchill and the Royal Navy'
John Fair (UT Kinesiology), 'The Diverse Roots of Physical Culture'
Ian Hancock (UT Romani Studies), 'The Historical Identity of "Gypsies"'
Roy Ritchie (Huntington Library), 'The Advent of Beach Culture in Britain'
Bernard Wasserstein (University of Chicago), 'The Men Who Ruled Palestine'
James Vaughn (History), 'The Ideological Origins of the American Revolution Revisited'
Steven Isenberg (Visiting Professor of the Humanities), 'The Literary Legacy of the Great War'
William Whyte (Oxford), 'A Hotbed of Cold Feet? Architecture in Oxford Since 1950'
George Christian (History), 'Scotland's Independence?'

Fall Semester 2014

Stephen Enniss (Harry Ransom Center), 'The Ransom Center Looks Ahead'
John Gurney (Oxford), 'Nancy Lambton and Iran'
James D. Garrison (English), 'Gray, Johnson, and Elegy'
General David Ramsbotham (House of Lords), 'The Last Colonial War'
Elena Schneider (University of California, Berkeley), 'Perspectives on Revolution'
Roger Billis (London), 'The Reform Club: Its Creation and Traditions'
Max Egremont (London), 'Siegfried Sassoon: A Reassessment'
William Meier (Texas Christian University), 'Drugs in Twentieth-Century Britain'
Richard Davenport-Hines (London), 'The Death of General Gordon in Khartoum'
Leah S. Marcus (Vanderbilt), '*Much Ado about Nothing* and *The Taming of the Shrew*'
Kenneth O. Morgan (House of Lords), 'Wales, Lloyd George, and the First World War'
Round Table Discussion, 'The Link between Psychology and History': Robert Abzug (Jewish Studies), Randy Diehl (Dean of Liberal Arts), Wm. Roger Louis (British Studies)
Jane Ridley (Buckingham University), 'George V, the Tsar, and the British Monarchy'
Richard Cleary (Architecture), 'Well Played! Sports Settings and the Perspective of Architecture'
Sir Keith Thomas (Oxford), 'Army Life in Jamaica'
Archie Brown (Oxford), 'The Scottish Referendum'
Miranda Seymour (Brown), 'Germany and England: Romantic Connections'

Spring Semester 2015

Kurt Heinzelman (English), 'The Disappearance of Dylan Thomas'
Michael Brenner (University of Pittsburgh), 'Blair and Bush: Partners in Reaction'

Bartholomew Sparrow (Government), 'Legacy of Colonialism: America's Forgotten Class'

Bain Attwood (Harvard), 'Indigenous Rights in Australia and New Zealand'

Bernard Porter (Newcastle), 'Genocide in Tasmania?'

Ingrid Norton (Harvard Divinity School), 'The Poetry of Valentine's Day'

Ferdinand Mount (London), 'Harold Macmillan'

Thomas Meaney (Columbia University), 'The United Nations and Colonial Independence'

Lawrence S. Graham (Government), 'Northern Ireland's Continuing Troubles: Reflections on the Belfast Agreement of 1998'

Gabriel Paquette (Johns Hopkins University), 'Allies yet Adversaries? Portugal and Britain in the Age of Empire'

Molly McCullers (University of West Georgia), 'South Africa and the Question of African Independence: The Case of South-West Africa (Namibia)'

Robert D. King (Liberal Arts), 'British Studies and Liberal Arts at UT'

Jane Ohlmeyer (Trinity College, Dublin), 'Making Ireland English'

Dane Kennedy (George Washington University), 'Lost Expeditions, Lost Histories'

Round Table Discussion, 'Racial and Social Prejudice in British and American Universities': Holly McCarthy (British Studies), Wm. Roger Louis (British Studies), and Tom Palaima (Classics)

Andrew O'Shaughnessy (University of Virginia), 'The Men Who Lost America'

John Milton Cooper (University of Wisconsin), 'Colonel House and the British'

Lawrence Goldman (Institute of Historical Research, London), 'The Oxford Dictionary of National Biography and National Identity'

Fall Semester 2015

Round Table Discussion, 'The Falklands War': Wm. Roger Louis (History), Bartholomew Sparrow (Government), and David Leal (Latino Politics)

The Austin Brass Band, '40th Anniversary of the British Studies Program at UT-Austin'

Jonathan Schneer (Georgia Tech), 'Churchill and the Second World War: A Reassessment'

Simon Green (Leeds University), 'The Myth of All Souls College'

James H. Dee (Visiting Scholar, Classics), 'Whiteness and Color-Based Racism'

J. K. Barret (English), 'A Midsummer Night's Dream'

Reba Soffer (California State University, Northridge), 'Newer Women and Newer Men after the Great War'

Deidre David (London), 'Pamela Hansford Johnson: "And have you ever written, Lady Snow?"'

Hans Mark (Chancellor of the University of Texas System, 1984–92), 'The Falklands War'

Geoffrey Wheatcroft (London), 'The Difficulties of Writing about Winston Churchill'

Brian Levack (History) and Martha Newman (History), 'The Magna Carta'

John D. Fair (Kinesiology), 'George Bernard Shaw and Physical Fitness'

Round Table Discussion, 'The Story of Alice: Lewis Carroll and the Secret History of Wonderland': Carol MacKay (English), Jerome Bump (English), George Scott Christian (English), and John Farrell (English)

Philip Mead (Harvard University), 'The Unjustifiable and the Imaginable: Politics and Fiction in Contemporary Aboriginal Life'

Spring Semester 2016

Round Table Discussion, 'The Best and Worst Books of 2015': Wm. Roger Louis (History), Al Martinch (Philosophy), Elizabeth Richmond-Garza (English), and Steve Weinberg (Physics)

Caroline Moorehead (London), 'Writing about the Resistance in World War II'

Boisfeuillet Jones, Jr. (Washington, D.C.), 'British and American Newspapers: How Long Will Print Copies Survive?'

Luise White (University of Florida), 'The Lost History of Rhodesia: Race and the Decolonization of Central Africa'

Martha Ann Selby (Asian Studies), 'Everyday Life in South India and the Tamil Short Story'

Rosemary Hill (London), 'British Propaganda in World War II'

Michael Holroyd (London), 'Kipling: Early Years and a Clue to His Personality'

Steve Hindle (Huntington Library), 'Labor and the Landscape in the Eighteenth Century'

Kenneth Fisher (Beverley Hills, California), 'Cecil Rhodes: The Man, the Scholarships, and the Protest Movement: Rhodes Must Fall'

Ron Heiferman (Quinnipiac University), 'China and India during World War II'

Joseph Epstein (Northwestern University), 'The Encyclopaedia Britannica'

Laura Mitchell (University of California, Irvine), 'The Colonial Hunt: Collecting Trophies and Knowledge'

Steven L. Isenberg, (Visiting Professor, Liberal Arts), 'The Poet Keith Douglas in the Tradition of Siegfried Sassoon'

Martin Stannard (Editor of OUP's 43-vol. *Complete Works of Evelyn Waugh*) 'Evelyn Waugh: His Visits to the United States'

Daniel Foliard (Paris Ouest University), 'Cartography and the Making of the Modern Middle East'

Rand Brandes (Lenoir-Rhyne University), 'Seamus Heaney: Irish Poet and Nobel Laureate'

Fall Semester 2016

James H. Dee (Visiting Scholar, Classics), 'Homo, Humanus, Humanitas—and the "Humanities"'

John Prados (National Security Archive), 'British and American Intelligence Services'

Round Table Discussion, 'Brexit': Jamie Galbraith (LBJ School), David Leal (Government), Philippa Levine (History), and Wm. Roger Louis (History)

Round Table Discussion, 'Shakespeare's Richard III': Alan Friedman (English), James Loehlin (English), Elizabeth Richmond-Garza (English), and David Kornhaber (English)

Annamaria Motrescu-Mayes (Cambridge), 'Re-illustrating the History of the British Empire'

Michelle Tusan (University of Nevada), 'Crimes against Humanity and the Armenian Genocide: How the British Invented Human Rights'

Andrew Lownie (London), 'Stalin's Englishman: Guy Burgess'

Barnaby Crowcroft (Harvard University), 'Britain's "Egyptian Allies" and the Suez Crisis of 1956'

James Scott (Statistics), 'Lost and Found: Bayes' Rule after 250 Years'

Geoffrey Wheatcroft (London), 'The Worst Thing since Suez? Tony Blair and Iraq'

Janine Barchas (English), '"Will & Jane": Shakespeare, Austen, and the Cult of Celebrity'

Richard Davenport-Hines (London), 'Jack the Ripper'

Terry Gifford (Bath Spa University) 'Six Stages in the Greening of Ted Hughes'

Steve Weinberg (Physics), 'The Whig History of Science'

John M. MacKenzie (Lancaster University), 'The British Empire: Ramshackle or Rampaging?'

David Edwards (Government), 'Post–November 8, Post-Brexit'

James Loehlin (English), 'Charles Dickens and Christmas'

Spring Semester 2017

Thomas Palaima (Classics), 'Bob Dylan and England'

Jane Ridley (Buckingham University), 'Harold Nicolson and the Biography of George V'

Wm. Roger Louis (History), 'Ernest Bevin and Palestine'

Jurgend Schmandt (LBJ School), 'Alexander King: Scientist and Environmentalist'

Caroline Elkins (Harvard University), 'British Colonial Violence and the End of Empire'

Al Martinich (Philosophy), 'Obedience and Some of Its Discontents'

Daniel Williams (Wales University), 'Assimilation and Its Discontents: Wales in British Literature'

Paul Kennedy (Yale University), 'Guglielmo Marconi and England'

James Epstein (Vanderbilt University), 'Writing from Newgate Prison, 1795: William Winterbotham's View of America'

Brian Levack (History), 'Trust and Distrust in Stuart England'

Kenneth O. Morgan (House of Lords), 'Brexit'

Sarah Beaver (Oxford), 'The Falklands Crisis: A Perspective from the Whitehall Operations Room'

John Rodden (Tunghai University, Taiwan), 'George Orwell's *1984* and His Subsequent Reputation'

Susan Napier (Tufts University), 'Where Shall We Adventure? Hayao Miyazaki Meets Robert Louis Stevenson'

Jason Parker (Texas A&M), 'The End of Empire: From "Divide and Conquer" to "Federate and Leave"'

Patrick French (Ahmedabad University, Gujarat), 'Writing the Biography of V. S. Naipaul'

Steven Isenberg (Visiting Professor, Liberal Arts), 'John Banville as Novelist and Critic: *The Untouchable*'